An R
COMPANION
to APPLIED
REGRESSION

2nd Edition

To the memory of my parents, Joseph and Diana
—J. F.

For my teachers, and especially Fred Mosteller, who I think would have liked this book
—S. W.

An R COMPANION to APPLIED REGRESSION

2nd Edition

John Fox
McMaster University

Sanford Weisberg
University of Minnesota

Los Angeles | London | New Delhi
Singapore | Washington DC

For information:

SAGE Publications, Inc.
2455 Teller Road
Thousand Oaks, California 91320
E-mail: order@sagepub.com

SAGE Publications India Pvt. Ltd.
B 1/I 1 Mohan Cooperative
     Industrial Area
Mathura Road, New Delhi 110 044
India

SAGE Publications Ltd.
1 Oliver's Yard
55 City Road,
London EC1Y 1SP
United Kingdom

SAGE Publications Asia-Pacific
     Pte. Ltd.
33 Pekin Street #02-01
Far East Square
Singapore 048763

Printed in the Unite*d States of America*

Library of Congress Cataloging-in-Publication Data

Fox, John, 1947-
An R companion to applied regression. — 2nd ed./John Fox, Sanford Weisberg.
     p. cm.
Rev. ed. of: An R and S-Plus companion to applied regression. c2002.
Includes bibliographical references and index.
ISBN 978-1-4129-7514-8 (pbk.)
     1. Regression analysis–Data processing. 2. R (Computer program language) I. Weisberg, Sanford, 1947- II. Fox, John, 1947- R and S-Plus companion to applied regression. III. Title.

QA278.2.F628 2011
519.5'3602855133—dc22   2010029245

This book is printed on acid-free paper.

10   11   12   13   14   10   9   8   7   6   5   4   3   2   1

Acquisitions Editor:	Vicki Knight
Associate Editor:	Lauren Habib
Editorial Assistant:	Kalie Koscielak
Production Editor:	Brittany Bauhaus
Permissions Editor:	Adele Hutchinson
Copy Editor:	QuADS PrePress (P) Ltd.
Typesetter:	C&M Digitals (P) Ltd.
Proofreader:	Charlotte J. Waisner
Cover Designer:	Candice Harman
Marketing Manager:	Dory Schrader

Contents

Preface

This book aims to provide a broad introduction to the R statistical computing environment (R Development Core Team, 2009a) in the context of applied regression analysis, which is typically studied by social scientists and others in a second course in applied statistics. We assume that the reader is learning or is otherwise familiar with the statistical methods that we describe; thus, this book is a *companion* to a text or course on modern applied regression, such as, but not necessarily, our own *Applied Regression Analysis and Generalized Linear Models*, second edition (Fox, 2008) and *Applied Linear Regression*, third edition (Weisberg, 2005). Of course, different texts and courses have somewhat different content, and if you encounter a topic that is unfamiliar or that is not of interest, feel free to skip it or to pass over it lightly. With a caveat concerning the continuity of examples within chapters, the book is designed to let you skip around and study only the sections you need.

The availability of cheap, powerful, and convenient computing has revolutionized the practice of statistical data analysis, as it has revolutionized other aspects of our society. Once upon a time, but well within living memory, data analysis was typically performed by statistical packages running on mainframe computers. The primary input medium was the punchcard, large data sets were stored on magnetic tapes, and printed output was produced by line printers; data were in rectangular case-by-variable format. The job of the software was to combine instructions for data analysis with a data set to produce a printed report. Computing jobs were submitted in batchmode, rather than interactively, and a substantial amount of time—hours, or even days—elapsed between the submission of a job and its completion.

Eventually, batch-oriented computers were superseded by interactive, time-shared, terminal-based computing systems and then successively by personal computers and workstations, networks of computers, and the Internet—and perhaps in a few years by cloud computing. But some statistical software still in use traces its heritage to the days of the card reader and line printer. Statistical packages, such as SAS and IBM SPSS,[1] have acquired a variety of accoutrements, including programming capabilities, but they are still principally oriented toward combining instructions with rectangular data sets to produce printed output.[2]

---

[1] SPSS was acquired by IBM in October 2009.

[2] With SAS, in particular, the situation is not so clear-cut, because there are several facilities for programming: The SAS DATA step is a simple programming language for manipulating data sets, the IML (interactive matrix language) procedure provides a programming language for matrix computations, and the macro facility allows the user to build applications that incorporate DATA steps and calls to SAS procedures. Nevertheless, programming in SAS is considerably less consistent and convenient than programming in a true statistical programming environment, and it remains fair to say that SAS principally is oriented toward processing rectangular data sets to produce printed output. Interestingly, both SAS and SPSS recently introduced facilities to link to R code.

The package model of statistical computing can work well in the application of standard methods of analysis, but we believe that it has several serious drawbacks, both for students and for practitioners of statistics. In particular, we think that the package approach of submitting code and getting output to decipher is not a desirable pedagogical model for learning new statistical ideas, and students can have difficulty separating the ideas of data analysis that are under study from the generally rigid implementation of those ideas in a statistical package. We prefer that students learn to request specific output, examine the result, and then modify the analysis or seek additional output. This feedback loop of intermediate examination forces students to think about what is being computed and why it is useful. Once statistical techniques are mastered, the data-analytic process of inserting the intelligence of the user in the middle of an analysis becomes second nature—in our view, a very desirable outcome.

The origins of R are in the S programming language, which was developed at Bell Labs by experts in statistical computing, including John Chambers, Richard Becker, and Allan Wilks (see, e.g., Becker et al., 1988, Preface). Like most good software, S has evolved considerably since its origins in the mid-1970s. Although Bell Labs originally distributed S directly, it is now available only as the commercial product S-PLUS. R is an independent, open-source, and free implementation of the S language, developed by an international team of statisticians, including John Chambers. As described in Ihaka and Gentleman (1996), what evolved into the R Project for Statistical Computing was originated by Ross Ihaka and Robert Gentleman at the University of Auckland, New Zealand. A key advantage of the R system is that it is free—simply download and install it, as we will describe shortly, and then use it.

R is a *statistical computing environment* and includes an *interpreter*, with which the user-programmer can interact in a conversational manner.[3] R is one of several statistical programming environments; others include Gauss, Stata, and Lisp-Stat (which are described, e.g., in Stine and Fox, 1996).

If you can master the art of typing commands, a good statistical programming environment allows you to have your cake and eat it too. Routine data analysis is convenient, but so are programming and the incorporation of new statistical methods. We believe that R balances these factors especially well:

- R is very capable out of the box, including a wide range of standard statistical applications. Contributed packages, which are easy to obtain and add to the basic R software, extend the range of routine data analysis both to new general techniques and to specialized methods, which are of interest only to users in particular areas of application.

---

[3] A *compiler* translates a program written in a programming language into an independently executable program in machine code. In contrast, an *interpreter* translates and executes a program under the control of the interpreter. Although it is in theory possible to write a compiler for a high-level, interactive language such as R, it is difficult to do so. Compiled programs usually execute more efficiently than interpreted programs. In advanced use, R has facilities for incorporating compiled programs written in Fortran and C.

- Once you get used to it, the R programming language is reasonably easy to use—as easy a programming language as we have encountered—and is finely tuned to the development of statistical applications.
- The S programming language and its descendant R are also carefully designed from the point of view of computer science as well as statistics. John Chambers, the principal architect of S, won the 1998 Software System Award of the Association for Computing Machinery (ACM) for the S System. Similarly, in 2010, Robert Gentleman and Ross Ihaka were awarded a prize for R by the Statistical Computing and Statistical Graphics sections of the American Statistical Association.
- The implementation of R is very solid under the hood—incorporating, for example, sound numerical algorithms for statistical computations—and it is regularly updated, currently at least twice per year.

One of the great strengths of R is that it allows users and experts in particular areas of statistics to add new capabilities to the software. Not only is it possible to write new programs in R, but it is also convenient to combine related sets of programs, data, and documentation in R *packages*. The previous edition of this book, published in 2002, touted the then "more than 100 contributed packages available on the R website, many of them prepared by experts in various areas of applied statistics, such as resampling methods, mixed models, and survival analysis" (p. xii). The Comprehensive R Archive Network (abbreviated CRAN and variously pronounced *see-ran* or *kran*) now holds more than 2,500 packages (see Figure 1, drawn, of course, with R); other R package archives—most notably the archive of the Bioconductor project, which develops software for bioinformatics—add several hundred more packages to the total. In the statistical literature, new methods are often accompanied by implementations in R; indeed, R has become a kind of *lingua franca* of statistical computing—at least among statisticians—although interest in R is also robust in other areas, including the social and behavioral sciences.

New in the Second Edition

Readers familiar with the first edition of this book will immediately notice two key changes. First, and most significant, there are now two authors, the first edition having been written by John Fox alone. Second, "S-PLUS" is missing from the title of the book (originally *An R and S-PLUS Companion to Applied Regression*), which now describes only R. In the decade since the first edition of the book was written, the open-source, free R has completely eclipsed its commercial cousin, S-PLUS. Moreover, where R and S-PLUS differ, we believe that the advantage generally goes to R. Although most of the contents of this second edition are applicable to S-PLUS as well as to R, we see little reason to discuss S-PLUS explicitly.

We have added a variety of new material—for example, with respect to transformations and effects plots—and in addition, virtually all the text has

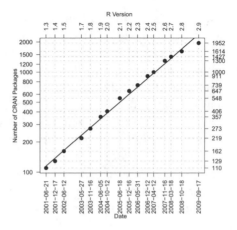

Figure 1 The number of packages on CRAN grew roughly exponentially since reliable data first became available in 2001 through 2009.
Source: Fox (2009).

been rewritten. We have taken pains to make the book as self-contained as possible, providing the information that a new user needs to get started. Many topics, such as R graphics (in Chapter 7) and R programming (in Chapter 8), have been considerably expanded in the second edition.

The book has a companion R package called **car**, and we have substantially added to, extended, and revised the functions in the **car** package to make them more consistent, easier to use, and, we hope, more useful. The new **car** package includes several functions inherited from the **alr3** package designed to accompany Weisberg (2005). The **alr3** package still exists, but it now contains mostly data.

Obtaining and Installing R

We assume that you're working on a single-user computer on which R has not yet been installed and for which you have administrator privileges to install software. To state the obvious, before you can start using R, you have to get it and install it. The good news is that R is free and runs under all commonly available computer operating systems—Windows, Mac OS X, and Linux and Unix—and that precompiled binary distributions of R are available for these systems. There is no bad news—at least not yet. It is our expectation that most readers of the book will use either the Windows or the Mac OS X implementations of R, and the presentation in the text reflects that assumption. Virtually everything in the text, however, applies equally to Linux and Unix systems, although the details of installing R vary across specific Linux distributions and Unix systems.

The best way to obtain R is by downloading it over the Internet from CRAN, at http://cran.r-project.org/. It is faster, and better netiquette, to download R from one of the many CRAN mirror sites than from the main CRAN site: Click on the "Mirrors" link near the top left of the CRAN home page and select a mirror near you.

Warning: The following instructions are current as of version 2.11.0 of R. Some of the details may change, so check for updates on the website for this book, and also consult the instructions on the CRAN site.

INSTALLING R ON A WINDOWS SYSTEM

Click on the "Windows" link in the "Download and Install R" section near the top of the CRAN home page. Then click on the "base" link on the "R for Windows" page. We recommend that you install the latest "patched build" of the current version of R; the patched release incorporates fixes to known bugs, usually small. Click on the link in "Patches to this release are incorporated in the r-patched snapshot build" and then on "Download R-x.y.z Patched build for Windows" to download the R Windows installer. "R-x.y.z" is the current version of R—for example, R-2.11.0.

R installs as a standard Windows application. We suggest that you take all the defaults in the installation, with one exception: We recommend that you select the *single-document interface (SDI)* in preference to the default *multiple-document interface (MDI)*. In the former, various R windows float freely on the desktop, while in the latter they are contained within a master window.

Once R is installed, you can start it as you would any Windows application, for example, by double-clicking on its desktop icon.

Whenever you start R, a number of files are automatically read and their contents executed. The start-up process provides the user with the ability to customize the program to meet particular needs or tastes, and as you gain experience with R, you may wish to customize the program in this way. On a single-user Windows system, probably the easiest route to customization is to edit the Rprofile.site file located in R's etc subdirectory. The possibilities for customization are nearly endless, but here are two useful steps, both of which assume that you have an active Internet connection:

- Permanently select a CRAN mirror site, so that you don't have to specify the mirror in each session that you install or update packages; just uncomment the following lines (with the exception of the first) in the Rprofile.site file by removing the pound signs (#):

```
# set a CRAN mirror
# local({r <- getOption("repos")
#        r["CRAN"] <- "http://my.local.cran"
#        options(repos=r)})
```

You must then replace the dummy site `http://my.local.cran` with a link to a real mirror site, such as `http://probability.ca/cran` for the CRAN mirror at the University of Toronto. This is, of course, just an example: You should pick a mirror site near you.

- Whenever you start R, automatically update any installed packages for which new versions are available on CRAN; just insert the following line into Rprofile.site:

```
utils::update.packages(ask=FALSE)
```

A disadvantage of the last change is that starting up R will take a bit longer. If you find the wait annoying, you can always remove this line from your Rprofile.site file.

Edit the Rprofile.site file with a plain-text (ASCII) editor, such as Windows Notepad; if you use a word-processing program, such as Word, make sure to save the file as plain text.

You can also customize certain aspects of the R graphical user interface via the *Edit → GUI preferences* menu.

INSTALLING R ON A MAC OS X SYSTEM

Click on the "Mac OS X" link in the "Download and Install R" section near the top of the CRAN home page. Click on the "R-x.y.z.pkg (latest version)" link on the "R for Mac OS X" page to download the R Mac OS X installer. "R-x.y.z," as mentioned earlier, is the current version of R—for example, R-2.11.0.

R installs as a standard Mac OS X application. Just double-click on the downloaded installer package, and follow the on-screen directions. Once R is installed, you can treat it as you would any Mac OS X application. For example, you can put the R.app program (or, on a 64-bit system, the R64.app program) on the Mac OS X Dock, from which it can conveniently be launched.

R is highly configurable under Mac OS X, but some of the details differ from the Windows details. The possibilities for customization are nearly endless. Here are the same two customizations that we suggested for Windows users:

- Permanently select a CRAN mirror site, so that you don't have to specify the mirror in each session that you install or update a package. From the menus in the *R Console*, select *R → Preferences*, and then select the *Startup* tab. Pick the URL of a mirror site near you.
- Whenever you start R, automatically update any installed packages for which new versions are available. Using a text editor capable of saving plain-text (ASCII) files (we recommend the free Text Wrangler, which can also be configured as a programming editor for R), create a file named .Rprofile in your home directory, being careful not to omit the initial period (.), and insert the following line in the file:

```
utils::update.packages(ask=FALSE)
```

INSTALLING AND USING THE CAR PACKAGE

Most of the examples in this book require the **car** package, which is not part of the standard R installation. The **car** package is available on CRAN. It "depends" on some other packages and "suggests" still others; the packages on which it depends will automatically be installed along with the **car** package.

Although both the Windows and the Mac OS X versions of R have menus for installing packages, the following command entered at the R command prompt will install the **car** package and all the other packages that it requires (i.e., both depends on and suggests):

```
> install.packages("car", dependencies=TRUE)
```

Installing a package does not make it available for use in a particular R session. When R starts up, it automatically loads a set of standard packages that are part of the R distribution. To access the programs and data in another package, you must first load the package using the `library` command:[4]

```
> library(car)
```

This command also loads all the packages on which the **car** package depends. If you want to use still other packages, you need to enter a separate `library` command for each. The process of loading packages as you need them will come naturally as you grow more familiar with R. You can also arrange to load packages automatically at the beginning of every R session by adding a pair of commands such as the following to your R profile:

```
pkgs <- getOption("defaultPackages")
options(defaultPackages = c(pkgs, "car", "alr3"))
```

The Website for the *R Companion*

There is a website for this book at `http://socserv.socsci.mc master.ca/jfox/Books/Companion/`.[5] If you are currently using R and are connected to the Internet, the `carWeb` command will open the website for the book in your browser:

```
> library(car)
> carWeb()
```

---

[4]The name of the `library` command is an endless source of confusion among new users of R. The command loads a *package*, such as **car**, which in turn resides in a *library* of packages. If you want to be among the R cognoscenti, never call a package a "library"!

[5]If you have difficulty accessing this website, please check the Sage Publications website at www .sagepub.com for up-to-date information. Search for "John Fox," and follow the links to the website for the book.

The website for the book includes the following materials:

- An appendix, referred to as the "online appendix" in the text, containing brief information on using R for various extensions of regression analysis not considered in the main body of the book: nonlinear regression; robust and resistant regression; nonparametric regression; time-series regression; Cox regression for survival data; multivariate linear models, including repeated-measures analysis of variance; mixed-effects models; structural-equation models; multiple imputation of missing data; and bootstrapping. We have relegated this material to a downloadable appendix in an effort to keep the text to a reasonable length. We plan to update the appendix from time to time as new developments warrant.
- Downloadable scripts for all the examples in the text.
- Exercises for the material on R in Chapters 1, 2, 7, and 8. As will be clear from the chapter synopses below, the remaining chapters deal with statistical material, for which a text on regression analysis should provide exercises.
- A few data files discussed in this *Companion* but not included in the **car** package.
- Errata and updated information about R.

All these can be accessed using the `carWeb` function; after loading the **car** package in R, type `help(carWeb)` for details.

Using This Book

This book is intended primarily as a companion for use with another textbook that covers linear and generalized linear models. For details on the statistical methods, particularly in Chapters 3 to 6, you will need to consult the regression textbook that you are using. To help you with this task, we provide sections of complementary readings, including references to Fox (2008) and Weisberg (2005).

While the *R Companion* is not intended as a comprehensive users' manual for R, we anticipate that most students learning regression methods and researchers already familiar with regression but interested in learning to use R will find this book sufficiently thorough for their needs.[6] Various features of R are introduced as they are needed, primarily in the context of detailed, worked-through examples. If you want to locate information about a particular feature, however, consult the index of functions and operators, or the

---

[6] A set of manuals in PDF and HTML format is distributed with R and can be accessed with Windows or Mac OS X through the *Help* menu. The manuals are also available on the R website. R has a substantial user community, which contributes to active and helpful email lists. See the previously mentioned website for details. And please remember to observe proper netiquette: Look for answers in the documentation and frequently-asked-questions (FAQ) lists before posting a question to an email discussion list; the people who answer your question are volunteering their time. Also, check the posting guide, at www.r-project.org/posting-guide.html, before posting a question to one of the R email lists.

subject index, at the end of the book; there is also an index of the data sets used in the text.

Occasionally, more demanding material (e.g., requiring a knowledge of matrix algebra or calculus) is marked with an asterisk; this material may be skipped without loss of continuity, as may the footnotes.[7]

Most readers will want to try out the examples in the text. You should therefore install R and the **car** package associated with this book before you start to work through the book. As you duplicate the examples in the text, feel free to innovate, experimenting with R commands that do not appear in the examples. Examples are often reused within a chapter, and so later examples in a chapter can depend on earlier ones in the same chapter; packages used in a chapter are loaded only once. The examples in *different* chapters are independent of each other; however, think of the R code in each chapter as pertaining to a separate R session.

Here are brief chapter synopses:

Chapter 1 explains how to interact with the R interpreter, introduces basic concepts, and provides a variety of examples, including an extended illustration of the use of R in data analysis. The chapter includes a brief presentation of R functions for basic statistical methods and concludes with a description of the **Rcmdr** (R Commander) package, which provides a basic point-and-click interface to R.

Chapter 2 shows you how to read data into R from several sources and how to work with data sets. There are also discussions of basic data structures, such as vectors, matrices, arrays, and lists; on handling character data; and on dealing with large data sets in R.

Chapter 3 discusses the exploratory examination and transformation of data, with an emphasis on graphical displays.

Chapter 4 describes the use of R functions for fitting, testing, manipulating, and displaying linear models, including simple- and multiple-regression models and linear models with categorical predictors (factors).

Chapter 5 focuses on generalized linear models (GLMs) in R. Particular attention is paid to GLMs for categorical data and to Poisson and related GLMs for counts.

Chapter 6 describes methods—often called "regression diagnostics"— for determining whether linear models and GLMs adequately

---

[7]Footnotes include references to supplementary material (e.g., cross-references to other parts of the text), elaboration of points in the text, and indications of portions of the text that represent (we hope) innocent distortion for the purpose of simplification. The objective is to present more complete and correct information without interrupting the flow of the text and without making the main text overly difficult.

describe the data to which they are fit. Many of these methods are implemented in the **car** package associated with this book.

Chapter 7   contains material on plotting in R, describing a step-by-step approach to constructing complex R graphs and introducing trellis displays constructed with the **lattice** package.

Chapter 8   is a general introduction to programming in R, including discussions of function definition, operators and functions for handling matrices, control structures, debugging and improving R programs, object-oriented programming, writing statistical-modeling functions, and the scoping rules of the R programming language.

With the possible exception of starred material, Chapters 1 and 2 contain general information that should be of interest to all readers. Chapters 3 to 6 cover material that will be contained in most regression courses. The material in Chapters 7 and 8 has less to do with regression specifically and more to do with using R in real-world applications, where the facilities provided either in the basic packages or in the **car** package need to be modified to meet a particular goal. Readers with an interest in programming may prefer to read the last two chapters before Chapters 3 to 6.

We employ a few simple typographical conventions:

- Input and output are printed in slanted and upright monospaced (typewriter) fonts, respectively—for example,

```
> mean(1:10)   # an input line

[1] 5.5
```

  The > prompt at the beginning of the input and the + prompt (not illustrated in this example), which begins continuation lines, are provided by R, not typed by the user.
- R input and output are printed as they appear on the computer screen, although we sometimes edit output for brevity or clarity; elided material in computer output is indicated by three widely spaced periods (. . .).
- Data set names, variable names, the names of R functions and operators, and R expressions that appear in the body of the text are in a monospaced (typewriter) font: `Duncan`, `income`, `mean`, `+`, `lm(prestige~income + education, data=Prestige)`.
- The names of R packages are in boldface: **car**.
- Occasionally, generic specifications (to be replaced by particular information, such as a variable name) are given in typewriter italics: `mean (variable-name)`.
- Menus, menu items, and the names of windows are set in an italic sansserif font: *File*, *Exit*, *R Console*.

- We use a sans-serif font for other names, such as names of operating systems, programming languages, software packages, and directories: Windows, R, SAS, c:\Program Files\R\R-2.11.0\etc.

Graphical output from R is shown in many figures scattered through the text; in normal use, graphs appear on the computer screen in graphics device windows that can be moved, resized, copied into other programs, saved, or printed (as described in Section 7.4).

There is, of course, much to R beyond the material in this book. The S language is documented in several books by John Chambers and his colleagues: *The New S Language: A Programming Environment for Data Analysis and Graphics* (Becker et al., 1988) and an edited volume, *Statistical Models in S* (Chambers and Hastie, 1992), describe what came to be known as S3, including the S3 object-oriented programming system, and facilities for specifying and fitting statistical models. Similarly, *Programming With Data* (Chambers, 1998) describes the S4 language and object system. The R dialect of S incorporates both S3 and S4, and so these books remain valuable sources.

Beyond these basic sources, there are now so many books that describe the application of R to various areas of statistics that it is impractical to compile a list here, a list that would inevitably be out-of-date by the time this book goes to press. We include complementary readings at the end of many chapters, however. There is nevertheless one book that is especially worthy of mention here: The fourth edition of *Modern Applied Statistics With S* (Venables and Ripley, 2002), though somewhat dated, demonstrates the use of R for a wide range of statistical applications. The book is associated with several R packages, including the **MASS** package, to which we make occasional reference. Venables and Ripley's text is generally more advanced and has a broader focus than our book. There are also some differences in emphasis: For example, the *R Companion* has more material on diagnostic methods.

Acknowledgments

We are grateful to a number of individuals who provided valuable assistance in writing this book and its predecessor:

- Several people have made contributions to the **car** package that accompanies the book; they are acknowledged in the package itself—see `help(package=car)`.
- Michael Friendly and three unusually diligent (and at the time anonymous) reviewers, Jeff Gill, J. Scott Long, and Bill Jacoby (who also commented on a draft of the second edition), made many excellent suggestions for revising the first edition of the book, as did eight anonymous reviewers of the second edition.
- C. Deborah Laughton, the editor at Sage responsible for the first edition, and Vicki Knight, the Sage editor responsible for the second edition, were both helpful and supportive.

- A draft of this book was used in Sociology 740 in the winter semester of 2010. Several students, most notably Arthur McLuhan, pointed out typographical and other errors in the text.
- The book was written in LaTeX using live R code compiled with the wonderful Sweave document preparation system. We are grateful to Fritz Leisch (Leisch, 2002) for Sweave.
- Finally, we wish to express our gratitude to the developers of R and to those who have contributed to R software for the wonderful resource that they have created with their collaborative and, in many instances, selfless efforts.

Getting Started With R

1

The purpose of this chapter is to introduce you to the R language and interpreter. After describing some of the basics of R, we will proceed to illustrate its use in a typical, if small, regression problem. We will then provide a brief description of R functions for familiar operations in basic statistics. The chapter concludes with an equally brief introduction to the *R Commander* graphical user interface (GUI) to R.

We know that many readers are in the habit of beginning a book at Chapter 1, skipping the Preface. The Preface to this *Companion* includes information about installing R and the **car** package on your computer. The **car** package, associated with the *R Companion to Applied Regression*, is necessary for many of the examples in the text. Moreover, the Preface includes information on the typographical and other conventions that we use in the text.

1.1 R Basics

Figure 1.1 shows the *RGui* (R *G*raphical *U*ser *I*nterface) for the Windows version of R. The most important element of the *Rgui* is the *R Console* window, which initially contains an opening message followed by a line with just a *command prompt*—the greater than (>) symbol. Interaction with R takes place at the command prompt. In Figure 1.1, we typed a simple command, 2 + 3, followed by the Enter key. R interprets and executes the command, returning the value 5, followed by another command prompt. Figure 1.2 shows the similar *R.app* GUI for the Mac OS X version of R.

The menus in *RGui* and *R.app* provide access to many routine tasks, such as setting preferences, various editing functions, and accessing documentation. We draw your attention in particular to the *Packages* menu in the Windows *RGui* and to the *Packages & Data* menu in the Mac OS X *R.app*, both of which provide dialogs for installing and updating R packages. Unlike

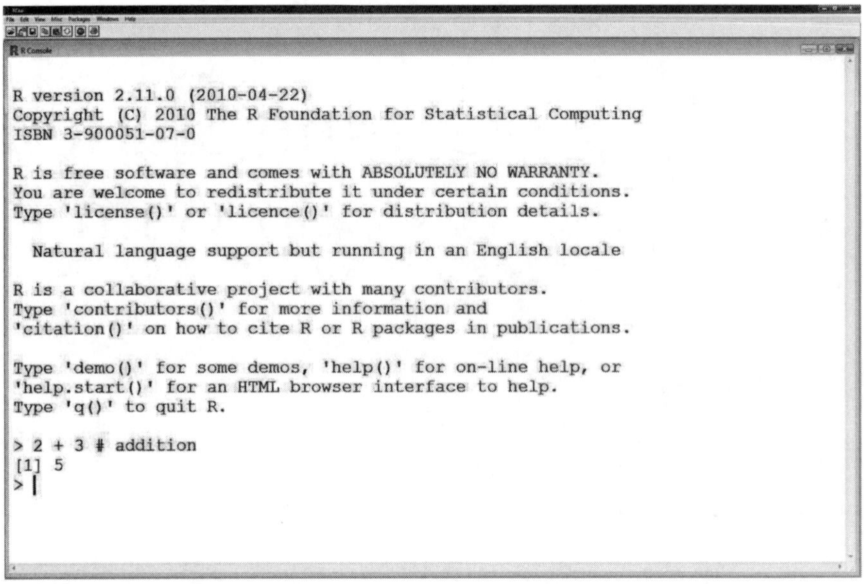

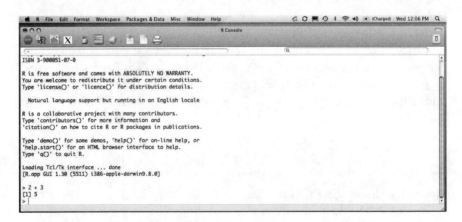

Figure 1.1 The *RGui* interface to the Windows version of R, shortly after the beginning of a session. This screen shot shows the default multiple-document interface (MDI); the single-document interface (SDI) looks similar but consists only of the *R Console* with the menu bar.

Figure 1.2 The *R.app* interface to the Mac OS X version of R.

many statistical analysis programs, the standard R menus do not provide direct access to the statistical functions in R, for which you will generally have to enter commands at the command prompt.

1.1.1 INTERACTING WITH THE INTERPRETER

Data analysis in R typically proceeds as an interactive dialogue with the interpreter. We type an R command at the > prompt, press the Enter key, and the interpreter responds by executing the command and, as appropriate, returning a result, producing graphical output, or sending output to a file or device.

The R language includes the usual arithmetic operators:

+	addition
−	subtraction
*	multiplication
/	division
^ or **	exponentiation

Here are some simple examples of arithmetic in R:

```
> 2 + 3 # addition

[1] 5

> 2 - 3 # subtraction

[1] -1

> 2*3    # multiplication

[1] 6

> 2/3    # division

[1] 0.6667

> 2^3    # exponentiation

[1] 8
```

Output lines are preceded by [1]. When the printed output consists of many values spread over several lines, each line begins with the index number of the first element in that line; an example will appear shortly. After the interpreter executes a command and returns a value, it waits for the next command, as signified by the > prompt. The pound sign (#) signifies a comment: Text to the right of # is ignored by the interpreter. We often take advantage of this feature to insert explanatory text to the right of commands, as in the examples above.

Several arithmetic operations may be combined to build up complex expressions:

```
> 4^2 - 3*2

[1] 10
```

In the usual notation, this command is $4^2 - 3 \times 2$. R uses standard conventions for precedence of mathematical operators. So, for example, exponentiation takes place before multiplication, which takes place before subtraction. If two operations have equal precedence, such as addition and subtraction, then they take place from left to right:

```
> 1 - 6 + 4

[1] -1
```

You can always explicitly specify the order of evaluation of an expression by using parentheses; thus, the expression $4\char94 2 - 3*2$ is equivalent to

```
> (4^2) - (3*2)

[1] 10
```

and

```
> (4 + 3)^2

[1] 49
```

is different from

```
> 4 + 3^2

[1] 13
```

Although spaces are not required to separate the elements of an arithmetic expression, judicious use of spaces can help clarify the meaning of the expression. Compare the following commands, for example:

```
> -2--3

[1] 1

> -2 - -3

[1] 1
```

Placing spaces around operators usually makes expressions more readable, as in the preceding examples. Readability of commands is generally improved by putting spaces around the binary arithmetic operators + and – but not around *, /, or ^.

1.1.2   R FUNCTIONS

In addition to the common arithmetic operators, R includes many—literally hundreds—of functions for mathematical operations, for statistical data analysis, for making graphs, and for other purposes. Function *arguments* are values passed to functions, and these are specified within parentheses after the function name. For example, to calculate the natural log of 100, that is $\log_e 100$ or ln 100, we type

```
> log(100)

[1] 4.605
```

To compute the log of 100 to the base 10, we specify

```
> log(100, base=10)

[1] 2

> log10(100) # equivalent

[1] 2
```

In general, arguments to R functions may be specified in the order in which they occur in the function definition or by the name of the argument followed by = (equals sign) and a value. In the command log(100, base=10), the value 100 is matched to the first argument in the log function. The second argument, base=10, explicitly matches the value 10 to the argument base.

Different arguments are separated by commas, and for clarity, we prefer to leave a space after each comma, although these spaces are not required. Argument names may be abbreviated, as long as the abbreviation is unique; thus, the previous example may be rendered more compactly as

```
> log(100, b=10)

[1] 2
```

To obtain information about a function, use the help function. For example,

```
> help(log)
```

The result of executing this command is shown in abbreviated form in Figure 1.3, where the three widely separated dots (. . .) mean that we have elided some information. An alternative that requires less typing is to use the equivalent ? (help) operator, ?log.

Figure 1.3 is a typical R help page, giving first a brief description of the functions documented in the help page, followed by a listing of the available arguments, and then a discussion of the arguments. The Details and Value sections generally describe what the function does. All functions return a value, and the log function returns the logarithm of its first argument. Some functions, particularly those that draw graphs, don't *appear* to return a value and are used instead for the *side effect* of drawing a graph. Help pages usually include references to related functions, along with examples that you can execute to see how the documented functions work. Reading R documentation is an acquired skill, but once you become familiar with the form of the documentation, you will likely find the help pages very useful.

Help can be displayed in a help window as a plain-text file, or as an HTML page in a web browser. The HTML help format has several useful features, such as live hypertext links to other help pages, and is selected by the command options(help_type="html"). HTML help is the default option when R is installed.

The help.start() command opens a page in your web browser that gives direct access to a variety of resources, including HTML versions of the

```
log                      package:base                    R Documentation
Logarithms and Exponentials
Description:
     'log' computes logarithms, by default natural logarithms,
     'log10' computes common (i.e., base 10) logarithms, and
     'log2' computes binary (i.e., base 2) logarithms.  The general
     form 'log(x, base)' computes logarithms with base 'base'.
.  .  .
     'exp' computes the exponential function.
.  .  .
Usage:
     log(x, base = exp(1))
     logb(x, base = exp(1))
     log10(x)
     log2(x)
.  .  .
     exp(x)
.  .  .
Arguments:
       x: a numeric or complex vector.
    base: a positive or complex number: the base with respect to which
          logarithms are computed.  Defaults to e='exp(1)'.
Details:
     All except 'logb' are generic functions: methods can be
     defined for them individually or via the 'Math' group generic.
.  .  .
Value:
     A vector of the same length as 'x' containing the transformed
     values.  'log(0)' gives '-Inf', and negative values give
     'NaN'.
.  .  .
See Also:
     'Trig', 'sqrt', 'Arithmetic'.
Examples:
     log(exp(3))
     log10(1e7)# = 7
     x <- 10^-(1+2*1:9)
     cbind(x, log(1+x), log1p(x), exp(x)-1, expm1(x))
```

Figure 1.3 The documentation returned by the command `help(log)`.
The ellipses (. . .) represent elided lines.

R manuals, hyperlinked help for all installed packages, a help search engine,
frequently-asked-questions (FAQ) lists, and more. The `help.start()` command is so useful that you may want to put it into a startup file so that the
help browser opens at the beginning of every R session (see the Preface and
`?Startup`).

A novel feature of the R help system is the facility it provides to execute
most examples in the help pages via the `example` command:

```
> example("log")

log> log(exp(3))
[1] 3

log> log10(1e7)   # = 7
```

```
[1] 7
. . .
```

The number `1e7` in the last example is given in scientific notation and represents $1 \times 10^7 = 10$ million.

A quick way to determine the arguments of many functions is to use the `args` function:

```
> args(log)
```

```
function (x, base = exp(1))
NULL
```

Because `base` is the second argument of the `log` function, we can also type

```
> log(100, 10)
```

```
[1] 2
```

specifying both arguments to the function (i.e., `x` and `base`) by position.

An argument to a function may have a *default* value—a value that the argument assumes if it is not explicitly specified in the function call. Defaults are shown in the function documentation and in the output of `args`. For example, the `base` argument to the `log` function defaults to `exp(1)` or $e^1 \approx 2.718$, the base of the natural logarithms.

R is largely a *functional programming language*, which means that both the standard programs that make up the language and the programs that users write are functions. Indeed, the distinction between standard and user-defined functions is somewhat artificial in R.[1] Even the arithmetic operators in R are really functions and may be used as such:

```
> '+'(2, 3)
```

```
[1] 5
```

We need to place back-ticks around `` ` + ` `` (single or double quotes also work) so that the interpreter does not get confused, but our ability to use + and the other arithmetic functions as *in-fix* operators, as in `2 + 3`, is really just syntactic "sugar," simplifying the construction of R expressions but not fundamentally altering the functional character of the language.

1.1.3 VECTORS AND VARIABLES

R would not be very convenient to use if we had to compute one value at a time. The arithmetic operators, and most R functions, can operate on more complex data structures than individual numbers. The simplest of these data structures is a numeric vector, or one-dimensional list of numbers.[2] In R an individual number is really a vector with a single element. A simple way to construct a vector is with the `c` function, which combines its elements:

---

[1] Section 1.1.6 briefly discusses user-defined functions; the topic is treated in greater depth in Chapter 8. Experienced programmers can also access programs written in Fortran and C from within R.

[2] We refer to vectors as "lists" using that term loosely, because *lists* in R are a distinct data structure (described in Section 2.3).

```
> c(1, 2, 3, 4)

[1] 1 2 3 4
```

Many other functions also return vectors as results. For example, the *sequence operator* (:) generates consecutive numbers, while the sequence function (seq) does much the same thing, but more flexibly:

```
> 1:4 # integer sequence

[1] 1 2 3 4

> 4:1

[1] 4 3 2 1

> -1:2

[1] -1  0  1  2

> seq(1, 4)

[1] 1 2 3 4

> seq(2, 8, by=2) # specify interval

[1] 2 4 6 8

> seq(0, 1, by=0.1) # non-integer sequence

 [1] 0.0 0.1 0.2 0.3 0.4 0.5 0.6 0.7 0.8 0.9 1.0

> seq(0, 1, length=11) # specify number of elements

 [1] 0.0 0.1 0.2 0.3 0.4 0.5 0.6 0.7 0.8 0.9 1.0
```

The standard arithmetic operators and functions apply to vectors on an element-wise basis:

```
> c(1, 2, 3, 4)/2

[1] 0.5 1.0 1.5 2.0

> c(1, 2, 3, 4)/c(4, 3, 2, 1)

[1] 0.2500 0.6667 1.5000 4.0000

> log(c(0.1, 1, 10, 100), 10)

[1] -1  0  1  2
```

If the operands are of different lengths, then the shorter of the two is extended by repetition, as in c(1, 2, 3, 4)/2 above; if the length of the longer operand is not a multiple of the length of the shorter one, then a warning message is printed, but the interpreter proceeds with the operation, *recycling* the elements of the shorter operand:

```
> c(1, 2, 3, 4) + c(4, 3) # no warning

[1] 5 5 7 7

> c(1, 2, 3, 4) + c(4, 3, 2) # produces warning

[1] 5 5 5 8

Warning message:
In c(1, 2, 3, 4) + c(4, 3, 2) :
  longer object length is not a multiple of shorter object length
```

R would also be of little use if we were unable to save the results returned by functions; we do so by *assigning* values to *variables*, as in the following example:

```
> x <- c(1, 2, 3, 4) # assignment
> x # print

[1] 1 2 3 4
```

The left-pointing arrow (<-) is the *assignment operator*; it is composed of the two characters < (less than) and - (dash or minus), with no intervening blanks, and is usually read as *gets*: "The variable x *gets* the value c(1, 2, 3, 4)." The equals sign (=) may also be used for assignment in place of the arrow (<-), except inside a function call, where = is exclusively used to specify arguments by name. Because reserving the equals sign for specification of function arguments leads to clearer and less error-prone R code, we encourage you to use the arrow for assignment, even where = is allowed.[3]

As the preceding example illustrates, when the leftmost operation in a command is an assignment, nothing is printed. Typing the name of a variable, as in the second command immediately above, causes its value to be printed.

Variable names in R are composed of letters (a–z, A–Z), numerals (0–9), periods (.), and underscores (_), and they may be arbitrarily long. The first character must be a letter or a period, but variable names beginning with a period are reserved by convention for special purposes.[4] Names in R are case sensitive; so, for example, x and X are distinct variables. Using descriptive names, for example, total.income rather than x2, is almost always a good idea.

Three common naming styles are conventionally used in R: (1) separating the parts of a name by periods, as in total.income; (2) separating them by underscores, as in total_income; or (3) separating them by uppercase letters, termed *camel case*, as in totalIncome. For variable names, we prefer the first style, but this is purely a matter of taste.

R commands using defined variables simply substitute the value of the variable for its name:

---

[3]R also permits a right-pointing arrow for assignment, as in 2 + 3 -> x.
[4]Nonstandard names may be used in a variety of contexts, including assignments, by enclosing the names in back-ticks, or in single or double quotes (e.g., 'first name' <- "John"). In most circumstances, however, nonstandard names are best avoided.

```
> x/2

[1] 0.5 1.0 1.5 2.0

> (y <- sqrt(x))

[1] 1.000 1.414 1.732 2.000
```

In the last example, sqrt is the square-root function, and thus sqrt(x) is equivalent to x^0.5. To obtain printed output without having to type the name of the variable y as a separate command, we enclose the command in parentheses so that the assignment is no longer the leftmost operation. We will use this trick regularly.

Unlike in many programming languages, variables in R are dynamically defined. We need not tell the interpreter in advance how many values x is to hold or whether it contains integers (whole numbers), real numbers, character values, or something else. Moreover, if we wish, we may *redefine* the variable x:

```
(x <- rnorm(100))   # 100 standard normal random numbers

  [1]   0.58553  0.70947 -0.10930 -0.45350  0.60589 -1.81796  0.63010
  [8]  -0.27618 -0.28416 -0.91932 -0.11625  1.81731  0.37063  0.52022
 [15]  -0.75053  0.81690 -0.88636 -0.33158  1.12071  0.29872  0.77962
 . . .
 [92]  -0.85508  1.88695 -0.39182 -0.98063  0.68733 -0.50504  2.15772
 [99]  -0.59980 -0.69455
```

The rnorm function generates standard-normal random numbers, in this case, 100 of them. Two additional arguments, not used in this example, allow us to sample values from a normal distribution with arbitrary mean and standard deviation; the defaults are mean=0 and sd=1, and because we did not specify these arguments, the defaults were used. When a vector prints on more than one line, as in the last example, the index number of the leading element of each line is shown in square brackets.

The function summary is an example of a *generic function*: How it behaves depends on its argument. Applied as here to a numeric vector,

```
> summary(x)

   Min. 1st Qu.  Median    Mean 3rd Qu.    Max.
 -2.380  -0.590   0.484   0.245   0.900   2.480
```

summary prints the minimum and maximum values of its argument, along with the mean, median, and first and third quartiles. Applied to another kind of object—a matrix, for example—summary gives different information, as we will see later.

1.1.4 NONNUMERIC VECTORS

Vectors may also contain nonnumeric values. For example,

```
> (words <- c("To", "be", "or", "not", "to", "be"))

[1] "To"  "be"  "or"  "not" "to"  "be"
```

is a *character vector* whose elements are character strings. There are R functions to work with character data. For example, to turn this vector into a single character string:

```
> paste(words, collapse=" ")

[1] "To be or not to be"
```

The very useful `paste` function pastes strings together (and is discussed, along with other functions for manipulating character data, in Section 2.4). The `collapse` argument, as its name implies, collapses the character vector into a single string, separating the elements with whatever is between the quotation marks, in this case one blank space.

A *logical vector* has all its elements either TRUE or FALSE:

```
> (vals <- c(TRUE, TRUE, FALSE, TRUE))

[1]  TRUE  TRUE FALSE  TRUE
```

The symbols T and F may also be used as logical values, but while TRUE and FALSE are *reserved symbols* in R, T and F are not, an omission that we regard as a design flaw in the language. For example, you can perniciously assign T <- FALSE and F <- TRUE (Socrates was executed for less!). For this reason, we suggest avoiding the symbols T and F.

Functions are available for working with logical vectors. For example, the ! operator negates a logical vector:

```
> !vals

[1] FALSE FALSE  TRUE FALSE
```

If we use logical values in arithmetic, R treats FALSE as if it were a zero and TRUE as if it were a one:

```
> sum(vals)

[1] 3
```

```
> sum(!vals)
```

```
[1] 1
```

More logical operators are described in the next section.

If we create a vector of mixed character strings, logical values, and numbers, we get back a vector of character strings:

```
> c("A", FALSE, 3.0)
```

```
[1] "A"       "FALSE" "3"
```

A vector of mixed numbers and logical values is treated as numeric, with FALSE becoming zero and TRUE becoming one. (Try it!) In the first case, we say that the logical and numeric values are *coerced* to character; in the second case, the logical values are coerced to numeric. In general, coercion in R takes place naturally and is designed to lose as little information as possible (see Section 2.6).

1.1.5   INDEXING VECTORS

If we wish to access—say, to print—only one of the elements of a vector, we can specify the index of the element within square brackets; for example, x[12] is the 12th element of the vector x:

```
> x[12]     # 12th element
```

```
[1] 1.817
```

```
> words[2] # second element
```

```
[1] "be"
```

```
> vals[3]     # third element
```

```
[1] FALSE
```

We may also specify a vector of indices:

```
> x[6:15] # elements 6 through 15
```

```
  [1] -1.8180  0.6301 -0.2762 -0.2842 -0.9193 -0.1162  1.8173  0.3706
  [9]  0.5202 -0.7505
```

Negative indices cause the corresponding values of the vector to be *omitted*:

```
> x[-(11:100)] # omit elements 11 through 100
```

```
  [1]  0.5855  0.7095 -0.1093 -0.4535  0.6059 -1.8180  0.6301 -0.2762
  [9] -0.2842 -0.9193
```

The parentheses around `11:100` serve to avoid generating numbers from −11 to 100, which would result in an error. (Try it!)

A vector can also be indexed by a logical vector of the same length. Logical values frequently arise through the use of *comparison operators*:

==	equals
!=	not equals
<=	less than or equals
<	less than
>	greater than
>=	greater than or equals

The double-equals sign (==) is used for testing equality, because = is reserved for specifying function arguments and for assignment.

Logical values may also be used in conjunction with the *logical operators*:

&	and
|	or

Here are some simple examples:

```
> 1 == 2

[1] FALSE

> 1 != 2

[1] TRUE

> 1 <= 2

[1] TRUE

> 1 < 1:3

[1] FALSE   TRUE   TRUE

> 3:1 > 1:3

[1]   TRUE FALSE FALSE

> 3:1 >= 1:3

[1]   TRUE   TRUE FALSE

> TRUE & c(TRUE, FALSE)

[1]   TRUE FALSE         .

> c(TRUE, FALSE, FALSE) | c(TRUE, TRUE, FALSE)

[1]   TRUE   TRUE FALSE
```

A somewhat more extended example illustrates the use of the comparison and logical operators:

```
> (z <- x[1:10])

 [1]  0.5855  0.7095 -0.1093 -0.4535  0.6059 -1.8180  0.6301 -0.2762
 [9] -0.2842 -0.9193
```

```
> z < -0.5

 [1] FALSE FALSE FALSE FALSE FALSE  TRUE FALSE FALSE FALSE  TRUE

> z > 0.5

 [1]  TRUE  TRUE FALSE FALSE  TRUE FALSE  TRUE FALSE FALSE FALSE

> z < -0.5 | z > 0.5  #  < and > of higher precedence than |

 [1]  TRUE  TRUE FALSE FALSE  TRUE  TRUE  TRUE FALSE FALSE  TRUE

> abs(z) > 0.5  # absolute value

 [1]  TRUE  TRUE FALSE FALSE  TRUE  TRUE  TRUE FALSE FALSE  TRUE

> z[abs(z) > 0.5]

[1]   0.5855  0.7095  0.6059 -1.8180  0.6301 -0.9193

> z[!(abs(z) > 0.5)]

[1] -0.1093 -0.4535 -0.2762 -0.2842
```

The last of these commands uses the ! operator, introduced in the last section, to negate the logical values returned by abs(z) > 0.5 and thus returns the observations for which the condition is FALSE.

A few pointers about using these operators:

- We need to be careful in typing z < -0.5; although most spaces in R commands are optional, the space after < is crucial: z <-0.5 would assign the value 0.5 to z. Even when spaces are not *required* around operators, they usually help to clarify R commands.
- Logical operators have lower precedence than comparison operators, and so z < -0.5 | z > 0.5 is equivalent to (z < -0.5) | (z > 0.5). When in doubt, parenthesize!
- The abs function returns the absolute value of its argument.
- As the last two commands illustrate, we can index a vector by a logical vector of the same length, selecting the elements with TRUE indices.

In addition to the vectorized *and* (&) and *or* (|) operators presented here, there are special *and* (&&) and *or* (||) operators that take individual logical values as arguments. These are often useful in writing programs (see Chapter 8).

1.1.6   USER-DEFINED FUNCTIONS

As you probably guessed, R includes functions for calculating many common statistical summaries, such as the mean of a vector:

```
> mean(x)

[1] 0.2452
```

Recall that x was previously defined to be a vector of 100 standard-normal random numbers. Were there no mean function, we could nevertheless have calculated the mean straightforwardly using sum and length:

```
> sum(x)/length(x)
```

```
[1] 0.2452
```

To do this repeatedly every time we need a mean would be inconvenient, and so in the absence of the standard R mean function, we could define our own mean function:

```
> myMean <- function(x) sum(x)/length(x)
```

- We define a function using the function function.[5] The arguments to function, here just x, are the *formal arguments* of the function being defined, myMean. As explained below, when the function myMean is called, an *actual argument* will appear in place of the formal argument. The remainder of the function definition is an R expression specifying the *body* of the function.
- The rule for naming functions is the same as for naming variables. We avoided using the name mean because we did not wish to *replace* the standard mean function, which is a generic function with greater utility than our simple version. For example, mean has an additional argument na.rm that tells R what to do if some of the elements of x are missing. We cannot overwrite the definitions of standard functions, but if we define a function of the same name, our version will be used in place of the standard function and is therefore said to *shadow* or *mask* the standard function. (This behavior is explained in Section 2.2.) In contrast to naming variables, in naming functions, we prefer using camel case (as in myMean) to separating words by periods (e.g., my.mean), because periods in function names play a special role in object-oriented programming in R (see Sections 1.4 and 8.7).
- The bodies of most user-defined functions are more complex than in this example, consisting of a *compound expression* comprising several simple R expressions, enclosed in braces and separated by semicolons or new-lines. We will introduce additional information about writing functions as required and take up the topic more systematically in Chapter 8.

Having defined the function myMean, we may use it in the same manner as the standard R functions. Indeed, most of the standard functions in R are themselves written in the R language.[6]

---

[5] We could not resist writing that sentence! Actually, however, function is a *special form*, not a true function, because its arguments (here, the formal argument x) are not evaluated. The distinction is technical, and it will do no harm to think of function as a function that returns a function as its result.

[6] Some of the standard R functions are *primitives*, in the sense that they are defined in code written in the lower-level languages C and Fortran.

```
> myMean(x)

[1] 0.2452

> y # from sqrt(c(1, 2, 3, 4))

[1] 1.000 1.414 1.732 2.000

> myMean(y)

[1] 1.537

> myMean(1:100)

[1] 50.5

> myMean(sqrt(1:100))

[1] 6.715
```

As these examples illustrate, there is no necessary correspondence between the name of the formal argument x of the function myMean and the actual argument to the function. Function arguments are evaluated by the interpreter, and it is the *value* of the argument that is passed to the function, not its name. Thus, in the last of the three examples above, the function call sqrt(1:100) must first be evaluated, and then the result is used as the argument to myMean. Function arguments, along with variables that are defined within a function, are *local* to the function: Local variables exist only while the function executes and are distinct from *global* variables of the same name. For example, the last call to myMean passed the value of sqrt(1:100) (i.e., the square roots of the integers from 1 to 100) to the argument x, but this argument did not change the contents of the global variable x (see p. 10):

```
> x

  [1]   0.58553   0.70947  -0.10930  -0.45350   0.60589  -1.81796   0.63010
. . .
 [99]  -0.59980  -0.69455
```

1.1.7   COMMAND EDITING AND OUTPUT MANAGEMENT

In the course of typing an R command, you may find it necessary to correct or modify the command before pressing Enter. The Windows *R Console* supports command-line editing:[7]

- You can move the cursor with the left and right arrow, Home, and End keys.
- The Delete key deletes the character under the cursor.
- The Backspace key deletes the character to the left of the cursor.
- The standard Windows *Edit* menu and keyboard shortcuts may be employed, along with the mouse, to block, copy, and paste text.

---

[7]The menu selection *Help* → *Console* will display these hints.

- In addition, R implements a command-history mechanism that allows you to recall and edit previously entered commands without having to retype them. Use the up and down arrow keys to move backward and forward in the command history. Press Enter in the normal manner to submit a recalled, and possibly edited, command to the interpreter.

The Mac OS X *R.app* behaves similarly, and somewhat more flexibly, in conformity with the usual OS X conventions.

Writing all but the simplest functions directly at the command prompt is impractical and possibly frustrating, and so using a programming editor with R is a good idea. Both the Windows and Mac OS X implementations of R include basic programming or script editors. We recommend that new users of R use these basic editors before trying a more sophisticated programming editor. You can open a new R script in the Windows *RGui* via the *File →New script* menu, or an existing script file via *File → Open script*. Similar *New Document* and *Open Document* selections are available under the Mac OS X *R.app File* menu. By convention, R script files have names that end with the extension or file type .R—for example, mycommands.R.

We also strongly recommend the use of an editor for data analysis in R, typing commands into the editor and then submitting them for execution rather than typing them directly at the command prompt. Using an editor simplifies finding and fixing errors, especially in multiline commands, and facilitates trying variations on commands. Moreover, when you work in the editor, you build a permanent, reusable record of input to your R session as a by-product.

Using the script editor in the Windows version of R, simply type commands into the editor, select them with the mouse, and then select *Edit → Run line or selection* or press the key combination Control-R to send the commands to the *R Console*. The procedure is similar in Mac OS X, except that commands are sent to the R interpreter by pressing the key combination command-return.

As you work, you can save text and graphical output from R in a word-processor (e.g., Microsoft Word or OpenOffice Writer) document. Simply block and copy the text output from the *R Console* and paste it into the word-processor document, taking care to use a monospaced (i.e., typewriter) font, such as `Courier New`, so that the output lines up properly. Word processors, however, make poor programming editors, and we recommend against their use for composing scripts of R commands.

Similarly, under Windows, you can copy and paste graphs: Right-clicking on a graphics window brings up a context menu that allows you to save the graph to a file or copy it to the Windows clipboard, from which it can be pasted into a word-processor document, for example. Alternatively, you can use the graphics window's *File* menu to save a graph. Copying the graph to the clipboard as a Windows Metafile rather than as a bitmap generally produces a more satisfactory result. Using *R.app* under Mac OS X, you can save the current plot in a *Quartz* graphics device window via the *File → Save as* menu, which by default saves a PDF file containing the graph; you can then import the PDF file into a word-processor document.[8]

For LATEX users, R supports a sophisticated system called Sweave for interleaving text and graphics with executable R code (for details, see Leisch, 2002, 2003). Indeed, we used Sweave to write this book!

1.1.8 WHEN THINGS GO WRONG

No one is perfect, and it is impossible to use a computer without making mistakes. Part of the craft of computing is learning to recognize the source of errors. We hope that the following advice and information will help you fix errors in R commands:

- Although it never hurts to be careful, do not worry too much about generating errors. An advantage of working in an interactive system is that you can proceed step by step, fixing mistakes as you go. R is also unusually forgiving in that it is designed to restore the workspace to its previous state when a command results in an error.
- If you are unsure whether a command is properly formulated or whether it will do what you intend, try it out and carefully examine the result. You can often debug commands by trying them on a scaled-down problem with an obvious answer. If the answer that you get differs from the one that you expected, focus your attention on the nature of the difference. Similarly, reworking examples from this *Companion*, from R help pages, or from textbooks or journal articles can help convince you that your programs are working properly.[9]
- When you do generate an error, don't panic! Read the error or warning message carefully. Although some R error messages are cryptic, others are informative, and it is often possible to figure out the source of the error from the message. Some of the most common errors are merely typing mistakes. For example, when the interpreter tells you that an object is not found, suspect a typing error, or that you have forgotten to load the package or read the file containing the object (e.g., a function).
- Sometimes, however, the source of an error may be subtle, particularly because an R command can generate a sequence of function calls of one function by another, and the error message may originate deep within this sequence. The `traceback` function, called with no arguments, provides information about the sequence of function calls leading up to an error. To create a simple example, we begin by writing a function to compute the variance of a variable, checking the output against the standard `var` function:

```
> myVar <- function(x) sum((x - myMean(x))^2)/(length(x) - 1)
> myVar(1:100)
```

---

[8]See Section 7.4 for more information on handling graphics devices in R.

[9]Sometimes, however, this testing may convince you that the published results are wrong, but that is another story.

```
[1] 841.7

> var(1:100) # check

[1] 841.7
```

We deliberately produce an error by foolishly calling `myVar` with a nonnumeric argument:

```
> letters

 [1] "a" "b" "c" "d" "e" "f" "g" "h" "i" "j" "k" "l" "m" "n" "o" "p"
[17] "q" "r" "s" "t" "u" "v" "w" "x" "y" "z"

> myVar(letters)

Error in sum(x) : invalid 'type' (character) of argument
```

The built-in variable `letters` contains the lowercase letters, and of course, calculating the variance of character data makes no sense. Although the source of the problem is obvious, the error occurs in the `sum` function, not directly in `myVar`; `traceback` shows the sequence of function calls culminating in the error:

```
> traceback()

2: myMean(x)
1: myVar(letters)
```

- Not all errors generate error messages. Indeed, the ones that do not are more pernicious, because you may fail to notice them. Always check your output for reasonableness, and follow up suspicious results.
- If you need to interrupt the execution of a command, you may do so by pressing the Esc (escape) key, by using the mouse to press the *Stop* button in the toolbar, or (under Windows) by selecting the *Misc → Stop current computation* menu item.
- There is much more information on debugging R code in Section 8.6.1.

1.1.9 GETTING HELP AND INFORMATION

We have already explained how to use the `help` function and `?` operator to get information about an R function. But what do you do if this information is insufficient or if you don't know the name of the function that you want to use? You may not even know whether a function to perform a specific task *exists* in the standard R distribution or in one of the contributed packages on CRAN. This is not an insignificant problem, for there are hundreds of functions in the standard R packages and literally thousands of functions in the more than 2,500 packages on CRAN.

Although there is no completely adequate solution to this problem, there are several R resources beyond `help` and `?` that can be of assistance:[10]

---

[10] In addition, we have already introduced the `help.start` command, and in Section 4.9, we describe the use of the `hints` function in the **hints** package to obtain information about functions that can be used with a particular R object.

- The `apropos` command searches for currently accessible objects whose names contain a particular character string. For example,

```
> apropos("log")

. . .
 [7] "dlogis"                "is.logical"
 [9] "log"                   "log10"
[11] "log1p"                 "log2"
[13] "logb"                  "Logic"
[15] "logical"               "logLik"
. . .
```

- Casting a broader net, the `help.search` command searches the titles and certain other fields in the help files of all R packages installed on your system, showing the results in a pop-up window. For example, try the command `help.search("loglinear")` to find functions related to loglinear models (discussed in Section 5.6). The `??` operator is a synonym for `help.search`—for example, `??loglinear`.
- If you have an active Internet connection, you can search even more broadly with the `RSiteSearch` function. For example, to look in all standard and CRAN packages—even those not installed on your system—for functions related to loglinear models, you can issue the command `RSiteSearch("loglinear", restrict="functions")`. The results appear in a web browser. See `?RSiteSearch` for details.
- The CRAN *task views* are documents that describe facilities in R for applications in specific areas such as Bayesian statistics, econometrics, psychometrics, social statistics, and spatial statistics. The approximately two-dozen task views are available via the command `carWeb("taskviews")`, which uses the `carWeb` function from the **car** package, or directly by pointing your browser at `http://cran.r-project.org/web/views/`.
- The command `help(package="package-name")`—for example, `help(package="car")`—shows information about an installed package, such as an index of help topics documented in the package.
- Some packages contain *vignettes*, discursive documents describing the use of the package. To find out what vignettes are available in the packages installed on your system, enter the command `vignette()`. The command `vignette(package="package-name")` displays the vignettes available in a particular installed package, and the command `vignette("vignette-name")` or `vignette("vignette-name", package="package-name")` opens a specific vignette.
- The *Help* menu in the Mac OS X and Windows versions of R provides self-explanatory menu items to access help pages, online manuals, the `apropos` function, and links to the R websites.
- As you might expect, help on R is available on the Internet from a wide variety of sources. The website `www.rseek.org` provides a custom Google search engine specifically designed to look for R-related

documents (try searching for **car** using this search site). The page www.
r-project.org/search.html lists other possibilities for web
searching.

- Finally, *Rhelp* is a very active email list devoted to answering users'
questions about R, and there are also several more specialized R mail-
ing lists (see www.r-project.org/mail.html). Before posting
a question to *Rhelp* or to one of the other email lists, however, *please*
carefully read the posting guide at www.r-project.org/posting
-guide.html.

1.1.10 CLEANING UP

User-defined variables and functions exist in R in a region of memory
called the *workspace*. The R workspace can be saved at the end of a session
or even during the session, in which case it is automatically loaded at the start
of the next session. Different workspaces can be saved in different directories,
as a means of keeping projects separate. Starting R in a directory loads the
corresponding workspace.[11]

The objects function lists the names of variables and functions residing
in the R workspace:

```
> objects()

[1] "myMean"   "myVar"    "vals"    "words"    "x"
[6] "y"        "z"
```

The function objects requires no arguments, but we nevertheless need to
type parentheses after the function name. Were we to type only the name of
the function, then objects would not be called—instead the *definition* of
the objects function would be printed. (Try it!) This is an instance of the
general rule that entering the name of an R object—in this case, the function
objects—causes the object to be printed.

It is natural in the process of using R to define variables—and occasionally
functions—that we do not want to retain. It is good general practice in R,
especially if you intend to save the workspace, to clean up after yourself from
time to time. To this end, we use the remove function to delete the variables
x, y, z, vals and words:

```
> remove(x, y, z, vals, words)

> objects()

[1] "myMean"   "myVar"
```

We keep the functions myMean and myVar, pretending that we still intend to
use them.

---

[11] See the R documentation for additional information on organizing separate projects.

1.1.11   ENDING THE R SESSION

The function quit or its equivalent, q, is used to exit from R:

```
> quit()

Save workspace image? [y/n/c]:
```

Answering y will save the workspace in the current directory, an operation that we generally do not recommend;[12] use n to avoid saving the workspace or c to cancel quitting. Entering quit(save="n") suppresses the question. You can also exit from R via the *File* menu or by clicking on the standard close-window button—the red button at the upper right in Windows and the upper left in Mac OS X.

1.2   An Extended Illustration: Duncan's Occupational-Prestige Regression

In this section, we illustrate how to read data from a file into an R *data frame* (data set), how to draw graphs to examine the data using both standard R functions and some of the specialized functions included in the **car** package, how to perform a linear least-squares regression analysis, and how to check the adequacy of the preliminary regression model using a variety of diagnostic methods. It is our intention both to introduce some of the capabilities of R and to convey the flavor of using R for statistical data analysis. All these topics are treated at length later in the book, so you should not be concerned if you don't understand all the details.

The data in the file Duncan.txt were originally analyzed by Duncan (1961).[13] The first few lines of the data file are as follows:

```
             type income education  prestige
accountant   prof 62        86      82
pilot        prof 72        76      83
architect    prof 75        92      90
author       prof 55        90      76
chemist      prof 64        86      90
minister     prof 21        84      87
professor    prof 64        93      93
dentist      prof 80       100      90
```

---

[12]A saved workspace will be loaded automatically in a subsequent session, a situation that often results in confusion, in our experience, especially among new users of R. We therefore recommend that you start each R session with a pristine workspace and instead save the script of the commands you use during a session that you may wish to recover (see the discussion of programming editors in Section 1.1.7). Objects can then conveniently be re-created as needed by executing the commands in the saved script. Admittedly, whether to save workspaces or scripts of commands is partly a matter of preference and habit.

[13]The Duncan.txt file, along with the other files used in this text, are available on the website for this *Companion*, at the web address given in the Preface. To reproduce the example, download the data file to a convenient location on your hard disk. Alternatively, you can open a copy of the file in your web browser with the command carWeb(data="Duncan.txt") and then save it to your disk.

```
reporter            wc   67      87         52
engineer            prof 72      86         88
 . . .
```

The first row of the file consists of variable (column) names: `type`, `income`, `education`, and `prestige`. Each subsequent row of the file contains data for one observation, with the values separated by spaces. The rows are occupations, and the first entry in each row is the name of the occupation. Because there is no variable name corresponding to the first column in the data file, the first value in each line will become a *row name* in the data frame that is constructed from the data in the file. There are 45 occupations in all, only 10 of which are shown.[14]

The variables are defined as follows:

- `type`: Type of occupation—bc (blue collar), wc (white collar), or prof (professional or managerial).
- `income`: Percentage of occupational incumbents in the 1950 U.S. Census who earned more than $3,500 per year (about $31,000 in 2008 U.S. dollars).
- `education`: Percentage of occupational incumbents in 1950 who were high school graduates (which, were we cynical, we would say is roughly equivalent to a PhD in 2008).
- `prestige`: Percentage of respondents in a social survey who rated the occupation as "good" or better in prestige.

Duncan used a linear least-squares regression of `prestige` on `income` and `education` to predict the prestige levels of occupations for which the income and educational levels were known but for which there were no direct prestige ratings. Duncan did not use occupational `type` in his analysis.

1.2.1   READING THE DATA

We will use the `read.table` function to read the data from the file Duncan.txt into a *data frame*—the standard R representation of a case-by-variable data set:

```
> Duncan <- read.table(file.choose(), header=TRUE)
```

The `file.choose` function brings up a standard open-file dialog box, allowing us to navigate to and select the Duncan.txt file; `file.choose` returns the path to this file, which becomes the first argument to `read.-table`. The second argument, `header=TRUE`, alerts `read.table` to the variable names appearing in the first line of the data file. The `read.table` function returns a data frame, which we assign to `Duncan`.

---

[14]As we will explain in Chapter 2, we can read data into R from a very wide variety of sources and formats. The format of the data in Duncan.txt is particularly simple, however, and furnishes a convenient initial example.

The generic `summary` function has a *method* that is appropriate for data frames. As described in Sections 1.4 and 8.7, generic functions know how to adapt their behavior to their arguments. Thus, a function such as `summary` may be used appropriately with diverse kinds of objects. This ability to reuse the same generic function for many similar purposes is one of the great strengths of R. When applied to the `Duncan` data-frame, `summary` produces the following output:

```
> summary(Duncan)

    type          income          education         prestige
 bc  :21    Min.   : 7.0    Min.   :  7.0    Min.   : 3.0
 prof:18    1st Qu.:21.0    1st Qu.: 26.0    1st Qu.:16.0
 wc  : 6    Median :42.0    Median : 45.0    Median :41.0
            Mean   :41.9    Mean   : 52.6    Mean   :47.7
            3rd Qu.:64.0    3rd Qu.: 84.0    3rd Qu.:81.0
            Max.   :81.0    Max.   :100.0    Max.   :97.0
```

In the input data file, the variable `type` contains character data, which `read.table` by default converts into a *factor*—an R representation of categorical data. The `summary` function simply counts the number of observations in each *level* (category) of the factor. The variables `income`, `education`, and `prestige` are numeric, and the `summary` function reports the minimum, maximum, median, mean, and first and third quartiles for each numeric variable.

To access a specific variable in the data frame, we need to provide its fully qualified name—for example, `Duncan$prestige` for the variable `prestige` in the `Duncan` data frame. Typing the full name can get tedious, and we can avoid this repetition by using the `attach` function. Attaching the `Duncan` data frame allows us to access its columns by name, much as if we had directly defined the variables in the R workspace:

```
> attach(Duncan)
> prestige

 [1] 82 83 90 76 90 87 93 90 52 88 57 89 97 59 73 38 76 81 45 92
[21] 39 34 41 16 33 53 67 57 26 29 10 15 19 10 13 24 20  7  3 16
[41]  6 11  8 41 10
```

Reading and manipulating data is the subject of Chapter 2, where the topic is developed in much greater detail. In particular, in Section 2.2 we will show you generally better ways to work with data frames than to attach them.

1.2.2 EXAMINING THE DATA

A sensible place to start any data analysis, including a regression analysis, is to examine the data using a variety of graphical displays. For example, Figure 1.4 shows a histogram for the response variable `prestige`, produced by a call to the `hist` function:

```
> hist(prestige)
```

Histogram of prestige

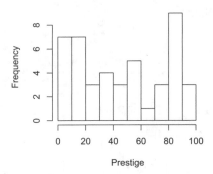

Figure 1.4 Histogram for `prestige` in Duncan's data.

The function `hist` doesn't return a value in the *R console* but rather is used for the side effect of drawing a graph, in this case a histogram.[15] The histogram may be copied to the clipboard, saved to a file, or printed (see Section 1.1.7).

The distribution of `prestige` appears to be bimodal, with observations stacking up near the lower and upper boundaries. Because `prestige` is a percentage, this behavior is not altogether unexpected—many occupations will either be low prestige, near the lower boundary, or high prestige, near the upper boundary, with fewer occupations in the middle. Variables such as this often need to be transformed, perhaps with a logit (log-odds) or similar transformation. As it turns out, however, it will prove unnecessary to transform `prestige`.

We should also examine the distributions of the predictor variables, along with the relationship between `prestige` and each predictor, and the relationship between the two predictors. The `pairs` function in R draws a scatterplot matrix. The `pairs` function is quite flexible, and we take advantage of this flexibility by placing histograms for the variables along the diagonal of the graph. To better discern the pairwise relationships among the variables, we augment each scatterplot with a least-squares line and with a nonparametric-regression smooth:[16]

```
> pairs(cbind(prestige, income, education),
+      panel=function(x, y){
+          points(x, y)
+          abline(lm(y ~ x), lty="dashed")
+          lines(lowess(x, y))
+      },
```

---

[15]Like all functions, `hist` *does* return a result; in this case, however, the result is *invisible* and is a list containing the information necessary to draw the histogram. To render the result visible, put parentheses around the command: `(hist(prestige))`. Lists are discussed in Section 2.3.

[16]Nonparametric regression is discussed in the online appendix to the book. Here, the method is used simply to pass a smooth curve through the data.

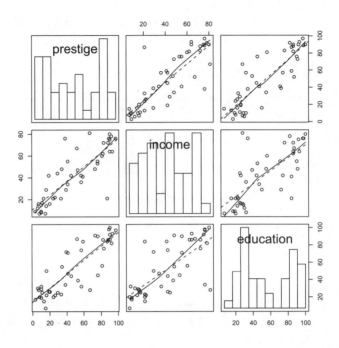

Figure 1.5 Scatterplot matrix for `prestige`, `income`, and `education` from Duncan's data.

```
+       diag.panel=function(x){
+           par(new=TRUE)
+           hist(x, main="", axes=FALSE)
+       }
+ )
```

Don't let the apparent complexity of this command worry you. Most graphs that you will want to draw are much simpler to produce than this one. Later in this *Companion*, we will describe functions in the **car** package that simplify the drawing of interesting graphs, including scatterplot matrices. Nevertheless, this call to `pairs` allows us to illustrate the structure of commands in R:

- The `cbind` (column-bind) function constructs a three-column matrix from the vectors `prestige`, `income`, and `education`, as required by the `pairs` function.
- The `panel` argument to `pairs` specifies a function that draws each off-diagonal panel of the scatterplot matrix. The function must have two arguments, which we call `x` and `y`, representing the horizontal and vertical variables in each plot. The panel function can be either a pre-defined function or—as here—a so-called *anonymous function*, defined on the fly.[17] Our panel function consists of three commands:

---

[17] The function is termed *anonymous* because it literally is never given a name: The function object returned by `function` is left unassigned.

1. `points(x, y)` plots the points.

2. `abline(lm(y ~ x), lty="dashed")` draws a broken line (specified by the line type[18] `lty="dashed"`) with intercept and slope given by a linear regression of y on x, computed by the `lm` (linear-model) function. The result returned by `lm` is passed as an argument to `abline`, which uses the intercept and slope of the regression to draw a line on the plot.

3. `lines(lowess(x, y))` draws a solid line, the default line type, showing the nonparametric regression of y on x. The `lowess` function computes and returns coordinates for points on a smooth curve relating y to x; these coordinates are passed as an argument to `lines`, which connects the points with line-segments on the graph.

Because there is more than one R command in the function body, these commands are enclosed as a *block* in curly braces, { and }. We indented the lines in the command to reveal the structure of the R code; this convention is optional but advisable. If no panel function is specified, then `panel` defaults to `points`. Try the simple command:

```
> pairs(cbind(prestige, income, education))
```

or, equivalently,

```
> pairs(Duncan[ ,-1])
```

This latter form uses all the columns in the `Duncan` data set except the first.

- The `panel.diagonal` argument similarly tells `pairs` what, in addition to the variable names, to plot on the diagonal of the scatterplot matrix. The function supplied must take one argument (x), corresponding to the current diagonal variable:

1. `par(new=TRUE)` prevents the `hist` function from trying to clear the graph. High-level R plotting functions, such as `plot`, `hist`, and `pairs`, by default clear the current graphics device prior to drawing a new plot. Lower-level plotting functions, such as `points`, `abline`, and `lines`, do not clear the current graphics device by default but rather add elements to an existing graph (see Section 7.1 for details).

2. `hist(x, main="", axes=FALSE)` plots a histogram for x, suppressing both the main title and the axes.

---

[18]Chapter 7 discusses the construction of R graphics, including the selection of line types.

The resulting scatterplot matrix for `prestige`, `income`, and `education` appears in Figure 1.5 (p. 26). The variable names on the diagonal label the axes: For example, the scatterplot in the upper-right-hand corner has `education` on the horizontal axis and `prestige` on the vertical axis.

Like `prestige`, `education` appears to have a bimodal distribution. The distribution of `income`, in contrast, is best characterized as irregular. The pairwise relationships among the variables seem reasonably linear, which means that as we move from left to right across the plot, the points more or less trace out a straight line, with scatter about the line. In addition, two or three observations appear to stand out from the others.

If you frequently want to make scatterplot matrices such as this, then it would save work to write a function to do the repetitive parts of the task:

```
> scatmat <- function(...) {
+     pairs(cbind(...),
+         panel=function(x, y){
+             points(x, y)
+             abline(lm(y ~ x), lty=2)
+             lines(lowess(x, y))
+         },
+         diag.panel=function(x){
+             par(new=TRUE)
+             hist(x, main="", axes=FALSE)
+         }
+     )
+ }
```

The special formal argument . . . (the *ellipses*) will match any number of actual arguments when the function is called—for example,

```
> scatmat(prestige, income, education)
```

produces a graph identical to the one in Figure 1.5. The `scatterplotMatrix` function in the **car** package (described in Section 3.3.2) is considerably more flexible than the `scatmat` function just defined.

In many graphs, we would like to identify unusual points by marking them with a descriptive label. Point identification in R is easier in a scatterplot than in a scatterplot matrix, and so we draw a separate scatterplot for `education` and `income`:

```
> plot(income, education)
> #   Use the mouse to identify points:
> identify(income, education, row.names(Duncan))

[1]   6 16 27

> row.names(Duncan)[c(6, 16, 27)]

[1] "minister"    "conductor"   "RR.engineer"
```

The `plot` function is the workhorse high-level plotting function in R. Called, as here, with two numeric vectors as arguments, `plot` draws a scatterplot of the variables given as arguments in the order first horizontal axis then vertical

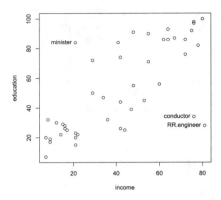

Figure 1.6   Scatterplot of income by education for Duncan's data. Three points were labeled interactively with the mouse.

axis. The identify function allows us subsequently to label points interactively with a mouse. The first two arguments to identify give the coordinates of the points, and the third argument gives point labels; row.names (Duncan) extracts the observation names from the Duncan data frame to provide the labels. The result is shown in Figure 1.6. The identify command returns the indices of the identified points, as we verify by indexing into the vector of names returned by row.names(Duncan). To duplicate this figure, you have to move the mouse cursor near each point to be identified, clicking the left mouse button; after identifying the points, in Windows click the right mouse button and select *Stop* to exit from identify, or click the *Stop* menu in the graphics device window and select *Stop locator*. In Mac OS X, press the esc key to stop identifying points.[19] In Section 3.5, we discuss both interactive and automatic point identification using the graphical functions in the **car** package.

Ministers are unusual in combining relatively low income with a relatively high level of education; railroad conductors and engineers are unusual in combining relatively high levels of income with relatively low education. None of these observations, however, are outliers in the *univariate* distributions of the three variables.

1.2.3   REGRESSION ANALYSIS

Duncan's interest in the data was in how prestige is related to income and education in combination. We have thus far addressed the distributions of the three variables and the pairwise—that is, *marginal*—relationships among them. Our plots don't directly address the *joint* dependence of

---

[19]Control doesn't return to the R command prompt until you exit from point-identification mode. New users of R occasionally think that R has frozen when they simply have failed to exit from identify.

prestige on education and income. Graphs for this purpose will be presented later. Following Duncan, we next fit a linear least-squares regression to the data to get numerical summaries for the joint dependence of prestige on the two predictors:

```
> (duncan.model <- lm(prestige ~ income + education))

Call:
lm(formula = prestige ~ income + education)

Coefficients:
(Intercept)          income     education
     -6.065           0.599         0.546
```

Because we previously attached the Duncan data frame, we can access the variables in it by name. The argument to lm is a *linear-model formula*, with the response variable, prestige, on the left of the tilde (~). The right-hand side of the model formula specifies the predictor variables in the regression, income and education. We read the formula as "prestige is regressed on income and education."

The lm function returns a linear-model object, which we assign to the variable duncan.model. As we explained in Section 1.1.3, enclosing the assignment in parentheses causes the assigned object to be printed, here producing a brief report of the results of the regression. The summary function produces a more complete report:

```
> summary(duncan.model)

Call:
lm(formula = prestige ~ income + education)

Residuals:
    Min      1Q  Median      3Q     Max
-29.538  -6.417   0.655   6.605  34.641

Coefficients:
            Estimate Std. Error t value Pr(>|t|)
(Intercept)  -6.0647     4.2719   -1.42     0.16
income        0.5987     0.1197    5.00  1.1e-05 ***
education     0.5458     0.0983    5.56  1.7e-06 ***
---
Signif. codes:  0 '***' 0.001 '**' 0.01 '*' 0.05 '.' 0.1 ' ' 1

Residual standard error: 13.4 on 42 degrees of freedom
Multiple R-squared: 0.828,        Adjusted R-squared: 0.82
F-statistic:  101 on 2 and 42 DF,  p-value: <2e-16
```

Both income and education have highly statistically significant, and rather large, regression coefficients: For example, holding education constant, a 1% increase in higher income earners is associated on average with an increase of about 0.6% in high prestige ratings.

R writes very small and very large numbers in scientific notation. For example, $1.1e-05$ is to be read as 1.1×10^{-5}, or 0.000011, and $2e-16 = 2 \times 10^{-16}$, which is effectively zero.

If you find the statistical significance asterisks that R prints annoying, as we do, you can suppress them, as we will in the remainder of this *Companion*, by entering the command:

```
> options(show.signif.stars=FALSE)
```

As usual, placing this command in one of R's start-up files will permanently banish the offending asterisks (see the discussion of configuring R in the Preface).[20] Linear models are described in much more detail in Chapter 4.

1.2.4   REGRESSION DIAGNOSTICS

Assuming that the regression in the previous section adequately summarizes the data does not make it so. It is therefore wise after fitting a regression model to check the fit using a variety of graphical and numeric procedures. The standard R distribution includes some facilities for regression diagnostics, and the **car** package associated with this book augments these capabilities. If you have not already done so, use the `library` command to load the **car** package:

```
> library(car)

Loading required package: MASS
Loading required package: nnet
Loading required package: leaps
Loading required package: survival
Loading required package: splines
```

Loading the **car** package also loads some other packages on which **car** depends.

The `lm` object `duncan.model` contains a variety of information about the regression. The `rstudent` function uses some of this information to calculate *Studentized residuals* for the model. A histogram of the Studentized residuals (Figure 1.7) is unremarkable:

```
> hist(rstudent(duncan.model))
```

Observe the sequence of operations here: `rstudent` takes the linear-model object `duncan.model`, previously returned by `lm`, as an argument and returns the Studentized residuals, which are passed to `hist`, which draws the histogram.

If the errors in the regression are normally distributed with zero means and constant variance, then the Studentized residuals are each *t*-distributed with $n - k - 2$ degrees of freedom, where k is the number of coefficients in the model excluding the regression constant and n is the number of observations. The generic `qqPlot` function from the **car** package, which makes *quantile-comparison plots*, has a method for linear models:

```
> qqPlot(duncan.model, labels=row.names(Duncan), id.n=3)

[1] "minister"   "reporter"   "contractor"
```

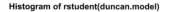

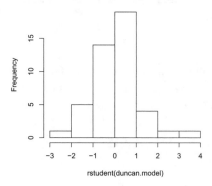

Figure 1.7 Histogram of the Studentized residuals from the regression of `prestige` on `income` and `education`.

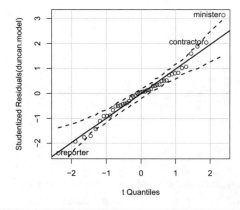

Figure 1.8 Quantile-comparison plot for the Studentized residuals from the regression of `prestige` on `income` and `education`. The broken lines show a bootstrapped pointwise 95% confidence envelope for the points.

The resulting plot is shown in Figure 1.8. The `qqPlot` function extracts the Studentized residuals and plots them against the quantiles of the appropriate t-distribution. If the Studentized residuals are t-distributed and $n - k - 2$ is large enough so that we can ignore the correlation between the Studentized residuals, then the points should lie close to a straight line. The comparison line on the plot is drawn by default by robust regression. In this case, the residuals pull away slightly from the comparison line at both ends, suggesting that the residual distribution is a bit heavy-tailed. By default, `qqPlot` produces a bootstrapped pointwise 95% confidence envelope for the

---

[20]If you like the significance stars, you may need to set `options(useFancyQuotes=FALSE)` to get the legend about the stars to print correctly in some cases, for example, in a L^AT_EX document.

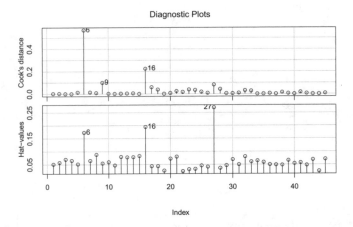

Figure 1.9   Index plots of Cook's distance and hat-values, from the regression of `prestige` on `income` and `education`.

Studentized residuals. The residuals nearly stay within the boundaries of the envelope at both ends of the distribution.

Most of the graphical methods in the **car** package have arguments that modify the basic plot. For example, the grid lines on the graph are added by default to most **car** graphics; you can suppress the grid lines with the argument `grid=FALSE`.[21]

The **car** graphics functions also have arguments that are used to identify points by their labels. In Figure 1.8 we set the argument `labels=row.-names(Duncan)` to tell the function the labels to use and the argument `id.n=3` to label three points with values on the horizontal axis farthest from the mean on the horizontal axis. The default in **car** graphical functions is `id.n=0`, to suppress point identification. Section 3.5 provides a more complete discussion of point labeling.

We proceed to check for high-leverage and influential observations by plotting *hat-values* (Section 6.3.2) and *Cook's distances* (Section 6.3.3) against the observation indices:

```
> influenceIndexPlot(duncan.model, vars=c("Cook", "hat"), id.n=3)
```

The plots are shown in Figure 1.9. We used the `id.n=3` argument to label the three most extreme points in each figure. Points are labeled by row number by default. Our attention is drawn to cases 6 and 16, which are flagged in both graphs, and which correspond to the following occupations:

```
> rownames(Duncan)[c(6, 16)]
```

```
[1] "minister"    "contractor"
```

---

[21] Grid lines can be added to most plots by first drawing using the `plot` function and then using the `grid` function to add the grid lines. In **car** graphics functions, we use `grid(lty=1)` to get solid-line grids rather than the dotted lines that are the default.

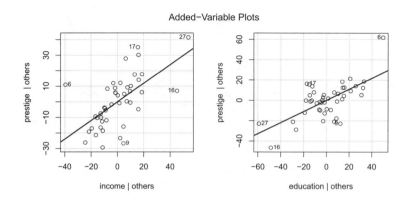

Figure 1.10 Added-variable plots for `income` and `education` in Duncan's occupational-prestige regression.

Because the observations in a regression can be jointly as well as individually influential, we also examine *added-variable plots* for the predictors, using the `avPlots` function in the **car** package (Section 6.2.3):

```
> avPlots(duncan.model, id.n=3, id.cex=0.75)
```

Each added-variable plot displays the conditional, rather than the marginal, relationship between the response and one of the predictors. Points at the extreme left or right of the plot correspond to points that are potentially influential, and possibly jointly influential. Figure 1.10 confirms and strengthens our previous observations: We should be concerned about the occupations `minister` (6) and `conductor` (16), which work together to decrease the `income` coefficient and increase the `education` coefficient. Occupation `RR.engineer` (27) has relatively high leverage on these coefficients but is more in line with the rest of the data. The argument `id.cex=0.75` makes the labels smaller to fit well into the plot. By specifying `id.n=3`, the `avPlots` function automatically labels the three most extreme points on the horizontal axis and the three points with the largest residuals.

We next use the `crPlots` function, also in the **car** package, to generate *component-plus-residual plots* for `income` and `education` (as discussed in Section 6.4.2):

```
> crPlots(duncan.model, span=0.7)
```

The component-plus-residual plots appear in Figure 1.11. Each plot includes a least-squares line, representing the regression plane viewed edge-on in the direction of the corresponding predictor, and a nonparametric-regression smoother, with the *span* of the smoother set to 0.7 (see Section 3.2). The purpose of these plots is to detect nonlinearity, evidence of which is slight here.

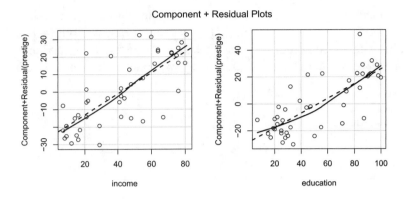

Figure 1.11   Component-plus-residual plots for income and education in Duncan's occupational-prestige regression. The span of the nonparametric-regression smoother was set to 0.7.

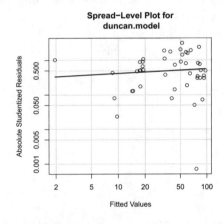

Figure 1.12   Spread-level plot of Studentized residuals from Duncan's regression of prestige on income and education.

We proceed to check whether the size of the residuals changes systematically with the fitted values, using the spreadLevelPlot function in the **car** package, which has a method for linear models (Section 6.5.1):

```
> spreadLevelPlot(duncan.model)

Suggested power transformation:   0.8653
```

The graph produced by spreadLevelPlot (Figure 1.12), shows little association of residual spread with level; and the suggested power transformation of the response variable, (prestige)$^{0.87}$, is essentially no transformation at all because the power is quite close to one. Using the ncvTest function in the **car** package (Section 6.5.2), we follow up with score tests for nonconstant variance, checking for an association of residual spread with the fitted values and with *any* linear combination of the predictors:

```
> ncvTest(duncan.model)

Non-constant Variance Score Test
Variance formula: ~ fitted.values
Chisquare = 0.3811     Df = 1      p = 0.537

> ncvTest(duncan.model, var.formula= ~ income + education)

Non-constant Variance Score Test
Variance formula: ~ income + education
Chisquare = 0.6976     Df = 2      p = 0.7055
```

Both tests are far from statistically significant, indicating that the assumption of constant variance is tenable.

Finally, on the basis of the influential-data diagnostics, we try removing the observations minister and conductor from the regression:

```
> summary(update(duncan.model, subset=-c(6, 16)))

Call:
lm(formula = prestige ~ income + education, subset = -c(6, 16))

Residuals:
   Min      1Q Median      3Q     Max
-28.61   -5.90   1.94    5.62   21.55

Coefficients:
             Estimate Std. Error t value Pr(>|t|)
(Intercept)   -6.4090     3.6526   -1.75   0.0870
income         0.8674     0.1220    7.11 1.3e-08
education      0.3322     0.0987    3.36   0.0017

Residual standard error: 11.4 on 40 degrees of freedom
Multiple R-squared: 0.876,         Adjusted R-squared: 0.87
F-statistic:  141 on 2 and 40 DF,  p-value: <2e-16
```

Rather than respecifying the regression model from scratch, we refit it using the update function, removing the two potentially problematic observations via the subset argument to update. The coefficients of income and education have changed substantially with the deletion of these two observations. Further work (not shown) suggests that removing occupations 27 (RR.engineer) and 9 (reporter) does not make much of a difference.

Chapter 6 has much more extensive information on regression diagnostics in R, including the use of the various functions in the **car** package.

1.3   R Functions for Basic Statistics

The focus of this *Companion* is on using R for regression analysis, broadly construed. In the course of developing this subject, we will encounter, and indeed already have encountered, a variety of R functions for basic statistical methods (mean, hist, etc.), but the topic is not addressed systematically.

Table 1.1 shows the names of some standard R functions for basic data analysis. Online help, through ? or help, provides information on the usage of these functions. Where there is a substantial discussion of a function in a later chapter in the present text, the location of the discussion is indicated in the column of the table marked *Reference*. The table is not meant to be complete.

1.4   Generic Functions and Their Methods*

Many of the most commonly used functions in R, such as summary, print, and plot, can have very different actions depending on the arguments passed to the function.[22] For example, the summary function applied to different columns of the Duncan data frame produces different output. The summary for the variable Duncan$type is the count in each level of this factor,

```
> summary(Duncan$type)

  bc prof   wc
  21   18    6
```

while for a numeric variable, the summary includes the mean, minimum, maximum, and several quantiles:

```
> summary(Duncan$prestige)

  Min. 1st Qu.  Median    Mean 3rd Qu.   Max.
   3.0    16.0    41.0    47.7    81.0    97.0
```

Similarly, the commands

```
> summary(Duncan)
> summary(lm(prestige ~ income + education, data=Duncan))
```

produce output appropriate to these objects—in the first case by summarizing each column of the Duncan data frame and in the second by returning a standard summary for a linear-regression model.

In R, allowing the same *generic function*, such as summary, to be used for many purposes is accomplished through an object-oriented programming

---

[22]The generic print function is invoked implicitly and automatically when an object is printed, for example, by typing the name of the object at the R command prompt, or in the event that the object returned by a function isn't assigned to a variable. The print function can also be called explicitly, however.

Table 1.1   Some R functions for basic statistical methods. All functions are in the standard R packages; chapter references are to this *Companion*.

Method	R Function(s)	Reference
histogram	hist	Ch. 3
stem-and-leaf display	stem	Ch. 3
boxplot	boxplot	Ch. 3
scatterplot	plot	Ch. 3
time-series plot	ts.plot	
mean	mean	
median	median	
quantiles	quantile	
extremes	range	
variance	var	
standard deviation	sd	
covariance matrix	var, cov	
correlations	cor	
normal density, distribution, quantiles, and random numbers	dnorm, pnorm, qnorm, rnorm	Ch. 3
t density, distribution, quantiles, and random numbers	dt, pt, qt, rt	Ch. 3
chi-square density, distribution, quantiles, and random numbers	dchisq, pchisq, qchisq, rchisq	Ch. 3
F density, distribution, quantiles, and random numbers	df, pf, qf, rf	Ch. 3
binomial probabilities, distribution, quantiles, and random numbers	dbinom, pbinom, qbinom, rbinom	Ch. 3
simple regression	lm	Ch. 4
multiple regression	lm	Ch. 4
analysis of variance	aov, lm, anova	Ch. 4
contingency tables	xtabs, table	Ch. 5
generating random samples	sample, rnorm, etc.	
t-tests for means	t.test	
tests for proportions	prop.test, binom.test	
chi-square test for independence	chisq.test	Ch. 5
various nonparametric tests	friedman.test, kruskal.test, wilcox.test, etc.	

technique called *object dispatch*. The details of object dispatch are implemented differently in the S3 and S4 object systems, so named because they originated in Versions 3 and 4, respectively, of the original S language on which R is based.

Almost everything created in R is an object, such as a vector, a matrix, a linear-regression model, and so on.[23] In the S3 object system, which we describe in this section, each object is assigned a *class*, and it is the class of

---

[23] Indeed, everything in R that is returned by a function is an object, but some functions have *side effects* that create nonobjects, such as files and graphs.

the object that determines how generic functions process the object. We defer
consideration of the S4 object system to a later chapter in the book, but it too
is class based and implements a version of object dispatch.[24]

The `class` function returns the class of an object:

```
> class(Duncan$type)

[1] "factor"

> class(Duncan$prestige)

[1] "integer"

> class(Duncan)

[1] "data.frame"
```

These objects are of classes `"factor"`, `"integer"`, and `"data.frame"`,
consecutively. When the function `lm` is used, an object of class `"lm"` is
returned:

```
> duncan.model <- lm(prestige ~ income + education)
> class(duncan.model)

[1] "lm"
```

Generic functions operate on their arguments indirectly by calling specialized functions, referred to as *method functions* or, more compactly, as *methods*. Which method function is invoked typically depends on the class of the
first argument to the generic function. For example, the generic `summary`
function has the following definition:

```
> summary

function (object, ...)
UseMethod("summary")
<environment: namespace:base>
```

The generic function `summary` has one required argument, `object`, and
the special argument . . . (the ellipses) for additional arguments that could be
different for each `summary` method. When `UseMethod("summary")` is
applied to an object of class `"lm"`, for example, R searches for a method
function named `summary.lm` and, if it is found, executes the command
`summary.lm(object, ...)`. It is, incidentally, perfectly possible to call
`summary.lm` directly; thus, the following two commands are equivalent:

```
> summary(duncan.model)
> summary.lm(duncan.model)
```

Although the generic `summary` function has only one explicit argument,
the method function `summary.lm` has additional arguments:

---

[24]More information on the S3 and S4 object systems is provided in Section 8.7.

```
> args(summary.lm)

function (object, correlation = FALSE, symbolic.cor = FALSE,
    ...)
NULL
```

Because the arguments correlation and symbolic.cor have default values (FALSE, in both cases), they need not be specified. Any additional arguments that are supplied, which are covered by ..., could be passed to functions that might be called by summary.lm.

Although in this instance we can call summary.lm directly, many method functions are hidden in the *namespaces* of packages and cannot normally be used directly.[25] In any event, it is good R form to use method functions indirectly through their generics.

Suppose that we invoke the hypothetical generic function fun with argument arg of class "cls". If there is no method function named fun.cls, then R looks for a method named fun=default. For example, objects belonging to classes without summary methods are printed by summary.-default. If, under these circumstances, there is no method named fun.-default, then R reports an error.

We can get a listing of all currently accessible method functions for the generic summary using the methods function, with hidden methods flagged by asterisks:

```
> methods(summary)

 [1] summary.aov           summary.aovlist      summary.aspell*
 [4] summary.connection    summary.data.frame   summary.Date
 [7] summary.default       summary.ecdf*        summary.factor
[10] summary.glm           summary.infl         summary.lm
. . .
[25] summary.stl*          summary.table        summary.tukeysmooth*

   Non-visible functions are asterisked
```

These methods may have different arguments beyond the first, and some method functions, for example, summary.lm, have their own help pages: ?summary.lm.

Method selection is slightly more complicated for objects whose class is a vector of more than one element. Consider, for example, an object returned by the glm function (anticipating a logistic-regression example developed in Section 5.3):

```
> mod.mroz <- glm(lfp ~ ., family=binomial, data=Mroz)
> class(mod.mroz)

[1] "glm" "lm"
```

---

[25]For example, the summary method summary.loess is hidden in the namespace of the **stats** package; to call this function directly to summarize an object of class "loess", we could reference the function with the nonintuitive name stats:::summary=loess.

If we invoke a generic function with `mod.mroz` as its argument, say `fun (mod.mroz)`, then the R interpreter will look first for a method named `fun.glm`; if a function by this name does not exist, then R will search next for `fun.lm`, and finally for `fun.default`. We say that the object `mod.mroz` is of *primary class* `"glm"`, and *inherits* from class `"lm"`. Inheritance permits economical programming through generalization, but it can also get us into trouble if, for example, there is no function `fun.glm` but `fun.lm` is inappropriate for `mod.mroz`. In a case such as this, the programmer of `fun.lm` should be careful to create a function `fun.glm`, which calls the default method or reports an error, as appropriate.

1.5   The R Commander Graphical User Interface

There are currently several statistical GUIs to R, the most extensive of which is the R Commander, implemented in the **Rcmdr** package.[26] The R Commander began as an interface to be used in an elementary statistics course but has expanded beyond that original purpose. Most of the statistical analysis described in this book can be carried out using menu items in the R Commander.

The R Commander, or any other well-designed statistical GUI, can help students learn new ideas, by separating the need for memorizing computer commands from the corresponding statistical concepts. A GUI can also assist a user who is familiar with the statistical ideas but not with R to make substantial and rapid progress. Finally, the infrequent user of R may find that a GUI provides access to the program without the burden of learning and relearning R commands.

With the good comes the bad:

- The R Commander provides access to only a small part of the capabilities of the standard R distribution and to a minuscule fraction of what's available in the more than 2,500 packages on CRAN. The user must trust that the writer of the GUI provided access to all the important functions, which is usually unlikely.
- Although the R Commander allows you to edit and reuse commands, it is generally quicker to type R commands than to generate them by drilling down through the R Commander menus.
- Learning to write R commands and to program in R will allow you to perform nonstandard tasks and to customize your work (e.g., drawing graphs—see Chapter 7) in a manner that's not possible with a GUI.

With these caveats in mind, the R Commander employs a standard menu-and-dialog-box interface that is meant to be largely self-explanatory. There are menus across the top of the main R Commander window, which is

---

[26] A disclaimer: We are not impartial, because one of us (Fox, 2005b) wrote the **Rcmdr** package and the other one insisted that it at least be mentioned in this chapter.

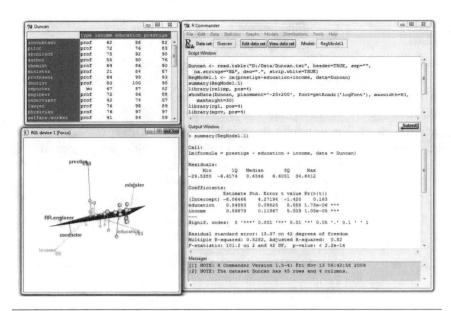

Figure 1.13   The R Commander in action.

shown, along with some other windows, at the right of the screen shot in Figure 1.13.

For example, to read the data from the file Duncan.txt into an R data frame, and to make that data frame the *active data set* in the R Commander, select *Data → Import data → from text file, clipboard, or URL*, and then complete the resulting dialog box, which allows you to navigate to the location of the data file. The R Commander generates and executes an appropriate command, which it also writes into its *Script Window*. Commands and associated printed output appear in the *Output Window*, and error and other messages in the *Messages* window. Graphs appear in a standard R graphics device window.

To continue the example, to perform a least-squares regression of prestige on income and education, select *Statistics → Fit models → Linear regression* (or *Linear model*), and complete the dialog. The R Commander generates an lm command. The linear-model object produced by the command becomes the *active model* in the R Commander, and various tests, graphs, and diagnostics can subsequently be accessed under the *Model* menu.

For more information, see the introductory manual provided by *Help → Introduction to the R Commander* and the help page produced by *Help → Commander help*. To install the **Rcmdr** package, use the command install.packages("Rcmdr", dependencies=TRUE), and be prepared to wait awhile as the many direct and indirect dependencies of the **Rcmdr** are downloaded from CRAN and installed on your system.

Reading and Manipulating Data 2

Traditional statistical computer packages such as SAS or SPSS are designed primarily to transform rectangular data sets into (sometimes very long) printed reports and graphs. A rectangular data set has rows representing observations and columns representing variables. In contrast, R is a programming language embedded in a statistical computing environment. It is designed to transform data objects into other data objects, (generally brief) printed reports, and graphs.

R supports rectangular data sets, in the form of *data frames*, but it also supports a variety of other data structures. One by-product of this generality is flexibility: Tasks not directly designed into the software are typically easier to carry out in R than in a statistical package. Another by-product of generality, however, is complexity. In this chapter, we attempt to eliminate some of the complexity:

- There are often many ways to accomplish a task in R. For common tasks such as reading data into an R data frame from a text file, we will generally explain a few good ways to proceed rather than aiming at an exhaustive treatment.
- We limit the presentation to those aspects of the R language that are most useful to practicing data analysts. For example, we avoid a fully general exposition of R modes and classes.
- Many functions in R, including those in the **car** package, have a dizzying array of options. We will generally only describe the most important options, or, in some cases, none of the options. As you gain experience with R you can learn about the options by reading the help pages that are included in R packages.
- We suggest that users of R adopt conventions that will facilitate their work and minimize confusion, even when the R language does not enforce these conventions. For example, in the **car** package we begin the names of data frames with uppercase letters and the names of variables in the data frames with lowercase letters.

Section 2.1 describes how to read data into R variables and data frames. Section 2.2 explains how to work with data stored in data frames. Section 2.3 introduces matrices, higher-dimensional arrays, and lists. Section 2.4 explains how to manipulate character data in R. Section 2.5 discusses how to handle large data sets in R. Finally, Section 2.6 deals more abstractly with the organization of data in R, explaining the notions of classes, modes, and attributes, and describing the problems that can arise with floating-point calculations.

2.1   Data Input

Although there are many ways to read data into R, we will concentrate on the most important ones: typing data directly at the keyboard, reading data from a plain-text (also known as *ASCII*) file into an R data frame, importing data saved by another statistical package, importing data from a spreadsheet, and accessing data from one of R's many packages. In addition, we will explain how to generate certain kinds of patterned data. In Section 2.5.3, we will briefly discuss how to access data stored in a database management system.

2.1.1   KEYBOARD INPUT

Entering data directly into R using the keyboard can be useful in some circumstances. First, if the number of values is small, keyboard entry can be efficient. Second, as we will see, R has a number of functions for quickly generating patterned data. For large amounts of data, however, keyboard entry is likely to be inefficient and error-prone.

We saw in Chapter 1 how to use the c (combine) function to enter a vector of numbers:

```
> (x <- c(1, 2, 3, 4))

[1] 1 2 3 4
```

Recall that enclosing the command in parentheses causes the value of x to be printed. The same procedure works for vectors of other types, such as character data or logical data:

```
> (names <- c("John", "Sandy", 'Mary'))

[1] "John"  "Sandy" "Mary"

> (v <- c(TRUE, FALSE))

[1]  TRUE FALSE
```

Character strings may be input between single or double quotation marks: for example, 'John' and "John" are equivalent. When R prints character

Table 2.1 Data from an experiment on anonymity and cooperation by Fox and Guyer (1978). The data consist of the number of cooperative choices made out of 120 total choices.

	Sex	
Condition	Male	Female
Public Choice	49	54
	64	61
	37	79
	52	64
	68	29
Anonymous	27	40
	58	39
	52	44
	41	34
	30	44

strings, it encloses them within double quotes, regardless of whether single or double quotes were used to enter the strings.

Entering data in this manner works well for very short vectors. You may have noticed in some of the previous examples that when an R statement is continued on additional lines, the > (greater than) prompt is replaced by the interpreter with the + (plus) prompt on the continuation lines. R recognizes that a line is to be continued when it is syntactically incomplete—for example, when a left parenthesis needs to be balanced by a right parenthesis or when the right argument to a binary operator, such as * (multiplication), has not yet been entered. Consequently, entries using c may be continued over several lines simply by omitting the terminal right parenthesis until the data are complete. It may be more convenient, however, to use the scan function, to be illustrated shortly, which prompts with the index of the next entry.

Consider the data in Table 2.1. The data are from an experiment (Fox and Guyer, 1978) in which each of 20 four-person groups of subjects played 30 trials of a prisoners' dilemma game in which subjects could make either cooperative or competitive choices. Half the groups were composed of women and half of men. Half the groups of each sex were randomly assigned to a public-choice condition, in which the choices of all the individuals were made known to the group after each trial, and the other groups were assigned to an anonymous-choice condition, in which only the aggregated choices were revealed. The data in the table give the number of cooperative choices made in each group, out of $30 \times 4 = 120$ choices in all.

To enter the number of cooperative choices as a vector, we could use the c function, typing the data values separated by commas, but instead we will illustrate the use of the scan function:

```
> (cooperation <- scan())
1:   49 64 37 52 68 54
7:   61 79 64 29
11:  27 58 52 41 30 40 39
18:  44 34 44
21:

Read 20 items
 [1] 49 64 37 52 68 54 61 79 64 29 27 58 52 41 30 40 39 44 34 44
```

The number before the colon on each input line is the index of the next observation to be entered and is supplied by scan; entering a blank line terminates scan. We entered the data for the Male, Public-Choice treatment first, followed by the data for the Female, Public-Choice treatment, and so on.

We could enter the condition and sex of each group in a similar manner, but because the data are patterned, it is more economical to use the rep (replicate) function. The first argument to rep specifies the data to be repeated; the second argument specifies the number of repetitions:

```
> rep(5, 3)

[1] 5 5 5

> rep(c(1, 2, 3), 2)

[1] 1 2 3 1 2 3
```

When the first argument to rep is a vector, the second argument can be a vector of the same length, specifying the number of times each entry of the first argument is to be repeated:

```
> rep(1:3, 3:1)

[1] 1 1 1 2 2 3
```

In the current context, we may proceed as follows:

```
> (condition <- rep(c("public", "anonymous"), c(10, 10)))

 [1] "public"    "public"    "public"    "public"    "public"
 [6] "public"    "public"    "public"    "public"    "public"
[11] "anonymous" "anonymous" "anonymous" "anonymous" "anonymous"
[16] "anonymous" "anonymous" "anonymous" "anonymous" "anonymous"
```

Thus, condition is formed by repeating each element of c("public", "anonymous") 10 times.

```
> (sex <- rep(rep(c("male", "female"), c(5, 5)), 2))

 [1] "male"   "male"   "male"   "male"   "male"   "female"
 [7] "female" "female" "female" "female" "male"   "male"
[13] "male"   "male"   "male"   "female" "female" "female"
[19] "female" "female"
```

The vector `sex` requires using `rep` twice, first to generate five `"male"` character strings followed by five `"female"` character strings, and then to repeat this pattern twice to get all 20 values.

Finally, it is convenient to put the three variables together in a data frame:

```
> (Guyer <- data.frame(cooperation, condition, sex))

    cooperation condition     sex
1            49     public    male
2            64     public    male
3            37     public    male
. . .
19           34  anonymous  female
20           44  anonymous  female
```

The original variables `condition` and `sex` are character vectors. When vectors of character strings are put into a data frame, they are converted by default into factors, which is almost always appropriate for subsequent statistical analysis of the data. (The important distinction between character vectors and factors is discussed in Section 2.2.4.)

R has a bare-bones, spreadsheet-like data editor that may be used to enter, examine, and modify data frames. We find this editor useful primarily for modifying individual values—for example, to fix an error in the data. If you prefer to enter data in a spreadsheet-like environment, we suggest using one of the popular and more general spreadsheet programs such as Excel or OpenOffice Calc, and then importing your data into R.

To enter data into a *new* data frame using the editor, we may type the following:

```
> Guyer <- edit(as.data.frame(NULL))
```

This command opens the data editor, into which we may type variable names and data values. An *existing* data frame can be edited with the `fix` function, as in `fix(Guyer)`.

The `fix` function can also be used to examine an existing data frame, but the `View` function is safer and more convenient: safer because `View` cannot modify the data, and more convenient because the `View` spreadsheet window can remain open while we continue to work at the R command prompt. In contrast, the R interpreter waits for `fix` or `edit` to terminate before returning control to the command prompt.

2.1.2   FILE INPUT TO A DATA FRAME

DELIMITED DATA IN A LOCAL FILE

The previous example shows how to construct a data frame from preexisting variables. More frequently, we read data from a plain-text (ASCII) file into an R data frame using the `read.table` function. We assume that the input file is organized in the following manner:

- The first line of the file gives the names of the variables separated by white space consisting of one or more blanks or tabs; these names are valid R variable names, and in particular must not contain blanks. If the first entry in each line of the data file is to provide row names for the data frame, then there is one fewer variable name than columns of data; otherwise, there is one variable name for each column.

- Each subsequent line contains data for one observation or case, with the data values separated by white space. The data values need not appear in the same place in each line as long as the *number* of values and their *order* are the same in all lines. Character data either contain no embedded blanks (our preference) or are enclosed in single or double quotes. Thus, for example, white.collar, 'white collar', and "white collar" are valid character data values, but white collar without quotes is not acceptable and will be interpreted as two separate values, white and collar. Character and logical data are converted to factors on input. You may avoid this conversion by specifying the argument as.is=TRUE to read.table, but representing categorical data as factors is generally desirable.

- Many spreadsheet programs and other programs create plain-text files with data values separated by commas—so-called *comma-delimited* or *comma-separated* files. Supplying the argument sep="," to read.- table accommodates this form of data. Alternatively, the function read.csv, a convenience interface to read.table that sets header=TRUE and sep="," by default, may be used to read comma-separated data files. In comma-delimited data, blanks *may* be included in unquoted character strings, but commas may not be included.

- Missing data appear explicitly, preferably encoded by the characters NA (Not Available); in particular, missing data are *not* left blank. There is, therefore, the same number of data values in each line of the input file, even if some of the values represent missing data. In a comma-separated file, however, missing values *may* be left blank. If characters other than NA are used to encode missing data, and if it is inconvenient to replace them in an editor, then you may specify the missing-data code in the na.strings argument to read.table. For example, both SAS and SPSS recognize the period (.) as an input missing-data indicator; to read a file with periods encoding missing data, use na.strings=".". Different missing-data codes can be supplied for different variables by specifying na.strings as a vector. For more details, see the online documentation for read.table.

This specification is more rigid than it needs to be, but it is clear and usually is easy to satisfy. Most spreadsheet, database, and statistical programs are capable of producing plain-text files of this format, or produce files that can be put in this form with minimal editing. Use a plain-text editor (such as Windows Notepad or a programming editor) to edit data files. If you use a word-processing program (such as Word or OpenOffice Writer), be careful to save the file as a plain-text file; `read.table` cannot read data saved in the default formats used by word-processing programs.

We use the data in the file Prestige.txt to illustrate.[1] This data set, with occupations as observations, is similar to the Duncan occupational-prestige data employed as an example in the previous chapter. Here are a few lines of the data file (recall that the ellipses represent omitted lines—there are 102 occupations in all):

	education	income	women	prestige	census	type
gov.administrators	13.11	12351	11.16	68.8	1113	prof
general.managers	12.26	25879	4.02	69.1	1130	prof
accountants	12.77	9271	15.70	63.4	1171	prof
. . .						
commercial.artists	11.09	6197	21.03	57.2	3314	prof
radio.tv.announcers	12.71	7562	11.15	57.6	3337	wc
athletes	11.44	8206	8.13	54.1	3373	NA
secretaries	11.59	4036	97.51	46.0	4111	wc
. . .						
elevator.operators	7.58	3582	30.08	20.1	6193	bc
farmers	6.84	3643	3.60	44.1	7112	NA
farm.workers	8.60	1656	27.75	21.5	7182	bc
rotary.well.drillers	8.88	6860	0.00	35.3	7711	bc

The variables in the data file are defined as follows:

- `education`: The average number of years of education for occupational incumbents in the 1971 Census of Canada.
- `income`: The average income of occupational incumbents, in dollars, in the 1971 Census.
- `women`: The percentage of occupational incumbents in the 1971 Census who were women.
- `prestige`: The average prestige rating for the occupation obtained in a sample survey conducted in Canada in 1966.
- `census`: The code of the occupation in the standard 1971 Census occupational classification.
- `type`: Professional and managerial (`prof`), white collar (`wc`), blue collar (`bc`), or missing (`NA`).

To read the data into R, we enter:

```
> (Prestige <- read.table("D:/data/Prestige.txt", header=TRUE))
```

	education	income	women	prestige	census	type
gov.administrators	13.11	12351	11.16	68.8	1113	prof
general.managers	12.26	25879	4.02	69.1	1130	prof
accountants	12.77	9271	15.70	63.4	1171	prof
. . .						
commercial.artists	11.09	6197	21.03	57.2	3314	prof
radio.tv.announcers	12.71	7562	11.15	57.6	3337	wc

---

[1] You can download this file and other data files referenced in this chapter from the website for the book, most conveniently with the `carWeb` function—see `?carWeb`. The data sets are also available, with the same names, in the **car** package.

athletes	11.44	8206	8.13	54.1	3373	NA
secretaries	11.59	4036	97.51	46.0	4111	wc
. . .						
elevator.operators	7.58	3582	30.08	20.1	6193	bc
farmers	6.84	3643	3.60	44.1	7112	NA
farm.workers	8.60	1656	27.75	21.5	7182	bc
rotary.well.drillers	8.88	6860	0.00	35.3	7711	bc

The first argument to read.table specifies the location of the input file, in this case the location in our local file system where we placed Prestige.txt. As we will see, with an active Internet connection, it is also possible to read a data file from a URL (web address). We suggest naming the data frame for the file from which the data were read and to begin the name of the data frame with an uppercase letter: Prestige.

Even though we are using R on a Windows system, the directories in the file system are separated by a / (forward slash) rather than by the standard Windows \ (back slash), because the back slash serves as a so-called *escape* character in an R character string, indicating that the next character has a special meaning: For example, \n represents a new-line character (i.e., go to the beginning of the next line), while \t is the tab character. Such special characters can be useful in creating printed output. A (single) back slash may be entered in a character string as \\.

You can avoid having to specify the full path to a data file if you first tell R where to look for data by specifying the *working directory*. For example, setwd("D:/data") sets the working directory to D:\data, and the command read.table("mydata.txt") would then look for the file mydata.txt in the D:\data directory. On Windows or Mac OS X, the command setwd(choose.dir()) allows the user to select the working directory interactively.[2] The command getwd() displays the working directory.

Under Windows or Mac OS X, you can also browse the file system to find the file you want using the file.choose function:

```
> Prestige <- read.table(file.choose(), header=TRUE)
```

The file.choose function returns the path to the selected file as a character string, which is then passed to read.table.

The second argument, header=TRUE, tells read.table that the first line in the file contains variable names. It is not necessary to specify header= TRUE when, as here, the initial variable-names line has one fewer entry than the data lines that follow. The first entry on each data line in the file is an observation label. Nevertheless, it does not hurt to specify header=TRUE, and getting into the habit of doing so will save you trouble when you read a file with variable names but *without* row names.

---

[2]Alternatively, you can use the menus to select *File* → *Change dir* under Windows or *Misc* → *Change Working Directory* under Mac OS X.

DATA FILES FROM THE INTERNET

If you have an active Internet connection, files can also conveniently be read from their URLs. For example, we can read the Canadian occupational-prestige data set from the website for the book:[3]

```
> Prestige <- read.table(
+    "http://socserv.socsci.mcmaster.ca/jfox/books/Companion/data/
        Prestige.txt",
+    header=TRUE)
```

DEBUGGING DATA FILES

Not all data files can be read on the first try. Here are some simple steps to follow to correct a problematic data file.

Whenever you read a file for the first time, it is a good idea to run a few checks to make sure the file doesn't have any problems. The summary function can be helpful for this purpose. For the Prestige data frame:

```
> summary(Prestige)

   education            income            women
 Min.    : 6.380    Min.    :  611    Min.    : 0.000
 1st Qu.: 8.445    1st Qu.: 4106    1st Qu.: 3.592
 Median :10.540    Median : 5930    Median :13.600
 Mean   :10.738    Mean    : 6798    Mean    :28.979
 3rd Qu.:12.648    3rd Qu.: 8187    3rd Qu.:52.203
 Max.   :15.970    Max.    :25879    Max.    :97.510
   prestige           census            type
 Min.    :14.80    Min.    :1113    bc  :44
 1st Qu.:35.23    1st Qu.:3120    prof:31
 Median :43.60    Median :5135    wc  :23
 Mean   :46.83    Mean    :5402    NA's: 4
 3rd Qu.:59.27    3rd Qu.:8312
 Max.   :87.20    Max.    :9517
```

From this output, we see that all the variables except type are numeric, because numeric summaries are reported, while type is a factor with levels bc, wc, and prof; furthermore, type has four missing values, given by the NAs.

If we had made an error in entering a numeric value—for example, typing the letter l ("ell") instead of the numeral 1 (one), or the letter O ("oh") instead of the numeral 0 (zero)—then the corresponding variable would have been made into a factor with many levels rather than a numeric variable, and we would have to correct the data in order to read them properly. Similarly, numbers with embedded commas, such as 2,000,000, are treated as character values rather than as numeric data, and so the corresponding variables would be incorrectly read as factors. Finally, if a value of type were entered incorrectly as BC rather than bc, then the type factor would acquire the additional level BC.

---

[3] The character string specifying the URL for the file Prestige.txt is broken across two lines to fit on the page but in fact must be given as one long string. Similar line breaks appear later in the chapter.

In some instances, an error in the data will prevent a file from being read at all, a problem that is usually caused by having too many or too few values in a line of the data file. Too many values can be produced by embedded blanks: For example, the characters - 2.3 in an input line, with a space between the minus sign and 2.3, would be read as two values, - and 2.3, not as the intended negative number −2.3. Too few items can be produced by coding missing data with blanks rather than with a proper missing-value indicator such as NA.

To simulate too few values in input lines, we prepared a version of the Prestige.txt data file in which NAs were erroneously replaced by blanks. Trying to read this file yields the following result:

```
> file <-
+ "http://socserv.socsci.mcmaster.ca/jfox/books/Companion/data/
     Prestige-bugged.txt"
> Prestige <- read.table(file, header=TRUE)

Error in scan(file = file, what = what, sep = sep, quote = quote, skip = 0,  :
line 34 did not have 7 elements
```

Because of the error, the data frame Prestige has not been created, and the error message tells us that at least one line in the file has the wrong number of elements. We can use the count.fields function to discover whether there are other errors as well, and, if there are, to determine their location:

```
> (counts <- count.fields(file))

 [1] 7 7 7 7 7 7 7 7 7 7 7 7 7 7 7 7 7 7 7 7 7 7 7 7 7 7 7 7 7 7
[31] 7 7 7 6 7 7 7 7 7 7 7 7 7 7 7 7 7 7 7 7 7 7 7 7 6 7 7 7 7 7
[61] 7 7 7 6 7 7 7 6 7 7 7 7 7 7 7 7 7 7 7 7 7 7 7 7 7 7 7 7 7 7
[91] 7 7 7 7 7 7 7 7 7 7 7 7

> which(counts != 7)

[1] 35 54 64 68
```

Once we know the location of the errors, it is simple to fix the input file in a text editor that keeps track of line numbers. Because the data file has column names in its first line, the 34*th* data line is the 35*th* line in the file.

FIXED-FORMAT DATA

Although they are no longer common, you may encounter *fixed-format* data files, in which the data values are not separated by white space or commas and in which variables appear in fixed positions within each line of the file. To illustrate the process of reading this kind of data, we have created a fixed-format version of the Canadian occupational-prestige data set, which we placed in the file Prestige-fixed.txt. The file looks like this:

```
gov.administrators            13.111235111.1668.81113prof
general.managers              12.2625879 4.0269.11130prof
```

```
accountants                12.77 927115.7063.41171prof
. . .
typesetters                10.00 646213.5842.29511bc
bookbinders                 8.55 361770.8735.29517bc
```

The first 25 characters in each line are reserved for the `occupation` name, the next five spaces for the `education` value, the next five for `income`, and so on. Most of the data values run together, making the file difficult to decipher. If you have a choice, fixed-format input is best avoided. The `read.fwf` (`read` fixed-width-format) function can be used to read this file into a data frame:

```
> file <-
+ "http://socserv.socsci.mcmaster.ca/jfox/books/Companion/data/
        Prestige-fixed.txt"
> Prestige <- read.fwf(file,
+     col.names=c("occupation", "education", "income", "women",
+         "prestige", "census", "type"),
+     row.names="occupation",
+     widths=c(25, 5, 5, 5, 4, 4, 4))
```

Our sample file does not have an initial line with variable names, and so the default value of `header=FALSE` is appropriate. The `col.names` argument to `read.fwf` supplies names for the variables, and the argument `row.-names` indicates that the variable `occupation` should be used to define row names. The `widths` argument gives the *field width* of each variable in the input file.

2.1.3 IMPORTING DATA

DATA FROM OTHER STATISTICAL PACKAGES

You are likely to encounter data sets that have been prepared in another statistical system, such as SAS or SPSS. If you have access to the other program, then exporting the data as a plain-text (ASCII) file for reading into R is generally quite straightforward. Alternatively, R provides facilities for *importing* data from other programs through functions in the **foreign** package, which is part of the standard R distribution. Currently, functions are available for importing data files from S version 3, SAS, SPSS, Minitab, Stata, and others. For example, the function `read.spss` is used to import SPSS data sets.

DATA FROM A SPREADSHEET

Raw data in a spreadsheet are probably the most common form of data that you will encounter. We can recommend three approaches to reading data from a spreadsheet. The simplest procedure may be to use the spreadsheet program to save the file in a format that can be read by `read.table`, usually a plain-text file with either white-space-delimited or comma-separated values. For this process to work, the data you want must be in the top-most worksheet of the spreadsheet, and the worksheet should look like a plain-text data file, with optional variable names in the first row, optional row names in the first column, and the row-by-column matrix of data values filled in completely. No extraneous information, such as variable labels requiring two rows, should be included.

The second approach is to copy the data you want to the clipboard and then to use an R function such as `read.table` to read the data from the clipboard. Select the data to be read in the spreadsheet program (e.g., by left-clicking and dragging the mouse over the data); the first row of the blocked data can contain variable names and the first column can contain row names. Next, copy the selected data to the clipboard (e.g., in Windows by the key combination Control-c and in Mac OS X by command-c). Finally, switch to R, and enter a command such as `Data <- read.table("clipboard", header=TRUE)` to read the data into the data frame `Data`. If the first selected row in the spreadsheet doesn't contain variable names, omit the argument `header=TRUE`.

On Windows, the **RODBC** package[4] can be used to read spreadsheets in Excel format directly. For example, the file Datasets.xls on the website for the book is an Excel file containing two worksheets: `Duncan`, with Duncan's occupational-prestige data, and `Prestige`, with the Canadian occupational-prestige data. We placed this file in D:\data\Datasets.xls. To read the `Prestige` data into R,

```
> library(RODBC)
> channel <- odbcConnectExcel("D:/data/Datasets.xls")
> Prestige <- sqlQuery(channel, "select * from [Prestige$]")
> odbcClose(channel)
> head(Prestige) # first 6 rows
```

	F1	education	income	women	prestige	census	type
gov.administrators	13.11	12351	11.16		68.8	1113	prof
general.managers	12.26	25879	4.02		69.1	1130	prof
accountants	12.77	9271	15.70		63.4	1171	prof
purchasing.officers	11.42	8865	9.11		56.8	1175	prof
chemists	14.62	8403	11.68		73.5	2111	prof
physicists	15.64	11030	5.13		77.6	2113	prof

Recall that everything to the right of the # (pound sign) is a comment and is ignored by the R interpreter. For Excel 2007 files, use `odbcConnect-Excel2007` in place of `odbcConnectExcel`.

The variable name "F1" was supplied automatically for the first column of the spreadsheet. We prefer to use this column to provide row names for the `Prestige` data frame:

```
> rownames(Prestige) <- Prestige$F1
> Prestige$F1 <- NULL  # remove F1 from Prestige
> head(Prestige)
```

---

[4]You can download and install this package from CRAN in the usual manner with the command `install.packages("RODBC")` or via the *Packages* menu. The **RODBC** package can also be made to work on other operating systems but not as conveniently as under Windows.

	education	income	women	prestige	census	type
gov.administrators	13.11	12351	11.16	68.8	1113	prof
general.managers	12.26	25879	4.02	69.1	1130	prof
accountants	12.77	9271	15.70	63.4	1171	prof
purchasing.officers	11.42	8865	9.11	56.8	1175	prof
chemists	14.62	8403	11.68	73.5	2111	prof
physicists	15.64	11030	5.13	77.6	2113	prof

```
> remove(Prestige)   # clean up
```

The **RODBC** package can also be used to connect R to a database management system (a topic that we will discuss briefly in Section 2.5.3).

2.1.4   ACCESSING DATA IN R PACKAGES

Many R packages, including the **car** and **alr3** packages, contain data sets. R provides two mechanisms for accessing the data in packages:

1. A data set can be read into the *global environment* (i.e., working memory) via the `data` command.[5] For example, to read the `Prestige` data frame from the **car** package into memory:

   ```
   > data(Prestige, package="car")
   > head(Prestige)   # first 6 rows
   ```

	education	income	women	prestige	census	type
gov.administrators	13.11	12351	11.16	68.8	1113	prof
general.managers	12.26	25879	4.02	69.1	1130	prof
accountants	12.77	9271	15.70	63.4	1171	prof
purchasing.officers	11.42	8865	9.11	56.8	1175	prof
chemists	14.62	8403	11.68	73.5	2111	prof
physicists	15.64	11030	5.13	77.6	2113	prof

   ```
   > remove(Prestige)   # clean up
   ```

   Had the **car** package already been loaded, the `package` argument to `data` could have been omitted.

2. Many packages allow data sets to be accessed directly, via the so-called *lazy-data* mechanism, without explicitly reading the data into memory. For example,

   ```
   library(car)
   ```

   . . .

   ```
   > head(Prestige)
   ```

	education	income	women	prestige	census	type
gov.administrators	13.11	12351	11.16	68.8	1113	prof
general.managers	12.26	25879	4.02	69.1	1130	prof
accountants	12.77	9271	15.70	63.4	1171	prof
purchasing.officers	11.42	8865	9.11	56.8	1175	prof
chemists	14.62	8403	11.68	73.5	2111	prof
physicists	15.64	11030	5.13	77.6	2113	prof

---

[5]Environments in R are discussed in Section 8.9.1.

CLEANING UP

We have defined several variables in the course of this section, some of which are no longer needed, so it is time to clean up:

```
> objects()

[1] "channel"     "condition"    "cooperation" "Guyer"
[5] "names"       "sex"          "v"           "x"

> remove(channel, names, v, x)
> detach(package:RODBC)
```

We have retained the data frame `Guyer` and the vectors `condition`, `cooperation`, and `sex` for subsequent illustrations in this chapter. Because we are finished with the **RODBC** package, we have detached it.

2.1.5 GETTING DATA *OUT* OF R

We hope and expect that you will rarely have to get your data out of R to use with another program, but doing so is nevertheless quite straightforward. As in the case of reading data, there are many ways to proceed, but a particularly simple approach is to use the `write.table` or `write.csv` function to output a data frame to a plain-text file. The syntax for `write.table` is essentially the reverse of that for `read.table`. For example, the following command writes the `Duncan` data frame (from the attached **car** package) to a file:

```
> write.table(Duncan, "c:/temp/Duncan.txt")
```

By default, row labels and variable names are included in the file, data values are separated by blanks, and all character strings are in quotes, whether or not they contain blanks. This default behavior can be changed—see `?write.table`.

The **foreign** package also includes some functions for exporting R data to a variety of file formats: Consult the documentation for the **foreign** package, `help(package="foreign")`.

2.2   Working With Data Frames

It is perfectly possible in R to analyze data stored in vectors, but we generally prefer to begin with a data frame, typically read from a file via the `read.table` function or accessed from an R package. Almost all the examples in this *Companion* use data frames from the **car** package.

In many statistical packages, such as SPSS, a single data set is active at any given time; in other packages, such as SAS, individual statistical procedures typically draw their data from a single source, which by default in SAS is the last data set created. This is not the case in R, where data may be used simultaneously from several sources, providing flexibility but with the possibility of interference and confusion.

There are essentially two ways to work with data in a data frame, both of which we will explain in this section:

1. Attach the data frame to the search path via the `attach` command, making the variables in the data frame directly visible to the R interpreter.

2. Access the variables in the data frame as they are required without attaching the data frame.

New users of R generally prefer the first approach, probably because it is superficially similar to other statistical software in which commands reference an *active* data set. For reasons that we will explain, however, experienced users of R usually prefer *not* to attach data frames to the search path.

2.2.1 THE SEARCH PATH

When you type the name of a variable in a command, the R interpreter looks for an object of that name in the locations specified by the *search path*. We attach the Duncan data frame to the search path with the `attach` function and then use the `search` function to view the current path:

```
> attach(Duncan)
> search()

 [1] ".GlobalEnv"         "Duncan"             "package:car"
 [4] "package:survival"   "package:splines"    "package:leaps"
 [7] "package:nnet"       "package:MASS"       "package:stats"
[10] "package:graphics"   "package:grDevices"  "package:utils"
[13] "package:datasets"   "package:methods"    "Autoloads"
[16] "package:base"
```

Now if we type the name of the variable `prestige` at the command prompt, R will look first in the global environment (`.GlobalEnv`), the region of memory in which R stores working data. If no variable named `prestige` is found in the global environment, then the data frame Duncan will be searched, because it was placed by the `attach` command in the second position on the search list. There is in fact no variable named `prestige` in the working data, but there is a variable by this name in the Duncan data frame, and so when we type `prestige`, we retrieve the `prestige` variable from Duncan, as we may readily verify:

```
> prestige

 [1] 82 83 90 76 90 87 93 90 52 88 57 89 97 59 73 38 76 81 45 92
[21] 39 34 41 16 33 53 67 57 26 29 10 15 19 10 13 24 20  7  3 16
[41]  6 11  8 41 10
```

```
> Duncan$prestige
```

```
 [1] 82 83 90 76 90 87 93 90 52 88 57 89 97 59 73 38 76 81 45 92
[21] 39 34 41 16 33 53 67 57 26 29 10 15 19 10 13 24 20  7  3 16
[41]  6 11  8 41 10
```

Typing `Duncan$prestige` directly extracts the column named `pres-tige` from the Duncan data frame.[6]

Had `prestige` not been found in `Duncan`, then the sequence of attached packages would have been searched in the order shown, followed by a special list of objects (`Autoloads`) that are loaded automatically as needed (and which we will subsequently ignore), and finally the R **base** package. The packages in the search path shown above, beginning with the **stats** package, are part of the basic R system and are loaded by default when R starts up.

Suppose, now, that we attach the `Prestige` data frame to the search path. The default behavior of the `attach` function is to attach a data frame in the *second* position on the search path, after the global environment:

```
> attach(Prestige)

        The following object(s) are masked from Duncan :

        education income prestige type


        The following object(s) are masked from package:datasets :

        women

> search()
```

```
 [1] ".GlobalEnv"        "Prestige"           "Duncan"
 [4] "package:car"       "package:survival"   "package:splines"
 [7] "package:leaps"     "package:nnet"       "package:MASS"
[10] "package:stats"     "package:graphics"   "package:grDevices"
[13] "package:utils"     "package:datasets"   "package:methods"
[16] "Autoloads"         "package:base"
```

Consequently, the data frame `Prestige` is attached *before* the data frame `Duncan`; and if we now simply type `prestige`, then the `prestige` variable in `Prestige` will be located *before* the `prestige` variable in `Duncan` is encountered:

```
> prestige
```

```
  [1] 68.8 69.1 63.4 56.8 73.5 77.6 72.6 78.1 73.1 68.8
 [11] 62.0 60.0 53.8 62.2 74.9 55.1 82.3 58.1 58.3 72.8
 [21] 84.6 59.6 66.1 87.2 66.7 68.4 64.7 34.9 72.1 69.3
  . . .
 [91] 38.9 36.2 29.9 42.9 26.5 66.1 48.9 35.9 25.1 26.1
[101] 42.2 35.2
```

---

[6]Information on indexing data frames is presented in Section 2.3.4.

The `prestige` variable in `Duncan` is still there—it is just being *shadowed* or *masked* (i.e., hidden) by `prestige` in `Prestige`, as the `attach` command warned us:

```
> Duncan$prestige

 [1] 82 83 90 76 90 87 93 90 52 88 57 89 97 59 73 38 76 81 45 92
[21] 39 34 41 16 33 53 67 57 26 29 10 15 19 10 13 24 20  7  3 16
[41]  6 11  8 41 10
```

Because the variables in one data frame can shadow the variables in another, attaching more than one data frame at a time can lead to unanticipated problems and should generally be avoided. You can remove a data frame from the search path with the `detach` command:

```
> detach(Prestige)
> search()

 [1] ".GlobalEnv"         "Duncan"              "package:car"
 [4] "package:survival"   "package:splines"     "package:leaps"
 [7] "package:nnet"       "package:MASS"        "package:stats"
[10] "package:graphics"   "package:grDevices"   "package:utils"
[13] "package:datasets"   "package:methods"     "Autoloads"
[16] "package:base"
```

Calling `detach` with no arguments detaches the second entry in the search path and, thus, produces the same effect as `detach(Prestige)`.

Now that `Prestige` has been detached, `prestige` again refers to the variable by that name in the `Duncan` data frame:

```
> prestige

 [1] 82 83 90 76 90 87 93 90 52 88 57 89 97 59 73 38 76 81 45 92
[21] 39 34 41 16 33 53 67 57 26 29 10 15 19 10 13 24 20  7  3 16
[41]  6 11  8 41 10
```

The working data are the first item in the search path, and so globally defined variables shadow variables with the same names anywhere else along the path. This is why we use an uppercase letter at the beginning of the name of a data frame. Had we, for example, named the data frame `prestige` rather than `Prestige`, then the variable `prestige` within the data frame would have been shadowed by the data frame itself. To access the variable would then require a potentially confusing expression, such as `prestige$prestige`.

Our focus here is on manipulating data, but it is worth mentioning that R locates functions in the same way that it locates data. Consequently, functions earlier on the path can shadow functions of the same name later on the path.

In Section 1.1.3, we defined a function called `myMean`, avoiding the name `mean` so that the `mean` function in the **base** package would not be shadowed. The **base** function `mean` can calculate trimmed means as well as the ordinary arithmetic mean; for example,

```
> mean(prestige)
```

```
[1] 47.68889
```

```
> mean(prestige, trim=0.1)
```

```
[1] 47.2973
```

Specifying `mean(prestige, trim=0.1)` removes the top and bottom 10% of the data, calculating the mean of the middle 80% of observations. Trimmed means provide more efficient estimates of the center of a heavy-tailed distribution—for example, when outliers are present; in this example, however, trimming makes little difference.

Suppose that we define our own `mean` function, making no provision for trimming:

```
> mean <- function(x){
+     warning("the mean function in the base package is shadowed")
+     sum(x)/length(x)
+ }
```

The first line in our `mean` function prints a warning message. The purpose of the warning is simply to verify that our function executes in place of the mean function in the **base** package. Had we *carelessly* shadowed the standard mean function, we would not have politely provided a warning:

```
> mean(prestige)
```

```
[1] 47.68889
Warning message:
In mean(prestige):the mean function in the base package is shadowed
```

The essential point here is that because our `mean` function resides in the global environment, it is encountered on the search path *before* the mean function in the **base** package. Shadowing the standard mean function is inconsequential as long as our function is equivalent; but if, for example, we try to calculate a trimmed mean, our function does not work:

```
> mean(prestige, trim=0.1)
```

```
Error in mean(prestige, trim = 0.1):unused argument(s)(trim = 0.1)
```

Shadowing standard R functions is a practice generally to be avoided. Suppose, for example, that a robust-regression function tries to calculate a trimmed mean, but fails because the standard mean function is shadowed by our redefined mean function. If we are not conscious of this problem, the resulting error message may prove cryptic.

We can, however, use the same name for a variable and a function, as long as the two do not reside in the working data. Consider the following example:

```
> mean <- mean(prestige)   # uses then overwrites our mean function
> mean
```

```
[1] 47.68889
```

Specifying `mean <- mean(prestige)` causes our `mean` function to calculate the mean `prestige` and then stores the result in a variable called mean, which has the effect of destroying our `mean` function (and good riddance to it). The *variable* mean in the working data does not, however, shadow the *function* mean in the **base** package:

```
> mean(prestige, trim=0.1)
```

```
[1] 47.2973
```

Before proceeding, let us tidy up a bit:

```
> remove(mean)
> detach(Duncan)
```

2.2.2 AVOIDING `attach`

Here are some compelling reasons for *not* attaching data frames to the search path:

- Variables in attached data frames may mask other objects, and variables in attached data frames themselves may be masked by objects of the same name—for example, in the global environment.
- Attaching a data frame makes a *copy* of the data frame; the attached version is a snapshot of the data frame at the moment when it is attached. If changes are made to the data frame, these are *not* reflected in the attached version of the data. Consequently, after making such a change, it is necessary to detach and reattach the data frame. We find this procedure awkward, and inexperienced users of R may not remember to detach and reattach the data, leading to confusion about the current state of the attached data.
- We have observed that new users of R tend not to detach data frames after they are done with them. Often they will attach multiple versions of a data frame in the same session, which potentially results in confusion.

There are several strategies that we can use to avoid attaching a data frame:

- We can reference the variables in a data frame explicitly: for example,

  ```
  > mean(Duncan$prestige)
  ```

  ```
  [1] 47.68889
  ```

- Statistical-modeling functions in R usually include a `data` argument, which can be set to a data frame, conveniently specifying where the data for the model are to be found: for example,

  ```
  > (lm(prestige ~ income + education, data=Duncan))

  Call:
  lm(formula = prestige ~ income + education, data = Duncan)

  Coefficients:
  (Intercept)       income      education
      -6.0647       0.5987         0.5458
  ```

- The `with` command can be used to evaluate an R expression in the environment of a data frame: for example,

```
> with(Duncan, mean(prestige))

[1] 47.68889

> with(Duncan, lm(prestige ~ income + education))

Call:
lm(formula = prestige ~ income + education)

Coefficients:
(Intercept)        income      education
    -6.0647        0.5987         0.5458
```

We will use `with` frequently in the rest of this *Companion*.

2.2.3   MISSING DATA

Missing data are a regrettably common feature of real data sets. Two kinds of issues arise in handling missing data:

- There are relatively profound statistical issues concerning how best to use available information when missing data are encountered (see, e.g., Little and Rubin, 2002; and Schafer, 1997). We will ignore these issues here, except to remark that R is well designed to make use of sophisticated approaches to missing data.[7]
- There are intellectually trivial but often practically vexing mechanical issues concerning computing with missing data in R. These issues, which are the subject of the present section, arise partly because of the diverse data structures and kinds of functions available simultaneously to the R user. Similar issues arise in *all* statistical software, however, although they may sometimes be disguised.

As we have explained, on data input, missing values are typically encoded by the characters NA. The same characters are used to print missing information. Many functions in R know how to handle missing data, although sometimes they have to be explicitly told what to do.

To illustrate, let us examine the data set `Freedman` in the **car** package:

```
> head(Freedman)   # first 6 rows

            population nonwhite density crime
Akron              675      7.3     746  2602
Albany             713      2.6     322  1388
Albuquerque         NA      3.3      NA  5018
Allentown          534      0.8     491  1182
Anaheim           1261      1.4    1612  3341
Atlanta           1330     22.8     770  2805

> dim(Freedman)   # number of rows and columns

[1] 110    4
```

---

[7]Notable packages for handling missing data include **amelia**, **mi**, **mice**, and **norm**, which perform various versions of multiple imputation of missing data.

These data, on 110 U.S. metropolitan areas, were originally from the *1970 Statistical Abstract of the United States* and were used by Freedman (1975) as part of a wide-ranging study of the social and psychological effects of crowding. Freedman argues, by the way, that high density tends to intensify social interaction, and thus the effects of crowding are not simply negative. The variables in the data set are as follows:

- population: Total 1968 population, in thousands.
- nonwhite: Percent nonwhite population in 1960.
- density: Population per square mile in 1968.
- crime: Number of serious crimes per 100,000 residents in 1969.

Some of Freedman's data are missing—for example, the population and density for Albuquerque. Here are the first few values for density:

```
> head(Freedman$density, 20)   # first 20 values

 [1]  746  322   NA  491 1612  770   41  877  240  147  272 1831
[13] 1252  832  630   NA   NA  328  308 1832
```

Suppose, now, that we try to calculate the median density; as we will see shortly, the density values are highly positively skewed, so using the *mean* as a measure of the center of the distribution would be a bad idea:

```
> median(Freedman$density)

[1] NA
```

R tells us that the median density is missing. This is the pedantically correct answer: Several of the density values are missing, and consequently we cannot in the absence of those values know the median, but this is probably not what we had in mind when we asked for the median density. By setting the na.rm (NA-remove) argument of median to TRUE, we instruct R to calculate the median of the remaining, nonmissing values:

```
> median(Freedman$density, na.rm=TRUE)

[1] 412
```

Several other R functions that calculate statistical summaries, such as mean, var (variance), sd (standard deviation), and quantile (quantiles), also have na.rm arguments, but not all R functions handle missing data in this manner.

Most plotting functions simply ignore missing data. For example, to construct a scatterplot of crime against density, including only the observations with valid data for both variables, we enter

```
> with(Freedman, {
+     plot(density, crime)
+     identify(density, crime, row.names(Freedman))
+ })
```

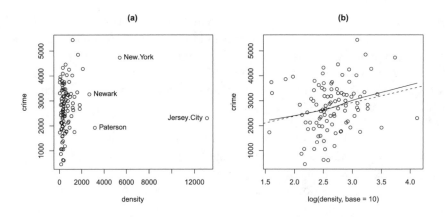

Figure 2.1   Scatterplot of `crime` by population `density` for Freedman's data. (a) Original density scale, with a few high-density cities identified interactively with the mouse, and (b) log-density scale, showing linear least-squares (broken) and lowess nonparametric-regression (solid) lines. Cases with one or both values missing are silently omitted from both graphs.

The resulting graph, including several observations identified with the mouse, appears in Figure 2.1a. Recall that we identify observations by pointing at them with the mouse and clicking the left mouse button; exit from `iden-tify` by pressing the esc key in Mac OS X or, in Windows, by clicking the right mouse button and selecting *Stop*. It is apparent that `density` is highly positively skewed, making the plot very difficult to read. We would like to try plotting `crime` against the log of `density` but wonder whether the missing data will spoil the computation.[8] The `log` function in R behaves sensibly, however: The result has a missing entry wherever—and only where—there was a missing entry in the argument:

```
> log(c(1, 10, NA, 100), base=10)

[1]  0  1 NA  2
```

Other functions that compute on vectors in an element-wise fashion—such as the arithmetic operators—behave similarly.

We, therefore, may proceed as follows, producing the graph in Figure 2.1b:[9]

```
> with(Freedman, plot(log(density, base=10), crime))
```

This graph is much easier to read, and it now appears that there is a weak, positive relationship between `crime` and `density`. We will address momentarily how to produce the lines in the plot.

Statistical-modeling functions in R have a special argument, `na.action`, which specifies how missing data are to be handled; `na.action` is set to

---

[8]Transformations, including the log transformation, are the subject of Section 3.4.

[9]An alternative would have been to plot `crime` against `density` using a log axis for `density`: `plot(density, crime, log="x")`. See Chapters 3 and 7 for general discussions of plotting data in R.

a function that takes a data frame as an argument and returns a similar data frame composed entirely of valid data (see Section 4.8.5). The default `na-.action` is `na.omit`, which removes all observations with missing data on *any* variable in the computation. All the examples in this *Companion* use `na.omit`. An alternative, for example, would be to supply an `na.action` that imputes the missing values.

The prototypical statistical-modeling function in R is `lm`, which is described extensively in Chapter 4. For example, to fit a linear regression of `crime` on the log of `density`, removing observations with missing data on either `crime` or `density`, enter the command

```
> lm(crime ~ log(density, base=10), data=Freedman)

Call:
lm(formula = crime ~ log(density, base = 10), data = Freedman)

Coefficients:
            (Intercept)   log(density, base = 10)
                 1297.3                     542.6
```

The `lm` function returns a linear-model object; because the returned object was not saved in a variable, the interpreter simply printed a brief report of the regression. To plot the least-squares line on the scatterplot in Figure 2.1:

```
> abline(lm(crime ~ log(density, base=10), data=Freedman),
   lty="dashed")
```

The linear-model object returned by `lm` is passed to `abline`, which draws the regression line; specifying the line type `lty="dashed"` produces a broken line.

Some functions in R, especially the older ones, make no provision for missing data and simply fail if an argument has a missing entry. In these cases, we need somewhat tediously to handle the missing data ourselves. A relatively straightforward way to do so is to use the `complete.cases` function to test for missing data, and then to exclude the missing data from the calculation.

For example, to locate all observations with valid data for both `crime` and `density`, we enter:

```
> good <- with(Freedman, complete.cases(crime, density))
> head(good, 20)   # first 20 values

 [1]  TRUE  TRUE FALSE  TRUE  TRUE  TRUE  TRUE  TRUE  TRUE  TRUE
[11]  TRUE  TRUE  TRUE  TRUE  TRUE FALSE FALSE  TRUE  TRUE  TRUE
```

We then use `good` to select the valid observations by indexing (a topic described in Section 2.3.4). For example, it is convenient to use the `lowess` function to add a nonparametric-regression smooth to our scatterplot (Figure 2.1b), but `lowess` makes no provision for missing data:[10]

---

[10]The `lowess` function is described in Section 3.2.1.

```
> with(Freedman,
+   lines(lowess(log(density[good], base=10), crime[good], f=1.0)))
```

By indexing the predictor `density` and response `crime` with the logical vector `good`, we extract only the observations that have valid data for *both* variables. The argument `f` to the `lowess` function specifies the *span* of the lowess smoother—that is, the fraction of the data included in each local-regression fit; large spans (such as the value `1.0` employed here) produce smooth regression curves.

Suppose, as is frequently the case, that we analyze a data set with a complex pattern of missing data, fitting several statistical models to the data. If the models do not all use exactly the same variables, then it is likely that they will be fit to different subsets of nonmissing observations. Then if we compare the models with a likelihood ratio test, for example, the comparison will be invalid.[11]

To avoid this problem, we can first use `na.omit` to filter the data frame for missing data, including all the variables that we intend to use in our data analysis. For example, for Freedman's data, we may proceed as follows, assuming that we want subsequently to use all four variables in the data frame:

```
> Freedman.good <- na.omit(Freedman)
> head(Freedman.good)   # first 6 rows

            population nonwhite density crime
Akron              675      7.3     746  2602
Albany             713      2.6     322  1388
Allentown          534      0.8     491  1182
Anaheim           1261      1.4    1612  3341
Atlanta           1330     22.8     770  2805
Bakersfield        331      7.0      41  3306

> dim(Freedman.good)   # number of rows and columns

[1] 100    4
```

A note of caution: Filtering for missing data on variables that we *do not* intend to use can result in discarding data unnecessarily. We have seen cases where students and researchers inadvertently and needlessly threw away most of their data by filtering an entire data set for missing values, even when they intended to use only a few variables in the data set.

Finally, a few words about testing for missing data in R: A common error is to assume that one can check for missing data using the == (equals) operator, as in

```
> NA == c(1, 2, NA, 4)

[1] NA NA NA NA
```

Testing equality of `NA` against *any* value in R returns `NA` as a result. After all, if the value is missing, how can we know whether it's equal to something else? The proper way to test for missing data is with the function `is.na`:

---

[11] How statistical-modeling functions in R handle missing data is described in Section 4.8.5.

```
> is.na(c(1, 2, NA, 4))
```

```
[1] FALSE FALSE  TRUE FALSE
```

For example, to count the number of missing values in the `Freedman` data frame:

```
> sum(is.na(Freedman))
```

```
[1] 20
```

This command relies on the automatic *coercion* of the logical values TRUE and FALSE to one and zero, respectively.

2.2.4   NUMERIC VARIABLES AND FACTORS

If we construct R data frames by reading data from text files using `read.-table` or from numeric and character vectors using `data.frame`, then our data frames will consist of two kinds of data: numeric variables and factors. Both `read.table` and `data.frame` by default translate character data and logical data into factors.

Before proceeding, let us clean up a bit:

```
> objects()
```

```
[1] "condition"     "cooperation"   "Freedman.good"
[4] "good"          "Guyer"         "sex"
```

```
> remove(good, Freedman.good)
```

Near the beginning of this chapter, we entered data from Fox and Guyer's (1978) experiment on anonymity and cooperation into the global variables `cooperation`, `condition`, and `sex`.[12] The latter two variables are character vectors, as we verify for `condition`:

```
> condition
```

```
 [1] "public"    "public"    "public"    "public"    "public"
 [6] "public"    "public"    "public"    "public"    "public"
[11] "anonymous" "anonymous" "anonymous" "anonymous" "anonymous"
[16] "anonymous" "anonymous" "anonymous" "anonymous" "anonymous"
```

We can confirm that this is a vector of character values using the *predicate function* `is.character`, which tests whether its argument is of mode `"character"`:

```
> is.character(condition)
```

```
[1] TRUE
```

---

[12] Variables created by assignment at the command prompt are global variables defined in the working data.

After entering the data, we defined the data frame `Guyer`, which also contains variables named `cooperation`, `condition`, and `sex`. We will remove the global variables and will work instead with the data frame:

```
> remove(cooperation, condition, sex)
```

Look at the variable `condition` in the `Guyer` data frame:

```
> Guyer$condition

 [1] public    public    public    public    public    public
 [7] public    public    public    public    anonymous anonymous
[13] anonymous anonymous anonymous anonymous anonymous anonymous
[19] anonymous anonymous
Levels: anonymous public
```

```
> is.character(Guyer$condition)
```

```
[1] FALSE
```

```
> is.factor(Guyer$condition)
```

```
[1] TRUE
```

As we explained, `condition` in the data frame is a *factor* rather than a character vector. A factor is a representation of a categorical variable; factors are stored more economically than character vectors, and the manner in which they are stored saves information about the *levels* (category set) of a factor. When a factor is printed, its values are not quoted, as are the values of a character vector, and the levels of the factor are listed.

Many functions in R, including statistical-modeling functions such as `lm`, know how to deal with factors. For example, when the generic `summary` function is called with a data frame as its argument, it prints various statistics for a numeric variable but simply counts the number of observations in each level of a factor:

```
> summary(Guyer)

  cooperation         condition      sex
 Min.    :27.00   anonymous:10   female:10
 1st Qu.:38.50   public   :10   male  :10
 Median :46.50
 Mean    :48.30
 3rd Qu.:58.75
 Max.    :79.00
```

Factors have unordered levels. An extension, called *ordered factors*, is discussed, along with factors, in the context of linear models in Section 4.6.

2.2.5   MODIFYING AND TRANSFORMING DATA

Data modification in R usually occurs naturally and unremarkably. When we wanted to plot `crime` against the log of `density` in Freedman's data, for example, we simply specified log(density, base=10).[13] Similarly, in regressing crime on the log of density, we just used log(density, base=10) on the right-hand side of the linear-model formula.

Creating new variables that are functions of other variables is straightforward. For example, the variable cooperation in the Guyer data set counts the number of cooperative choices out of a total of 120 choices. To create a new variable with the percentage of cooperative choices in each group:

```
> perc.coop <- 100*Guyer$cooperation/120
```

The new variable perc.coop resides in the working data, not in the Guyer data frame. It is generally advantageous to add new variables such as this to the data frame from which they originate: Keeping related variables together in a data frame avoids confusion, for example.

```
> Guyer$perc.coop <- 100*Guyer$cooperation/120
> head(Guyer)   # first 6 rows

  cooperation condition    sex perc.coop
1          49    public   male  40.83333
2          64    public   male  53.33333
3          37    public   male  30.83333
4          52    public   male  43.33333
5          68    public   male  56.66667
6          54    public female  45.00000
```

A similar procedure may be used to *modify* an existing variable in a data frame. The following command, for example, replaces the original cooperation variable in Guyer with the logit (log-odds) of cooperation:

```
> Guyer$cooperation <- with(Guyer, log(perc.coop/(100 - perc.coop)))
> head(Guyer)

  cooperation condition    sex perc.coop
1  -0.3708596    public   male  40.83333
2   0.1335314    public   male  53.33333
3  -0.8079227    public   male  30.83333
4  -0.2682640    public   male  43.33333
5   0.2682640    public   male  56.66667
6  -0.2006707    public female  45.00000
```

The transform function can be used to create and modify several variables in a data frame at once. For example, if we have a data frame called Data with variables named a, b, and c, then the command

```
> Data <- transform(Data, c=-c, asq=a^2, a.over.b=a/b)
```

replaces Data by a new data frame in which the variables a and b are included unchanged, c is replaced by -c, and two new variables are added—asq, with the squares of a, and a.over.b, with the ratios of a to b.

---

[13] We did not have to create a new variable, say log.density <- log(density, 10), as one may be required to do in a typical statistical package such as SAS or SPSS.

Transforming numeric data is usually a straightforward operation—simply using mathematical operators and functions. Categorizing numeric data and recoding categorical variables are often more complicated matters. Several functions in R are employed to create factors from numeric data and to manipulate categorical data, but we will limit our discussion to three that we find particularly useful: (1) the standard R function `cut`, (2) the `recode` function in the **car** package, and (3) the standard `ifelse` function.

The `cut` function dissects the range of a numeric variable into class intervals, or *bins*. The first argument to the function is the variable to be binned; the second argument gives either the number of equal-width bins or a vector of cut points at which the division is to take place. For example, to divide the range of `perc.coop` into four equal-width bins, we specify

```
> Guyer$coop.4 <- cut(Guyer$perc.coop, 4)
> summary(Guyer$coop.4)


(22.5,33.3] (33.3,44.2]   (44.2,55]   (55,65.9]
         6           7           5           2
```

R responds by creating a factor, the levels of which are named for the end points of the bins. In the example above, the first level includes all values with `Guyer$perc.coop` greater than 22.5 (which is slightly smaller than the minimum value of `Guyer$perc.coop`) and less than or equal to 33.3, the cut point between the first two levels. Because `perc.coop` is not uniformly distributed across its range, the several levels of `coop.4` contain different numbers of observations. The output from the `summary` function applied to a factor gives a one-dimensional table of the number of observations in each level of the factor.

Suppose, alternatively, that we want to bin `perc.coop` into three levels containing roughly equal numbers of observations[14] and to name these levels `"low"`, `"med"`, and `"high"`; we may proceed as follows:

```
> Guyer$coop.groups <- with(Guyer, cut(perc.coop,
+      quantile(perc.coop, c(0, 1/3, 2/3, 1)),
+      include.lowest=TRUE,
+      labels=c("low", "med", "high")))
> summary(Guyer$coop.groups)

 low  med high
   7    6    7
```

The `quantile` function is used to locate the cut points. Had we wished to divide `perc.coop` into four groups, for example, we would simply have specified different quantiles, `c(0, .25, .5, .75, 1)`, and of course supplied four values for the `labels` argument.

---

[14]*Roughly* equal numbers of observations in the three bins are the best we can do because $n = 20$ is not evenly divisible by 3.

The `recode` function in the **car** package, which is more flexible than `cut`, can also be used to dissect a quantitative variable into class intervals: for example,

```
> (Guyer$coop.2 <- recode(Guyer$perc.coop, "lo:50=1; 50:hi=2"))
```

```
[1] 1 2 1 1 2 1 2 2 2 1 1 1 1 1 1 1 1 1 1 1
```

The `recode` function works as follows:

- The first argument is the variable to be recoded, here `perc.coop`.
- The second argument is a character string, enclosed in single or double quotes, containing the recode specifications.
- Recode specifications are of the form *old.values=new.value*. There may be several recode specifications, separated by semicolons.
- The *old.values* may be a single value, including NA; a range, of the form *minimum:maximum*, as in the example, where the special values `lo` and `hi` have been used to stand in for the smallest and largest values of the variable; a vector of values, typically specified with the `c` (combine) function; or the special symbol `else`, which, if present, should appear last.
- An observation that fits into more than one recode specification is assigned the value of the first one encountered. For example, a group with `perc.coop` exactly equal to 50 would get the new value 1.
- Character data may appear both as *old.values* and as *new.value*. You must be careful with quotation marks, however: If single quotes are employed to enclose the recode specifications, then double quotes must be used for the values (and vice versa).
- When a factor is recoded, the *old.values* should be specified as character strings; the result is a factor, even if the *new.values* are numbers, unless the argument `as.factor.result` is set to FALSE.
- Character data may be recoded to numeric, and vice versa. To recode a character or numeric variable to a factor, set `as.factor.result` =TRUE.
- If an observation does not satisfy any of the recode specifications, then the *old.value* for that observation is carried over into the result.

To provide a richer context for additional illustrations of the use of `recode`, we turn our attention to the `Womenlf` data frame from the **car** package:

```
> set.seed(12345)  # for reproducibility
> (sample.20 <- sort(sample(nrow(Womenlf), 20)))  # 20 random obs.
```

```
 [1]    1    9   39   43   44   84   96   98  100  115  119  131  185  186  190
[16]  199  230  231  233  252
```

```
> Womenlf[sample.20, ]  # 20 randomly selected rows
```

```
        partic hincome children   region
1     not.work      15  present  Ontario
9     not.work      15  present  Ontario
39    not.work       9  present Atlantic
43    parttime      28   absent  Ontario
44    not.work      23  present  Ontario
84    fulltime      17  present  Ontario
96    not.work      17  present  Ontario
98    fulltime      15   absent  Ontario
100   not.work      15  present  Ontario
115   parttime      13  present  Prairie
119   fulltime      15   absent       BC
131   parttime      19  present  Ontario
185   not.work      13   absent  Ontario
186   parttime      15  present       BC
190   not.work      23  present       BC
199   fulltime      10   absent   Quebec
230   parttime      23  present   Quebec
231   not.work       7  present   Quebec
233   fulltime      15   absent   Quebec
252   not.work      23   absent   Quebec
```

The `sample` function is used to pick a random sample of 20 rows in the data frame, selecting 20 random numbers without replacement from one to the number of rows in `Womenlf`; the numbers are placed in ascending order by the `sort` function.[15]

We use the `set.seed` function to specify the seed for R's pseudo-random number generator, ensuring that if we repeat the `sample` command, we will obtain the same sequence of pseudo-random numbers. Otherwise, the seed of the random-number generator will be selected unpredictably based on the system clock when the first random number is generated in an R session. Setting the random seed to a known value before a random simulation makes the result of the simulation reproducible. In serious work, we generally prefer to start with a known but randomly selected seed, as follows:

```
> (seed <- sample(2^31 - 1, 1))

[1] 974373618

> set.seed(seed)
```

The number $2^{31} - 1$ is the largest integer representable as a 32-bit binary number on most of the computer systems on which R runs (see Section 2.6.2).

The data in `Womenlf` originate from a social survey of the Canadian population conducted in 1977 and pertain to married women between the ages of 21 and 30, with the variables defined as follows:

- `partic`: Labor-force participation, `parttime`, `fulltime`, or `not.work` (not working outside the home).

---

[15]If the objective here were simply to sample 20 rows from `Womenlf`, then we could more simply use the `some` function in the **car** package, `some(Womenlf, 20)`, but we will reuse this sample to check on the results of our recodes.

- hincome: Husband's income, in $1,000s (actually, family income minus wife's income).
- children: Presence of children in the household: present or absent.
- region: Atlantic, Quebec, Ontario, Prairie (the Prairie provinces), or BC (British Columbia).

Now consider the following recodes:

```
> # recode in two ways:
> Womenlf$working <- recode(Womenlf$partic,
+     ' c("parttime", "fulltime")="yes"; "not.work"="no" ')
> Womenlf$working.alt <- recode(Womenlf$partic,
+     ' c("parttime", "fulltime")="yes"; else="no" ')
> Womenlf$working[sample.20]   # 20 sampled observations

 [1] no  no  no  yes no  yes no  yes no  yes yes yes no  yes no
[16] yes yes no  yes no
Levels: no yes

> with(Womenlf, all(working == working.alt))   # check

[1] TRUE

> Womenlf$fulltime <- recode(Womenlf$partic,
+     ' "fulltime"="yes"; "parttime"="no"; "not.work"=NA ')
> Womenlf$fulltime[sample.20]   # 20 sampled observations

 [1] <NA> <NA> <NA> no   <NA> yes  <NA> yes  <NA> no   yes  no
[13] <NA> no   <NA> yes  no   <NA> yes  <NA>
Levels: no yes

> Womenlf$region.4 <- recode(Womenlf$region,
+     ' c("Prairie", "BC")="West" ')
> Womenlf$region.4[sample.20]   # 20 sampled observations

 [1] Ontario  Ontario  Atlantic Ontario  Ontario  Ontario
 [7] Ontario  Ontario  Ontario  West     West     Ontario
[13] Ontario  West     West     Quebec   Quebec   Quebec
[19] Quebec   Quebec
Levels: Atlantic Ontario Quebec West
```

In all these examples, factors (either partic or region) are recoded, and consequently, recode returns factors as results:

- The first two examples yield identical results, with the second example illustrating the use of else. To verify that all the values in working and working.alt are the same, we use the all function along with the element-wise comparison operator == (equals).
- In the third example, the factor fulltime is created, indicating whether a woman who works outside the home works full-time or part-time; fulltime is NA (missing) for women who do not work outside the home.
- The fourth and final example illustrates how values that are *not* recoded (here Atlantic, Quebec, and Ontario in the factor region) are simply carried over to the result.

The standard R ifelse command (discussed further in Section 8.3.1) can also be used to recode data. For example,

```
> Womenlf$working.alt.2 <- factor(with(Womenlf,
+     ifelse(partic %in% c("parttime", "fulltime"), "yes", "no")))
> with(Womenlf, all.equal(working, working.alt.2))

[1] TRUE

> Womenlf$fulltime.alt <- factor(with(Womenlf,
+     ifelse(partic == "fulltime", "yes",
+         ifelse(partic == "parttime", "no", NA))))
> with(Womenlf, all.equal(fulltime, fulltime.alt))

[1] TRUE
```

The first argument to ifelse is a logical vector, containing the values TRUE and FALSE; the second argument gives the value assigned where the first argument is TRUE; and the third argument gives the value assigned when the first argument is FALSE. We used cascading ifelse commands to create the variable fulltime.alt, assigning the value "yes" to those working "fulltime", "no" to those working "parttime", and NA otherwise (i.e., where partic takes on the value "not.work").

We employed the *matching operator*, %in%, which returns a logical vector containing TRUE if a value in the vector before %in% is a member of the vector after the symbol and FALSE otherwise. See help("%in%") for more information; the quotes are required because of the % character. We also used the function all.equal to test the equality of the alternative recodings. When applied to numeric variables, all.equal tests for *approximate* equality, within the precision of floating-point computations (discussed in Section 2.6.2); more generally, all.equal not only reports whether two objects are approximately equal but, if they are not equal, provides information on how they differ.

An alternative to the first test is all(working == working.alt.2), but this approach won't work properly in the second test because of the missing data:

```
> with(Womenlf, all(fulltime == fulltime.alt))

[1] NA
```

We once more clean up before proceeding by removing the copy of Womenlf that was made in the working data:

```
> remove(Womenlf)
```

2.3   Matrices, Arrays, and Lists

We have thus far encountered and used several data structures in R:

- *Vectors:* One-dimensional arrays of numbers, character strings, or logical values. Single numbers, character strings, and logical values in R are treated as vectors of length one.

- *Factors:* One-dimensional arrays of levels.
- *Data frames:* Two-dimensional data tables, with the rows defining observations and the columns defining variables. Data frames are heterogeneous, in the sense that some columns may be numeric and others factors and some may even contain character data or logical data.

In this section, we describe three other common data structures in R: *matrices*, *arrays*, and *lists*.

2.3.1 MATRICES

A matrix in R is a two-dimensional array of elements all of which are of the same *mode*—for example, real numbers, integers, character strings, or logical values. Matrices can be constructed using the `matrix` function, which reshapes its first argument into a matrix with the specified number of rows (the second argument) and columns (the third argument): for example,

```
> (A <- matrix(1:12, nrow=3, ncol=4))

     [,1] [,2] [,3] [,4]
[1,]    1    4    7   10
[2,]    2    5    8   11
[3,]    3    6    9   12

>(B <- matrix(c("a", "b", "c"), 4, 3, byrow=TRUE))# 4 rows,3 columns

     [,1] [,2] [,3]
[1,] "a"  "b"  "c"
[2,] "a"  "b"  "c"
[3,] "a"  "b"  "c"
[4,] "a"  "b"  "c"
```

A matrix is filled by columns, unless the optional argument `byrow` is set to TRUE. The second example illustrates that if there are fewer elements in the first argument than are required, then the elements are simply recycled, extended by repetition to the required length.

A defining characteristic of a matrix is that it has a `dim` (dimension) *attribute* with two elements: the number of rows and the number of columns:[16]

```
> dim(A)

[1] 3 4

> dim(B)

[1] 4 3
```

As we have seen before, a vector is a one-dimensional array of numbers. For example, here is a vector containing a random permutation of the first 10 integers:

---

[16]More correctly, a matrix is a vector with a two-element `dim` attribute.

```
> set.seed(54321) # for reproducibility
> (v <- sample(10, 10))   # permutation of 1 to 10

 [1]  5 10  2  8  7  9  1  4  3  6
```

A vector has a `length` attribute but not a `dim` attribute:

```
> length(v)

[1] 10

> dim(v)

NULL
```

R often treats vectors differently than matrices. You can turn a vector into a one-column matrix using the `as.matrix` *coercion* function:

```
> as.matrix(v)

         [,1]
 [1,]     5
 [2,]    10
 [3,]     2
 [4,]     8
 [5,]     7
 [6,]     9
 [7,]     1
 [8,]     4
 [9,]     3
[10,]     6
```

R includes extensive facilities for matrix computation, some of which are described later in this chapter and in Section 8.2.

2.3.2 ARRAYS

Higher-dimensional arrays of homogeneous elements are encountered much less frequently than matrices. If needed, higher-dimensional arrays may be created with the `array` function; here is an example generating a three-dimensional array:

```
> (array.3 <- array(1:24, dim=c(4, 3, 2))) # 4 rows, 3 columns, 2 layers

, , 1

     [,1] [,2] [,3]
[1,]    1    5    9
[2,]    2    6   10
[3,]    3    7   11
[4,]    4    8   12

, , 2

     [,1] [,2] [,3]
[1,]   13   17   21
[2,]   14   18   22
[3,]   15   19   23
[4,]   16   20   24
```

The order of the dimensions is row, column, and layer. The array is filled with the index of the first dimension changing most quickly—that is, row, then column, then layer.

2.3.3 LISTS

Lists are data structures composed of potentially heterogeneous elements. The elements of a list may be complex data structures, including other lists. Because a list can contain other lists as elements, each of which can also contain lists, lists are *recursive* structures. In contrast, the elements of an ordinary vector—such as an individual number, character string, or logical value—are *atomic* objects.

Here is an example of a list, constructed with the `list` function:

```
> (list.1 <- list(mat.1=A, mat.2=B, vec=v))  # a 3-item list

$mat.1
     [,1] [,2] [,3] [,4]
[1,]    1    4    7   10
[2,]    2    5    8   11
[3,]    3    6    9   12

$mat.2
     [,1] [,2] [,3]
[1,] "a"  "b"  "c"
[2,] "a"  "b"  "c"
[3,] "a"  "b"  "c"
[4,] "a"  "b"  "c"

$vec
 [1]  5 10  2  8  7  9  1  4  3  6
```

This list contains a numeric matrix, a character matrix, and a numeric vector. We named the arguments in the call to the `list` function; these are arbitrary names that we chose, not standard arguments to `list`. The argument names supplied became the names of the list elements.

Because lists permit us to collect related information regardless of its form, they provide the foundation for the class-based S3 object system in R.[17] Data frames, for example, are lists with some special properties that permit them to behave somewhat like matrices.

2.3.4 INDEXING

A common operation in R is to extract some of the elements of a vector, matrix, array, list, or data frame by supplying the indices of the elements to be extracted. Indices are specified between square brackets, " [" and "] ". We have already used this syntax on several occasions, and it is now time to consider indexing more systematically.

---

[17]Classes are described in Sections 2.6 and 8.7.

INDEXING VECTORS

A vector can be indexed by a single number or by a vector of numbers; indeed, indices may be specified out of order, and an index may be repeated to extract the corresponding element more than once:

```
> v

 [1]   5 10  2  8  7  9  1  4  3  6

> v[2]

[1] 10

> v[c(4, 2, 6)]

[1]   8 10  9

> v[c(4, 2, 4)]

[1]   8 10  8
```

Specifying *negative* indices suppresses the corresponding elements of the vector:

```
> v[-c(2, 4, 6, 8, 10)]

[1] 5 2 7 1 3
```

If a vector has a names attribute, then we can also index the elements by name:[18]

```
> names(v) <- letters[1:10]
> v

 a  b  c  d  e  f  g  h  i  j
 5 10  2  8  7  9  1  4  3  6

> v[c("f", "i", "g")]

f i g
9 3 1
```

Finally, a vector may be indexed by a logical vector of the same length, retaining the elements corresponding to TRUE and omitting those corresponding to FALSE:

```
> v < 6

    a     b     c     d     e     f     g     h     i     j
 TRUE FALSE  TRUE FALSE FALSE FALSE  TRUE  TRUE  TRUE FALSE

> v[v < 6]   # all entries less than 6
```

---

[18] The vector letters contains the 26 lowercase letters from "a" to "z"; LETTERS similarly contains the uppercase letters.

```
a c g h i
5 2 1 4 3
```

Any of these forms of indexing may be used on the left-hand side of the assignment operator to replace the elements of a vector—an unusual and convenient feature of the R language: for example,

```
> (vv <- v)   # make copy of v

a  b  c  d  e  f  g  h  i  j
5 10  2  8  7  9  1  4  3  6

> vv[c(1, 3, 5)] <- 1:3
> vv

a  b  c  d  e  f  g  h  i  j
1 10  2  8  3  9  1  4  3  6

> vv[c("b", "d", "f", "h", "j")] <- NA
> vv

a  b  c  d  e  f  g  h  i  j
1 NA  2 NA  3 NA  1 NA  3 NA

> remove(vv)
```

INDEXING MATRICES AND ARRAYS

Indexing extends straightforwardly to matrices and to higher-dimensional arrays. Indices corresponding to the different dimensions of an array are separated by commas; if the index for a dimension is left unspecified, then all the elements along that dimension are selected. We demonstrate with the matrix A:

```
> A

     [,1] [,2] [,3] [,4]
[1,]    1    4    7   10
[2,]    2    5    8   11
[3,]    3    6    9   12

> A[2, 3]   # element in row 2, column 3

[1] 8

> A[c(1, 2), 2]   # rows 1 and 2, column 2

[1] 4 5

> A[c(1, 2), c(2, 3)] # rows 1 and 2, columns 2 and 3

     [,1] [,2]
[1,]    4    7
[2,]    5    8
```

```
> A[c(1, 2), ]   # rows 1 and 2, all columns

     [,1] [,2] [,3] [,4]
[1,]    1    4    7   10
[2,]    2    5    8   11
```

The second example above, A[2, 3], returns a single-element vector rather than a 1×1 matrix; likewise, the third example, A[c(1, 2), 2], returns a vector with two elements rather than a 2×1 matrix. *More generally, in indexing a matrix or array, dimensions of extent one are automatically dropped.* In particular, if we select elements in a single row or single column of a matrix, then the result is a vector, not a matrix with a single row or column, a convention that will occasionally give an R programmer headaches. We can override this default behavior with the argument drop=FALSE:

```
> A[ , 1]

[1] 1 2 3

> A[ , 1, drop=FALSE]

     [,1]
[1,]    1
[2,]    2
[3,]    3
```

In both of these examples, the row index is missing and is therefore taken to be all rows of the matrix.

Negative indices, row or column names (if they are defined), and logical vectors of the appropriate length may also be used to index a matrix or a higher-dimensional array:

```
> A[ , -c(1, 3)]   # omit columns 1 and 3

     [,1] [,2]
[1,]    4   10
[2,]    5   11
[3,]    6   12

> A[-1, -2]        # omit row 1 and column 2

     [,1] [,2] [,3]
[1,]    2    8   11
[2,]    3    9   12

> rownames(A) <- c("one", "two", "three")   # set row names
> colnames(A) <- c("w", "x", "y", "z")       # set column names
> A

      w x y  z
one   1 4 7 10
two   2 5 8 11
three 3 6 9 12
```

```
> A[c("one", "two"), c("x", "y")]

    x y
one 4 7
two 5 8

> A[c(TRUE, FALSE, TRUE), ]

      w x y  z
one   1 4 7 10
three 3 6 9 12
```

Used on the left of the assignment arrow, we may replace indexed elements in a matrix or array:

```
> (AA <- A)   # make a copy of A

      w x y  z
one   1 4 7 10
two   2 5 8 11
three 3 6 9 12

> AA[1, ] <- 0  # set first row to zeros
> AA

      w x y  z
one   0 0 0  0
two   2 5 8 11
three 3 6 9 12

> remove(AA)
```

INDEXING LISTS

Lists may be indexed in much the same way as vectors, but some special considerations apply. Recall the list that we constructed earlier:

```
> list.1

$mat.1
     [,1] [,2] [,3] [,4]
[1,]    1    4    7   10
[2,]    2    5    8   11
[3,]    3    6    9   12

$mat.2
     [,1] [,2] [,3]
[1,] "a"  "b"  "c"
[2,] "a"  "b"  "c"
[3,] "a"  "b"  "c"
[4,] "a"  "b"  "c"

$vec
 [1]  5 10  2  8  7  9  1  4  3  6
```

```
> list.1[c(2, 3)]   # elements 2 and 3

$mat.2
     [,1] [,2] [,3]
[1,] "a"  "b"  "c"
[2,] "a"  "b"  "c"
[3,] "a"  "b"  "c"
[4,] "a"  "b"  "c"

$vec
 [1]  5 10  2  8  7  9  1  4  3  6

> list.1[2]   # returns a one-element list

$mat.2
     [,1] [,2] [,3]
[1,] "a"  "b"  "c"
[2,] "a"  "b"  "c"
[3,] "a"  "b"  "c"
[4,] "a"  "b"  "c"
```

Even when we select a single element of the list, as in the last example, we get a *single-element list* rather than (in this case) a matrix. To extract the matrix in position 2 of the list, we can use double-bracket notation:

```
> list.1[[2]]   # returns a matrix

     [,1] [,2] [,3]
[1,] "a"  "b"  "c"
[2,] "a"  "b"  "c"
[3,] "a"  "b"  "c"
[4,] "a"  "b"  "c"
```

The distinction between a one-element list and the element itself is subtle but important, and it can trip us up if we are not careful.

If the list elements are named, then we can use the names in indexing the list:

```
> list.1["mat.1"]   # produces a one-element list

$mat.1
     [,1] [,2] [,3] [,4]
[1,]    1    4    7   10
[2,]    2    5    8   11
[3,]    3    6    9   12

> list.1[["mat.1"]]   #  extracts a single element

     [,1] [,2] [,3] [,4]
[1,]    1    4    7   10
[2,]    2    5    8   11
[3,]    3    6    9   12
```

An element name may also be used—either quoted or, if it is a legal R name, unquoted—after the $ (dollar sign) to extract a list element:

```
> list.1$mat.1
```

```
     [,1] [,2] [,3] [,4]
[1,]    1    4    7   10
[2,]    2    5    8   11
[3,]    3    6    9   12
```

Used on the left-hand side of the assignment arrow, dollar-sign indexing allows us to replace list elements, define new elements, or delete an element (by assigning NULL to the element):

```
> list.1$mat.1 <- matrix(1, 2, 2)       # replace element
> list.1$title <- "an arbitrary list"   # new element
> list.1$mat.2 <- NULL                   # delete element
> list.1

$mat.1
     [,1] [,2]
[1,]    1    1
[2,]    1    1

$vec
 [1]  5 10  2  8  7  9  1  4  3  6

$title
[1] "an arbitrary list"
```

Setting a list element to NULL is trickier:

```
> list.1["title"] <- list(NULL)
> list.1

$mat.1
     [,1] [,2]
[1,]    1    1
[2,]    1    1

$vec
 [1]  5 10  2  8  7  9  1  4  3  6

$title
NULL
```

Once a list element is extracted, it may itself be indexed: for example,

```
> list.1$vec[3]

[1] 2

> list.1[["vec"]][3:5]

[1] 2 8 7
```

Finally, extracting a nonexistent element returns NULL:

```
> list.1$foo

NULL
```

This behavior is potentially confusing because it is not possible to distinguish by the value returned between a NULL element, such as list.1$title in the example, and a nonexistent element, such as list.1$foo.

INDEXING DATA FRAMES

Data frames may be indexed either as lists or as matrices. Recall the Guyer data frame:

```
> head(Guyer)   # first 6 rows

  cooperation condition    sex perc.coop       coop.4 coop.groups
1  -0.3708596    public   male 40.83333 (33.3,44.2]         med
2   0.1335314    public   male 53.33333  (44.2,55]        high
3  -0.8079227    public   male 30.83333 (22.5,33.3]         low
4  -0.2682640    public   male 43.33333 (33.3,44.2]         med
5   0.2682640    public   male 56.66667  (55,65.9]        high
6  -0.2006707    public female 45.00000  (44.2,55]        high
  coop.2
1      1
2      2
3      1
4      1
5      2
6      1
```

Because no row names were specified when we entered the data, the row names are simply the character representation of the row numbers. Indexing Guyer as a matrix:

```
> Guyer[ , 1]   # first column

 [1] -0.37085958  0.13353139 -0.80792270 -0.26826399  0.26826399
 [6] -0.20067070  0.03333642  0.65587579  0.13353139 -1.14356368
[11] -1.23676263 -0.06669137 -0.26826399 -0.65587579 -1.09861229
[16] -0.69314718 -0.73088751 -0.54654371 -0.92798677 -0.54654371

> Guyer[ , "cooperation"]   # equivalent

 [1] -0.37085958  0.13353139 -0.80792270 -0.26826399  0.26826399
 [6] -0.20067070  0.03333642  0.65587579  0.13353139 -1.14356368
[11] -1.23676263 -0.06669137 -0.26826399 -0.65587579 -1.09861229
[16] -0.69314718 -0.73088751 -0.54654371 -0.92798677 -0.54654371

> Guyer[c(1, 2), ]   # rows 1 and 2

  cooperation condition  sex perc.coop       coop.4 coop.groups
1  -0.3708596    public male 40.83333 (33.3,44.2]         med
2   0.1335314    public male 53.33333  (44.2,55]        high
  coop.2
1      1
2      2

> Guyer[c("1", "2"), "cooperation"] # by row and column names

[1] -0.3708596  0.1335314

> Guyer[-(6:20), ]   # drop rows 6 through 20

  cooperation condition  sex perc.coop       coop.4 coop.groups
1  -0.3708596    public male 40.83333 (33.3,44.2]         med
2   0.1335314    public male 53.33333  (44.2,55]        high
3  -0.8079227    public male 30.83333 (22.5,33.3]         low
```

```
4   -0.2682640     public male   43.33333  (33.3,44.2]              med
5    0.2682640     public male   56.66667    (55,65.9]             high
    coop.2
1      1
2      2
3      1
4      1
5      2
```

```
> with(Guyer, Guyer[sex == "female" & condition == "public", ])
```

```
    cooperation condition     sex perc.coop         coop.4 coop.groups
6   -0.20067070    public female  45.00000     (44.2,55]         high
7    0.03333642    public female  50.83333     (44.2,55]         high
8    0.65587579    public female  65.83333     (55,65.9]         high
9    0.13353139    public female  53.33333     (44.2,55]         high
10  -1.14356368    public female  24.16667   (22.5,33.3]          low
    coop.2
6      1
7      2
8      2
9      2
10     1
```

We require `with` in the last example to access the variables `sex` and `condi-tion`, because the data frame `Guyer` is not attached to the search path. More conveniently, we can use the `subset` function to perform this operation:

```
> subset(Guyer, sex == "female" & condition == "public")
```

```
    cooperation condition     sex perc.coop         coop.4 coop.groups
6   -0.20067070    public female  45.00000     (44.2,55]         high
7    0.03333642    public female  50.83333     (44.2,55]         high
8    0.65587579    public female  65.83333     (55,65.9]         high
9    0.13353139    public female  53.33333     (44.2,55]         high
10  -1.14356368    public female  24.16667   (22.5,33.3]          low
    coop.2
6      1
7      2
8      2
9      2
10     1
```

Alternatively, indexing the data frame `Guyer` as a list:

```
> Guyer$cooperation
```

```
 [1] -0.37085958  0.13353139 -0.80792270 -0.26826399  0.26826399
 [6] -0.20067070  0.03333642  0.65587579  0.13353139 -1.14356368
[11] -1.23676263 -0.06669137 -0.26826399 -0.65587579 -1.09861229
[16] -0.69314718 -0.73088751 -0.54654371 -0.92798677 -0.54654371
```

```
> Guyer[["cooperation"]]
```

```
 [1] -0.37085958  0.13353139 -0.80792270 -0.26826399  0.26826399
 [6] -0.20067070  0.03333642  0.65587579  0.13353139 -1.14356368
[11] -1.23676263 -0.06669137 -0.26826399 -0.65587579 -1.09861229
[16] -0.69314718 -0.73088751 -0.54654371 -0.92798677 -0.54654371
```

```
> head(Guyer["cooperation"])  # first six rows

  cooperation
1  -0.3708596
2   0.1335314
3  -0.8079227
4  -0.2682640
5   0.2682640
6  -0.2006707
```

Specifying `Guyer["cooperation"]` returns a one-column data frame rather than a vector.

As has become our habit, we clean up before continuing:

```
> remove(A, B, v, array.3, list.1)
```

2.4   Manipulating Character Data

One of the most underappreciated capabilities of R is its facility in handling text. Indeed, for many applications, R is a viable alternative to specialized text-processing tools, such as the PERL scripting language and the Unix utilities sed, grep, and awk. Most of the text-processing functions in R make use of so-called *regular expressions* for matching text in character strings. In this section, we provide a brief introduction to manipulating character data in R, primarily by example. More complete information may be found in the online help for the various text-processing functions; in `?regexp`, which describes how regular expressions are implemented in R; and in the sources cited at the end of the chapter.

We'll turn to the familiar "To Be or Not To Be" soliloquy from Shakespeare's *Hamlet*, in the plain-text file Hamlet.txt, as a source of examples. We begin by using the `readLines` function to read the lines of the file into a character vector, one line per element:

```
> file <- "http://socserv.socsci.mcmaster.ca/jfox/books/
      Companion/data/Hamlet.txt"
> Hamlet <- readLines(file)

> head(Hamlet)       # first 6 lines

[1] "To be, or not to be: that is the question:"
[2] "Whether 'tis nobler in the mind to suffer"
[3] "The slings and arrows of outrageous fortune,"
[4] "Or to take arms against a sea of troubles,"
[5] "And by opposing end them? To die: to sleep;"
[6] "No more; and by a sleep to say we end"

> length(Hamlet)     # number of lines

[1] 35

> nchar(Hamlet)      # number of characters per line
```

```
 [1] 42 41 44 42 43 37 46 42 40 50 47 43 39 36 48 49 44 38 41 38
[21] 43 38 44 41 37 43 39 44 37 47 40 42 44 39 26

> sum(nchar(Hamlet)) # number of characters in all

[1] 1454
```

The `length` function counts the number of character strings in the character vector `Hamlet`—that is, the number of lines in the soliloquy—while the `nchar` function counts the number of characters in each string—that is, in each line.

The `paste` function is useful for joining character strings into a single string. For example, to join the first six lines:

```
(lines.1_6 <- paste(Hamlet[1:6], collapse=" "))

[1] "To be, or not to be: that is the question: . . . to say we end"
```

Here, and elsewhere in this section, we've edited the R output where necessary so that it fits properly on the page. Alternatively, we can use the `strwrap` function to wrap the text (though this once again divides it into lines),

```
> strwrap(lines.1_6)

[1] "To be, or not to be: that is the question: Whether 'tis"
[2] "nobler in the mind to suffer The slings and arrows of"
[3] "outrageous fortune, Or to take arms against a sea of"
[4] "troubles, And by opposing end them? To die: to sleep; No"
[5] "more; and by a sleep to say we end"
```

and the `substring` function, as its name implies, to select parts of a character string—for example, to select the characters 1 through 42:

```
> substring(lines.1_6, 1, 42)

[1] "To be, or not to be: that is the question:"
```

Suppose, now, that we want to divide `lines.1_6` into words. As a first approximation, let's split the character string at the blanks:

```
> strsplit(lines.1_6, " ")

[[1]]
 [1] "To"         "be,"         "or"        "not"
 [5] "to"         "be:"         "that"      "is"
 [9] "the"        "question:"   "Whether"   "'tis"
 . . .
[49] "sleep"      "to"          "say"       "we"
[53] "end"
```

The `strsplit` (string-split) function takes two required arguments: (1) a character vector of strings to be split, here consisting of one element, and (2) a quoted *regular expression* specifying a pattern that determines where the splits will take place. In this case, the regular expression contains the single character " " (space). Most characters in regular expressions, including spaces, numerals, and lowercase and uppercase alphabetic characters, simply match themselves. The `strsplit` function returns a list as its result, with one element for each element of the first argument—in this case, a one-element list corresponding to the single string in `lines.1_6`.

Our first attempt at dividing `lines.1_6` into words hasn't been entirely successful: Perhaps we're willing to live with words such as "`'tis`" (which is a contraction of "it is"), but it would be nice to remove the punctuation from `"be:"`, `"troubles,"` and `"them?"`, for example.

Characters enclosed in square brackets in a regular expression represent *alternatives*; thus, for example, the regular expression `"[ ,;:.?!]"` will match a space, comma, semicolon, colon, period, question mark, or exclamation point. Because some words are separated by more than one of these characters (e.g., a colon followed by a space), we add the *quantifier* + (plus sign) immediately to the right of the closing bracket; the resulting regular expression, `"[ ,;:.?!]+"`, will match *one or more* adjacent spaces and punctuation characters:

```
> strsplit(lines.1_6, "[ ,;:.?!]+")[[1]]

 [1] "To"         "be"         "or"         "not"
 [5] "to"         "be"         "that"       "is"
 [9] "the"        "question"   "Whether"    "'tis"
. . .
[49] "sleep"      "to"         "say"        "we"
[53] "end"
```

Other quantifiers in regular expressions include * (asterisk), which matches the preceding expression *zero or more* times, and ? (question mark), which matches the preceding expression *zero or one* time. Special characters, such as square brackets and quantifiers, that don't represent themselves in regular expressions are called *meta-characters*. We can, for example, divide the text into sentences by splitting at any of ., ?, or !, followed by zero or more spaces:

```
> strsplit(lines.1_6, "[.?!] *")[[1]]

[1] "To be, or not to be: that is the question: . . . end them"
[2] "To die: to sleep; No more; and by a sleep to say we end"
```

And we can divide the text into individual characters by splitting at the *empty string*, `""`:

```
> characters <- strsplit(lines.1_6, "")[[1]]
> length(characters)     # number of characters

[1] 254

> head(characters, 20)   # first 20 characters

 [1] "T" "o" " " "b" "e" "," " " " " "o" "r" " " "n" "o" "t" " " "t"
[16] "o" " " "b" "e" ":"
```

Let us turn now to the whole soliloquy, dividing the text into words at spaces (a strategy that, as we have seen, is flawed):

```
> all.lines <- paste(Hamlet, collapse=" ")
> words <- strsplit(all.lines, " ")[[1]]
> length(words)     # number of words

[1] 277

> head(words, 20)  # first 20 words

 [1] "To"        "be,"      "or"       "not"      "to"
 [6] "be:"       "that"     "is"       "the"      "question:"
[11] "Whether"   "'tis"     "nobler"   "in"       "the"
[16] "mind"      "to"       "suffer"   "The"      "slings"
```

We can fix the words that have extraneous punctuation by substituting the empty string for the punctuation, using the function sub (substitute):

```
> words <- sub("[,;:.?!]", "", words)
> head(words, 20)

 [1] "To"        "be"       "or"       "not"      "to"
 [6] "be"        "that"     "is"       "the"      "question"
[11] "Whether"   "'tis"     "nobler"   "in"       "the"
[16] "mind"      "to"       "suffer"   "The"      "slings"
```

The sub function takes three required arguments: (1) a regular expression matching the text to be replaced, (2) the replacement text (here, the empty string), and (3) a character vector in which the replacement is to be performed. If the pattern in the regular expression matches more than one substring in an element of the third argument, then only the first occurrence is replaced. The gsub function behaves similarly, except that *all* occurrences of the pattern are replaced:

```
> sub("me", "you", "It's all, 'me, me, me' with you!")

[1] "It's all, 'you, me, me' with you!"

> gsub("me", "you", "It's all, 'me, me, me' with you!")

[1] "It's all, 'you, you, you' with you!"
```

Returning to the soliloquy, suppose that we want to determine and count the different words that Shakespeare used. A first step is to use the tolower function to change all the characters to lowercase, so that, for example, "the" and "The" aren't treated as distinct words:

```
> head(words <- tolower(words), 20)  # first 20 words

 [1] "to"        "be"       "or"       "not"      "to"
 [6] "be"        "that"     "is"       "the"      "question"
[11] "whether"   "'tis"     "nobler"   "in"       "the"
[16] "mind"      "to"       "suffer"   "the"      "slings"

> word.counts <- sort(table(words), decreasing=TRUE)
> word.counts[word.counts > 2]  # words used more than twice
```

```
words
  the    of    to   and  that      a sleep     be    we  bear      in
   22    15    15    12     7       5     5      4     4     3       3
   is    us  with
    3     3     3

> head(sort(unique(words)), 20)  # first 20 unique words

 [1] "-"           "a"            "action"    "after"      "against"
 [6] "all"         "and"          "arms"      "arrows"     "awry"
[11] "ay"          "bare"         "be"        "bear"       "bodkin"
[16] "bourn"       "but"          "by"        "calamity"   "cast"

> length(unique(words))    # number of unique words

[1] 167
```

We used the `table` command to obtain the word counts, `unique` to remove duplicate words, and `sort` to order the words from the most to the least used and to arrange the unique words in alphabetical order. The alphabetized words reveal a problem, however: We're treating the hyphen ("-") as if it were a word.

The function `grep` may be used to search character strings for a regular expression, returning the indices of the strings in a character vector for which there is a match. For our example,

```
> grep("-", words)

[1]   55 262

> words[grep("-", words)]

[1] "heart-ache" "-"
```

We found matches in two character strings: the valid, hyphenated word `"heart-ache"` and the spurious word `"-"`. We would like to be able to differentiate between the two, because we want to discard the latter from our vector of words but retain the former. We can do so as follows:

```
> grep("^-", words)

[1] 262

> words <- words[- grep("^-", words)] # negative index to delete
> head(sort(unique(words)), 20)

 [1] "a"          "action"     "after"     "against"    "all"
 [6] "and"        "arms"       "arrows"    "awry"       "ay"
[11] "bare"       "be"         "bear"      "bodkin"     "bourn"
[16] "but"        "by"         "calamity"  "cast"       "coil"
```

The meta-character ^ (caret) is an *anchor* representing the beginning of a text string, and thus, the regular expression "^-" only matches first-character hyphens. The meta-character $ is similarly an anchor representing the end of a text string:

```
> grep("!$", c("!10", "wow!"))

[1] 2

> grep("^and$", c("android", "sand", "and", "random"))

[1] 3

> grep("and", c("android", "sand", "and", "random"))

[1] 1 2 3 4
```

A hyphen (–) may be used as a meta-character within square brackets to represent a range of characters, such as the digits from 0 through 9;[19] in the following command, for example, we pick out the elements of a character vector that is composed of numerals, periods, and minus signs:

```
> data <- c("-123.45", "three hundred", "7550",
+       "three hundred 23", "Fred")
> data[grep("^[0-9.-]*$", data)]

[1] "-123.45" "7550"
```

Here, the hyphen before the closing bracket represents itself and will match a minus sign.

Used after an opening square bracket, the meta-character "^" represents negation, and so, for example, to select elements of the vector data that *do not* contain any numerals, hyphens, or periods:

```
> data[grep("^[^0-9.-]*$", data)]

[1] "three hundred" "Fred"
```

Parentheses are used for grouping in regular expressions, and the bar character (|) means *or*. To find all the articles in the soliloquy, for example:

```
> words[grep("^(the|a|an)$", words)]

 [1] "the" "the" "the" "a"   "a"   "the" "the" "a"   "the" "the"
[11] "the" "the" "the" "the" "the" "the" "the" "the" "a"   "a"
[21] "the" "the" "the" "the" "the" "the" "the"
```

To see why the parentheses are needed here, try omitting them.

What happens if we want to treat a meta-character as an ordinary character? We have to *escape* the meta-character by using a back slash (\), and because the back slash is the escape character for R as well as for regular expressions, we must, somewhat awkwardly, double it: for example,

```
> grep("\\$", c("$100.00", "100 dollars"))

[1] 1
```

---

[19]Using the hyphen to represent ranges of characters can be risky, because character ranges can vary from one locale to another—say between English and French. Thus, for example, we cannot rely on the range a-zA-Z to contain all the alphabetic characters that may appear in a word—it will miss the accented letters, for example. As a consequence, there are special character classes defined for regular expressions, including [:alpha:], which matches all the alphabetic characters in the current locale.

Cleaning up,

```
> remove(Hamlet, lines.1_6, characters, all.lines, word.counts, data)
```

2.5   Handling Large Data Sets in R*

R has a reputation in some quarters for choking on large data sets. This reputation is only partly deserved. We will explain in this section why very large data sets may pose a problem for R and suggest some strategies for dealing with such data sets.

The most straightforward way to write functions in R is to access data that reside in the computer's main memory. This is true, for example, of the statistical-modeling functions in the standard R distribution, such as the `lm` function for fitting linear models (discussed in Chapter 4) and the `glm` function for fitting generalized linear models (Chapter 5). The size of computer memory then becomes a limitation on the size of statistical analyses that can be handled successfully.

A computer with a 32-bit operating system can't address more than 4 GB (gigabytes) of memory, and depending on the system, not all this memory may be available to R.[20] Computers with 64-bit operating systems can address vastly larger amounts of memory. The current version of R is freely available in 64-bit implementations for Linux, Mac OS X and Windows systems. As memory gets cheaper and 64-bit systems become more common, analyzing very large data sets directly in memory will become more practical.

Handling large data sets in R is partly a matter of programming technique. Although it is *convenient* in R to store data in memory, it is not *necessary* to do so. There are many R programs designed to handle very large data sets, such as those used in genomic research, most notably the R packages distributed by Bioconductor (at `www.bioconductor.org`). Similarly, the **biglm** package on CRAN has functions for fitting linear and generalized linear models that work serially on chunks of the data rather than all the data at once. Moreover, some packages, such as **biglm** and the **survey** package for the analysis of data from complex sample surveys, are capable of accessing data in database management systems (see Section 2.5.3).

Inefficient programming, such as unnecessarily looping over the observations of a data set or allocating very large sparse matrices consisting mostly of zeros, can waste computer time and memory.[21]

---

[20] One *gigabyte* is a little more than 1 billion bytes, and 1 *byte* is 8 *bits* (i.e., binary digits); *double-precision floating-point numbers* in R are stored in 8 bytes (64 bits) each. In a data set composed of floating-point numbers, then, 4 GB corresponds to $4 \times 1024^3/8$, or somewhat more than 500 million data values.

[21] We describe how to avoid these problems in Sections 8.4.1 and 8.6.2.

2.5.1 HOW LARGE IS "LARGE"?

Problems that are quite large by social science standards can be handled routinely in R, and don't require any special care or treatment. In the following examples, we will fit linear least-squares and logistic regressions to a data set with 100,000 observations and 100 explanatory variables. All this is done on our 32-bit Windows Vista system, which has the maximum 4 GB of memory. By default, about 1.5 GB is allocated to the R process, and this is sufficient for the computations below. If necessary, the memory allocated to R can be increased: See ?memory.limit.

We begin by constructing a model matrix for the regression by sampling $100,000 \times 100$ values from the standard-normal distribution and then reshaping these values into a matrix with 100,000 rows and 100 columns:

```
> set.seed(123456789) # for reproducibility
> X <- rnorm(100000*100)
> X <- matrix(X, 100000, 100)
```

Under Windows, the memory.size and memory.limit functions allow us to check the amount of memory in MB (megabytes—approximately 1 million bytes, or 0.001 of a GB) that we've used and the amount available to the R process, respectively:

```
> memory.size()

[1] 10.59

> memory.limit()

[1] 1535
```

Thus, we've used less than 10% of the memory available to R. Next, we generate values of the response variable y, according to a linear-regression model with normally distributed errors that have a standard deviation of 10:

```
> y <- 10 + as.vector(X %*% rep(1, 100) + rnorm(100000, sd=10))
```

In this expression, %*% is the matrix multiplication operator (see Section 8.2), and the coercion function as.vector is used to *coerce* the result to a vector, because matrix multiplication of a matrix by a vector in R returns a one-column matrix. The vector of population regression coefficients consists of ones—rep(1, 100)—and the regression intercept is 10.

To fit the regression model to the data,

```
> system.time(m <- lm(y ~ X))

   user  system elapsed
   5.01    1.02    6.05

> head(coef(m))   # first 6 coefficients

(Intercept)          X1          X2          X3          X4          X5
  9.9896470   1.0803639   1.0325304   1.0354325   0.9190081   1.0549449
```

We print the first six regression coefficients: The intercept and the first five slopes are close to the population values of the coefficients, as we would expect in a sample of $n = 100{,}000$ observations. The `system.time` command times the computation, which took about 6 seconds on our computer. More information on `system.time` is provided in Section 8.6.2.

For a logistic regression (see Section 5.3), we first generate the response vector `yy` of 0s and 1s according to a model with an intercept of 0 and slope coefficients of $1/4$:

```
> p <- as.vector(1/(1 + exp(-X %*% rep(0.25, 100))))
> summary(p)

      Min.    1st Qu.     Median       Mean    3rd Qu.       Max.
 1.743e-05  1.583e-01  4.994e-01  5.004e-01  8.432e-01  1.000e+00

> yy <- rbinom(100000, 1, prob=p)
> table(yy)

yy
    0     1
49978 50022
```

Then, to fit the model,

```
> system.time(m <- glm(yy ~ X, family=binomial))

   user  system elapsed
  19.47    2.34   21.99

> head(coef(m))   # first 6 coefficients

(Intercept)          X1          X2          X3          X4          X5
-0.00194165  0.25235613  0.24011919  0.24634113  0.23995316  0.26141005
```

Again, the computation goes through in a reasonable amount of time (22 seconds) and in the available memory; the results are as expected.

2.5.2 SPEEDING UP `read.table`

In Section 2.1.2, we suggested using `read.table` to input data from ASCII files into R, but `read.table` can be very slow in reading large data sets. To provide a simple example, we create a data frame from our simulated data and output the data frame to an ASCII file with the `write.table` function:

```
> D <- data.frame(X, y, yy)
> dim(D)

[1] 100000    102

> object.size(D)

81611176 bytes

> write.table(D, "C:/temp/largeData.txt")
```

The data frame D consists of 100,000 rows and 102 columns, and uses about 80 MB of memory. To read the data back into memory from the ASCII file takes about 3 minutes on our Windows Vista computer:

```
> system.time(DD <- read.table("C:/temp/largeData.txt", header=TRUE))

   user   system elapsed
 183.77    1.31  185.25
```

The read.table function is slow because it has to figure out whether data should be read as numeric variables or as factors. To determine the class of each variable, read.table reads *all* the data in character form and then examines each column, converting the column to a numeric variable or a factor, as required. We can make this process considerably more efficient by explicitly telling read.table the class of each variable, via the col-Classes argument:

```
> system.time(DD <- read.table("C:/temp/largeData.txt", header=TRUE,
+     colClasses=c("character", rep("numeric", 102))))

   user   system elapsed
  30.67    0.47   31.28
```

Reading the data now takes about 30 seconds. The "character" class specified for the first column is for the row name in each line of the file created by write.table; for example, the name of the first row is "1" (with the quotation marks included). For more details about specifying the col-Classes argument, see ?read.table.

The save function allows us to store data frames and other R objects in a non-human-readable format, which can be reread—using the load function—much more quickly than an ASCII data file. For our example, the time to read the data is reduced to only about 3 seconds:

```
> save(DD, file="C:/temp/DD.Rdata")
> remove(DD)
> system.time(load("C:/temp/DD.Rdata"))

   user   system elapsed
   2.97    0.12    3.14

> dim(DD)

[1] 100000    102
```

Before continuing, we clean up the workspace:

```
> remove(D, DD, p, X, y, yy)
```

2.5.3 ACCESSING DATA IN DATABASES

In large problems, the variables to be used at any given time are often many fewer than the variables available. For example, there may be hundreds of variables in a data set from a social survey with tens of thousands of observations, but a regression model fit to the data will likely use only a small fraction of these variables.

Very large data sets may not fit into the memory of a 32-bit system, and manipulating very large data sets in memory may well prove awkward and slow even on a 64-bit system. We could use `read.table` to input only the variables that we intend to use, but the process of specifying these variables is tedious and error-prone, and if we decide to add a variable to the analysis, we would have to read the data again.

A better solution is to store the data in a database management system (DBMS), retrieving subsets of the data as they are required. There are several packages on CRAN for interfacing R with DBMSs, including the **RODBC** package (which we introduced in Section 2.1.3 to import data from an Excel spreadsheet).

2.6   More on the Representation of Data in R*

This section deals more abstractly with data in R. We aim to introduce the topic rather than to cover it exhaustively. The information here is rarely needed in routine data analysis, but it is occasionally useful for programming in R; you may safely skip this section on first reading.

2.6.1   LENGTH, CLASS, MODE, AND ATTRIBUTES

All objects in R have a *length*, a *class*, and a *mode*.[22] Consider the following examples.

- A vector of integers:

```
> (x <- 1:5)

[1] 1 2 3 4 5

> length(x)

[1] 5

> class(x)

[1] "integer"

> mode(x)

[1] "numeric"
```

---

[22]Objects also have a *storage mode*, but we will not make use of that.

- A vector of floating-point numbers:

```
> (y <- log(x))

[1] 0.0000000 0.6931472 1.0986123 1.3862944 1.6094379

> length(y)

[1] 5

> class(y)

[1] "numeric"

> mode(y)

[1] "numeric"
```

- A character vector:

```
> (cv <- c("Abel", "Baker", "Charlie"))

[1] "Abel"    "Baker"    "Charlie"

> length(cv)

[1] 3

> class(cv)

[1] "character"

> mode(cv)

[1] "character"
```

- A list:

```
> (lst <- list(x=x, y=y, cv=cv))

$x
[1] 1 2 3 4 5

$y
[1] 0.0000000 0.6931472 1.0986123 1.3862944 1.6094379

$cv
[1] "Abel"    "Baker"    "Charlie"

> length(lst)

[1] 3

> class(lst)

[1] "list"

> mode(lst)

[1] "list"
```

- A matrix:

```
> (X <- cbind(x, y))

     x         y
[1,] 1 0.0000000
[2,] 2 0.6931472
[3,] 3 1.0986123
[4,] 4 1.3862944
[5,] 5 1.6094379
```

```
> length(X)

[1] 10

> class(X)

[1] "matrix"

> mode(X)

[1] "numeric"
```

- A data frame:

```
> head(Duncan)

            type income education prestige
accountant  prof     62        86       82
pilot       prof     72        76       83
architect   prof     75        92       90
author      prof     55        90       76
chemist     prof     64        86       90
minister    prof     21        84       87

> length(Duncan)

[1] 4

> class(Duncan)

[1] "data.frame"

> mode(Duncan)

[1] "list"
```

- A factor:

```
> Duncan$type

 [1] prof prof prof prof prof prof prof prof wc   prof prof prof
[13] prof prof prof wc        prof prof prof prof wc   wc   wc   wc
[25] bc   bc   bc   bc   bc   bc   bc   bc   bc bc   bc   bc
[37] bc   bc   bc   bc   bc   bc   bc   bc   bc
Levels: bc prof wc

> length(Duncan$type)

[1] 45

> class(Duncan$type)

[1] "factor"

> mode(Duncan$type)

[1] "numeric"
```

- A function:

```
> length(lm)

[1] 1

> class(lm)

[1] "function"

> mode(lm)

[1] "function"
```

- An object returned by the function `lm`:

```
> (mod <- lm(prestige ~ income + education, data=Duncan))

Call:
lm(formula = prestige ~ income + education, data = Duncan)

Coefficients:
(Intercept)        income        education
    -6.0647        0.5987          0.5458

> length(mod)

[1] 12

> class(mod)

[1] "lm"

> mode(mod)

[1] "list"
```

The class of an object is most important in *object-oriented programming in R* (discussed in Sections 1.4 and 8.7), where *generic functions* are written to invoke different *methods* depending on the class of their arguments. A familiar example is the generic `summary` function, which works differently for vectors, data frames, and regression models, among other classes of objects.

Some objects have additional *attributes*, which store information about the object: for example,

```
> X # a matrix

     x         y
[1,] 1 0.0000000
[2,] 2 0.6931472
[3,] 3 1.0986123
[4,] 4 1.3862944
[5,] 5 1.6094379

> attributes(X)

$dim
[1] 5 2

$dimnames
$dimnames[[1]]
NULL

$dimnames[[2]]
[1] "x" "y"

> attributes(Duncan) # a data frame

$names
[1] "type"      "income"    "education" "prestige"

$class
[1] "data.frame"
```

```
$row.names
 [1] "accountant"            "pilot"            "architect"
 [4] "author"                "chemist"          "minister"
 . . .
[43] "janitor"               "policeman"        "waiter"

> attributes(mod) # a linear-model object

$names
 [1] "coefficients"  "residuals"       "effects"
 [4] "rank"          "fitted.values"   "assign"
 [7] "qr"            "df.residual"     "xlevels"
[10] "call"          "terms"           "model"

$class
[1] "lm"
```

There is an important distinction between the printed representation of an object (such as the linear-model object mod) and its internal structure. That said, we do not normally interact directly with an object produced by a modeling function and therefore do not need to see its internal structure; interaction with the object is the province of functions created for that purpose (e.g., the generic summary function). The invaluable str function, however, allows us to examine the internal structure of an object in abbreviated form:

```
> str(Duncan) # a data frame

'data.frame':         45 obs. of  4 variables:
 $ type     : Factor w/ 3 levels "bc","prof","wc":
                       2 2 2 2 2 2 2 2 3 2 ...
 $ income   : int  62 72 75 55 64 21 64 80 67 72 ...
 $ education: int  86 76 92 90 86 84 93 100 87 86 ...
 $ prestige : int  82 83 90 76 90 87 93 90 52 88 ...
```

The output from str gives us a variety of information about the object: that it is a data frame composed of four variables, including the factor type, with levels "bc", "wc", and "prof" and initial values 2 2 2 2 2 2 2 2 3 2; and so on.[23]

Standard R functions exist to create data of different modes and for many classes (*constructor functions*), to test for modes and classes (*predicate functions*), and to convert data to a specific mode or class (*coercion functions*).

- Constructor functions conventionally have the same name as their mode or class: for example,

```
> (num <- numeric(5))# create numeric vector of 0s of length 5

[1] 0 0 0 0 0

> (fac <- factor(c("a","b","c","c","b","a")))# create factor

[1] a b c c b a
Levels: a b c
```

---

[23]The str function is used extensively in Chapter 8 on programming in R.

There is also the general constructor function `vector`, whose first argument specifies the `mode` of the object to be created and whose second argument specifies the object's `length`:

```
> vector(mode="numeric", length=5)

[1] 0 0 0 0 0

> vector(mode="list", length=2)

[[1]]
NULL

[[2]]
NULL
```

- By convention, predicates in R prefix the characters "`is.`" to the name of a mode or class:

```
> is.numeric(num)   # predicate for mode numeric

[1] TRUE

> is.numeric(fac)

[1] FALSE

> is.factor(fac)   # predicate for class factor

[1] TRUE
```

The general predicate `is` takes a class or mode as its second argument:

```
> is(fac, "factor")

[1] TRUE

> is(fac, "numeric")

[1] FALSE
```

- The names of coercion functions use the prefix "`as.`":

```
> (char <- as.character(fac))   # coerce to mode character

[1] "a" "b" "c" "c" "b" "a"

> (num <- as.numeric(fac))   # coerce to mode numeric

[1] 1 2 3 3 2 1

> (as.factor(num)) # coerce to class factor

[1] 1 2 3 3 2 1
Levels: 1 2 3

> as.numeric(char)

[1] NA NA NA NA NA NA

Warning message:
NAs introduced by coercion
```

The last example illustrates that coercion may cause information to be lost.

There is also a general coercion function, `as`:

```
> as(fac, "character")

[1] "a" "b" "c" "c" "b" "a"

> as(fac, "numeric")

[1] 1 2 3 3 2 1
```

2.6.2   PITFALLS OF FLOATING-POINT ARITHMETIC

The designers of R have paid a great deal of attention to the numerical accuracy of computations in the language, but they have not been able to repeal the laws of computer arithmetic. We usually need not concern ourselves with the details of how numbers are stored in R; occasionally, however, these details can do us in if we're not careful.

Integers—that is, the positive and negative whole numbers and zero—are represented exactly in R. There are, however, qualifications. Computers represent numbers in binary form, and on a typical computer, R uses 32 binary digits (*bits*) to store an integer, which usually means that integers from $-2^{31} = -2,147,483,648$ to $2^{31} - 1 = +2,147,483,647$ can be represented. Smaller and larger integers can't be represented. Moreover, just because a number *looks like* an integer doesn't mean that it *is represented as* an integer in R:

```
> is.integer(2)

[1] FALSE

> is.integer(2L)

[1] TRUE
```

Integer constants are entered directly by appending the character L to the number.[24] As well, some operations produce integers:

```
> is.integer(1:100)

[1] TRUE
```

Unlike in some programming languages, arithmetic involving integers in R doesn't necessarily produce an integer result, even when the result could be represented exactly as an integer:

```
> is.integer(2L + 3L)

[1] TRUE

> is.integer(2L*3L)

[1] TRUE

> is.integer(4L/2L)

[1] FALSE

> is.integer(sqrt(4L))

[1] FALSE
```

Furthermore, R silently coerces integers to floating-point numbers (described below), when both kinds of numbers appear in an arithmetic expression:

---

[24]Integers in R are so-called *long integers*, occupying 32 bits, hence the L.

```
> is.integer(2L + 3)
```

```
[1] FALSE
```

Most numbers in R are represented as *floating-point numbers*. A floating-point number consists of three parts: a *sign*, either $+$ or $-$; a *significand*; and an *exponent*. You're probably already familiar with this idea from scientific notation; for example, the number -2.3×10^{12} has the sign $-$, significand 2.3, and exponent 12.

On a computer, floating-point numbers are represented in binary rather than in decimal form. R stores floating-point numbers as double-precision binary numbers, which typically use 64 bits for each number, including one bit for the sign, 11 bits for the exponent, and 52 bits for the significand. This allows R to represent numbers with magnitudes between about 5×10^{-324} and 2×10^{308}. If you work with numbers outside this range, then you're out of our league!

You're probably also familiar with the idea that not all numbers have exact decimal representations. For example, the *irrational numbers* $\pi \approx 3.14159$, $e \approx 2.71828$, and $\sqrt{2} \approx 1.41421$ cannot be represented exactly as decimal numbers. Even many *rational numbers*, such as $1/3 = 0.33333\cdot$, do not have exact decimal representations. The same is true in binary representation, where, for example, $1/10$ does not have an exact representation because 10 is not a power of 2. This fact, and the fact that floating-point arithmetic can result in round-off errors, means that you cannot rely on R to produce exact floating-point results: for example,

```
> (sqrt(2))^2 == 2
```

```
[1] FALSE
```

```
> (sqrt(2))^2 - 2
```

```
[1] 4.440892e-16
```

Recall that `4.440892e-16` represents 4.440892×10^{-16}, a number very close to 0.

It is, consequently, not a good idea to test for exact equality of numbers produced by floating-point operations. The *machine double-epsilon* for a computer gives the maximum relative error that can result from rounding floating-point numbers and depends on the number of bits in the significand; thus, on a typical computer, the machine double-epsilon is $2^{-52} \approx 2 \times 10^{-16}$.

When comparing floating-point numbers for equality, we should allow for a tolerance of about the square root of the machine double-epsilon, that is, typically $2^{-26} \approx 1.5 \times 10^{-8}$. The `all.equal` function in R uses this tolerance by default:

```
> all.equal((sqrt(2))^2, 2)
```

```
[1] TRUE
```

Moreover, when objects are not essentially equal, `all.equal` tries to provide useful information about how they differ:

```
> all.equal(2, 4)

[1] "Mean relative difference: 1"

> all.equal(2, "2")

[1] "Modes: numeric, character"
[2] "target is numeric, current is character"
```

R can also represent and compute with complex numbers, which occasionally have statistical applications:

```
> (z <- complex(real=0, imaginary=1))

[1] 0+1i

> (w <- 2 + 2*z) # 2 is coerced to complex

[1] 2+2i

> w*z

[1] -2+2i

> w/z

[1] 2-2i
```

See `?complex` for more information.

Finally, arithmetic operations can produce results that are not (ordinary) numbers:

```
> 1/0

[1] Inf

> -1/0

[1] -Inf

> 0/0

[1] NaN
```

where `Inf` stands for ∞ (infinity) and `NaN` stands for "Not a Number."

We do not bother to clean up at the end of the current chapter because we will not save the R workspace. More generally, and as we mentioned in the Preface, in this book we assume that each chapter represents an independent R session.

2.7 Complementary Reading and References

- The *R Data Import/Export* manual, which is part of the standard R distribution and is also available on the R website (at `http://cran.r-project.org/doc/manuals/R-data.html`), provides a great deal of information about getting data into and out of R, including on database interfaces. For the latter topic, see also Ripley (2001).
- Spector (2008) provides a reasonably broad treatment of data management in R, a dry topic but one that is vital for the effective day-to-day use of R (or of any statistical data-analysis system).
- Both Gentleman (2009, chap. 5) and Chambers (2008, chap. 8) have extensive discussions of manipulating character data in R. Further information about regular expressions is available in many sources, including the *Wikipedia* (at `http://en.wikipedia.org/wiki/Regular_expression`).
- A good place to learn more about floating-point operations is the *Wikipedia* article on the subject (at `http://en.wikipedia.org/wiki/Floating_point`), which also has useful references.

Exploring and Transforming Data 3

Statistical graphs play three important roles in data analysis. Graphs provide an initial look at the data, a step that is skipped at the peril of the data analyst. At this stage, we learn about the data, its oddities, outliers, and other interesting features. John Tukey (Tukey, 1977) coined the term *exploratory data analysis* for this phase of an analysis. Graphs are also employed during model building and model criticism, particularly in diagnostic methods used to understand the fit of a model. Finally, *presentation graphics* can summarize a fitted model for the benefit of others.

In the first two applications, we need to be able to draw many graphs quickly and easily, while in the presentation phase we should be willing to spend more time on a graph to get it just right for publication. In this chapter, we present some basic tools for exploratory graphs, such as histograms, boxplots, and scatterplots. Some of these tools are standard to R, while others are in the **car** package associated with this book. We will return to regression graphics in Chapter 6, with equally easy to use functions for various diagnostic methods, which differ from the basic graphs of this chapter mostly in the quantities that are graphed, not in the graphing paradigm. Finally, in Chapter 7 we show how to produce customized, potentially elaborate, graphs suitable for almost any purpose.

3.1 Examining Distributions

3.1.1 HISTOGRAMS

The most common graph of the distribution of a quantitative variable is the *histogram*. A histogram dissects the range of the variable into class intervals, called *bins*, and counts the number of observations falling in each bin. The counts—or percentages, proportions, or densities calculated from the

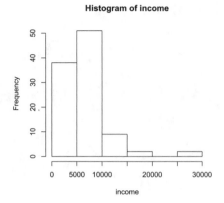

Figure 3.1   Default histogram of `income` in the Canadian occupational-prestige data.

counts—are plotted in a bar graph. An example, constructed by the following R commands, appears in Figure 3.1:[1]

```
> library(car)
> head(Prestige) # first 6 rows

                    education income women prestige census type
gov.administrators      13.11  12351 11.16     68.8   1113 prof
general.managers        12.26  25879  4.02     69.1   1130 prof
accountants             12.77   9271 15.70     63.4   1171 prof
purchasing.officers     11.42   8865  9.11     56.8   1175 prof
chemists                14.62   8403 11.68     73.5   2111 prof
physicists              15.64  11030  5.13     77.6   2113 prof

> with(Prestige, hist(income))
```

The first of these commands loads the **car** package, giving us access to the `Prestige` data. The second command displays the initial six lines of the data set. The histogram is drawn by the `hist` function, in this case with no arguments other than the variable to be plotted, `income`. The `with` command allows `hist` to access `income` from the `Prestige` data frame (as explained in Section 2.2.2).

The default histogram, produced by `hist` with no extra arguments, has bins of equal width, and the height of each bar is equal to the *frequency*—the number of observations—in the corresponding bin. In an alternative definition of the histogram, the height of each bar is selected so that its *area* is equal to the fraction of the data in the corresponding bin. To distinguish it from the more common frequency histogram, we call this latter graph a *density histogram*. The `hist` function draws density histograms if the argument `freq`

----

[1]The Canadian occupational-prestige data set, on which this example is based, was introduced in Section 2.1.2.

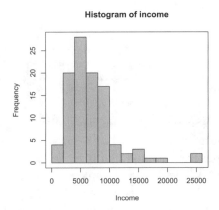

Figure 3.2 Revised histogram of `income`.

is set to `FALSE` or if the `breaks` argument is used to define bins of unequal width.

The shape of the histogram is determined in part by the number of bins—too few and the plot hides interesting features of the data, too many and the histogram is too rough, displaying spurious features of the data. The default method for selecting the number of bins, together with the effort to locate nice cut points between the bins, can produce too few bins. An alternative rule, proposed by Freedman and Diaconis (1981), sets the target number of bins to

$$\left\lceil \frac{n^{1/3}(\max - \min)}{2(Q_3 - Q_1)} \right\rceil$$

where n is the number of observations, $\max - \min$ is the range of the data, $Q_3 - Q_1$ is the interquartile range, and the ceiling brackets indicate rounding up to the next integer. Applying this rule to `income` in the Canadian occupational-prestige data produces the histogram in Figure 3.2:

```
> with(Prestige, hist(income, breaks="FD", col="gray"))
> box()
```

Setting `col="gray"` specifies the color of the histogram bars.[2] The `box` function draws a box around the histogram and could have been omitted. In this example, both histograms suggest that the distribution of income has a single mode near $5,000 and is skewed to the right, with several occupations that have relatively large incomes.

As with most of the graphics functions in R, `hist` has a dizzying array of arguments that can change the appearance of the graph:

---

[2]The general use of color in R is discussed in Section 7.1.4.

```
> args(hist.default)

function (x, breaks = "Sturges", freq = NULL, probability = !freq,
 include.lowest = TRUE, right = TRUE, density = NULL, angle = 45,
 col = NULL, border = NULL, main = paste("Histogram of", xname),
 xlim = range(breaks), ylim = NULL, xlab = xname, ylab, axes = TRUE,
 plot = TRUE, labels = FALSE, nclass = NULL, ...)
```

The `args` command (Section 1.1.2) displays all the arguments of a function. We asked for the arguments for `hist.default` rather than just `hist` because `hist` is a generic function and it is the default method that actually draws the graph.[3] While a more complete description is available from `?hist`, here are some of the key arguments. The `breaks` argument is used to specify the edges of the bins. We can choose these values ourselves [e.g., `breaks=c(0, 5000, 10000, 15000, 20000, 25000)`], give the number of bins we want (e.g., `breaks=10`), or set `breaks` equal to the name of a rule that will determine the number of equal-size bins (e.g., `breaks ="FD"`). The possible settings are given on the help page for the function. The `xlab`, `ylab`, and `main` arguments are used, as in most graphical functions in R, to label the horizontal axis, vertical axis, and plot title, respectively. If we don't set these arguments, then `hist` will construct labels that are often reasonable. The remaining arguments generally change the appearance of the graph.

You may be familiar with *stem-and-leaf displays*, which are histograms that encode the numeric data directly in their bars. We believe that stem-leaf-displays, as opposed to more traditional histograms, are primarily useful for what Tukey (1977) called *scratching down* numbers—that is, paper-and-pencil methods for visualizing small data sets. That said, stem-and-leaf displays may be constructed by the standard R function `stem`; a more sophisticated version, corresponding more closely to Tukey's original stem-and-leaf display, is provided by the `stemleaf` function in the **aplpack** package.

If you are looking for fancy three-dimensional effects and other chart junk (an apt term coined by Tufte, 1983) that are often added by graphics programs to clutter up histograms and other standard graphs, you will have to look elsewhere: The basic R graphics functions intentionally avoid chart junk.

3.1.2 DENSITY ESTIMATION

Nonparametric density estimation often produces a more satisfactory representation of a distribution by smoothing the histogram. The *kernel-density estimate* at the value x of a variable X is defined as

$$\widehat{p}(x) = \frac{1}{nh} \sum_{i=1}^{n} K\left(\frac{x - x_i}{h}\right)$$

---

[3]See Sections 1.4 and 8.7 on object-oriented programming in R for a detailed explanation of generic functions and their methods.

where $\widehat{p}(x)$ is the estimated density at the point x, the x_i are the n observations on the variable, and K is a *kernel function*—generally a symmetric, single-peaked density function, such as the normal density. The quantity h is called the *bandwidth*, and it controls the degree of smoothness of the density estimate: If h is too large then the density estimate is smooth but biased as an estimator of the true density, while if h is too small then bias is low but the estimate is too rough—that is, the variance of the estimator is large.

The density function in R implements kernel-density estimation, by default using a normal kernel and a reasonable method for selecting h to balance variance and bias.[4] Applying the density function to income in the Prestige data:

```
> with(Prestige, {
+     hist(income, breaks="FD", freq=FALSE, ylab="Density")
+     lines(density(income), lwd=2)
+     lines(density(income, adjust=0.5), lwd=1)
+     rug(income)
+     box()
+ })
```

This example, which produces Figure 3.3, illustrates how an R graph can be built up by successive calls to graphics functions. The hist function constructs the histogram, with freq=FALSE to specify density scaling and ylab="Density" furnishing the label for the vertical axis of the graph. The lines function draws the density estimate on the graph, the coordinates of which are calculated by the call to density. The argument lwd=2 draws a double-thick line. The second call to density, with adjust=0.5, specifies a bandwidth half the default value and therefore produces a rougher density estimate, shown in the figure as a lighter line, lwd=1. The rug function is used to draw a one-dimensional *scatterplot* or *rug-plot* at the bottom of the graph. The curly braces { } define a *compound command* as the second argument to with, allowing us to specify several commands that use the Prestige data. In this case, the default bandwidth appears to do a good job of balancing detail against roughness, and using half the default bandwidth produces a density estimate that is too rough.

3.1.3 QUANTILE-COMPARISON PLOTS

We may want to compare the distribution of a variable with a theoretical reference distribution, such as the normal distribution. A *quantile-comparison plot*, or *quantile-quantile plot (QQ-plot)*, provides an effective graphical means of making the comparison, plotting the ordered data on the vertical axis against the corresponding quantiles of the reference distribution on the horizontal axis. If the data conform to the reference distribution, then the quantile-comparison plot should be a straight line, within sampling error.

---

[4]Several freely available R packages provide more sophisticated facilities for density estimation. See, in particular, the **sm** package (Bowman and Azzalini, 1997) and the **locfit** package (Loader, 1999).

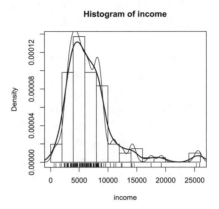

Histogram of income

Figure 3.3 Nonparametric kernel-density estimates for the distribution of income, using the default bandwidth (heavier line) and half the default bandwidth (lighter line).

R provides the `qqnorm` function for making quantile-comparison plots against the normal distribution, but we prefer the `qqPlot` function in the **car** package. By default, `qqPlot` compares the data with the normal distribution and provides a 95% pointwise *confidence envelope* around a line fit to the plot; the reference line is drawn by default between the pairs of quartiles Q_1 and Q_3 of the two distributions. Figure 3.4 shows a normal QQ-plot for `income` in the `Prestige` data:

```
> with(Prestige, qqPlot(income, labels=row.names(Prestige), id.n=3))

[1] "general.managers" "physicians"        "lawyers"
```

As do most of the graphics functions in the **car** package, `qqPlot` supports both interactive and automatic marking of extreme points. The `labels` argument is used to provide labels to mark the points, here the row names of the `Prestige` data frame. By setting `id.n=3`, automatic point marking is turned on, and the three most extreme points are labeled on the plot. The labels of the marked points are returned in the R console.[5]

The `qqPlot` function can be used more generally to plot the data against *any* reference distribution for which there are quantile and density functions in R, which includes just about any distribution that you may wish to use. Simply specify the root word for the distribution. For example, the root for the normal distribution is `norm`, with density function `dnorm` and quantile function `qnorm`. The root for the chi-square distribution is `chisq`, with density and quantile functions `dchisq` and `qchisq`, respectively. Root words for some other commonly used distributions are `binom` and `pois` for the binomial and Poisson distributions, respectively (which, as discrete distribution, have probability-mass functions rather than density functions), `f` for the *F* distribution, `t` for the *t* distribution, and `unif` for the uniform distribution.

---

[5]See Section 3.5 for further discussion of point labeling.

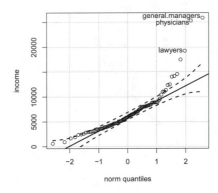

Figure 3.4 Normal quantile-comparison plot for `income`. The broken lines give a pointwise 95% confidence envelope around the fitted solid line. Three points were labeled automatically. Because many points, especially at the right of the graph, are outside the confidence bounds, we have evidence that the distribution of `income` is not like a sample from a normal population.

Table 3.1 Arguments for some standard probability functions in R. Most of the arguments are self-explanatory. For the binomial distribution, `size` represents the number of binomial trials, while `prob` represents the probability of success on each trial. For the Poisson distribution, `lambda` is the mean. Not all arguments are shown for all functions; consult the R help pages for details.

Distribution	Density or Mass Function	Quantile Function
normal	dnorm(x, mean=0, sd=1)	qnorm(p, mean=0, sd=1)
chi-square	dchisq(x, df)	qchisq(p, df)
F	df(x, df1, df2)	qf(p, df1, df2)
t	dt(x, df)	qt(p, df)
binomial	dbinom(x, size, prob)	qbinom(p, size, prob)
Poisson	dpois(x, lambda)	qpois(p, lambda)
uniform	dunif(x, min=0, max=1)	qunif(p, min=0, max=1)

Distribution	Distribution Function	Random Number Function
normal	pnorm(q, mean=0, sd=1)	rnorm(n, mean=0, sd=1)
chi-square	pchisq(q, df)	rchisq(n, df)
F	pf(q, df1, df2)	rf(n, df1, df2)
t	pt(q, df)	rt(n, df)
binomial	pbinom(q, size, prob)	rbinom(n, size, prob)
Poisson	ppois(q, lambda)	rpois(n, lambda)
uniform	punif(q, min=0, max=1)	runif(n, min=0, max=1)

In addition to density and quantile functions, R also provides cumulative distribution functions, with the prefix p, and pseudo-random number generators, with prefix r. For example, pnorm gives cumulative probabilities for the normal distributions, while rnorm generates normal random variables. Table 3.1 summarizes the principal arguments to these probability functions.

To illustrate, we use the rchisq function to generate a random sample from the chi-square distribution with 3 *df* and then plot the sample against

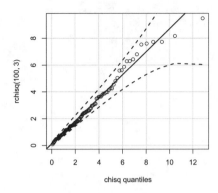

Figure 3.5   Quantile-comparison plot of a sample of size $n = 100$ from the $\chi^2(3)$ distribution against the distribution from which the sample was drawn.

the distribution from which it was drawn, producing Figure 3.5:

```
> set.seed(124) # for reproducibility
> qqPlot(rchisq(100, 3), distribution="chisq", df=3)
```

The points should, and do, closely match the straight line on the graph, with the fit a bit worse for the larger values in the sample. The confidence envelope suggests that these deviations for large values are to be expected, as they reflect the long right tail of the $\chi^2(3)$ density function.

3.1.4   BOXPLOTS

The final univariate display that we describe is the *boxplot*. Although boxplots are most commonly used to compare distributions among groups (as in Section 3.2.2), they can also be drawn to summarize a single sample, providing a quick check of symmetry and the presence of outliers. Figure 3.6 shows a boxplot for income, produced by the Boxplot function in the **car** package:[6]

```
> Boxplot(~ income, data=Prestige)

[1] "general.managers"          "lawyers"
[3] "physicians"                "veterinarians"
[5] "osteopaths.chiropractors"
```

The variable to be plotted is given in a *one-sided formula*: a tilde (~) followed by the name of the variable. This variable is contained in the data frame Prestige, and the data argument is used to tell the function where to find the data. Most graphical functions that use a formula accept a data argument.

---

[6]The standard R boxplot function can also be used to draw boxplots, but Boxplot is more convenient, automatically identifying outliers, for example; indeed, Boxplot is simply a front-end to boxplot.

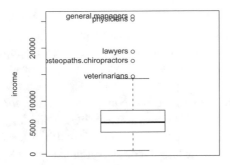

Figure 3.6 Boxplot of `income`. Several outlying observations were labeled automatically.

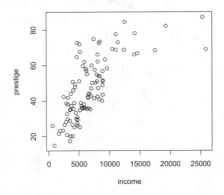

Figure 3.7 Simple scatterplot of `prestige` versus `income` for the Canadian occupational-prestige data.

3.2 Examining Relationships

3.2.1 SCATTERPLOTS

A *scatterplot* is the familiar graph of points with one quantitative variable on the horizontal or *x*-axis and a second quantitative variable on the vertical or *y*-axis. Understanding, and using, scatterplots is at the heart of regression analysis. There is typically an asymmetric role of the two axes, with the *y*-axis reserved for a response variable and the *x*-axis for a predictor.

The generic `plot` function is the primary tool in R for drawing graphs in two dimensions. What this function produces depends on the values of its first one or two arguments.[7] If the first two arguments to `plot` are numeric vectors, then we get a scatterplot, as in Figure 3.7:

```
> with(Prestige, plot(income, prestige))
```

---

[7]The behavior of generic functions such as `plot` is discussed in Sections 1.4 and 8.7, and more information about the `plot` function is provided in Section 3.2.3 and in Chapter 7 on R graphics.

The *first* argument to `plot` is the *x*-axis variable, and the *second* argument is the *y*-axis variable. The scatterplot in Figure 3.7 is a *summary graph* for the regression problem in which `prestige` is the response and `income` is the predictor. As our eye moves from left to right across the graph, we see how the distribution of `prestige` changes as `income` increases. In technical terms, we are visualizing the *conditional distributions* of `prestige` given values of `income`. The overall story here is that as `income` increases, so does `prestige`, at least up to about $10,000, after which the value of `prestige` stays more or less fixed on average at about 80.

We write E(`prestige|income`) to represent the mean value of `prestige` as the value of `income` varies and call this the *conditional mean function* or the *regression function*. The qualitative statements in the previous paragraph therefore concern the regression function. The *variance function*, Var(`prestige|income`), traces the conditional variability in `prestige` as `income` changes—that is, the spread of *y* in vertical strips in the plot. As in Figure 3.7, when the tilt of a scatterplot changes, it is difficult to judge changes in conditional variability from a simple scatterplot.

Scatterplots are useful for studying the mean and variance functions in the regression of the *y*-variable on the *x*-variable. In addition, scatterplots can help us identify *outliers*—points that have values of the response far different from the expected value—and *leverage points*—cases with extremely large or small values of the predictor. How these ideas relate to multiple regression is a topic discussed in Chapter 6.

PLOT ENHANCEMENTS

Scatterplots can be enhanced by adding curves to the graphs and by identifying unusual points. A *scatterplot smoother* provides a visual estimate of the regression function, either using a statistical model such as simple linear regression or nonparametrically, without specifying the shape of the regression curve explicitly.

The `scatterplot` function in the **car** package draws scatterplots with smoothers, as in Figure 3.8:

```
> scatterplot(prestige ~ income, span=0.6, lwd=3,
+     id.n=4, data=Prestige)

[1] "general.managers" "physicians"       "lawyers"
[4] "ministers"
```

The variables in the scatterplot are given in a *formula*, separated by a tilde (~), with the response variable on the left and the predictor on the right. If, as in this example, the `scatterplot` is specified via a formula, we can use the `data` argument to supply a data frame in which the variables in the formula are located; this is also true for the standard `plot` function.

There are two smoothers on the scatterplot in Figure 3.8. The first is a straight line fit by ordinary least squares (OLS); we can suppress this line with the argument `reg.line=FALSE`. The second, the solid curved line, is

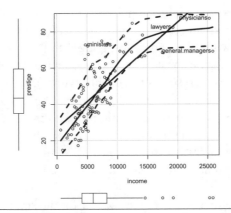

Figure 3.8 Enhanced scatterplot of `prestige` by `income`. Several points were identified automatically.

a nonparametric-regression smoother produced by the `lowess` function in R; the lowess smoother can be suppressed by the argument `smooth=FALSE`.

Lowess is an acronym for *lo*cally *we*ighted *s*catterplot *s*moother, which implements a form of *local linear regression*: Each point along the regression curve is produced by a weighted linear least-squares fit to data in the neighborhood of the focal point, with the weights declining as the *x* values get farther from the *x* value of the focal point. The degree of smoothness of the lowess line is controlled by a smoothing parameter, called the *span*, representing the fraction of the data included in each local-regression fit; larger spans produce a smoother regression line. The span is analogous to the bandwidth of the kernel-density estimator (described in Section 3.1.2). We generally want to use the smallest span that produces a reasonably smooth result, to achieve a favorable trade-off of bias against variance—balancing roughness against fidelity to the data. In the command above, the span was changed from the default value `span=0.5` to `span=0.6`. One advantage to the lowess smooth is that the fit is relatively insensitive to the choice of smoothing parameter, and values of the span from about 0.3 to about 0.7 generally give useful fitted lines. In very large samples, however, we can often use a smaller span than 0.3, and in very small samples, we may need a larger span than 0.7. In Figure 3.8, the least-squares line cannot match the obvious curve in the regression function that is apparent in the lowess fit.[8]

In addition to the least-squares and lowess lines, by default, `scatterplot` displays a nonparametric estimate of the variance function, showing how the conditional spread of the *y*-values changes with *x*. The broken lines in the graph are based on smoothing the residuals from the lowess line. By smoothing the positive and negative residuals separately, `scatterplot` also

---

[8]We use a smoother here and in most of this book as a plot enhancement, designed to help us derive information from a graph. Nonparametric regression, in which smoothers are substituted for more traditional regression models, is described in the online appendix to the book. *Kernel regression*, which is similar to lowess, is described in Section 7.2.

helps us detect asymmetry in the conditional distribution of y. In interpreting the conditional spread, however, we must be careful to focus on the *vertical* separation of the two broken lines. In Figure 3.8, the conditional spread of `prestige` remains quite constant as `income` increases, and the conditional distribution of `prestige` seems reasonably symmetric.

The graph in Figure 3.8 also includes marginal boxplots for the two variables, and these can be suppressed with `boxplots=FALSE`. As with the other graphical functions in the **car** package, point labeling is available either automatically or interactively (see Section 3.5); setting `id.n=4` identifies the four most extreme points, rather than the default `id.n=0`, which suppresses point identification.

For clarity, we set the line-width to `lwd=3` for the smoothers in Figure 3.8 to make the regression lines on the plot thicker than they would be by default (`lwd=1`). The default color of nonparametric-regression lines plotted by `scatterplot` is red. To get black points and lines, we can specify the argument `col="black"`. See `?scatterplot` for details.

CODED SCATTERPLOTS FOR GROUPED DATA

Using the categorical variable `type` (type of occupation) in the `Prestige` data set, we could simultaneously condition on both `type` and `income` by drawing a separate plot of `prestige` versus `income` for each level of `type`. When, as here, the categorical variable has only a few levels, we can achieve the same result in a single graph by using distinct colors or symbols for points in the different levels of the categorical variable, fitting separate smoothers to each group. We call the resulting graph a *coded scatterplot*. An example appears in Figure 3.9:

```
> scatterplot(prestige~income|type, data=Prestige, boxplots=FALSE,
+             span=0.75, col=gray(c(0, 0.5, 0.7)), id.n=0)
```

The variables for the coded scatterplot are given in a formula as $y \sim x \mid g$, which we read as plotting y on the vertical axis and x on the horizontal axis and marking points according to the value of g (or "y vs. x given g").

We selected a large span, `span=0.75`, for the lowess smoothers because of the small number of observations in the occupational groups. The legend for the graph, automatically generated by the `scatterplot` function, can be suppressed with `legend.plot=FALSE`. We set the colors for points and lines with the argument `col=gray(c(0, 0.5, 0.7))`, which generates three levels of gray for the three occupational types. If we omit the `col` argument, `scatterplot` will select the colors for us. The argument `id.n=0` was included as a reminder that we could have specified automatic point marking by setting `id.n` to the number of points to be labeled; this argument was unnecessary because `id.n=0` is the default value.

Figure 3.9 allows us to examine three regression functions simultaneously: $E(\text{prestige}|\text{income}, \text{type} = \text{bc})$, $E(\text{prestige}|\text{income}, \text{type} =$

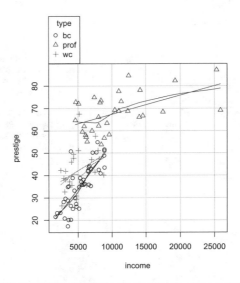

Figure 3.9 Scatterplot of `prestige` by `income`, coded by `type` of occupation.

`wc`), and E(`prestige|income, type = prof`). The nonlinear relationship in Figure 3.8 has disappeared, and we now have three reasonably linear regressions with different slopes. The slope of the relationship between `prestige` and `income` looks steepest for blue-collar occupations and looks least steep for professional and managerial occupations.

JITTERING SCATTERPLOTS

Discrete, quantitative variables typically result in uninformative scatterplots. The example in Figure 3.10a was produced by the `plot` command:

```
> head(Vocab)

         year     sex education vocabulary
20040001 2004 Female         9          3
20040002 2004 Female        14          6
20040003 2004   Male        14          9
20040005 2004 Female        17          8
20040008 2004   Male        14          1
20040010 2004   Male        14          7

> nrow(Vocab)

[1] 21638

> plot(vocabulary ~ education, data=Vocab)
```

The data for this illustration, from the `Vocab` data frame in the **car** package, come from the U.S. General Social Surveys, 1972–2004, conducted by the National Opinion Research Center. The two variables in the plot are education in years and the respondent's score on a 10-word `vocabulary` test.

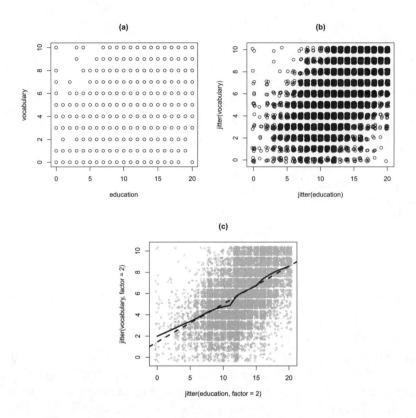

Figure 3.10 Scatterplots of vocabulary by education: (a) unjittered, (b) default jittering, and (c) twice default jittering, with least-squares and lowess lines.

Because education can take on only 21 distinct values and vocabulary only 11 distinct values, most of the nearly 22,000 observations in the data set are overplotted; indeed, almost all the possible $21 \times 11 = 231$ plotting positions are occupied, producing a meaningless rectangular grid of dots.

Jittering the data by adding a small random quantity to each coordinate serves to separate the overplotted points. We can use the jitter function in R for this purpose:

```
> plot(jitter(vocabulary) ~ jitter(education), data=Vocab)
```

The result is shown in Figure 3.10b. We can control the degree of jittering via the argument factor; for example, specifying factor=2 doubles the jitter, yielding a more satisfactory result for the current example:

```
> plot(jitter(vocabulary, factor=2) ~ jitter(education, factor=2),
+    col="gray", cex=0.5, data=Vocab)
```

To render the individual points less prominent, we plot them in gray and use the argument cex=0.5 to make the points half the default size. To complete the picture, we add least-squares and nonparametric-regression lines, using the original *unjittered* data for these computations, producing Figure 3.10c:

```
> with(Vocab, {
+     abline(lm(vocabulary ~ education), lwd=3, lty="dashed")
+     lines(lowess(education, vocabulary, f=0.2), lwd=3)
+     })
```

The least-squares line on the graph is computed by `lm` and drawn by `abline`; the argument `lwd` to `abline` sets the width of the regression line, while the line type `lty="dashed"` specifies a broken line. The `lowess` function returns the coordinates for the local-regression curve, which is drawn by `lines`; the span of the local regression is set by the argument `f` to `lowess`, and we take advantage of the very large data set by using a small span. The relationship between `vocabulary` and `education` appears nearly linear, and we can also discern other features of the data that previously were hidden by over plotting, such as the relatively large number of respondents with 12 years of education.

We could have more conveniently used the `jitter` argument to the `scatterplot` function in the **car** package to make the graphs in Figures 3.10b and c, but we wanted to demonstrate how to construct a simple plot from its components (a topic described in detail in Chapter 7).

3.2.2 PARALLEL BOXPLOTS

Parallel boxplots help us visualize the conditional distributions of a quantitative response for each of several values of a discrete predictor. We illustrate with data from Ornstein (1976) on interlocking directorates among 248 major Canadian corporations:

```
> some(Ornstein) # sample 10 rows
```

	assets	sector	nation	interlocks
3	113230	BNK	CAN	94
29	11090	MAN	US	21
57	5021	MIN	OTH	27
123	1427	HLD	CAN	1
150	830	MIN	UK	1
153	802	MAN	CAN	0
154	798	AGR	CAN	11
156	789	MAN	US	6
160	761	WOD	US	1
211	376	MER	CAN	5

```
> nrow(Ornstein)
```

```
[1] 248
```

The variables in the data set include the `assets` of the corporation in millions of dollars; the corporation's `sector` of operation, a *factor* (i.e., categorical variable) with 10 *levels* (categories); the `nation` in which the firm is controlled, CAN (Canada), OTH (other), UK, and US; and the number of interlocking directorate and executive positions (`interlocks`) maintained between each company and others in the data set. Figure 3.11a shows a boxplot of the number of `interlocks` for each level of `nation`:

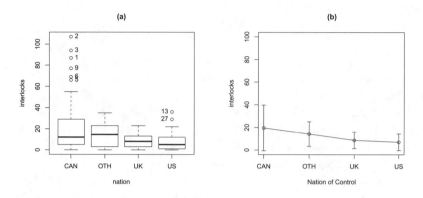

Figure 3.11 (a) Parallel boxplots of interlocks by nation of control, for Ornstein's interlocking-directorate data. (b) A mean/standard deviation plot of the same data.

```
> Boxplot(interlocks ~ nation, data=Ornstein, main="(a)")

[1] "1"   "2"   "3"   "5"   "6"   "9"   "13"  "27"
```

Because the names of the companies are not given in the original source, the points are labeled by case numbers. The firms are in descending order by assets, and thus, the identified points are among the largest companies.

A more common plot in the scientific literature is a graph of group means with error bars showing ±1 SD around the means. This plot can be drawn conveniently using the plotCI function in the **plotrix** package, as shown, for example, in Figure 3.11b:[9]

```
> library(plotrix)
> means <- with(Ornstein, tapply(interlocks, nation, mean))
> sds <- with(Ornstein, tapply(interlocks, nation, sd))
> plotCI(1:4, means, sds, xaxt="n", xlab="Nation of Control",
+     ylab="interlocks", main="(b)", ylim=c(0, 100))
> lines(1:4, means)
> axis(1, at=1:4, labels = names(means))
```

The tapply function (described in Section 8.4) is used here to compute the means and SDs for each level of nation. The graph is drawn with plotCI. The first argument gives the coordinates on the horizontal axis, the second gives the coordinates on the vertical axis, and the third is the vector of SDs. The standard graphical argument xaxt="n" suppresses the x-axis tick marks

---

[9]These plots are sometimes drawn with intervals of ±1 standard error rather than ±1 SD, and sometimes these error bars are added to bar charts rather than to a scatterplot of means. We discourage the use of bar charts for means because interpretation of the length of the bars, and therefore the visual metaphor of the graph, depends on whether or not a meaningful origin exists for the measured variable and whether or not the origin is included in the graph. The error bars can also lead to misinterpretation because neither the standard-error bars nor the standard-deviation bars are the appropriate measure of variation for comparing means between groups, because they make no allowance or correction for multiple testing, among other potential problems.

and labels, and the `ylim` argument is used here to match the vertical axis of Panel b with that of Panel a. The `lines` function joins the means with lines, and the `axis` function labels the horizontal axis with the names of the groups.

The parallel boxplots in Figure 3.11a and the mean/SD plot in Figure 3.11b purport to provide similar information, but the impression one gets from the two graphs is very different. The boxplots allow us to identify outliers and recognize skewness, with a few larger values in each level of `nation`. The mean/SD graph is misleading: Instead of showing the outliers, the graph inflates both the mean and the SD for Canada and disguises the skewness that is obvious in the boxplots. Both graphs, however, suggest that the variation among firms within nations is greater than the differences between nations.

3.2.3 MORE ON `plot`

The generic `plot` function is used in various ways in R. Suppose that x and y are numeric variables, that g is a factor, and that m is an object produced, for example, by one of the many statistical modeling functions in R, such as `lm`, for fitting linear models (discussed in Chapter 4), or `glm`, for fitting generalized linear models (Chapter 5). Then:

- `plot(y ~ x)` or `plot(x, y)` produces a basic scatterplot with y on the vertical axis and x on the horizontal axis. If x and y are two variables in the data frame D, then we can type `plot(y ~ x, data=D)`, `plot(D$x, D$y)`, or `with(D, plot(x, y))`. If we employ a formula to specify the plot, then we can use the `data` argument, but we can't use the `data` argument if the plotted variables are given as two arguments.
- `plot(x)` produces a scatterplot with x on the *vertical* axis and case numbers on the horizontal axis, which is called an *index plot*.
- `plot(y ~ g)` is the same as `boxplot(y ~ g)`.
- What `plot(m)` does depends on the *class* of the object m.[10] For example if m is a linear-model object created by a call to `lm`, then the `plot` function draws several graphs that are commonly associated with linear-regression models fit by least squares. In contrast, `plot(density(x))` draws a plot of the density estimate for the numeric variable x.

The `plot` function takes many additional arguments that control the appearance of the plot, the labeling of the axes, the fonts used, and so on. We can set some of these options globally with the `par` function, or just for the current graph by including the arguments in the `plot` command. We defer discussion of these details to Chapter 7; you can also look at `?par` for a description of the various graphical parameters.

---

[10]The class-based object-oriented programming system in R and its implementation through generic functions such as `plot` are explained in Sections 1.4 and 8.7.

3.3   Examining Multivariate Data

Scatterplots provide summaries of the conditional distribution of a numeric response variable given a numeric predictor and with coding can also condition on the value of a categorial predictor. When there is more than one numeric predictor, we would like to be able to draw a plot, in $m+1$ dimensions, of the response versus all m predictors simultaneously. Because the media on which we draw graphs (paper, computer displays) are two dimensional, and because in any event we can only perceive objects in three dimensions, examining multivariate data is intrinsically more difficult than examining univariate or bivariate data.

3.3.1   THREE-DIMENSIONAL PLOTS

Perspective and motion can convey a sense of depth, enabling us to examine data in three dimensions on a two-dimensional computer display. The most effective software of this kind allows the user to manipulate—for example, rotate—the display, to mark points, and to plot surfaces—such as regression surfaces.

The **rgl** package links R to the OpenGL three-dimensional graphics library, which is widely used in animated films, for example. Using **rgl**, the scatter3d function in the **car** package provides a three-dimensional generalization of the scatterplot function. The command

```
> scatter3d(prestige ~ income + education, id.n=3, data=Duncan)
```

produces Figure 3.12, which is a three-dimensional scatterplot for Duncan's occupational-prestige data (introduced in Section 1.2). The graph shows the least-squares regression plane for the regression of the variable on the vertical or y-axis, prestige, on the two variables on the horizontal or x- and z-axes, education and income; three observations (minister, conductor, and railroad engineer) were identified automatically as the most unusual based on their *Mahalanobis distances* from the centroid (i.e., the point of means) of the three variables.[11] The three-dimensional scatterplot can be rotated by left-clicking and dragging with the mouse. Color is used by default, with perspective, sophisticated lighting and translucency, and fog-based depth cuing. The overall effect is quite striking on the computer screen.

The scatter3d function has a variety of additional capabilities, including the ability to plot other regression surfaces (e.g., nonparametric regressions), to identify points interactively and according to other criteria, to plot concentration ellipsoids, and to rotate the plot automatically. Because three-dimensional dynamic graphs depend on color, perspective, and motion for

---

[11]Unlike simple Euclidean distance, which is inappropriate when the variables are scaled in different units, the Mahalanobis distance takes into account the variation and correlational structure of the data.

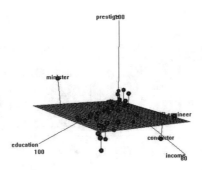

Figure 3.12 Three-dimensional scatterplot for Duncan's occupational-prestige data, showing the least-squares regression plane. Three unusual points were labeled automatically.

their effectiveness, we refer the reader to the help file for scatter3d and to the examples therein.

There are also facilities in R for drawing three-dimensional static graphs, including the standard R persp function, and the cloud and wireframe functions in the **lattice** package. The **rggobi** package links R to the GGobi system for visualizing data in three and more dimensions (Swayne et al., 1998; Cook and Swayne, 2009).

3.3.2 SCATTERPLOT MATRICES

Scatterplot matrices are graphical analogs of correlation matrices, displaying bivariate scatterplots of all pairs of variables—predictors and response—in a two-dimensional graphical array. Because each panel in a scatterplot matrix is just a two-dimensional scatterplot, each is the appropriate summary graph for the regression of the *y*-axis variable on the *x*-axis variable. In standard R, scatterplot matrices are constructed by the pairs function or by the splom function in the **lattice** package. The scatterplotMatrix function in the **car** package provides a variety of enhancements and bears the same relationship to pairs that scatterplot bears to plot.

An example, using the Canadian occupational-prestige data, appears in Figure 3.13:

```
> scatterplotMatrix(~ prestige + income + education + women,
+       span=0.7, data=Prestige)
```

The first argument to scatterplotMatrix is a one-sided formula, specifying the variables to be plotted separated by + signs. We previously saw the plot of prestige versus income, in the first row and second column (cf. Figure 3.8 on page 117), and this graph summarizes the regression of prestige on income. In contrast, the plot of income versus prestige, in the second row, first column, is for the regression of income on prestige.

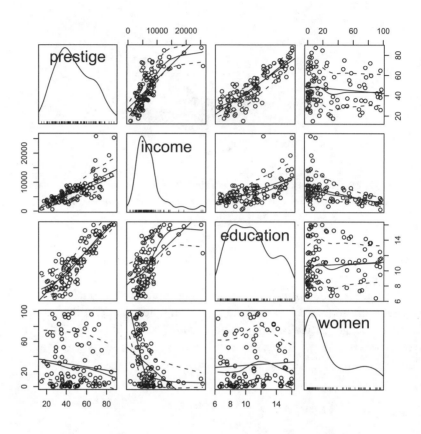

Figure 3.13   Scatterplot matrix for the Canadian occupational-prestige data, with density estimates on the diagonal.

It can be helpful to augment the scatterplots in a scatterplot matrix with fitted lines, and to use the diagonal of the array to display graphical summaries of the marginal distribution of each of the variables. The `scatterplotMatrix` function provides these and other amenities, by default placing density estimates on the diagonal and plotting least-squares and lowess lines in each panel. In the example, we increased the `span` of the lowess smoothers from the default value of 0.5 to 0.7 after examining a preliminary version of the graph. Many of the arguments to `scatterplotMatrix` are similar to those for `scatterplot`; see `?scatterplotMatrix` for details.

3.4   Transforming Data

The way we measure data may not necessarily reflect the way we should use the data in a regression analysis. For example, automobile fuel usage in the

United States is measured in miles per gallon. In most of the rest of the world, fuel usage is measured in liters per 100 km, which is the *inverse* of miles per gallon times a factor to account for the change in the units of measurement from gallons to liters and from miles to kilometers. More fuel-efficient cars have larger values of miles per gallon and smaller values of liters per 100 km. If we are interested in a regression in which fuel usage is either the response or a predictor, the choice between these two measures is not obvious.

As a second example, suppose that we are interested in the variable annual salary, measured in dollars. An increase in salary from, say, $10,000 to $12,000 is a substantial increase to the person receiving it, whereas an increase from $110,000 to $112,000, still $2,000, is much less substantial. Replacing salary by a nonlinear transformation of the variable, probably by its logarithm, can reflect the different effects we expect for changes in salary from different base values.

Similar ideas apply when a variable is a percentage or fraction, such as the percentage of an audience that responds to an advertising campaign. An increase from 2% to 4% is a substantial change, whereas an increase from 40% to 42%, still an increase of 2%, is much less substantial. Percentages often need to be transformed for this reason.

Learning to use transformations effectively—to *reexpress* variables, as Tukey (1977) put it—is part of the subtle craft of data analysis. Good computational tools, such as those described in this section, facilitate this endeavor.

3.4.1 LOGARITHMS

The single most important transformation of a strictly positive variable is the logarithmic transformation.[12] You will encounter *natural logs* to the base $e \approx 2.718$, *common logs* to the base 10, and sometimes logs to the base 2, but the choice of base is inconsequential for statistical applications because logs to different bases differ only by multiplication by a constant. For example, $\log_e(x) = \log_2(x) / \log_2(e) \approx 0.692 \log_2(x)$. That said, common logs and logs to the base 2 can simplify the interpretation of results: For example, increasing the common log by 1 multiplies the original quantity by 10, and increasing $\log_2$ by one multiplies the original quantity by 2.

The R functions `log`, `log10`, and `log2` compute the natural, base-10, and base-2 logarithms, respectively:

```
> log(7) # natural logarithm

[1] 1.946

> log10(7) # base-10 logarithm

[1] 0.8451

> log2(7) # base-2 logarithm

[1] 2.807
```

[12]If you are unfamiliar with logarithms, see the complementary readings cited at the end of the chapter.

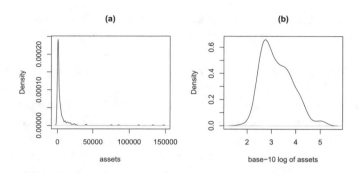

Figure 3.14   Distribution of `assets` in the Ornstein data set (a) before and (b) after log transformation.

```
> log2(7)/log2(exp(1)) # again the natural logarithm

[1] 1.946
```

The `exp` (exponential) function computes powers of *e*, and thus, `exp(1)` = *e*.

The `log` and `logb` functions can also be used to compute logs to any base:

```
> log(7, base=10)   # equivalent to log10(7)

[1] 0.8451

> logb(7, 10)

[1] 0.8451
```

The log functions in R work on numeric vectors, matrices, and data frames. They return `NA` for missing values, `NaN` (not a number) for negative values, and `-Inf` ($-\infty$) for zeros.

The `Ornstein` data set (introduced in Section 3.2.2) includes measurements of the assets of $n = 248$ large Canadian companies. Density plots of assets and their logs are shown in Figure 3.14:

```
> par(mfrow=c(1, 2))
> with(Ornstein, plot(density(assets), xlab="assets", main="(a)"))
> with(Ornstein, plot(density(log10(assets)),
+       xlab="base-10 log of assets", main="(b)"))
```

The command `par(mfrow=c(1, 2))` produces two panels in the graph, displayed horizontally (see Section 7.1). Figure 3.14a is a typical distribution of a variable that represents the size of objects—what Tukey (1977) calls an *amount*. In this case, size is measured in dollars. Most of the data values are reasonably similar, but a few values are very large, and the distribution is consequently positively skewed. Logarithms spread out the small values and compress the large ones, producing the more symmetric distribution seen in Figure 3.14b. The log transformation does not achieve perfect symmetry,

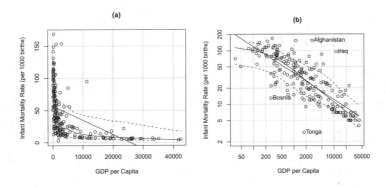

Figure 3.15 Infant mortality rate and gross domestic product per capita, from the United Nations data set: (a) untransformed data and (b) both variables log-transformed.

however, and there is a suggestion that the distribution of the log-transformed variable has more than one mode, a property of the data that is disguised by the skew in Figure 3.14a. Nevertheless the log-transformed data are far better behaved than the untransformed data.

Logarithms are sufficiently important in data analysis to have a rule: For any strictly positive variable with no fixed upper bound whose values cover two or more orders of magnitude (i.e., powers of 10), replacement of the variable by its logarithm is likely helpful. Conversely, if the range of a variable is considerably less than an order of magnitude, then transformation by logarithms, or indeed any simple transformation, is unlikely to make much of a difference.

The data frame UN in the **car** package, with data obtained from the United Nations, contains the `infant.mortality` rate (infant deaths per 1,000 live births) and `gdp` [per capita gross domestic product (GDP), in U.S. dollars] for 207 countries in 1998:[13]

```
> scatterplot(infant.mortality ~ gdp, data=UN, xlab="GDP per Capita",
+       ylab="Infant Mortality Rate (per 1000 births)", main="(a)",
+       boxplot=FALSE)

> scatterplot(infant.mortality ~ gdp, data=UN, xlab="GDP per capita",
+       ylab="Infant Mortality Rate (per 1000 births)", main="(b)",
+       log="xy", boxplots=FALSE, id.n=4)

[1] "Tonga"        "Iraq"         "Afghanistan" "Bosnia"
```

The graph in Figure 3.15a simply plots the data as provided. In Panel b, we used the argument `log="xy"`, which also works with `plot`, to draw both axes on log scales but to label the axes in the units of the original variables.

The dominant feature of the plot in Figure 3.15a is that many of the countries are very poor, and the poorer countries have highly variable infant mortality rates. There is very little visual resolution, as nearly all the data points

---

[13] Some data are missing, however, and only 193 of the 207 countries have valid data for both variables.

congregate at the far left of the graph. The lowess smooth, however, suggests that average `infant.mortality` decreases with `gdp`, steeply at first and then at a decreasing rate. The log-scale plot tells a clearer story, as the points now fall close to a straight line with a negative slope, also suggesting that increasing `gdp` corresponds to decreasing `infant.mortality`. A few of the points, however, are relatively far from the least-squares line, with Tonga and (perhaps surprisingly) Bosnia having relatively low infant mortality rates for their GDP, and Iraq and Afghanistan having relatively high infant mortality. The transformations to log scales achieve visual interpretability, near-linearity, and constant variance across the plot.

From Figure 3.15b, we can posit a regression model of the form

$$\log(\texttt{infant.mortality}) = \beta_0 + \beta_1 \log(\texttt{gdp}) + \varepsilon$$

where ε is an additive *error*, with mean zero and constant variance. Once again, the base of the logarithms doesn't matter, and so for convenience, we use natural logarithms in this equation. If we exponentiate both sides, we get[14]

$$
\begin{aligned}
\texttt{infant.mortality} &= \exp(\beta_0 + \beta_1 \log \texttt{gdp} + \varepsilon) \\
&= \exp(\beta_0) \times \texttt{gdp}^{\beta_1} \times \exp(\varepsilon) \\
&= \alpha_0 \left(\texttt{gdp}^{\beta_1}\right) \times \delta
\end{aligned}
$$

where we have defined $\alpha_0 = \exp(\beta_0)$, and $\delta = \exp(\varepsilon)$ is a *multiplicative error* with typical value (actually, geometric mean) $\exp(0) = 1$. Additive errors in the log scale imply multiplicative errors in the original scale. According to this model, an increase in `gdp` is associated with a *proportional*, not an *absolute*, decrease in `infant.mortality`. Fitting the regression model to the data produces the following results:

```
> lm(log(infant.mortality) ~ log(gdp), data=UN)

Call:
lm(formula = log(infant.mortality) ~ log(gdp), data = UN)

Coefficients:
(Intercept)        log(gdp)
      7.045          -0.493
```

If `gdp` actually caused `infant.mortality` and we could increase the `gdp` in a country by 1% to $1.01 \times \texttt{gdp}$, the expected `infant.mortality` would be

$$\alpha_0 (1.01 \times \texttt{gdp})^{\beta_1} = 1.01^{\beta_1} \times \alpha_0 \left(\texttt{gdp}^{\beta_1}\right)$$

For the estimated slope $b_1 = -0.493$, we have $1.01^{-0.493} = 0.995$, and so the estimated `infant.mortality` would be 0.5% smaller—a substantial amount. Put another way, if we compare pairs of countries that differ by 1% in their `gdp`, on average the country with the 1% higher `gdp` will have a

---

[14]The $\exp(\cdot)$ notation represents raising the constant e to a power: Thus, $\exp(\beta_0) = e^{\beta_0}$.

0.5% lower `infant.mortality`, a percentage approximately equal to the estimated regression coefficient, $b_1 = -0.493$. Economists call a coefficient such as β_1 in a log-log regression an *elasticity*.

3.4.2 POWER TRANSFORMATIONS

We define a *simple power transformation* as the replacement of a variable x by x^λ. Depending on the context, x may be a predictor or the response variable in a regression.

This use of powers is distinct from *polynomial regression*. In polynomial regression, the highest-order power, say p, is a small positive integer, usually two or three, and rather than *replacing* a predictor x by x^p, we also include all lower-order powers of x in the regression model. For example, for $p = 3$, we would include the regressors x, x^2, and x^3. Polynomial regression in R can be accomplished with the `poly` function (introduced in Section 4.6.3).

Often, powers λ in the range $[-2, 3]$ are useful. The power $\lambda = -1$ is the reciprocal or inverse transformation, $1/x$. We have seen, for example, that the two competing measures of fuel consumption differ by $\lambda = -1$. Similarly, if we measure $x =$ time to an event, then x^{-1} is the *speed* at which the event occurs, and the appropriate scaling of the variable—elapsed time or speed—is at issue here as well. The power $\lambda = 1/3$ can convert a volume measure to a linear measure, which may be appropriate in some problems. Likewise, $\lambda = 3$ can convert a linear measure to a volume; $\lambda = 1/2$, an area to a linear measure; and $\lambda = 2$, a linear measure to an area.

More generally, we can treat λ either as an estimable parameter or as a value selected by guided trial and error to make the data better behaved. In either context, it is convenient to define a family of *scaled-power transformations* by

$$T_{BC}(x, \lambda) = x^{(\lambda)} = \begin{cases} \dfrac{x^\lambda - 1}{\lambda} & \text{when } \lambda \neq 0 \\ \log_e x & \text{when } \lambda = 0 \end{cases} \quad (3.1)$$

For $\lambda \neq 0$, the scaled power transformations are essentially x^λ, because the scaled-power family only subtracts 1 and divides by the constant λ. One can show that as λ approaches 0, $T_{BC}(x, \lambda)$ approaches $\log_e(x)$, and so the scaled-power family includes the invaluable log transformation as a special case, whereas the basic power family doesn't. Also, the scaled power $T_{BC}(x, \lambda)$ preserves the order of the x values, while the basic powers preserve order only when λ is positive and *reverse* the order of x when λ is negative.

The family of scaled-power transformations was first used in a seminal paper by Box and Cox (1964), and this family is often called the *Box-Cox (BC) transformations* in their honor.[15] Box and Cox used the scaled powers to help determine the transformation of the response in linear regression (a topic that we will discuss in Section 6.4.1).

---

[15]*Box and Cox* is also the title of an operetta by Gilbert and Sullivan and an 1847 farce by John Maddison Morton, although the operetta and the play have nothing whatever to do with regression or statistics.

The scaled-power family can be computed using the bcPower function in the **car** package; for example, for $\lambda = 0.5$,

```
> bcPower(1:5, 0.5)
```

```
[1] 0.0000 0.8284 1.4641 2.0000 2.4721
```

The families of basic and Box-Cox powers are applicable only when the data to be transformed are all positive and generally not when the data contain negative values or 0s: Some of the power transformations—for example, square root and log—are undefined for negative values, and others—for example, square—won't preserve the order of the data when both positive and negative values are present. A simple solution is to add a sufficiently large positive constant, called a *start* by Mosteller and Tukey (1977), to the data to make all the data positive prior to transformation.

Transformations are effective only when the data span a sufficiently large range. When the ratio of the largest to the smallest data value is not much higher than 1, the transformations are nearly linear and thus don't bend the data. A negative start can be used to move the data closer to 0, increasing the ratio of the largest to the smallest value and making the transformations more effective.

The **car** package also includes a function for a second family of power transformations, $T_{YJ}(x, \lambda)$, due to Yeo and Johnson (2000), which can be used when the variable to be transformed is not strictly positive. The Yeo-Johnson family is defined as $T_{BC}(x + 1, \lambda)$ for nonnegative values of x and $T_{BC}(-x + 1, 2 - \lambda)$ for negative values of x. Yeo-Johnson powers are computed by the yjPower function:

```
> yjPower(-5:5, 0.5)
```

```
 [1] -9.1313 -6.7869 -4.6667 -2.7974 -1.2190  0.0000  0.8284
 [8]  1.4641  2.0000  2.4721  2.8990
```

In all discussions of the scaled-power family and bcPower in this *Companion*, the Yeo-Johnson family and yjPower can be substituted.

Moving down what Tukey (1977) calls the *ladder of powers*—from $\lambda = 1$ (no transformation) to, for example, $\lambda = 1/2$ (square root), $\lambda = 0$ (log), or $\lambda = -1$ (inverse)—serves to spread out the small values of a variable relative to the large ones. Consequently, transformations down the ladder of powers can be used to correct a positive skew. Negatively skewed data are much less common but can be made more symmetric by transformation *up* the ladder of powers—for example, $\lambda = 2$ (square) or $\lambda = 3$ (cube).

The symbox function in the **car** package is useful for finding a transformation to approximate symmetry by trial and error—for example, for gdp in the UN data:

```
> symbox(~ gdp, data=UN)
```

The resulting graph is shown in Figure 3.16. By default, symbox uses the function bcPower and displays boxplots of the transformed variable for several transformations down the ladder of powers; here, the log transformation of gdp does the best job of making the distribution of the variable symmetric.

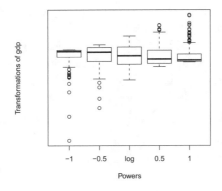

Figure 3.16 Boxplots of various power transformations of gdp in the United Nations data.

3.4.3 TRANSFORMING RESTRICTED-RANGE VARIABLES

Variables with ranges bounded both below and above may require different transformations, because of ceiling or floor effects, in which values tend to accumulate near the boundaries of the variable. The most common kinds of restricted-range variable are percentages and proportions. Because small changes in a proportion near 0 or 1 are much more important than small changes near 0.5, potentially useful transformations will spread out both large and small proportions relative to proportions near 0.5. If a proportion has a more limited range, however, say between 0.25 and 0.75, transformations are unlikely to be helpful.

The *arcsine square-root* is a commonly used transformation for proportions. For a proportion x, this transformation is defined by

$$T_{\text{asinsqrt}}(x) = \sin^{-1}(\sqrt{x})$$

and is computed in R as, for example,

```
> asin(sqrt(seq(0, 1, length=11)))
```

```
 [1] 0.0000 0.3218 0.4636 0.5796 0.6847 0.7854 0.8861 0.9912
 [9] 1.1071 1.2490 1.5708
```

The arcsine square-root transformation has the following justification: If $x_1/n, \ldots, x_m/n$ is a sample of proportions, where each x_i is a binomial random variable with n trials and probability of success p, then the sample SD of the proportions will be close to the theoretical value $\sqrt{p(1-p)/n}$, which is highly dependent on p. The SD of the arcsine square root of the x_is is approximately $0.5/\sqrt{n}$ for any value of p, and hence, $T_{\text{asinsqrt}}(x)$ is a variance-stabilizing transformation.

For x in the interval $(0,1)$, the *logit* or *log-odds* transformation is an alternative to the arcsine square-root transformation:

$$T_{\text{logit}}(x) = \text{logit}(x) = \log_e\left(\frac{x}{1-x}\right)$$

The logit transformation is not defined for sample proportions exactly equal to 0 or 1, however. We can get around this limitation by remapping proportions from the interval [0, 1] to [.025, .975], for example, taking the logit of .025 + .95 × *p* rather than the logit of *p*. The `logit` function in the **car** package takes care of remapping proportions or percentages when there are 0s or 1s, or 0% or 100% for percentage data, printing a warning if remapping is required:

```
> logit(seq(0.1, 0.9, 0.1))

[1] -2.1972 -1.3863 -0.8473 -0.4055  0.0000  0.4055  0.8473
[8]  1.3863  2.1972

> logit(seq(0, 1, 0.1))

[1] -3.6636 -1.9924 -1.2950 -0.8001 -0.3847  0.0000  0.3847
[8]  0.8001  1.2950  1.9924  3.6636

Warning message:
In logit(seq(0, 1, 0.1)) : Proportions remapped to (0.025,0.975)
```

Even better, if we have access to the original data from which the proportions are calculated, we can avoid proportions of 0 or 1 by computing *empirical logits*, $\log[(x + 1/2)/(n + 1)]$, where x is the number of successes in n trials.

We apply the logit and arcsine square-root transformations to the distribution of the gender composition of occupations in the Canadian occupational-prestige data:

```
> par(mfrow=c(1, 3))
> with(Prestige, {
+       plot(density(women, from=0, to=100),
+           main="(a) Untransformed")
+       plot(density(logit(women), adjust=0.75),
+           main="(b) Logit")
+       plot(density(asin(sqrt(women/100))),
+           adjust=0.75), main="(c) Arcsine square-root")
+ })
```

The resulting density plots are shown in Figure 3.17. The density plot for the untransformed percentages is confined to the domain 0 to 100. The untransformed data, in Panel a, stack up near the boundaries, especially near 0. The logit-transformed data, in Panel b, appear better behaved, and the density plot reveals three apparent concentrations or groups of occupations. The arcsine square-root transformed data, in Panel c, are similar. We adjusted the bandwidth of the density estimators for the transformed data to resolve the third peak in the distribution. When there are multiple modes in a distribution, the default bandwidth is often too large.

3.4.4   OTHER TRANSFORMATIONS

The transformations that we have discussed thus far are hardly a complete catalog. Here are a few other possibilities:

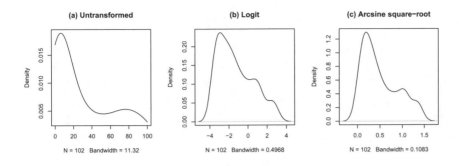

Figure 3.17 Distribution of women in the Canadian occupational-prestige data: (a) untransformed, (b) logit transformed, and (c) arcsine square-root transformed.

1. People's height and weight are combined in the *body mass index*, BMI = weight/(height^2), which is intended to measure body composition.

2. A variable like `month.number` can be replaced by sin(`month-.number`/12) and cos(`month.number`/12) to model seasonal time trends.

3. In a study of highway accident rates, a variable giving the number of signals in a highway segment is converted to the number of signals per mile by dividing by the length of the segment. More generally, measures of total size often need to be converted to size per unit—for example, converting GDP to a per capita basis by dividing by population.

The upshot of these examples is that one should think carefully about how variables are expressed in the substantive context in which they are used in research.

3.4.5 TRANSFORMATIONS TO EQUALIZE SPREAD

In Figure 3.11 (p. 122) we examined the relationship between number of interlocks and nation of control among the 248 large Canadian corporations in Ornstein's interlocking-directorate data. That graph reveals an association between *level* and *spread*: Nations with a relatively high level of interlocks (Canada, other) show more variation than nations with fewer interlocks on average (United States, United Kingdom). The term *level* is meant to imply an average or typical value, such as a mean, and *spread* is meant to imply variability. These terms are used in exploratory data analysis in preference to more technical terms such as mean and variance because level and spread may be measured using other statistics—such as (in the current context) the median and interquartile range—that are resistant to outlying values.

A *spread-level plot* (Tukey, 1977) is a scatterplot of the logarithm of the interquartile range, which measures spread, versus the logarithm of the within-group median, which measures level. Interquartile ranges and medians are

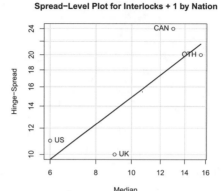

Figure 3.18   Spread-level plot for the relationship between number of interlocks and nation of control in Ornstein's interlocking-directorate data.

insensitive to a few outliers, and so the spread-level plot provides a robust representation of the dependence of level on spread.

Using the `spreadLevelPlot` function in the **car** package produces Figure 3.18, along with a printed report:

```
> spreadLevelPlot(interlocks + 1 ~ nation, Ornstein)
```

	LowerHinge	Median	UpperHinge	Hinge-Spread
US	2	6.0	13	11
UK	4	9.0	14	10
CAN	6	13.0	30	24
OTH	4	15.5	24	20

```
Suggested power transformation:  0.1534
```

Because Tukey's method requires a strictly positive response variable, we added a start of 1 to `interlocks` to avoid 0 values. The function returns a table giving the first quartile (Tukey's *lower hinge*), median, third quartile (*upper hinge*), and interquartile range (*hinge-spread*), along with the suggested power transformation of `interlocks + 1`. When, as here, there is an association between spread and level, we can make the spreads more nearly equal by a power transformation of the response. Suppose that a line is fit to the spread-level plot and the slope of the line is b; a spread-stabilizing power transformation is then given by the power $1 - b$. When b is positive, reflecting a tendency of spread to increase with level—a common situation—the suggested power transformation will be less than 1; in the example, the suggested power is $p = 0.15$, close to the log transformation (i.e., $p = 0$).

Figure 3.19 shows parallel boxplots for the log-transformed data:

```
> oldmar <- par(mar=c(5.1, 4.1, 4.1, 4.1))
> Boxplot(log10(interlocks + 1) ~ nation, data=Ornstein)
```

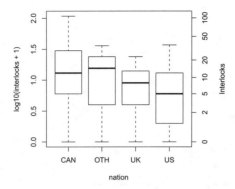

Figure 3.19 Parallel boxplots for $\log_{10}$(interlocks $+1$) by nation of control.

```
> basicPowerAxis(power=0, base=10, at=c(1, 3, 6, 11, 21, 51, 101),
+       start=1, axis.title="Interlocks")
> par(oldmar)
```

The spreads in the transformed data for the four groups are much more similar than the spreads in the untransformed data shown in Figure 3.11 (p. 122).

We used two arguments in the call to `Boxplot`: a formula with the base-10 logarithm of `interlocks + 1` on the left-hand side and the factor `nation` on the right-hand side; and the data frame in which these variables reside, `Ornstein`. The remaining commands make the graph more elaborate, by first increasing the right-side margin of the plot and then adding a second axis on the right, labeled in the original units of `interlocks`, produced by the `basicPowerAxis` function in the **car** package.[16] The argument `power=0` to `basicPowerAxis` specifies the log transformation; `base=10`, the base used for the logs; `at=c(1, 3, 6, 11, 21, 51, 101)`, where the tick marks are to appear on the `interlocks + 1` scale; and `start=1`, the start that was used, so that the tick labels can be adjusted to the original `interlocks` scale. The functions `bcPowerAxis`, `yjPowerAxis`, and `probabilityAxis` in the **car** package may be used similarly to produce axes on the untransformed scale corresponding to Box-Cox, Yeo-Johnson, and logit transformations. Finally, we restored the graphical settings in `par` to their original values so that future graphs will not have extra space on the right. An alternative would have been simply to close the graphics device window, because a subsequently opened graphics device would revert to the default settings of graphical parameters such as `mar`.

A variance-stabilizing (or spread-stabilizing) transformation can also be selected formally by estimating a transformation parameter (described in Section 3.4.7).

---

[16]Many global graphics parameters in R are set or queried with the `par` function. The `mar` setting is for the plot margins; see `?par` for details. Graphics parameters are also discussed in Section 7.1.

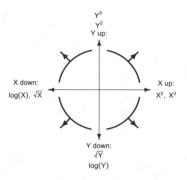

Figure 3.20 Mosteller and Tukey's *bulging rule* for finding linearizing transformations: When the bulge points *down*, transform *y down* the ladder of powers; when the bulge points *up*, transform *y up*; when the bulge points *left*, transform *x down*; when the bulge points *right*, transform *x up*.

3.4.6 TRANSFORMATIONS TOWARD LINEARITY

It is often possible to straighten a monotone (i.e., strictly increasing or strictly decreasing) nonlinear relationship by transforming *x*, *y*, or both. We will describe two simple methods for selecting a transformation, one based on guided trial and error and the other treating the transformation as a least-squares problem. In Section 3.4.7, we will consider more sophisticated methods for selecting transformations by formal estimation.

MOSTELLER AND TUKEY'S BULGING RULE

If a relationship is nonlinear but monotone and simple (in the sense that the curvature of the regression function is relatively constant), Mosteller and Tukey's *bulging rule* (Mosteller and Tukey, 1977), illustrated in Figure 3.20, can guide the selection of linearizing transformations. When the bulge points down and to the right, for example, as in the lower-right quadrant of Figure 3.20, we move *y down* the ladder of powers, *x up* the ladder of powers, or both, to straighten the relationship between the two variables.

Consider, for example, the U. N. data graphed in Figure 3.15 (p. 129). In Panel a, the nonlinear relationship between `infant.mortality` and `gdp` is simple and monotone; the bulge in the scatterplot points down and to the left, suggesting the transformation of `infant.mortality` or `gdp`, or both, down the ladder of powers. In this case, the log transformation of both variables produces a nearly linear relationship, as shown in Panel b of Figure 3.15.

INVERSE TRANSFORMATION PLOTS

Figure 3.7 (p. 115) is a scatterplot of `prestige` versus `income` for the Canadian occupational-prestige data. The relationship between the two

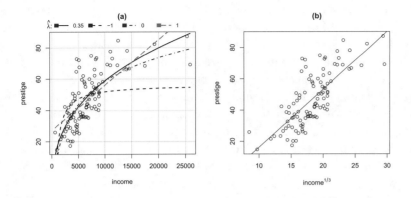

Figure 3.21 (a) Inverse transformation plot for the relationship of `prestige` to `income` in the `Prestige` data, and (b) scatterplot of `prestige` versus `income`$^{1/3}$.

variables in this plot is plainly nonlinear. We may be able to induce a linear relationship between the variables by transforming just the x-variable, `income`.

More generally, imagine fitting a regression for generic y and x variables that is made linear by a yet-to-be-determined Box-Cox power transformation of x,

$$y = \beta_0 + \beta_1 T_{\text{BC}}(x, \lambda) + \varepsilon \qquad (3.2)$$

where ε is an additive error. Unless $\lambda = 1$, the regression equation describes a curve as a function of x, which, we assume here, reproduces the nonlinear pattern in the data.

The function `invTranPlot` in the **car** package can be used to select a transformation of the x variable by fitting Equation 3.2 for λ equal to -1, 0, and 1 and for the value of λ estimated in a nonlinear least-squares regression. For example, the following commands produce Figure 3.21, for the relationship of `prestige` to `income` in the Canadian occupational-prestige data:

```
> par(mfrow=c(1, 2))
> invTranPlot(prestige ~ income, data=Prestige, lwd=2,
+     xlab="income", main="(a)", col.lines=gray((0:3)/6))

   lambda   RSS
1  0.3491 12724
2 -1.0000 22166
3  0.0000 13478
4  1.0000 14616

> plot(prestige ~ I(income^(1/3)), data=Prestige,
+     xlab=expression(income^{1/3}), main="(b)")
> abline(lm(prestige ~ I(income^(1/3)), data=Prestige))
```

In Figure 3.21a, we explicitly set the label for the horizontal axis of the graphs, and set `col.lines` to be shades of gray for printing in this book. The `invTranPlot` function also produces printed output, displaying the values of λ that it used and the corresponding residual sums of squares for the regression specified by Equation 3.2. Small values of the residual sum of squares indicate better agreement between the fitted line and the data.

In the code to draw Figure 3.21b, we used the `I` (identity) function so that `income^(1/3)` produces the cube root of `income`; otherwise the `^` operator has a special meaning in a model formula (see Section 4.8.1); and we use the `expression` function to typeset the superscript $1/3$ in the x-axis label.

As shown in Figure 3.21a, none of the curves produced by λ in $(-1, 0, 1)$, with the possible exception of 0 (i.e., log), match the data well, but λ close to $1/3$ does a good job, except perhaps at the highest levels of `income`. Figure 3.21b shows the result of taking the cube root of income.

In light of our earlier discussion, a cube-root transformation rather than a log transformation of `income` is unexpected. We saw, however, in Section 3.2.1 that the relationship between `income` and `prestige` is different for each level of `type`, so choosing a transformation ignoring `type`, as we have done here, can be misleading.

3.4.7   FAMILIES OF TRANSFORMATIONS*

In our discussion so far, we have avoided an important question: When fitting regression models, do transformations matter? If we have a formal mathematical model for the determination of the response—a rarity in the social sciences—then the model will specify the correct transformations of the variables. If, however, our model is intended simply as an approximate description of the data—a much more common situation—then scaling can matter, and acceptable approximations may be available with predictors and the response correctly transformed.

A reasonable goal in many problems is to *transform numeric variables— response and predictors—so that they are as close to multivariate normal as possible.* One justification for this approach is that if the data are multivariate normal, then the conditional distribution of the response given the predictors can be modeled using multiple linear regression. Because data that are multivariate normal satisfy all the assumptions of linearity, constant variance, and normality of errors in the resulting regression problem, the automatic procedures described here can be used to achieve any of these goals.

Box and Cox (1964) first presented methodology for estimating a transformation of the response that, given the values of the predictors, has a distribution as close as possible to a normal distribution. Velilla (1993) generalized Box and Cox's approach by transforming a *set* of variables to multivariate normality, and we have implemented and slightly extended his method in the `powerTransform` function in the **car** package. Given variables $x_1, \ldots, x_k$, `powerTransform` provides estimates of parameters $\lambda_1, \ldots, \lambda_k$ such that $T(x_1, \widehat{\lambda}_1), \ldots, T(x_k, \widehat{\lambda}_k)$ are as close to multivariate normal as possible, where $T(x_j, \lambda_j)$ denotes a member of a one-parameter transformation family with parameter λ_j, usually either the Box-Cox or the Yeo-Johnson family.

```
> summary(powerTransform(UN))

bcPower Transformations to Multinormality

                 Est.Power Std.Err. Wald Lower Bound
infant.mortality   -0.0009   0.0655          -0.1293
gdp                 0.0456   0.0365          -0.0260
                 Wald Upper Bound
infant.mortality           0.1275
gdp                        0.1171

Likelihood ratio tests about transformation parameters
                             LRT df    pval
LR test, lambda = (0 0)    1.649  2 0.4385
LR test, lambda = (1 1)  680.250  2 0.0000
```

Because the UN data frame has only two numeric columns, we can simply use the data frame as the first argument to `powerTransform`. An equivalent command would be

```
> with(UN, summary(powerTransform(cbind(infant.mortality, gdp))))
```

The `cbind` function turns the two variables into a two-column matrix, and a scaled-power transformation parameter is estimated for each column. Were there more variables in the data frame, we could also select the variables of interest by indexing the data frame (see Section 2.3.4), as in

```
> summary(powerTransform(UN[ , c("infant.mortality", "gdp")]))
```

The estimated powers for both variables are near 0, and $\lambda = 0$ (the log transformation) is within the marginal confidence interval for each transformation parameter. Also given in the output are two likelihood ratio tests, the first that logs are appropriate for *all* the variables simultaneously, and the second that no transformation, $\lambda = 1$, is necessary for any variable, against the alternative that at least one variable requires transformation. The first test has a large p value, suggesting that logs will work well here, as we have seen in Figure 3.15 (p. 129), and the second has a tiny p value, suggesting that using the untransformed data is a bad idea.

The `powerTransform` function also allows for estimating transformations of variables after conditioning on a set of predictors that are not transformed. The most common example of this situation is the transformation of one or more numeric variables after adjusting for a grouping factor or factors. For example, we used a transformation of number of interlocks in Ornstein's Canadian interlocking-directorate data (in Section 3.4.5) in an attempt to equalize the variance within each national group. The `powerTransform` function can be used to find a variance-stabilizing transformation:

```
> summary(powerTransform(interlocks ~ nation,
+     data=Ornstein, family="yjPower"))

yjPower Transformation to Normality
```

```
          Est.Power Std.Err. Wald Lower Bound Wald Upper Bound
Y1        0.1397    0.052           0.0378            0.2416

Likelihood ratio tests about transformation parameters
                               LRT df      pval
LR test, lambda = (0)    7.143  1 0.007526
LR test, lambda = (1)  265.647  1 0.000000
```

The variables to the left of the ~ in the formula—in this case, just
interlocks—will be transformed, while the variables to the right are the
conditioning variables—in this case, just the single predictor nation. This
command suggests a Yeo-Johnson power transformation of interlocks
so that the data are as close as possible to normally distributed within each
nation and so that the variances in the several nations are as similar as possible. By using family="yjPower", we avoid explicitly having to add 1
to the variable, because the Yeo-Johnson family permits 0 values.

The indicated power is about 0.14, which is close to the value of 0 for a
log transformation, although 0 is excluded by both the Wald interval and the
likelihood ratio test. Whether one would actually use an unusual power such
as $\lambda = 0.14$ in preference to the similar log transformation, however, is partly
a matter of taste. We will return to Ornstein's data in Chapters 5 and 6.

TRANSFORM BEFORE MODELING

A useful early step in any regression analysis is considering transformations
toward linearity and normality of all the quantitative predictors, without at this
point including the response. For the Canadian occupational-prestige data,
the scatterplot matrix in Figure 3.13 (p. 126) suggests nonlinear relationships
between some of the predictors and between the predictors and the response.
We will not consider power-transforming women because it is a percentage,
bounded between 0 and 100, and because, from Figure 3.13, women is at best
weakly related to the other predictors and to the response. We will, however,
try to transform income and education toward bivariate normality:

```
> summary(p1 <- with(Prestige,
+       powerTransform(cbind(income, education))))

bcPower Transformations to Multinormality

            Est.Power Std.Err. Wald Lower Bound Wald Upper Bound
income        0.2617    0.1014          0.0629           0.4604
education     0.4242    0.4033         -0.3663           1.2146

Likelihood ratio tests about transformation parameters
                               LRT df      pval
LR test, lambda = (0 0)     7.694  2 2.134e-02
LR test, lambda = (1 1)    48.873  2 2.440e-11
LR test, lambda = (0.33 1)  2.406  2 3.003e-01
```

Looking at the likelihood ratio tests, untransformed variables, $\lambda =(1,1)'$,
and all logarithms, $\lambda =(0,0)'$, both have small significance levels, suggesting

that neither of these choices is appropriate. The estimated transformation for income is $\widehat{\lambda}_1 = 0.26$, and the cube root ($\lambda_1 = 1/3$) is in the Wald confidence interval, while the log transformation, $\lambda_1 = 0$, is just outside the interval. In contrast, the value $\lambda_2 = 1$, representing no transformation of educa-tion, is inside the marginal confidence interval for λ_2, which is very broad. Because rounding to nice powers is standard practice, we test the hypothesis that $\lambda = (1/3, 1)'$:

```
> testTransform(p1, lambda=c(0.33, 1))

                            LRT df    pval
LR test, lambda = (0.33 1) 2.406   2 0.3003
```

The p-value is about 0.30. This test is also shown in the summary output for powerTransform. Because we favor logarithms, let's also try $\lambda = (0, 1)'$:

```
> testTransform(p1, lambda=c(0, 1))

                         LRT df    pval
LR test, lambda = (0 1) 9.278   2 0.009666
```

The p value is about 0.01, suggesting that the log transformation of income is not adequate. Nevertheless, we suggest using log(income) as a starting point for analysis because this is the standard transformation for a variable such as income. A prudent approach would be to repeat the analysis employ-ing the cube root of income to see if any differences result. In Figure 3.22, we have used base-2 logarithms:

```
> scatterplotMatrix(~ prestige + log2(income) + education + women,
+       span=0.7, data=Prestige)
```

The panels in this scatterplot matrix show little nonlinearity, although in the plot of prestige versus log2(income), the two occupations with the lowest income appear not to fit the trend in the rest of the data.

We can retrieve the estimated transformations using the coef function:

```
> coef(p1)

  income education
  0.2617    0.4242
```

Rounded estimates of the transformations are available as well:

```
> coef(p1, round=TRUE)

  income education
    0.33      1.00
```

where the rounded value is the first element of $(1, 0, 0.5, 0.33, -0.5, -0.33, 2, -2)$ in the confidence interval for a transformation parameter. If none of these values are in the confidence interval for the transformation parameter, the unrounded estimate is provided.

We can add transformed variables to the data using the transform function (as discussed in Section 2.2.5):

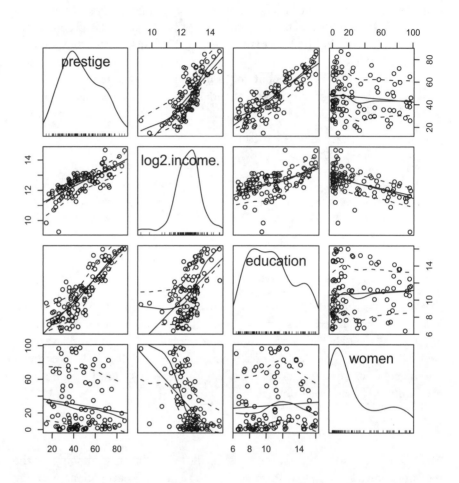

Figure 3.22 Scatterplot matrix with transformed predictors for the Prestige data set.

```
> Prestige <- transform(Prestige, log2income = log2(income))
```

The variable `type` is a factor that divides occupations into white collar, blue collar, and professional/managerial categories. We can also seek transformations that will normalize the distributions of the numeric predictors within each level of `type`, as would be desirable if `type` were to be included as a predictor:

```
> summary(p2 <- powerTransform(cbind(income, education) ~ type,
+     data=Prestige))

bcPower Transformations to Multinormality
```

	Est.Power	Std.Err.	Wald Lower Bound	Wald Upper Bound
income	-0.0170	0.1310	-0.2738	0.2398
education	0.7093	0.2946	0.1318	1.2867

```
Likelihood ratio tests about transformation parameters
                              LRT df        pval
LR test, lambda = (0 0)   5.7228  2 5.719e-02
LR test, lambda = (1 1)  64.0196  2 1.255e-14
LR test, lambda = (0 1)   0.9838  2 6.115e-01

> testTransform(p2, c(0, 1))

                           LRT df    pval
LR test, lambda = (0 1) 0.9838  2 0.6115
```

After conditioning on `type`, the log transformation of `income` is clearly indicated, while `education` is untransformed, producing the revised scatterplot matrix in Figure 3.23:

```
> scatterplotMatrix(~ prestige + log2(income) + education
+           + women | type,
+        data=Prestige, by.group=TRUE, id.n=0, smooth=FALSE,
+        col=gray(c(0, 0.5, 0.7)))
```

We set the argument `by.group=TRUE` to get separate least-squares fits for each group and specified gray-scale colors appropriate for this book. We suppressed the lowess smooths with the argument `smooth=FALSE` to minimize clutter in the graph. Approximate within-group linearity is apparent in most of the panels of Figure 3.23. The plotted points are the same in Figures 3.22 and 3.23—only the point marking and the fitted lines are different. In particular, the two points with low `income` no longer appear exceptional when we control for `type`.

3.5   Point Labeling and Identification

Identifying extreme points can be particularly valuable in graphs used for model building and diagnostics. Standard R includes one function for this purpose, `identify`, which allows interactive point identification. Many users find `identify` inconvenient, and so the ability to mark extreme points automatically can be helpful, even if it is not as desirable in general as interactive identification. The graphical functions in the **car** package—including the `scatterplot`, `scatterplotMatrix`, `scatter3d`, and `invTranPlot` functions discussed in this chapter and others to be introduced subsequently— employ a common strategy for identifying points. In this section, we describe both the `identify` function and the point identification scheme used in the **car** package.

3.5.1   THE `identify` FUNCTION

Figure 2.1 (p. 64) provides an example of the use of the `identify` function:

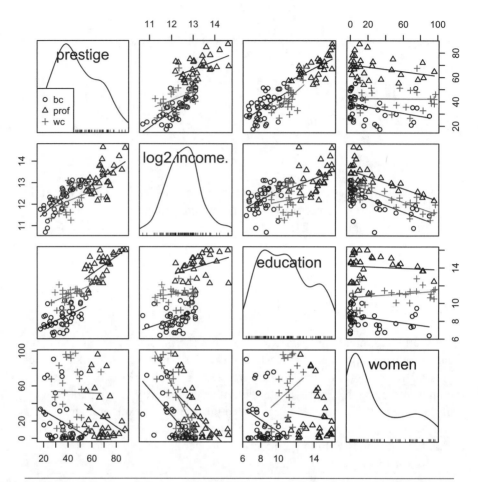

Figure 3.23   Scatterplot matrix with transformed predictors for the `Prestige` data set, conditioned on `type`.

```
> with(Freedman, {
+     plot(density, crime)
+     identify(density, crime, row.names(Freedman))
+ })
```

After a plot is created—in this case, a scatterplot of `crime` versus `density`—`identify` is called with three principal arguments: the variable on the horizontal axis of the plot, the variable on the vertical axis, and finally a vector of labels of the same length as the two variables. The mouse is used to select the points to be identified: Left click near a point to label it.

Labeling points continues until we explicitly stop the process, and *we cannot execute any other R commands until we exit from point-identification mode*. In Windows, we can return control to the R console either by right-clicking the mouse and selecting *Stop* from the resulting pop-up context menu or via the *Stop* menu associated with the graphics device window. Under Mac OS X, we can exit by clicking the right mouse button if we have a two-button mouse; otherwise, control-click, command-click, or esc all produce the same result.

The `identify` function has several other arguments that can modify the size and location of the labels that are printed; you can learn about these arguments by typing `?identify`.

3.5.2 AUTOMATIC LABELING OF POINTS

All the graphical functions in the **car** package employ similar mechanisms for point identification, using the `showLabels` function to label potentially noteworthy points. Labeling can be either automatic or interactive, depending on how we set arguments to the function. The arguments to `showLabels` are as follows:

```
> args(showLabels)

function (x, y, labels = NULL, id.method = "identify",
    id.n = length(x), id.cex = 1, id.col = palette()[1], ...)
NULL
```

Except for x, y, and . . ., these arguments can also be set in **car** higher-level plotting functions such as `scatterplot` or `invTranPlot`. When you call `showLabels` directly, the default is to use the `identify` function to label as many cases as you like using the mouse as described in the last section. Usually, you will use this function by setting arguments to the **car** graphics functions, and for these, the defaults are different. All **car** graphics functions have `id.n=0` by default for no point identification. The default `id.method` for **car** functions depends on the function. To get any point identification, you need to set `id.n` to a positive number or set `method="identify"` for interactive point identification (see below). Here is a description of the various arguments to `showLabels`:

labels is a vector of labels to be used for the points. Most higher-level plotting functions will find reasonable labels on their own, but sometimes we are required to supply labels. In these instances, if no labels are provided, then case numbers are used.

id.method selects the method for identifying points. There are several built-in methods selected by setting `id.method` to a quoted string, or you can make up your own method. The options `"x"` and `"y"` will select extreme values on the *x*-axis and the *y*-axis, respectively. If you want both types of extremes identified, set `id.method=list("x"`, `"y")`. For use with the `scatter3d` function, there is also an argument `"z"`. The argument `id.method="mahal"` labels points with the largest Mahalanobis distance from the point $(\bar{x}, \bar{y})$. This is most appropriate when studying the joint distribution of the two plotted variables. Labeling by Mahalanobis distance is the default for `scatterplot`, `scatterplotMatrix`, and (employing three-dimensional

Mahalanobis distances) `scatter3d`; other functions may use different defaults.

If `m1` is a regression model, then `id.method=abs(residuals(m1))` will select the cases with the largest absolute residuals. Finally, as long as `id.n` is a positive value, setting `id.method=c(1, 4, 7)` would label cases number 1, 4, and 7 only, regardless of the value of `id.n`.

`id.n` controls the number of points marked. The value `id.n=0` turns off point marking.

`id.cex, id.col` determine the relative size and the color of the point labels, respectively.

`...` allows additional arguments that can be passed to either the `identify` function or the `text` function.

3.6   Complementary Reading and References

- Mosteller and Tukey (1977) and Tukey (1977) were very influential in convincing applied statisticians of the necessity of looking at their data through a variety of graphs.
- Most of the material in this chapter on examining data is covered in Fox (2008, chap. 3). Power transformations (Section 3.4.2) are discussed in Fox (2008, chap. 4).
- Plotting in general and scatterplot matrices in particular are also covered in Weisberg (2005, chap. 1). Much of the material in Section 3.4 is covered in Weisberg (2005, chaps. 7–8), although some of the discussion in this section on transformations to multivariate normality conditioning on other variables is new material.
- There is a vast literature on density estimation, including Bowman and Azzalini (1997) and Silverman (1986).
- The lowess smoother used in the `scatterplot` function and elsewhere in the **car** package was introduced by Cleveland (1979) and is but one of many scatterplot smoothers, including regression and smoothing splines, kernel regression, and others (see, e.g., Fox, 2000b). Jittering was apparently proposed by Chambers et al. (1983).
- The OpenGL graphics standard is discussed at `http://www.opengl.org`. Cook and Weisberg (1999) includes an extended treatment of three-dimensional plots in regression.
- The *Wikipedia* article on logarithms (at `http://en.wikipedia.org/wiki/Logarithms`) provides a nice introduction to the topic. Fox (2000a) describes logarithms, powers, and other mathematics for social statistics.

Fitting Linear Models 4

A *statistical model* is a collection of assumptions that has sufficient structure to allow us to estimate interesting quantities, to use past data to predict future values, and to perform many other tasks. We assume general familiarity with the standard *linear-regression model* but briefly summarize the essential characteristics of the model, most of which are assumptions made about the process generating the data:

1. We have a set of m predictors and a response variable y observed on each of n units or cases. In real data sets, there may be missing values.[1]

2. The observations of the variables for one case are independent of the observations for all other cases.

3. The predictors can be numerical variables, such as age or score on an exam; qualitative variables, such as sex, country of origin, or treatment group; or ordinal variables, such as a subject's assessment of an item on a 5-point scale. The predictors are converted to *regressor variables*, which are numeric variables, in the model. For example, a qualitative predictor with d distinct levels typically requires $d - 1$ regressors. A numeric predictor usually corresponds to just one regressor given by the predictor itself, but it could require a transformation to another scale such as logarithms, or generate several regressors—for example, if it is to be used in a polynomial of degree higher than 1. Additional regressor variables can be generated using *interactions*, as we will illustrate later in this chapter. In all, the m predictors generate k regressors, which we generically name $x_1, \ldots, x_k$.

---

[1] How missing data are represented in R is described in Section 2.2.3. When there is more than a small proportion of missing data, simply ignoring missing values can be seriously problematic. One principled approach to missing data, multiple imputation, is described in the online appendix to the text.

4. The dependence of the response on the predictors is through the conditional expected value,

$$E(y|x_1, \ldots, x_k) = \beta_0 + \beta_1 x_1 + \cdots + \beta_k x_k \qquad (4.1)$$

The vertical bar "|" is read as *given*, and thus $E(y|x_1, \ldots, x_k)$ is the conditional expectation of the response y *given* fixed values of the regressors. The quantity $\eta(\mathbf{x}) = \beta_0 + \beta_1 x_1 + \cdots + \beta_k x_k$ on the right-hand side of Equation 4.1 is called the *linear predictor*.[2] Equation 4.1 specifies a linear-regression model because its right-hand side is a linear combination of the parameters, that is, the βs.

5. The conditional variance of the response given the predictors is constant,

$$\text{Var}(y|x_1, \ldots, x_k) = \sigma^2 > 0 \qquad (4.2)$$

An alternative, common specification of the model in Equations 4.1 and 4.2 is as

$$y = \beta_0 + \beta_1 x_1 + \cdots + \beta_k x_k + \varepsilon$$

The quantity ε is called an *error*, with $E(\varepsilon|x_1, \ldots, x_k) = 0$ and $\text{Var}(\varepsilon|x_1, \ldots, x_k) = \sigma^2$.

Changing assumptions changes the model. For example, it is common to add a normality assumption,

$$(y|x) \sim \text{N}(\beta_0 + \beta_1 x_1 + \cdots + \beta_k x_k, \sigma^2)$$

producing the *normal linear model*. The normal linear model provides more structure than is required for fitting linear models by least squares, although it furnishes a strong justification for doing so.

Another common extension to the linear model is to modify the constant variance assumption to

$$\text{Var}(y|x_1, \ldots, x_k) = \sigma^2/w$$

for known positive weights w, producing the *weighted linear model*. There are myriad other changes that might be made to the basic assumptions of the linear model, each possibly requiring a modification in methodology.

The basic R function for fitting linear-regression models by *ordinary least squares (OLS)* or *weighted least squares (WLS)* is the lm function, which is the primary focus of this chapter.

---

[2]If you are unfamiliar with vector notation, simply think of $\mathbf{x} = (x_1, \ldots, x_k)$ as the collection of regressors.

4.2 Linear Least-Squares Regression

4.2.1 SIMPLE REGRESSION

The `Davis` data set in the **car** package contains data on the measured and reported heights and weights of 200 men and women engaged in regular exercise. A few of the data values are missing, however, and there are only 183 complete observations for the variables that are used in the analysis reported below.

We start by taking a quick look at some of the data:

```
> library(car)
> head(Davis) # first 6 rows

  sex weight height repwt repht
1   M     77    182    77   180
2   F     58    161    51   159
3   F     53    161    54   158
4   M     68    177    70   175
5   F     59    157    59   155
6   M     76    170    76   165

> nrow(Davis)

[1] 200
```

The variables `weight` and `repwt` are in kilograms, and `height` and `repht` are in centimeters. One of the goals of the researcher who collected these data (Davis, 1990) was to determine whether the reports of height and weight are sufficiently accurate to replace the actual measurements, which suggests regressing each measurement on the corresponding report. We focus here on measured weight (`weight`) and reported weight (`repwt`).

This problem has response $y = $ `weight` and one predictor, `repwt`, from which we obtain the regressor variable $x_1 = $ `repwt`. The *simple linear-regression model* is a special case of Equation 4.1 with $k = 1$. Simple linear regression is fit in R via OLS, using the `lm` function:

```
> davis.mod <- lm(weight ~ repwt, data=Davis)
```

The basic form of the `lm` command is

```
> mod <- lm(formula, data)
```

The `formula` argument describes the response and the linear predictor, and is the only required argument. The `data` argument optionally gives a data frame that includes the variables to be used in fitting the model.[3]

The `formula` syntax was originally proposed by Wilkinson and Rogers (1973) specifically for use with linear models. Formulas are used more generally in R, but their application is clearest for regression models with linear

---

[3] Alternatives to using the `data` argument are discussed in Section 2.2. The full set of arguments for `lm` is described in Section 4.8.

predictors, such as the linear-regression models discussed in this chapter and the generalized linear models taken up in the next.

A model `formula` consists of three parts: the *left-hand side*, the ~ (*tilde*), and the *right-hand side*. The left-hand side of the formula specifies the response variable; it is usually a variable name (`weight`, in the example) but may be an expression that evaluates to the response (e.g., `sqrt(weight)`, `log(income)`, or `income/hours.worked`). The tilde is a separator. The right-hand side of the formula is a special expression including the names of the predictors that R evaluates to produce the regressors for the model. As we will see later in this chapter, the arithmetic operators, +, -, *, /, and ^, have special meaning on the right-hand side of a model formula; they retain their ordinary meaning, however, on the left-hand side of the formula.

R will use any numeric predictor on the right-hand side of the model formula as a regressor variable, as is desired here for simple regression. The intercept is included in the model without being specified directly. We can put the intercept in explicitly using `weight ~ 1 + repwt`, however, or force the regression through the origin using `weight ~ -1 + repwt` or `weight ~ repwt - 1`. A minus sign explicitly removes a term—here the intercept—from the linear predictor. Using 0 in a formula also suppresses the intercept: `weight ~ 0 + repwt`. As subsequent examples illustrate, model formulas can be much more elaborate (and are described in detail in Section 4.8.1).

The `lm` function returned a *linear-model object*, which we saved in `davis.mod`. We call other functions with `davis.mod` as an argument to produce and display useful results. As with any R object, we can print `davis-.mod` by typing its name at the R command prompt:

```
> davis.mod

Call:
lm(formula = weight ~ repwt, data = Davis)

Coefficients:
(Intercept)         repwt
      5.336         0.928
```

Printing a linear-model object simply shows the estimated regression coefficients. A more complete report is obtained from the `summary` function:

```
> summary(davis.mod)

Call:
lm(formula = weight ~ repwt, data = Davis)

Residuals:
    Min      1Q  Median      3Q     Max
 -7.048  -1.868  -0.728   0.601 108.705

Coefficients:
            Estimate Std. Error t value Pr(>|t|)
(Intercept)   5.3363     3.0369    1.76     0.08
repwt         0.9278     0.0453   20.48   <2e-16
```

```
Residual standard error: 8.42 on 181 degrees of freedom
  (17 observations deleted due to missingness)
Multiple R-squared: 0.699,         Adjusted R-squared: 0.697
F-statistic:  420 on 1 and 181 DF,  p-value: <2e-16
```

The output produced by summary is similar for most statistical-modeling functions in R. A brief summary of the residuals is provided first. Next is a *coefficient table*, giving estimates of the regression coefficients in the Estimate column and their standard errors in the Std. Error column. The column marked t value is the ratio of the estimate to its standard error and is a *Wald test* of the hypothesis that the corresponding regression coefficient is equal to 0. If the errors are normally distributed or the sample size is large enough, then these t statistics are distributed under the null hypothesis as t random variables with degrees of freedom (df) equal to the residual df under the model. The column marked Pr(>|t|) is the two-sided p value assuming that the t distribution is appropriate. For example, the hypothesis that $\beta_0 = 0$ versus $\beta_0 \neq 0$, with the value of β_1 unspecified, has a p value of about .08, providing weak evidence against the null hypothesis that $\beta_0 = 0$, if the assumptions of the model hold.

Below the coefficient table is additional summary information including the residual standard error, which is an estimate of σ. For the example, $\hat{\sigma} \approx$ 8.4 kg. This error is so large that, if correct, it is unlikely that predictions of actual weight from the reported weight would be of any practical value. The residual df are $n - 2$ for simple regression, here $183 - 2 = 181$. The Multiple R-squared, $R^2 \approx .70$, is the square of the correlation between the response and the fitted values. The reported F statistic tests the hypothesis that all the regression coefficients in Equation 4.1, except for the intercept, are equal to 0, versus the alternative that at least one of the β_j is nonzero. If the errors are normal or n is large enough, then this test statistic has an F distribution with the degrees of freedom shown. Because simple regression has only one parameter beyond the intercept, the F test is equivalent to the t test that $\beta_1 = 0$, with $t^2 = F$. In other models, such as the GLMs of the next chapter or normal nonlinear models, Wald tests and the generalization of the F test may test the same hypotheses, but they need not give the same inferences.

If individuals are unbiased reporters of their weight, then the regression intercept should be near 0 and the slope near 1. To assess this expectation, we can examine *confidence intervals* for the estimates using the confint function:

```
> confint(davis.mod)

             2.5 %  97.5 %
(Intercept) -0.6560 11.329
repwt        0.8385  1.017
```

The values of $\beta_0 = 0$ and $\beta_1 = 1$ are *marginally* (i.e., individually) consistent with the unbiased estimation of weight because these values are included in their respective confidence intervals, although the interval for the intercept is

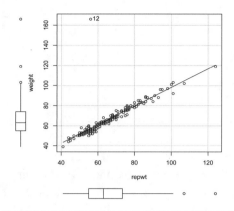

Figure 4.1 Scatterplot of measured weight (`weight`) by reported weight (`repwt`) for Davis's data.

so wide that these estimates are unlikely to be of much value. The *separate* confidence intervals, however, do not address the hypothesis that *simultaneously* $\beta_0 = 0$ and $\beta_1 = 1$, versus the alternative that either or both of the intercept and slope differ from these values. We will provide the relevant test in Section 4.4.5.

We should have started (of course!) by plotting the data, and we now do so belatedly, using the `scatterplot` function from the **car** package:

```
> scatterplot(weight ~ repwt, data=Davis, smooth=FALSE, id.n=1)

[1] "12"
```

The graph, shown in Figure 4.1, reveals an extreme outlier, Observation 12, flagged on the graph by the argument `id.n=1`. The argument `smooth=FALSE` suppresses the lowess smoother (see Section 3.2.1). It seems bizarre that an individual who weighs more than 160 kg would report her weight as less than 60 kg, but there is a simple explanation: On data entry, Subject 12's height in centimeters and weight in kilograms were inadvertently exchanged.

The proper course of action would be to correct the data, but to extend the example, we instead will use the `update` function to refit the model by removing the 12*th* observation:

```
> davis.mod.2 <- update(davis.mod, subset=-12)
> summary(davis.mod.2)

Call:
lm(formula = weight ~ repwt, data = Davis, subset = -12)

Residuals:
   Min     1Q Median     3Q    Max
-7.530 -1.101 -0.132  1.129  6.389

Coefficients:
            Estimate Std. Error t value Pr(>|t|)
(Intercept)   2.7338     0.8148    3.36  0.00097
```

```
repwt          0.9584     0.0121    78.93   < 2e-16

Residual standard error: 2.25 on 180 degrees of freedom
  (17 observations deleted due to missingness)
Multiple R-squared: 0.972,         Adjusted R-squared: 0.972
F-statistic: 6.23e+03 on 1 and 180 DF,  p-value: <2e-16
```

The `update` function can be used in many circumstances to create a new model object by changing one or more arguments. In this case, setting `subset=-12` refits the model by omitting the 12*th* observation. (See Section 4.8.3 for more on the `subset` argument.)

Extreme outliers such as this one have several effects on a fitted model, which will be explored more fully in Chapter 6. They can sometimes determine the value of the estimated coefficients:

```
> cbind(Original=coef(davis.mod), NoCase12=coef(davis.mod.2))

            Original NoCase12
(Intercept)   5.3363   2.7338
repwt         0.9278   0.9584
```

The `cbind` (column `bind`) function binds the two vectors of coefficient estimates into a two-column matrix. The first column gives the coefficient estimates using all the data and the second after deleting Case 12. Only the intercept changes, and not dramatically at that, because Case 12 is a relatively low-leverage point, meaning that its value for the predictor is near the center of the distribution of predictor values (see Section 6.3). In contrast, there is a major change in the residual standard error, reduced from an unacceptable 8.4 kg to a possibly acceptable 2.2 kg. Also, the value of R^2 is greatly increased. Finally, the F and t tests discussed previously are not reliable when outliers are present.

4.2.2 MULTIPLE REGRESSION

Multiple regression extends simple regression to allow for more than one regressor. To provide an illustration, we return to the Canadian occupational-prestige data (introduced in Chapter 2):

```
> head(Prestige)

                   education income women prestige census type
gov.administrators     13.11  12351 11.16     68.8   1113 prof
general.managers       12.26  25879  4.02     69.1   1130 prof
accountants            12.77   9271 15.70     63.4   1171 prof
purchasing.officers    11.42   8865  9.11     56.8   1175 prof
chemists               14.62   8403 11.68     73.5   2111 prof
physicists             15.64  11030  5.13     77.6   2113 prof

> nrow(Prestige)

[1] 102
```

Just as simple regression should start with a graph of the response versus the predictor, multiple regression should start with the examination of appropriate graphs, such as a scatterplot matrix. In Section 3.4, we constructed a scatterplot matrix for the predictors education (the average number of years of education of the occupational incumbents), income (their average income), and women (the percentage of women in the occupation), and the response variable prestige (Figure 3.13, p. 126); based on this graph, we suggested replacing income by its logarithm. The resulting scatterplot matrix (Figure 3.22, p. 144), in which little or no curvature is observed in any of the panels of the plot, suggests that this is a good place to start regression modeling.

We fit Equation 4.1 for the response variable $y =$ prestige, and from the three predictors we derive $k = 3$ regressors, $x_1 =$ education, $x_2 = \log_2(\text{income})$, and $x_3 =$ women. Thus, two of the three predictors are directly represented in the model as regressors, and the other regressor is derived from the remaining predictor, income. As in simple regression, we fit the model with the lm function:

```
> prestige.mod <- lm(prestige ~ education + log2(income) + women,
+      data=Prestige)
```

The only difference between fitting a simple and multiple linear regression in R is in the model formula: In a multiple regression, there are several predictors, and their names are separated in the formula by + signs. R recognizes education, log2(income), and women as numeric variables and uses them as the three regressors.

```
> summary(prestige.mod)

Call:
lm(formula = prestige ~ education + log2(income) +
    women, data = Prestige)

Residuals:
    Min      1Q  Median      3Q     Max
-17.364  -4.429  -0.101   4.316  19.179

Coefficients:
              Estimate Std. Error t value Pr(>|t|)
(Intercept)  -110.9658    14.8429   -7.48  3.3e-11
education       3.7305     0.3544   10.53  < 2e-16
log2(income)    9.3147     1.3265    7.02  2.9e-10
women           0.0469     0.0299    1.57     0.12

Residual standard error: 7.09 on 98 degrees of freedom
Multiple R-squared: 0.835,        Adjusted R-squared: 0.83
F-statistic:  165 on 3 and 98 DF,  p-value: <2e-16
```

In multiple regression, the regression coefficients are called *partial slopes*, and they can only be interpreted in the context of the other regressors in the model. For example, the estimate[4] $b_1 \approx 3.7$ suggests that for any fixed values

---

[4]In this *Companion*, we indicate an estimated regression coefficient by replacing a Greek letter with the corresponding Roman letter, as in b_1 for β_1.

of income and women, the average increment in prestige for an additional year of education is 3.7 prestige units. Interpreting the coefficient of a logged predictor is more complicated, but it is somewhat easier when base-2 logarithms are used: Increasing $\log_2(\text{income})$ by 1 unit corresponds to *doubling* income, and so doubling income, holding the other predictors constant, is associated on average with an increase of about 9.3 prestige units.

We will revisit the Prestige data set later in this chapter and in Chapter 6 on regression diagnostics.

4.2.3 MODELS WITH FACTORS AND INTERACTIONS

FACTORS

The values of qualitative variables are category labels rather than measurements. Examples of qualitative variables are gender, treatment in a clinical trial, country of origin, and job title. Qualitative variables can have as few as two categories or a very large number of categories. An *ordinal* categorical variable has categories that have a natural ordering, such as age class, highest degree attained, or response on a 5-point scale with values from *strongly disagree* to *strongly agree*.

We (and R) call qualitative variables *factors* and their categories, *levels*. In some statistical packages, including SAS and SPSS, factors are called *class variables*. Regardless of what they are called, factors are very common, and statistical software should make some provision for including them in regression models.

As explained in Section 2.1.2, when the read.table function reads a column of a data file that includes at least some values that are neither numbers nor missing-value indicators, it by default turns that column into a factor. An example is the variable type (type of occupation) in the Prestige data frame:

```
> Prestige$type

 [1] prof prof prof prof prof prof prof prof prof prof prof prof
[13] prof prof prof prof prof prof prof prof prof prof prof prof
[25] prof prof prof bc   prof prof wc   prof wc   <NA> wc   wc
[37] wc   wc   wc   wc   wc   wc   wc   wc   wc   wc   wc   wc
[49] wc   wc   wc   wc   <NA> bc   wc   wc   wc   bc   bc   bc
[61] bc   bc   <NA> bc   bc   bc   <NA> bc   bc   bc   bc   bc
[73] bc   bc   bc   bc   bc   bc   bc   bc   bc   bc   bc   bc
[85] bc   bc   bc   bc   bc   bc   bc   bc   bc   bc   bc   prof
[97] bc   bc   bc   bc   bc   bc
Levels: bc prof wc
```

```
> class(Prestige$type)
```

```
[1] "factor"
```

The three levels of the factor type represent blue-collar (bc), professional and managerial (prof), and white-collar (wc) occupations. The missing-value symbol, NA, is not counted as a level of the factor. The levels were automatically alphabetized when the factor was created, but the order of the factor levels can be changed:

```
> levels(Prestige$type)

[1] "bc"    "prof" "wc"

> Prestige$type <- with(Prestige, factor(type,
+     levels=c("bc", "wc", "prof")))
> select <- c(1, 2, 35, 36, 61, 62) # a few rows
> Prestige$type[select]  # a few values

[1] prof prof wc   wc   bc   bc
Levels: bc wc prof
```

The reordered levels are in a more natural order. We can also *coerce* a factor into a numeric vector:[5]

```
> type.number <- as.numeric(Prestige$type)
> type.number[select]

[1] 3 3 2 2 1 1

> class(type.number)

[1] "numeric"
```

The `as.numeric` function replaces each level of the factor by its level number, producing a `"numeric"` result. It is also possible to coerce `type` into a vector of character strings:

```
> type.character <- as.character(Prestige$type)
> type.character[select]

[1] "prof" "prof" "wc"   "wc"   "bc"   "bc"

> class(type.character)

[1] "character"
```

Finally, we can turn `type.character` back into a factor with naturally ordered levels:

```
> type.factor <- factor(type.character, levels=c("bc", "wc", "prof"))
> type.factor[select]

[1] prof prof wc   wc   bc   bc
Levels: bc wc prof
```

Suppose that we have a data frame named `Drug` with a discrete variable called `dosage`, whose values are numeric—say 1, 2, 4, 8—indicating the dose of a drug. When the data are read from a file, `read.table` by default

---

[5]See Section 2.6 for a general discussion of coercion from one type of data to another.

will not make this variable a factor, because all its values are numbers.[6] We can turn dosage into a factor using any of the following commands:

```
> Drug$dosage <- factor(Drug$dosage)
> Drug$dosage <- factor(Drug$dosage,
+     levels=c("8", "4", "2", "1"))
> Drug$dosage <- factor(Drug$dosage,
+     labels=c("D1", "D2", "D4", "D8"))
```

The first of these commands creates a factor with the levels "1", "2", "4", "8", treating the numbers as text. The second command orders the levels differently. The third command keeps the default ordering but assigns customized labels to the levels of the factor via the labels argument.

When a factor is included in a model formula, R automatically creates regressors, called *contrasts*, to represent the levels of the factor. The default contrast coding in R is produced by the function contr.treatment: If a factor has m distinct levels, then contr.treatment creates $m - 1$ regressors, each of which is *dummy-coded*, with values consisting only of 0s and 1s. For example, suppose we have a factor z with four levels:

```
> (z <- factor(rep(c("a", "b", "c", "d"), c(3, 2, 4, 1))))

 [1] a a a b b c c c c d
Levels: a b c d
```

We can see the dummy variables that will be created using the model-.matrix function, specifying a model formula with z on the right-hand side:

```
> model.matrix(~ z)

   (Intercept) zb zc zd
1            1  0  0  0
2            1  0  0  0
3            1  0  0  0
4            1  1  0  0
5            1  1  0  0
6            1  0  1  0
7            1  0  1  0
8            1  0  1  0
9            1  0  1  0
10           1  0  0  1
```

The first column of the model matrix is a columns of 1s, representing the intercept. The remaining three columns are the dummy regressors constructed from the factor z. To put it more compactly,

```
> contrasts(z)

  b c d
a 0 0 0
b 1 0 0
c 0 1 0
d 0 0 1
```

---

[6]As explained in Section 2.5.2, we can alter the default behavior of read.table via its col-Classes argument.

When $z =$ "a", all the dummy variables are equal to 0; when $z =$ "b", the dummy variable $zb = 1$; when $z =$ "c", $zc = 1$; and, finally, when $z =$ "d", $zd = 1$. Each level of z is therefore uniquely identified by a combination of the dummy variables.

R has several other functions apart from `contr.treatment` for coding contrasts, and if you don't like the standard contrast codings, you can make up your own. The results of an analysis generally don't depend on the choice of contrasts to define a factor, except in some testing situations that we will describe later. Section 4.6 provides an extended discussion of contrast selection.

A LINEAR MODEL WITH ONE FACTOR: ONE-WAY ANALYSIS OF VARIANCE

The simplest linear model with factors, known as *one-way analysis of variance* (ANOVA), has just one factor and no numeric predictors. For example, Baumann and Jones (as reported in Moore and McCabe, 1993) conducted an experiment in which 66 children were assigned at random to one of three experimental groups. The groups represent different methods of teaching reading: a standard method called `Basal` and two new methods called `DTRA` and `Strat`. The researchers conducted two pretests and three post tests of reading comprehension. We focus here on the third post test. The data for the study are in the data frame `Baumann` in the **car** package:

```
> some(Baumann) # sample 10 observations

   group pretest.1 pretest.2 post.test.1 post.test.2 post.test.3
1  Basal          4         3           5           4          41
8  Basal         12         7           5           5          32
14 Basal         12         2           8           8          44
30  DRTA          8         7          13           5          53
39  DRTA          9         5          12           6          54
40  DRTA         13         6          10           6          41
41  DRTA         10         2          11           6          49
54 Strat          9         5           7          11          42
63 Strat         14         4          15           7          49
64 Strat          8         2           9           5          33

> nrow(Baumann)

[1] 66
```

Like the head function, the `some` function in the **car** package prints rows of its argument: `head`, the first few rows, and `some`, a random few rows.

The researchers were interested in whether the new methods produce better results than the standard method, and whether the new methods differ in their effectiveness.

```
> xtabs(~ group, data=Baumann)

group
Basal  DRTA Strat
   22    22    22
```

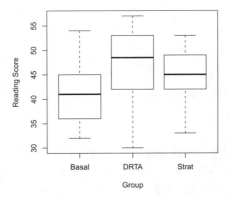

Figure 4.2 Post-test reading score by condition, for Baumann and Jones's data.

When `xtabs` is used with a one-sided formula, as it is here, it will count the number of cases in the data set at each level or combination of levels of the right-hand-side variables, in this case just the factor `group`. The experimental design has the same number, 22, of subjects in each group.

```
> with(Baumann, tapply(post.test.3, group, mean))

Basal  DRTA Strat
41.05 46.73 44.27

> with(Baumann, tapply(post.test.3, group, sd))

Basal  DRTA Strat
5.636 7.388 5.767
```

The `tapply` function (described in Section 8.4) computes the means and SDs for each level of `group`. The means appear to differ, while the within-group SDs are similar. Plotting a numeric variable against a factor produces a parallel boxplot, as in Figure 4.2:

```
> plot(post.test.3 ~ group, data=Baumann, xlab="Group",
+       ylab="Reading Score")
```

The means and boxplots suggest that there may be differences among the groups, particularly between the new methods and the standard one.

The one-way ANOVA model can be fit with `lm`:

```
> baum.mod.1 <- lm(post.test.3 ~ group, data=Baumann)
> summary(baum.mod.1)

Call:
lm(formula = post.test.3 ~ group, data = Baumann)

Residuals:
   Min    1Q Median    3Q    Max
-16.73  -3.61   1.11  3.95  12.95
```

```
Coefficients:
            Estimate Std. Error t value Pr(>|t|)
(Intercept)    41.05       1.35   30.49   <2e-16
groupDRTA       5.68       1.90    2.98    0.004
groupStrat      3.23       1.90    1.70    0.095

Residual standard error: 6.31 on 63 degrees of freedom
Multiple R-squared: 0.125,       Adjusted R-squared: 0.0967
F-statistic: 4.48 on 2 and 63 DF,  p-value: 0.0152
```

We specify the predictor `group` in the formula for the linear model. Because R recognizes that `group` is a factor, it is replaced with dummy regressors. The coefficients for the two regressors are the estimates of the *difference* in means between the groups shown and the baseline group. For example, the estimated mean difference between `DRTA` and `basal` is 5.68. The *t* value is the Wald test that the corresponding population mean difference is equal to 0. The intercept is the estimated mean for the baseline `basal` group. No test is directly available in the summary output to compare the groups `DRTA` and `Strat`, but such a test could be easily generated by refitting the model with a releveled factor, using the `relevel` function to set `"DRTA"` as the baseline (or reference) level of `group`:

```
> summary(update(baum.mod.1, . ~ . - group +
+     relevel(group, ref="DRTA")))

Call:
lm(formula = post.test.3 ~ relevel(group, ref = "DRTA"),
    data = Baumann)

Residuals:
   Min    1Q Median    3Q    Max
-16.73  -3.61   1.11  3.95  12.95

Coefficients:
                                     Estimate Std. Error t value
(Intercept)                             46.73       1.35   34.71
relevel(group, ref = "DRTA")Basal       -5.68       1.90   -2.98
relevel(group, ref = "DRTA")Strat       -2.45       1.90   -1.29
                                     Pr(>|t|)
(Intercept)                            <2e-16
relevel(group, ref = "DRTA")Basal       0.004
relevel(group, ref = "DRTA")Strat       0.202

Residual standard error: 6.31 on 63 degrees of freedom
Multiple R-squared: 0.125,       Adjusted R-squared: 0.0967
F-statistic: 4.48 on 2 and 63 DF,  p-value: 0.0152
```

The periods (".") in the updated model formula represent the previous left- and right-hand sides of the formula; we, therefore, updated the model by removing the factor `group` and replacing it with its releveled version. The *t* test for the comparison between `DRTA` and `Strat` has a *p* value close to .2.[7]

---

[7]There are many other ways of producing this test: See, for example, Section 4.4.5 on testing linear hypotheses.

MODELS WITH NUMERIC PREDICTORS AND FACTORS BUT NO INTERACTIONS

Regression with factors and numeric variables is often called *analysis of covariance* or *dummy-variable regression*. To illustrate, we return to the Prestige data set, but this time, we exclude the predictor women and add the factor type:

```
> prestige.mod.1 <- update(prestige.mod, ~ . - women + type)
> summary(prestige.mod.1)

Call:
lm(formula = prestige ~ education + log2(income) +
    type, data = Prestige)

Residuals:
   Min     1Q Median     3Q    Max
-13.51  -3.75   1.01   4.36  18.44

Coefficients:
              Estimate Std. Error t value Pr(>|t|)
(Intercept)    -81.202     13.743   -5.91  5.6e-08
education        3.284      0.608    5.40  5.1e-07
log2(income)     7.269      1.190    6.11  2.3e-08
typewc          -1.439      2.378   -0.61   0.546
typeprof         6.751      3.618    1.87   0.065

Residual standard error: 6.64 on 93 degrees of freedom
  (4 observations deleted due to missingness)
Multiple R-squared: 0.855,          Adjusted R-squared: 0.849
F-statistic:  138 on 4 and 93 DF,  p-value: <2e-16
```

We once again used the update function rather than typing in a model from scratch. The output indicates that four observations were deleted because of missing data—that is, four of the occupations have the value NA for type. This model has three predictors (education, income, and type), which produce four regressors plus an intercept—effectively one intercept for each level of type and one slope for each of the numeric predictors (called *covariates*).

The estimate for typewc is the difference in intercepts between wc and the baseline bc. The corresponding *t* value tests the hypothesis that these two levels of type have the same intercept. Similarly, the typeprof coefficient is the difference in intercepts between prof and bc. A test of the natural hypothesis that *all* the group intercepts are equal will be given in Section 4.4.4.

There is a slope for each of the two numeric regressors, and according to this model, the slopes are the same for each level of the factor type, producing parallel regressions, or an *additive model* with *no interactions*. Because the regression planes for the three levels of type are parallel, the typewc and typeprof coefficients represent not only the differences in intercepts among the groups but also the constant separation of the regression planes at fixed levels of income and education.

It is common to compute *adjusted means* for the levels of a factor in an analysis of covariance: Adjusted means are simply fitted values at the various levels of a factor, when the means of the covariates are substituted into the linear predictor of the estimated model. The adjusted means can be computed by the `effect` function in the **effects** package:[8]

```
> library(effects)
> effect("type", prestige.mod.1)

 type effect
type
   bc    wc  prof
45.53 44.09 52.28
```

For the no-interaction dummy-regression model, the differences among the adjusted means are the same as the corresponding differences among the intercepts.

MODELS WITH NUMERIC PREDICTORS, FACTORS, AND INTERACTIONS

Thus far, we have allowed each level of a factor in a linear-regression model to have its own intercept, but the slopes for the numeric predictors in the model are constrained to be the same for each level of the factor. Including interactions in the model allows for different slopes at each level of the factor— "different slopes for different folks."

Interactions in an R model formula are specified using the `:` (*colon*) operator. The interaction between `type` and `education`, for example, literally multiplies each of the two `type` dummy variables by `education` to produce two additional interaction regressors. To see the regressors computed from the factors and interactions, we examine a few rows of the `model.matrix`:

```
> select # defined previously

[1]  1   2 35 36 61 62

> model.matrix(~ type + education + education:type,
+    data=Prestige)[select, ]
```

	(Intercept)	typewc	typeprof	education
gov.administrators	1	0	1	13.11
general.managers	1	0	1	12.26
typists	1	1	0	11.49
bookkeepers	1	1	0	11.32
launderers	1	0	0	7.33
janitors	1	0	0	7.11

	typewc:education	typeprof:education
gov.administrators	0.00	13.11
general.managers	0.00	12.26
typists	11.49	0.00
bookkeepers	11.32	0.00
launderers	0.00	0.00
janitors	0.00	0.00

---

[8]The more general use of the **effects** package for displaying fitted linear models is developed in Section 4.3.3.

The first column of the model matrix is for the intercept. Because `typewc` is either 0 or 1, `typewc:education` is 0 whenever `typewc` is 0 and is equal to `education` whenever `typewc` is 1; similarly, `typeprof:education` is 0 whenever `typeprof` is 0 and is equal to `education` whenever `typeprof` is 1.

We add interactions between `income` and `type` and between `education` and `type` and refit the model:

```
> prestige.mod.2 <- update(prestige.mod.1,
+       . ~ . + log2(income):type + education:type)
> summary(prestige.mod.2)

Call:
lm(formula = prestige ~ education + log2(income) +
    type + log2(income):type + education:type, data = Prestige)

Residuals:
   Min     1Q Median    3Q    Max
-13.97  -4.12   1.21  3.83  18.06

Coefficients:
                        Estimate Std. Error t value Pr(>|t|)
(Intercept)             -120.046     20.158   -5.96  5.1e-08
education                  2.336      0.928    2.52   0.0136
log2(income)              11.078      1.806    6.13  2.3e-08
typewc                    30.241     37.979    0.80   0.4280
typeprof                  85.160     31.181    2.73   0.0076
log2(income):typewc       -5.653      3.052   -1.85   0.0673
log2(income):typeprof     -6.536      2.617   -2.50   0.0143
education:typewc           3.640      1.759    2.07   0.0414
education:typeprof         0.697      1.290    0.54   0.5900

Residual standard error: 6.41 on 89 degrees of freedom
  (4 observations deleted due to missingness)
Multiple R-squared: 0.871,          Adjusted R-squared: 0.859
F-statistic: 75.1 on 8 and 89 DF,  p-value: <2e-16
```

The regression model still has only three *predictors*, but it includes eight *regressors* in addition to the intercept. There are effectively one intercept and two slopes for each level of the factor `type`. In this model,

- For the baseline level bc, the intercept is -120.05, the slope for education is 2.34, and the slope for `log2(income)` is 11.08.
- For level wc, the intercept is $-120.05 + 30.24 = -89.81$, the slope for `log2(income)` is $11.08 + (-5.65) = 5.43$, and the slope for education is $2.34 + 3.64 = 5.98$.
- For level prof, the intercept is $-120.05 + 85.16 = -34.89$, the slope for `log2(income)` is $11.08 + (-6.54) = 4.54$, and the slope for education is $2.34 + 0.70 = 3.04$.

The dummy-regression model with interactions can alternatively and equivalently be specified using the * (*crossing*) operator:

```
> prestige.mod.2a <- lm(prestige ~ education*type +
+                            log2(income)*type, data=Prestige)
```

To put it even more compactly,

```
> prestige.mod.2b <- lm(prestige ~ type*(education + log2(income)),
+                  data=Prestige)
```

We generally recommend using * to specify models with interactions because it is easy to make mistakes using the : operator: For example, the model formula

```
prestige ~ education:type + log2(income):type
```

is *not* equivalent to

```
prestige ~ education*type + log2(income)*type
```

(as the reader can verify).[9]

MODELS WITH MANY FACTORS: MULTIWAY ANOVA

Linear models with many factors and no numerical predictors are often termed *multiway* ANOVA, but they could just as accurately be described as multifactor regression models. We draw an example from a social-psycho-logical experiment on conformity reported by Moore and Krupat (1971):

```
> some(Moore)   # sample 10 rows
```

	partner.status	conformity	fcategory	fscore
4	low	7	low	20
7	low	12	medium	51
8	low	4	medium	44
15	low	9	high	65
17	low	6	low	28
21	low	8	low	17
34	high	20	medium	44
36	high	12	low	22
37	high	14	high	52
42	high	13	high	57

```
> nrow(Moore)
```

```
[1] 45
```

The 45 subjects in the experiment interacted with a partner who was of either relatively low or relatively high status as recorded in the factor partner.status. In the course of the experiment, the subjects made intrinsically ambiguous judgments and shared these judgments with their partners. The partners were confederates of the experimenter, and their judgments were manipulated so that they disagreed with the subjects on 40 critical trials.

---

[9]The model prestige ~ education:type + log2(income):type fits a common intercept for the three occupational groups and different education and log2(income) slopes for the groups, not a generally sensible specification; see Section 4.8.1.

After exchanging initial judgments, the subjects were given the opportunity to change their minds. The variable `conformity` records the number of times in these 40 trials that each subject deferred to his or her partner's judgment. The variable `fscore` is a measure of the subject's authoritarianism, and `fcategory` is a categorized version of this variable, dissecting `fscore` into thirds, labeled `low`, `medium`, and `high`.

Using `partner.status` and `fcategory` as factors, Moore and Krupat performed a two-way ANOVA of `conformity`.[10] We start by reordering the levels of the factors because the default alphabetical order is not what we want:

```
> Moore$fcategory <- factor(Moore$fcategory,
+     levels=c("low", "medium", "high"))
> Moore$partner.status <- relevel(Moore$partner.status, ref="low")
```

A table of the number of observations in each *cell*, or combination of factor levels, is called a *contingency table*. The `xtabs` function can be used to generate this table:

```
> xtabs(~ fcategory + partner.status, data=Moore)

          partner.status
fcategory low high
    low        10     5
    medium      4    11
    high        8     7
```

The first argument to the `xtabs` function is a one-sided formula, where the + operator now separates the dimensions of the contingency table. The `data` argument is optional and supplies a data frame to which the formula is applied. All six cells have entries, although the cell counts are not all the same. In the language of ANOVA models, this is an *unbalanced* design. We can also calculate the means and standard deviations for conformity within cells using the `tapply` function:

```
> with(Moore, tapply(conformity,
+     list(Authoritarianism=fcategory,
+         "Partner's Status"=partner.status),
+     mean))

                   Partner's Status
Authoritarianism    low   high
            low     8.90 17.40
            medium  7.25 14.27
            high   12.62 11.86
```

---

[10] Actually, Moore and Krupat categorized authoritarianism *separately* within each level of partner's status. The results we present here are similar to theirs, but our procedure is more defensible.

The reader may want to consider variations on the analysis: Using `fscore`, the quantitative version of authoritarianism, in place of the factor `fcategory` produces a dummy-variable regression. Because `conformity` is a disguised proportion (i.e., the number of conforming responses out of 40), a logit or similar transformation of `conformity`/40 might be tried. See Section 3.4.3 on transforming restricted-range variables.

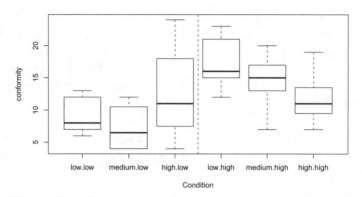

Figure 4.3   Conformity by authoritarianism and partner's status, for Moore and Krupat's data.

```
> with(Moore, tapply(conformity,
+       list(Authoritarianism=fcategory,
+            "Partner's Status"=partner.status),
+       sd))

                  Partner's Status
Authoritarianism   low   high
            low   2.644 4.506
         medium   3.948 3.952
           high   7.347 3.934
```

Mean conformity appears to decrease on average with authoritarianism in the high-partner-status condition but appears to increase with authoritarianism (at least comparing low and medium authoritarianism with high authoritarianism) in the low-status condition. Variability appears to be greatest in the high-authoritarianism, low-status condition.

A graphical view of the data can guide us in subsequent statistical modeling. In this case, we examine parallel boxplots of the response variable `conformity` within the six combinations of levels of the factors `fcategory` and `partner.status` (Figure 4.3):

```
> boxplot(conformity ~ fcategory:partner.status, data=Moore,
+       xlab="Condition", ylab="conformity")
> abline(v=3.5, lty="dashed")
```

We used the formula `conformity ~ fcategory:partner.-status`, and consequently, the boxplots were drawn with the levels of `fcategory` changing faster than those of `partner.status`. We separated the boxplots at the low level of `partner.status` from those at the high level by adding a vertical broken line midway between the third and fourth boxplots.[11]

We can see from Figure 4.3, first, that the treatment combinations may well differ because the centers of the boxes are all different; moreover, the patterns within the two levels of `partner.status` are different, suggesting

---

[11]This graph can be drawn more elegantly using the `bwplot` function in the **lattice** package; see Section 7.3.1.

an `fcategory`-by-`partner.status` interaction. As we noted in examining the SDs, variability may also be somewhat different in different groups, and appears especially large in the `"high.low"` (high authoritarianism, low partner status) group. With small samples sizes, however, only gross differences in within-group variability are likely to be important (but see our further discussion of the Moore and Krupat data below).

We are now ready to start modeling the data. Because we anticipate that the interaction between `fcategory` and `partner.status` may be important, we fit a model including the main effects for the two factors and the interaction between them, using the * (crossing) operator to specify the model, as in dummy-variable regression:

```
> mod.moore.1 <- lm(conformity ~ fcategory*partner.status, data=Moore)
> summary(mod.moore.1)

Call:
lm(formula = conformity ~ fcategory * partner.status,
    data = Moore)

Residuals:
    Min     1Q  Median     3Q     Max
 -8.625 -2.900 -0.273  2.727  11.375

Coefficients:
                                   Estimate Std. Error t value
(Intercept)                            8.90       1.45    6.15
fcategorymedium                       -1.65       2.71   -0.61
fcategoryhigh                          3.72       2.17    1.71
partner.statushigh                     8.50       2.51    3.39
fcategorymedium:partner.statushigh    -1.48       3.67   -0.40
fcategoryhigh:partner.statushigh      -9.27       3.45   -2.69
                                   Pr(>|t|)
(Intercept)                        3.2e-07
fcategorymedium                     0.5460
fcategoryhigh                       0.0943
partner.statushigh                  0.0016
fcategorymedium:partner.statushigh  0.6892
fcategoryhigh:partner.statushigh    0.0106

Residual standard error: 4.58 on 39 degrees of freedom
Multiple R-squared: 0.324,        Adjusted R-squared: 0.237
F-statistic: 3.73 on 5 and 39 DF,  p-value: 0.0074
```

The six coefficient estimates can be combined to give the estimated means for all six combinations of `fcategory` and `partner.status`, according to the following table:

	partner.status	
fcategory	low	high
low	b_0	$b_0 + b_3$
medium	$b_0 + b_1$	$b_0 + b_1 + b_3 + b_4$
high	$b_0 + b_2$	$b_0 + b_2 + b_3 + b_5$

Because we fit the six cell means with six parameters, the reader can verify that the sums shown in the table are identical to the directly computed cell means, which were shown previously.

An additive (i.e., main effects only) model can be conveniently produced from the full, two-way ANOVA model by removing the interactions:

```
> mod.moore.2 <- update(mod.moore.1,
+     . ~ . - fcategory:partner.status)
> summary(mod.moore.2)

Call:
lm(formula = conformity ~ fcategory + partner.status,
    data = Moore)

Residuals:
   Min     1Q Median     3Q    Max
-7.724 -3.198 -0.198  2.883 13.883

Coefficients:
                    Estimate Std. Error t value Pr(>|t|)
(Intercept)          10.1978     1.3727    7.43  4.1e-09
fcategorymedium      -1.1760     1.9020   -0.62   0.5398
fcategoryhigh        -0.0809     1.8092   -0.04   0.9646
partner.statushigh    4.6067     1.5565    2.96   0.0051

Residual standard error: 4.92 on 41 degrees of freedom
Multiple R-squared: 0.179,     Adjusted R-squared: 0.118
F-statistic: 2.97 on 3 and 41 DF,  p-value: 0.0428
```

The fitted cell means for the no-interaction model are not in general equal to the directly calculated sample cell means, because the fitted means are based on only four parameters:

	partner.status	
fcategory	low	high
low	b_0	$b_0 + b_3$
medium	$b_0 + b_1$	$b_0 + b_1 + b_3$
high	$b_0 + b_2$	$b_0 + b_2 + b_3$

In problems with all the factors and no numeric predictors, it is usual for the analysis to center on examination of the estimated cell means under various models and on tests summarized in an ANOVA table. We will discuss testing in Section 4.4.

Plots of cell means in R can be conveniently constructed by the `interaction.plot` function. In the graph for Moore and Krupat's data in Figure 4.4, we also show the data values themselves, and so this graph provides an alternative visualization of the data to the boxplots in Figure 4.3.

```
> with(Moore, {
+   interaction.plot(fcategory, partner.status, conformity, type="b",
+       pch=c(1, 16), cex=2, ylim=range(conformity), leg.bty="o")
+   points(jitter(as.numeric(fcategory), factor=0.5), conformity,
+       pch=ifelse(partner.status == "low", "L", "H"))
+   })
```

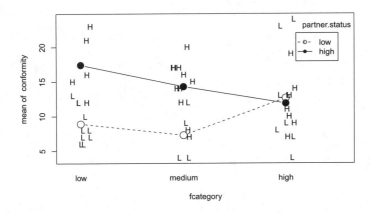

Figure 4.4 Conformity by authoritarianism and partner's status, for Moore and Krupat's data.

Here is a brief explanation of the commands used to construct this graph:[12]

- The `interaction.plot` command creates the basic graph, with the means for low partner's status given by empty circles, `pch=1` (where the argument `pch` specifies the plotting character to be used), and those for high partner's status given by filled circles, `pch=16`. Setting `ylim=range(conformity)` leaves room in the graph for the data. Setting `leg.bty="o"` puts a box around the legend.
- The `points` function adds the data points to the graph, using `"L"` and `"H"` for low- and high-status partners, respectively; `jitter` adds a small random quantity to the horizontal coordinates of the points, to avoid overplotting.

Two points in the upper right of Figure 4.3, in the low-status, high-authoritarianism group, have conformity scores that are much higher than those of the other six members of their group; we could use the `identify` function to find their case numbers. These points were not identified as outliers in the boxplot of the data, but they jointly increase both the mean and the standard deviation of conformity in their group.

4.3 Working With Coefficients

For an `lm` object, and indeed for most fitted models computed in R, additional functions are used to extract useful information from the model object. We describe a few of these functions that are useful for working with coefficient estimates.

---

[12]See `?interaction.plot`, `?points`, and `?jitter` for more information on each of the functions used in this example. The construction of graphs in R is described in detail in Chapter 7.

4.3.1 CONFIDENCE INTERVALS

The confint function returns the confidence intervals for coefficient estimates; for example:

```
> confint(prestige.mod.1)

                 2.5 %    97.5 %
(Intercept)  -108.4929  -53.911
education       2.0769    4.492
log2(income)    4.9063    9.632
typewc         -6.1616    3.283
typeprof       -0.4347   13.937
```

For a linear model such as prestige.mod.1, these are Wald confidence intervals, of the familiar form of estimate plus or minus a multiplier from the t distribution times the standard error of the coefficient, where the multiplier depends on the confidence level and on the residual degrees of freedom. The default level is 95%, but this can be changed to 99%, for example, by adding the argument level=0.99 to the confint command. The confint function can be used with many types of regression models in R, including the GLMs discussed in the next chapter.

4.3.2 ESTIMATED COEFFICIENTS

The coef function returns the coefficient estimates:

```
> coef(prestige.mod.1)

(Intercept)     education log2(income)       typewc      typeprof
    -81.202         3.284        7.269       -1.439         6.751
```

We can use the cbind function to show the coefficient estimates and confidence limits simultaneously:

```
> cbind(Estimate=coef(prestige.mod.1), confint(prestige.mod.1))

              Estimate     2.5 %    97.5 %
(Intercept)    -81.202  -108.4929  -53.911
education        3.284     2.0769    4.492
log2(income)     7.269     4.9063    9.632
typewc          -1.439    -6.1616    3.283
typeprof         6.751    -0.4347   13.937
```

4.3.3 EFFECT DISPLAYS FOR LINEAR MODELS

In models with no interactions or transformations, coefficient estimates can provide a good summary of the dependence of a response on predictors. Transformation and interactions can make parameters much more difficult to interpret. Moreover, certain kinds of models, such as those using regression splines (introduced later in this section), are essentially impossible to understand directly from the coefficient estimates.

Effect displays (Fox, 1987, 2003) are tables or, more commonly, graphs of fitted values computed from an estimated model that allow us to see how the expected response changes with the predictors in the model. Effect displays are an alternative to interpreting linear models directly from the estimated coefficients, which is often a difficult task when the structure of the model is complicated.

We typically use the following strategy to construct effect displays: Identify the *high-order terms* in the model—that is, terms that are not marginal to others. For example, in a model of the form y ~ x*a + x*b, which includes the terms 1 for the regression constant, x, a, b, x:a, and x:b, the high-order terms are the interactions x:a and x:b. You can imagine for this example that x is a numeric predictor and a and b are factors, but the essential idea is more general.

To form an effect display, we allow the predictors in a high-level term to range over the combinations of their values, while the other regressors in the model are held to typical values. The default for the effect function in the **effects** package is to replace each regressor by its mean in the data, which is equivalent to setting each numerical predictor to its mean and each transformed predictor to the mean of its transformed values. For factors, this choice of a typical value averages each of the contrasts that represent the factor, which in a linear model is equivalent to setting the proportional distribution of the factor to the distribution observed in the data; this approach gives the same results regardless of the contrasts used to represent the factor. We proceed to compute the fitted value of the response for each such combination of regressor values. Because effect displays are collections of fitted values, it is straightforward to estimate the standard errors of the effects.

The effect function can produce numeric and graphical effect displays for many kinds of models, including linear models. For example, we have seen (p. 164) how the effect function can be used to calculate adjusted means for a factor in an analysis of covariance. Applied to a one-way ANOVA model, effect recovers the group means. We illustrate with the one-way ANOVA fit to Baumann and Jones's data on methods of teaching reading (described in Section 4.2.3), producing Figure 4.5:

```
> plot(effect("group", baum.mod.1))
```

The first argument to effect is the quoted name of the effect that we wish to compute, here "group"; the second argument is the fitted model object, baum.mod.1. The effect function returns an effect object, for which the plot function has a suitable method. It is also possible to print or summarize effect objects to produce tables of effects, as we have seen in the case of adjusted means (p. 164). The broken lines in the effect plot show 95% confidence intervals around the means, computed using the estimated error variance from the fitted model—that is, assuming equal within-group variances. Because the numbers of subjects in the three levels of group are equal, the confidence intervals are all the same size.

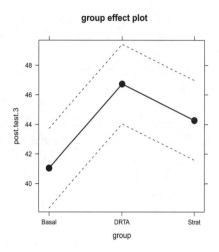

Figure 4.5   The effect display for the one-way ANOVA model fit to the `Baumann` data set simply recovers the group means. The broken lines give 95% confidence intervals around the means.

The `effect` function applied to a simple-regression model calculates the least-squares regression line. For a multiple linear regression, we can use the `allEffects` function to compute the effect of each predictor, setting the others to average values. To illustrate, we produce effect plots for the three predictors in the regression model fit to the `Prestige` data in Section 4.2.2 (Figure 4.6):

```
> plot(allEffects(prestige.mod, default.levels=50), ask=FALSE)
```

The argument `ask=FALSE` causes the `plot` function to show the graphs for all three predictors in the same display, while the argument `default-.levels=50` asks the `effect` function, which is called by `allEffects`, to evaluate the effects at 50 evenly spaced values across the range of each numeric predictor, rather than the default 10, producing a smoother fitted curve for `income`. The broken lines in the panels of the display represent pointwise 95% confidence intervals around the fits. The rug-plot at the bottom of each panel represents the marginal distribution of the corresponding predictor.

The graphs in Figure 4.6 are for the predictors in the model, not for the corresponding regressors. The second plot, therefore, has the predictor `income` rather than `log2(income)` on the horizontal axis, displaying a fitted curve in the original income scale rather than a straight line in the transformed scale. Both `income` and `education` influence `prestige` considerably, as is clear from the wide ranges of the vertical scales of the effect plots, and the small pointwise confidence envelopes around the fitted lines reflect the relative precision of estimation of these effects. The response `prestige`, on the other hand, is not strongly related to `women`, as is similarly clear from the

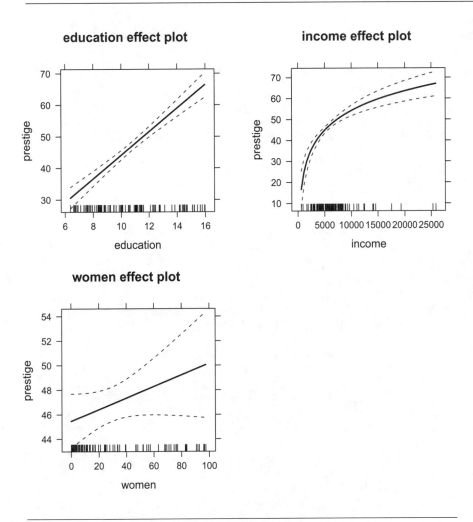

Figure 4.6 Effect displays for the predictors in the multiple linear regression of `prestige` on `education`, log `income`, and `women`.

vertical axis of the effect display; the pointwise confidence envelope around the fitted line for women is wide compared to the slope of the line, and indeed, a horizontal line would fit inside the confidence band, reflecting the fact that the coefficient for women may not differ from 0.

In a two-way ANOVA model with interactions, the effect display for the interaction term recovers the cell means. For an additive model, however, we obtain adjusted means for each factor. We use the additive model fit to Moore and Krupat's conformity data in Section 4.2.3 to illustrate, producing Figure 4.7:

```
> plot(allEffects(mod.moore.2), ask=FALSE)
```

By plotting the absent `fcategory-by-partner.status` interaction, we can combine the main effects, which are marginal to the interaction, producing fitted cell means under the additive model (Figure 4.8):

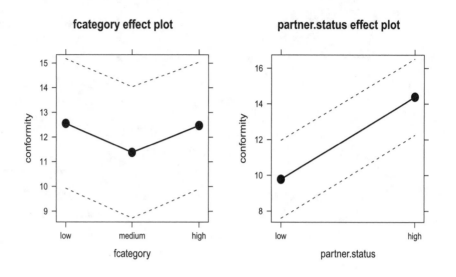

Figure 4.7 Effect displays for the factors `fcategory` and `partner.status` in the additive model fit to the `Moore` data.

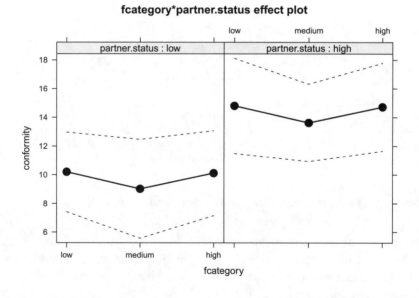

Figure 4.8 Effect plot for `fcategory:partner.status` in the additive model fit to the `Moore` data.

```
> plot(effect("fcategory:partner.status", mod.moore.2))

Warning message:
In analyze.model(term, mod, xlevels, default.levels) :
  fcategory:partner.status does not appear in the model
```

The profiles of the means at the two levels of `partner.status` are parallel, reflecting the additivity of the two predictors in the model. The `effect`

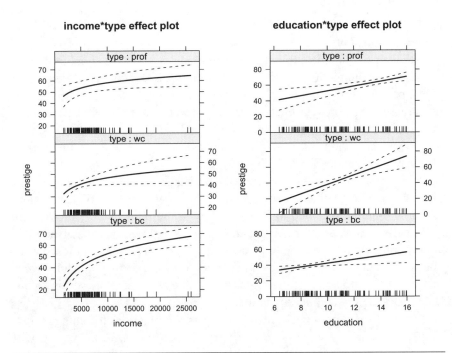

Figure 4.9 Effect displays for the interactions between education and type and between income and type for the Prestige data.

function reports a warning because the fcategory:partner.status interaction is not in the model.

Consider the more complex model fit to the Prestige data in Section 4.2.3, with the numeric predictors log2(income) and education and the factor type of occupation, in which there are interactions between income and type and between education and type. Here, the high-order terms are the two sets of interactions (see Figure 4.9):

```
> plot(allEffects(prestige.mod.2, default.levels=50), ask=FALSE,
+       layout=c(1, 3))
```

The effect display for the income-by-type interaction, for example, which appears at the left of Figure 4.9, is computed at the average level of education. The **lattice**-graphics layout argument is used to arrange the panels in each effect display into one column and three rows.[13]

REGRESSION SPLINES

Displaying fitted models graphically is especially important when the coefficients of the model don't have straightforward interpretations. This issue arises in models with complex interactions, for example, as it does in models

---

[13]The layout argument reverses the usual convention for the order of rows and columns. There is more information about **lattice** graphics in Section 7.3.1.

with polynomial regressors. The problem is even more acute in models that use regression splines.

Although polynomials may be used to model a variety of nonlinear relationships, polynomial regression is highly nonlocal: Data in one region of the predictor space can strongly influence the fit in remote regions, preventing the fitted regression from flexibly tracing trends through the data. One solution to this problem is nonparametric regression, which doesn't make strong assumptions about how the mean of y changes with the xs.[14] Another solution is to use *regression splines*.

Regression splines are piecewise polynomials fit to nonoverlapping regions dissecting the range of a numeric predictor. The polynomials—typically cubic functions—are constrained to join smoothly at the points where the regions meet, called *knots*, and further constraints may be placed on the polynomials at the boundaries of the data. Regression splines often closely reproduce what one would obtain from a nonparametric regression, but they are fully parametric. The coefficients of the regression-spline regressors, however, do not have easily understood interpretations.

The standard **splines** package in R provides two functions for fitting regression splines, bs, for so-called *B-splines*, and ns for *natural splines*. We will illustrate the use of regression splines with data from the 1994 Canadian Survey of Labour and Income Dynamics (the SLID) for the province of Ontario; the data are in the data frame SLID in the **car** package:

```
> some(SLID)

      wages education age     sex language
1235  17.46       9.0  45    Male  English
2412     NA      13.0  72  Female  English
3388     NA       8.0  35  Female  English
3778     NA      13.0  34  Female  English
5353  12.11       8.0  62    Male  English
5398  14.00      12.5  36  Female  English
5649  18.43      12.0  32    Male  English
6502  18.76      18.0  31  Female  English
6577   6.75      12.0  18    Male  English
7340   8.40      12.0  24  Female  English

> nrow(SLID)

[1] 7425
```

The missing values for wages primarily represent respondents to the survey who have no earnings. We perform a regression of the log of individuals' composite hourly wages on their years of education, age, and sex, restricting our attention to those between age 18 and 65 with at least 6 years of education. The numeric predictors education and age are modeled using natural splines with 6 *df* each. Natural splines with 6 *df* have four knots, dividing each predictor into five regions.

---

[14]Nonparametric regression in R is described in the online appendix to the text.

```
> library(splines)
> mod.slid.1 <- lm(log(wages) ~ sex + ns(education, df=6) +
+      ns(age, df=6), data=SLID,
+      subset = age >= 18 & age <= 65 & education >= 6)
> Anova(mod.slid.1)

Anova Table (Type II tests)

Response: log(wages)
                     Sum Sq   Df F value Pr(>F)
sex                      50    1     322 <2e-16
ns(education, df = 6)    79    6      85 <2e-16
ns(age, df = 6)         210    6     225 <2e-16
Residuals               598 3840

> summary(mod.slid.1)

Call:
lm(formula = log(wages) ~ sex + ns(education, df = 6) +
    ns(age, df = 6), data = SLID, subset = age >= 18 &
    age <= 65 & education >= 6)

Residuals:
    Min      1Q  Median      3Q     Max
-2.0507 -0.2350  0.0234  0.2585  1.8061

Coefficients:
                        Estimate Std. Error t value Pr(>|t|)
(Intercept)               1.8423     0.5159    3.57  0.00036
sexMale                   0.2294     0.0128   17.95  < 2e-16
ns(education, df = 6)1   -0.1324     0.4995   -0.27  0.79090
ns(education, df = 6)2   -0.1182     0.5226   -0.23  0.82115
ns(education, df = 6)3   -0.0682     0.5120   -0.13  0.89397
ns(education, df = 6)4    0.3598     0.3070    1.17  0.24136
ns(education, df = 6)5   -0.1314     1.0577   -0.12  0.90110
ns(education, df = 6)6    0.4952     0.1907    2.60  0.00945
ns(age, df = 6)1          0.8678     0.0392   22.15  < 2e-16
ns(age, df = 6)2          0.8359     0.0570   14.66  < 2e-16
ns(age, df = 6)3          1.0122     0.0605   16.74  < 2e-16
ns(age, df = 6)4          0.4233     0.1926    2.20  0.02803
ns(age, df = 6)5          1.7893     1.2562    1.42  0.15440
ns(age, df = 6)6          1.7288     2.2712    0.76  0.44660

Residual standard error: 0.394 on 3840 degrees of freedom
  (2121 observations deleted due to missingness)
Multiple R-squared: 0.367,       Adjusted R-squared: 0.364
F-statistic:  171 on 13 and 3840 DF,  p-value: <2e-16
```

It is unsurprising in a sample this large that all the terms in the model are highly statistically significant; the model as a whole accounts for a respectable 37% of the variation in log(wages).[15]

There are two obstacles to interpreting the coefficients in the model summary: (1) the response variable is expressed on the log scale and (2) the B-spline regressors do not have a simple description. Instead, we construct effect plots for the terms in the model (shown in Figure 4.10):

---

[15]The interactions between sex and education and between sex and age are also statistically significant but relatively small, increasing the R^2 for the model by only about 1%. The general use of the Anova function for testing linear models is described in Section 4.4.4.

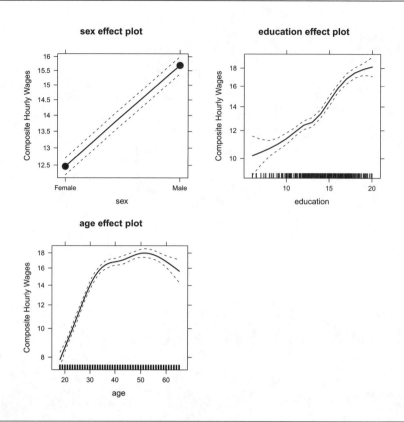

Figure 4.10 Effect displays for the predictors in the `SLID` regression of `log(wages)` on `sex`, `education`, and `age`, using 6-*df* B-splines for education and age.

```
> plot(allEffects(mod.slid.1,
+         xlevels=list(age=18:65, education=6:20),
+         given.values=c(sexMale=0.5),
+         transformation=list(link=log, inverse=exp)),
+     ylab="Composite Hourly Wages", ask=FALSE)

Warning messages:
1: In effect.lm(c("sex", "ns(education,df=6)",  :
   There is a discrepancy of 1.888 percent
      in the 'safe' predictions used to generate effect sex
. . .
```

The `xlevels` argument to `allEffects` sets the values of the predictors at which effects are computed; the default is to use 10 evenly spaced values across the range of each predictor. The `given.values` argument fixes the `sex` dummy regressor to `0.5`, representing a group composed equally of males and females; the default is to use the mean of the dummy regressor, which is the proportion of males in the data. The `transformation` argument serves to relabel the vertical axis on the dollar rather than log-dollar scale. Finally, the `ylab` argument to the `plot` function provides a title for the vertical axis. The `effect` function, called by `allEffects` for each term in the model, reports warnings about the computations. Regressors such as natural splines and orthogonal polynomials have bases that depend on the data. In cases like this, there can be "slippage" in computing the effects, as reflected in the warnings.

The effect plots in Figure 4.10 suggest that the partial relationship between `log(wages)` and `age` is nearly quadratic, while the relationship between `log(wages)` and `education` is not far from linear. We therefore fit an alternative model to the data:

```
> mod.slid.2 <- lm(log(wages) ~ sex + education
+          + poly(age, 2), data=SLID,
+       subset = age >= 18 & age <= 65 & education >= 6)
```

The `poly` function fits a second-degree (i.e., quadratic), orthogonal polynomial for age, in which the linear and quadratic terms are uncorrelated (see Section 4.6.3). The new model is simpler than `mod.slid.1`, using just 1 *df* for `education` and 2 *df*s for `age`; moreover, the R^2 for `slid.mod.2` is just 1% smaller than that for `mod.slid.1`. Effect plots for the terms in `mod.slid.2` are shown in Figure 4.11:

```
> plot(allEffects(mod.slid.2,
+          xlevels=list(age=18:65, education=6:20),
+          given.values=c(sexMale=0.5),
+          transformation=list(link=log, inverse=exp)),
+       ylab="Composite Hourly Wages", ask=FALSE)
```

4.3.4 COEFFICIENT STANDARD ERRORS*

The estimated covariance matrix of the coefficient estimates is given by $\hat{\sigma}^2(X'X)^{-1}$, where X is the model matrix, typically including a column of 1s for the regression intercept. The coefficient-covariance matrix is returned by the `vcov` function:

```
> (V <- vcov(prestige.mod.1))
```

	(Intercept)	education	log2(income)	typewc	typeprof
(Intercept)	188.871722	-0.009295	-15.2917	-2.2155	13.2870
education	-0.009295	0.369782	-0.2509	-1.0049	-1.8834
log2(income)	-15.291676	-0.250948	1.4160	0.7829	0.1185
typewc	-2.215465	-1.004851	0.7829	5.6549	6.0249
typeprof	13.286993	-1.883351	0.1185	6.0249	13.0935

The square roots of the diagonal elements of this matrix are the coefficient standard errors:

```
> sqrt(diag(V))
```

(Intercept)	education	log2(income)	typewc	typeprof
13.7431	0.6081	1.1900	2.3780	3.6185

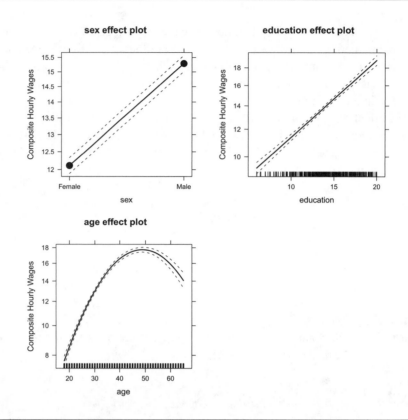

Figure 4.11 Effect displays for the predictors in the `SLID` regression of `log(wages)` on `sex`, `education`, and `age`, using a linear term for `education` and a quadratic for `age`.

The pairwise correlations among the estimated coefficients are given by

```
> round(cov2cor(V), 3)
```

	(Intercept)	education	log2(income)	typewc	typeprof
(Intercept)	1.000	-0.001	-0.935	-0.068	0.267
education	-0.001	1.000	-0.347	-0.695	-0.856
log2(income)	-0.935	-0.347	1.000	0.277	0.028
typewc	-0.068	-0.695	0.277	1.000	0.700
typeprof	0.267	-0.856	0.028	0.700	1.000

The large negative correlation between the coefficient for `log2(income)` and the intercept, incidentally, is not a cause for alarm but simply reflects the fact that the values of `log2(income)` are far from 0.

The `summary` function applied to a regression object returns, among other things, a *coefficient matrix*, containing estimates, standard errors, t values, and p values. We can extract this matrix from the model summary for use in further computations:

```
> (coefmat <- summary(prestige.mod.1)$coef)

            Estimate Std. Error t value  Pr(>|t|)
(Intercept)  -81.202    13.7431 -5.9086 5.627e-08
```

```
education      3.284    0.6081  5.4013 5.058e-07
log2(income)   7.269    1.1900  6.1089 2.312e-08
typewc        -1.439    2.3780 -0.6053 5.465e-01
typeprof       6.751    3.6185  1.8657 6.524e-02
```

For example, `coefmat[ , 2]` is the vector of standard errors.

4.3.5 STANDARDIZED REGRESSION COEFFICIENTS

Standardized regression coefficients are obtained when the predictors and the response are standardized to have sample means of 0 and SDs of 1. As long as the model includes no factors, standardized coefficients can be obtained using the `scale` function to standardize the variables in the regression; for example:

```
> Prestige.1 <- with(Prestige, data.frame(
+    prestige=prestige, log2income=log2(income), education=education,
+    women=women))
> Prestige.scaled <- data.frame(scale(Prestige.1))
> head(Prestige.scaled)

  prestige log2income education  women
1   1.2768     1.2866    0.8693 -0.5617
2   1.2942     2.5373    0.5578 -0.7867
3   0.9629     0.8017    0.7447 -0.4186
4   0.5793     0.7259    0.2499 -0.6263
5   1.5500     0.6354    1.4228 -0.5453
6   1.7883     1.0954    1.7966 -0.7517

> summary(lm(prestige ~ log2income + education + women,
+     data=Prestige.scaled))

Call:
lm(formula = prestige ~ log2income + education + women,
    data = Prestige.scaled)

Residuals:
     Min       1Q   Median       3Q      Max
-1.00927 -0.25745 -0.00587  0.25087  1.11479

Coefficients:
             Estimate Std. Error t value Pr(>|t|)
(Intercept) -4.55e-17   4.08e-02 -1.1e-15     1.00
log2income   4.62e-01   6.58e-02    7.02  2.9e-10
education    5.92e-01   5.62e-02   10.53  < 2e-16
women        8.65e-02   5.51e-02    1.57     0.12

Residual standard error: 0.412 on 98 degrees of freedom
Multiple R-squared: 0.835,      Adjusted R-squared: 0.83
F-statistic:  165 on 3 and 98 DF,  p-value: <2e-16
```

The code required to standardize the data is convoluted because we want to scale the regressors, not the original predictors. We first create a new data frame with the logged `income` variable. If no transformations are required, this step can be skipped. The `scale` function then linearly transforms each of the variables in its argument to have a mean of 0 and an SD of 1, but it also converts the data frame into a matrix. Finally, we use the `data.frame` function to turn the matrix back into a data frame.

When the predictors and response are standardized, the intercept is always within rounding error of 0. Scale-invariant statistics such as t values, F tests, and R^2 are the same as for the unscaled variables. All that changes is the interpretation of the regression coefficients. For example, the expected change in `prestige` in SD units for a 1-SD change in `education`, holding `income` and `women` constant, is 0.63. Using standardized predictors apparently permits comparing regression coefficients for different predictors, but this is an interpretation that we believe does not stand up to close scrutiny. Also, you should be careful *not* to standardize dummy regressors and interaction regressors.

4.3.6   SANDWICH ESTIMATES OF COEFFICIENT STANDARD ERRORS*

When the assumption of constant error variance σ^2 is violated, OLS estimates of coefficients remain consistent and unbiased, as long as the mean function in the regression model is correctly specified, but coefficient standard errors, and hence test statistics, can be seriously biased. One approach to this problem is to replace the usual coefficient standard errors with standard errors that are consistent even when the error variance isn't constant.

If we let ε be the vector of regression errors, then the usual assumption for OLS is that $\mathrm{Var}(\varepsilon) = \sigma^2 \mathbf{I}_n$, where $\mathbf{I}_n$ is the order-n identity matrix. Suppose that we use the OLS estimator but that $\mathrm{Var}(\varepsilon) = \boldsymbol{\Sigma}$ for some matrix $\boldsymbol{\Sigma}$. If $\mathbf{b}$ is the OLS estimator, then one can show that

$$\mathrm{Var}(\mathbf{b}) = (\mathbf{X}'\mathbf{X})^{-1}\mathbf{X}'\boldsymbol{\Sigma}\mathbf{X}(\mathbf{X}'\mathbf{X})^{-1} \tag{4.3}$$

When $\boldsymbol{\Sigma} = \sigma^2 \mathbf{I}_n$, this equation reduces to the usual result,

$$\mathrm{Var}(\mathbf{b}) = \sigma^2(\mathbf{X}'\mathbf{X})^{-1}$$

but in general it is different. Equation 4.3 is not computable as it stands because it depends on $\boldsymbol{\Sigma}$, which is unspecified. The idea then is to estimate $\boldsymbol{\Sigma}$ by some function of the residuals e_i from the OLS fit and to use the estimate to compute standard errors. The resulting coefficient covariance matrix is called a *sandwich estimator*, with the two outer identical terms in Equation 4.3 representing the "bread" and the inner term the "contents" of the sandwich.

In the context of nonconstant error variance, where $\boldsymbol{\Sigma}$ is a diagonal matrix, reflecting uncorrelated but possibly heteroscedastic errors, White (1980) proposed the diagonal matrix $\mathrm{diag}(e_i^2)$ for the center of the sandwich. Work by

Long and Ervin (2000) suggests that it is advantageous to use a slightly modified version of the White sandwich estimator, which they term HC3, based on $\text{diag}[e_i^2/(1 - h_i^2)]$; here h_i is the ith diagonal entry of the *hat-matrix* $\mathbf{X}(\mathbf{X}'\mathbf{X})^{-1}\mathbf{X}'$ (see Section 6.3.2).

To develop an example, we will use the `Transact` data set from the **car** package:

```
> some(Transact)

     t1   t2  time
43  525 4658 13404
83   32  623  1548
118 471 3783  9430
130   0 1561  2721
185 712 3075 10587
189 278 1626  4618
198 280 2103  5974
228 640 2534 10083
229 856 4525 13961
250 331 3143  8537

> nrow(Transact)

[1] 261
```

This data set has two predictors, `t1` and `t2`, the number of transactions of two types performed by the branches of a large bank, to account for the response variable, `time`, the total minutes of labor in the bank.

For brevity, we skip the crucial step of drawing graphs of the data and begin by regressing `time` on `t1` and `t2`:

```
> summary(trans.mod <- lm(time ~ t1 + t2, data=Transact))

Call:
lm(formula = time ~ t1 + t2, data = Transact)

Residuals:
     Min       1Q   Median       3Q      Max
-4652.38  -601.30     2.41   455.71  5607.37

Coefficients:
            Estimate Std. Error t value Pr(>|t|)
(Intercept) 144.3694   170.5441    0.85      0.4
t1            5.4621     0.4333   12.61   <2e-16
t2            2.0345     0.0943   21.57   <2e-16

Residual standard error: 1140 on 258 degrees of freedom
Multiple R-squared: 0.909,        Adjusted R-squared: 0.908
F-statistic: 1.29e+03 on 2 and 258 DF,  p-value: <2e-16
```

Each of the regression coefficients in this model has a straightforward interpretation: The intercept of 144 minutes is the fixed number of minutes that a branch requires for nontransaction business, and the slopes are the number of minutes for transactions of each type, about 5.5 minutes per Type 1 transaction and 2.0 minutes per Type 2 transaction. Cunningham and Heath-cote (1989) suggest, however, that the errors for these data are unlikely to be close to normally distributed with constant variance. Consequently, the usual asymptotic theory used to compute standard errors and tests may not apply, and the usual estimated covariance matrix of the coefficient estimates,

```
> vcov(trans.mod)

              (Intercept)         t1          t2
(Intercept)      29085.29   23.58169   -12.68329
t1                  23.58    0.18772    -0.03154
t2                 -12.68   -0.03154     0.00890
```

is likely to be incorrect; the diagonal elements in particular, which are the estimated variances of the parameter estimates, are probably too small.

The function hccm in the **car** package computes a sandwich estimate of the coefficient covariance matrix, assuming that Σ is a diagonal matrix and by default employing the HC3 modification to White's estimator:[16]

```
> hccm(trans.mod)

              (Intercept)         t1          t2
(Intercept)      41273.51   98.3536   -30.21684
t1                  98.35    0.5312    -0.10556
t2                 -30.22   -0.1056     0.02672
```

In our example, the sandwich estimate of the coefficient covariance matrix has substantially larger diagonal entries than the usual estimate.

Approximate Wald t tests for the coefficients can be obtained using the coeftest function in the **lmtest** package:

```
> library(lmtest)
> coeftest(trans.mod, vcov=hccm)

t test of coefficients:

              Estimate Std. Error t value Pr(>|t|)
(Intercept)  144.369     203.159    0.71     0.48
t1             5.462       0.729    7.49   1.1e-12
t2             2.035       0.163   12.45   < 2e-16
```

The values of the t statistics are reduced by about 40% for the slopes and 15% for the intercept compared to the t values based on the constant variance assumption. The sandwich estimate of the coefficient covariance matrix can be used with functions in the **car** package including deltaMethod (described in Section 4.4.6), linearHypothesis (Section 4.4.5), and Anova (Section 4.4.4).

---

[16]hccm is an acronym for *heteroscedasticity-corrected covariance matrix*.

4.3.7   BOOTSTRAPPING REGRESSION MODELS

R is well suited for the bootstrap and other computationally intensive statistics. The **boot** package, associated with Davison and Hinkley (1997), and the **bootstrap** package, associated with Efron and Tibshirani (1993), provide comprehensive facilities in R for bootstrapping.[17] Several other R packages are available for using the bootstrap in specialized situations. In this section, we use the simpler bootCase function in the **car** package, which implements case resampling.

The bootstrap provides a computational method for obtaining standard errors for the Transact data introduced in the previous section. The essential idea of the case-resampling bootstrap is simple:

1. Refit the regression with modified data, obtained by *sampling from the rows of the original data with replacement*. As a consequence, some of the rows in the data will be sampled several times and some not at all. Compute and save summary statistics of interest from this bootstrap sample.

2. Repeat Step 1 a large number of times, say $B = 999$.

The bootCase function does the work for us:[18]

```
> set.seed(3435) # for reproducibility
> betahat.boot <- bootCase(trans.mod, B=999)
```

The bootCase function takes up to three arguments. In the example above, we used two of them, the linear-model object, trans.mod, and the number of bootstrap replications, B=999. The third argument, called f, is a function to be evaluated on each bootstrap sample. The default is the standard R coef function, which returns the coefficient estimates; because we did not specify a value for f, the default is used. The coefficient estimates are saved for each bootstrap replication.

The result returned by bootCase, which we assigned to betahat-.boot, is a matrix with $B = 999$ rows. The number of columns in the result depends on the argument f, and for the default of the coefficient vector, the result therefore has one column for each regression coefficient, including the intercept.

We can use common R tools to summarize the bootstrap estimates:

```
> usualEsts <- summary(trans.mod)$coef[ , 1:2]
> bootSD <- apply(betahat.boot, 2, sd) # bootstrap standard errors
> bootEst <- colMeans(betahat.boot)
> bootBias <- (bootEst - usualEsts[ , 1])/usualEsts[ , 2]
> bootCI <- apply(betahat.boot, 2,
+    function(x) quantile(x, c(.025,.975)))
> print(cbind(usualEsts, bootSD, bootEst, bootBias, t(bootCI)),
+    digits=3)
```

---

[17]The use of the **boot** package is described in the online appendix to the text.

[18]The bootCase function can be used with most regression models in R, but it may not be appropriate in all instances; see ?bootCase.

	Estimate	Std. Error	bootSD	bootEst	bootBias	2.5%	97.5%
(Intercept)	144.37	170.5441	195.212	152.38	0.0470	-223.09	548.37
t1	5.46	0.4333	0.702	5.48	0.0358	4.06	6.80
t2	2.03	0.0943	0.157	2.03	-0.0687	1.73	2.33

We began by using the `summary` function to extract the large-sample-theory estimates and standard errors from the linear-model object `trans.mod`; the coefficients and standard errors are located in the first two columns of the coefficient matrix returned by `summary`. The names of the coefficients are the row names of the coefficient matrix, and so the output will be appropriately labeled. The column labeled `bootSD` is the bootstrap estimate of the standard error, simply the SD of the bootstap estimates, while `bootEst` is the average of the bootstrap estimates. The column labeled `bootBias`, the bootstrap estimate of bias in the least-squares estimate, is the difference between the usual estimate and the average of the bootstrap estimates, scaled by the standard error. Finally, we computed a simple, quantile-based 95% confidence interval for the coefficients based on the bootstrap replications.[19] We could also have looked at histograms, scatterplots, or other summaries of the bootstrap estimates.

The bootstrap estimates of bias in the least-squares estimates are relatively small—just small fractions of the standard errors. This result is expected because the unbias of the OLS estimates doesn't depend on the assumptions of normality and constant variance. The usual estimates of the coefficient standard errors, however, are uniformly too small relative to the bootstrap standard errors, although the bootstrap estimates are very similar to the sandwich estimates (obtained in Section 4.3.6). Confidence intervals based on the bootstrap will likely be more appropriate for statistical inference than the usual intervals.

4.3.8   CONFIDENCE ELLIPSES AND DATA ELLIPSES*

The `confint` function computes a *marginal* confidence interval for each regression coefficient. In this section, we discuss computing *simultaneous* confidence regions for regression coefficients. We will concentrate on confidence regions for two coefficients at a time so that we can draw pictures, and will work with Duncan's occupational-prestige data (introduced in Chapter 1), treating `prestige` as the response and `income` and `education` as predictors:

```
> duncan.mod <- lm(prestige ~ income + education, data=Duncan)
> (ci <- confint(duncan.mod))

            2.5 % 97.5 %
(Intercept) -14.6858 2.5565
income       0.3572 0.8402
education    0.3476 0.7441
```

---

[19]More complicated rules for computing bootstrap confidence intervals that are somewhat better behaved in practice are discussed in the online appendix to the text.

Generalization of these intervals to more than one dimension, assuming normality, produces *joint confidence regions*, called *confidence ellipses* in two dimensions and *confidence ellipsoids* in more than two dimensions.

The `confidenceEllipse` function in the **car** package can be used to draw a confidence ellipse for the coefficients of the two predictors in Duncan's regression, as shown in Figure 4.12a:

```
> confidenceEllipse(duncan.mod, levels=c(0.85, 0.95))
> for (j in 1:2) abline(v=ci[2, j], lty=2) # CI for education
> for (j in 1:2) abline(h=ci[3, j], lty=2) # CI for income
```

The outer ellipse in this graph is a 95% joint confidence region for the population regression coefficients β_1 and β_2: With repeated sampling, 95% of such ellipses will simultaneously include β_1 and β_2, if the fitted model is correct and normality holds. The orientation of the ellipse reflects the negative correlation between the estimates. Contrast the 95% confidence ellipse with the marginal 95% confidence intervals, also shown on the plot. Some points within the marginal intervals—with larger values for both of the coefficients, for example—are implausible according to the joint region. Similarly, the joint region includes values of the coefficient for `income`, for example, that are excluded from the marginal interval. The inner ellipse, generated with a confidence level of 85% and termed the *confidence-interval-generating ellipse*, has perpendicular shadows on the parameter axes that correspond to the marginal 95% confidence intervals for the coefficients.

In addition to confidence ellipses for estimates, we can also plot *data ellipses*. When variables have a multivariate-normal distribution, data ellipses and ellipsoids represent estimated probability contours, containing expected fractions of the data. The `dataEllipse` function in the **car** package draws data ellipses for a pair of variables. We illustrate with `income` and `education` in Duncan's occupational-prestige data:

```
> with(Duncan, {
+       dataEllipse(income, education, levels=c(0.5, 0.75, 0.9, 0.95))
+       identify(income, education, rownames(Duncan))
+       })
```

The result can be seen in Figure 4.12b. The contours are set to enclose 50%, 75%, 90%, and 95% of bivariate-normal data. Three observations identified with the mouse—representing ministers, railroad conductors, and railroad engineers—are outside the 95% normal contour. Recall that to exit from the `identify` function in Windows you must right-click and select *Stop*; in Mac OS X, press the esc key.

The 95% ellipses in the two panels of Figure 4.12 differ in shape by only a 90° rotation, because the data ellipse is based on the sample covariance matrix of the predictors, while the confidence ellipse is based on the sample covariance matrix of the slope coefficients, which is proportional to the inverse of the sample covariance matrix of the predictors.

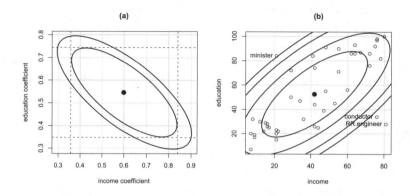

Figure 4.12 (a) 95% (outer) and 85% (inner) joint confidence ellipses for the coefficients of income and education in Duncan's regression of prestige on these predictors, augmented by the marginal 95% confidence intervals (broken lines). (b) 50%, 75%, 90%, and 95% data ellipses for income and education. In (b), three observations were identified interactively with the mouse.

4.4 Testing Hypotheses About Regression Coefficients

Significance levels for standard hypothesis tests about linear-regression models depend on either the normality of the errors or large sample size. Under these circumstances, the test statistics generally have t or F distributions, at least approximately. For example, if $x_1, x_2, \ldots, x_n$ are the values of the predictor in a simple regression, then the large-sample distribution of the t statistic for testing the hypothesis that the slope is 0 will be normally distributed as long as $\max_i [(x_i - \bar{x})^2 / \sum(x_j - \bar{x})^2]$ gets close to 0 as n increases (Huber and Ronchetti, 2009).

4.4.1 WALD TESTS

Wald tests, named for Abraham Wald (1902–1950), are based on a Wald statistic, which is the ratio of an estimate that has a mean of 0 under the null hypothesis to its standard error. The t values in the R regression output and the associated p values are Wald tests that each coefficient is 0 against a two-sided alternative, while the other regression coefficients are left unspecified. We also can easily compute a Wald test that a coefficient has any other specified value. For the Davis data (discussed in Section 4.2.1), for example, we test that the slope is equal to 1:

```
> tval <- (coef(davis.mod.2)[2] - 1)/sqrt(vcov(davis.mod.2)[2, 2])
> pval <- 2*pt(abs(tval), df.residual(davis.mod.2), lower.tail=FALSE)
> c(tval=tval, pval=pval)
```

```
tval.repwt pval.repwt
-3.4280342  0.0007535
```

Here, vcov(davis.mod.2)[2, 2] is the estimated variance of the slope coefficient, extracted from the coefficient covariance matrix, which is returned by the vcov function. The pt function is used to compute a two-tailed p value, by taking the area to the right of $|t|$ and doubling it. Wald tests such as this, as well as tests for several parameters simultaneously, can also be computed conveniently using the linearHypothesis function in the **car** package (see Section 4.4.5).

Wald tests for coefficients in linear models are equivalent to likelihood ratio tests of the same hypotheses (described in the next section), but this is not necessarily true for other kinds of regression models, such as the GLMs described in the next chapter.

4.4.2 LIKELIHOOD RATIO TESTS AND THE ANALYSIS OF VARIANCE

One of the fundamental ideas in hypothesis testing is that of model comparison according to the following paradigm: As with all tests, we compare a null and an alternative hypothesis. The two hypotheses differ only by the terms in the model, with the null-hypothesis model obtainable from the alternative-hypothesis model by setting some of the parameters in the latter to 0 or to other, prespecified values. We have already seen one instance of this approach in the overall F test (p. 153), for which the null model has the mean function $E(y|\mathbf{x}) = \beta_0$ versus the alternative given by $E(y|\mathbf{x}) = \beta_0 + \beta_1 x_1 + \cdots + \beta_k x_k$, testing that all the coefficients with the exception of the intercept β_0 are 0. The null hypothesis is tested by fitting both models and then computing an incremental F statistic.

We use the Prestige data to provide examples. First, we compute the overall F-test statistic:

```
> prestige.mod.1 <- lm(prestige ~ education + log2(income) + type,
+     data=na.omit(Prestige)) # full model
> prestige.mod.0 <- update(prestige.mod.1, . ~ 1) # intercept only
> anova(prestige.mod.0, prestige.mod.1) # compare models

Analysis of Variance Table

Model 1: prestige ~ 1
Model 2: prestige ~ education + log2(income) + type
  Res.Df    RSS Df Sum of Sq    F Pr(>F)
1     97  28347
2     93   4096  4     24251  138 <2e-16
```

The test requires that each model fit to the data uses the same observations. Because the variable type in the Prestige data set has some missing values, we were careful to use na.omit to filter the Prestige data frame for missing data prior to fitting the models, ensuring that both models are fit to the same subset of cases, with complete data on all four variables in the larger model.[20]

The overall F test is based on the difference between the residual sums of squares for the two models, on the difference in degrees of freedom for error, and on the estimate of the error variance σ^2 from the larger model. In this case, F has $(4, 93)$ df. The overall F statistic is also printed in the summary output for a linear model. Here, the p value is essentially 0, and so the null hypothesis is emphatically rejected.

We can use this method for any comparison of nested models, where one model is a specialization of the other. For example, to test the null hypothesis that only the coefficient for log2(income) is 0 against the same alternative hypothesis as before we enter the following commands:

```
> prestige.mod.0inc <- update(prestige.mod.1, . ~ . - log2(income))
> anova(prestige.mod.0inc, prestige.mod.1) # compare models

Analysis of Variance Table

Model 1: prestige ~ education + type
Model 2: prestige ~ education + log2(income) + type
  Res.Df  RSS Df Sum of Sq    F  Pr(>F)
1     94 5740
2     93 4096  1      1644 37.3 2.3e-08
```

Once again, the null hypothesis is clearly rejected. For a test such as this of a single coefficient, the F statistic is just t^2 from the corresponding Wald test.

The standard anova function is a generic function, with methods for many classes of statistical models.[21] In the next chapter, we will use the anova function to obtain likelihood ratio chi-square tests for GLMs.

4.4.3   SEQUENTIAL ANALYSIS OF VARIANCE

As we gave seen, the anova function is useful for comparing two nested models. We can also apply anova to an individual lm object, producing a *sequential ANOVA table*:

```
> anova(prestige.mod.1)

Analysis of Variance Table

Response: prestige
              Df Sum Sq Mean Sq F value  Pr(>F)
education      1  21282   21282  483.19 < 2e-16
log2(income)   1   2499    2499   56.74 3.2e-11
type           2    469     235    5.32  0.0065
Residuals     93   4096      44
```

Sequential analysis of variance (abbreviated *ANOVA*) is sometimes known by the less descriptive name *SAS Type I ANOVA*, or just *Type I ANOVA*. The

---

[20]See Section 2.2.3 on handling missing data in R.

[21]Generic functions and their methods are discussed in Sections 1.4 and 8.7.

table shows three tests, produced by fitting a sequence of models to the data; these tests are for (1) education *ignoring* log2(income) and type; (2) log2(income) *after* education but *ignoring* type; and (3) type *after* education and log2(income). The successive lines in the table show tests for comparing the following models, as specified by their formulas:

```
prestige ~ 1 versus prestige ~ education
prestige ~ education versus prestige ~ education + log2(income)
prestige ~ education + log2(income) versus
                prestige ~ education + log2(income) + type
```

The first two of these hypothesis tests are generally not of interest, because the test for education fails to control for log2(income) and type, while the test for log2(income) fails to control for type. The third test *does* correspond to a sensible hypothesis, for equality of intercepts of the three levels of type—that is, no effect of type controlling for education and log2(income).

A more subtle difference between the sequential tests produced by the anova function applied to a single model and the incremental F test produced when anova is applied to a pair of nested models has to do with the manner in which the error variance σ^2 in the denominator of the F statistics is estimated: When we apply anova to a pair of nested models, the error variance is estimated from the residual sum of squares and degrees of freedom for the larger of the two models, which corresponds to the alternative hypothesis. In contrast, *all* the F statistics in the sequential table produced when anova is applied to a single model are based on the estimated error variance from the full model—prestige ~ education + log2(income) + type in our example—which is the largest model in the sequence. Although this model includes terms that are extraneous to (i.e., excluded from the alternative hypothesis for) all but the last test in the sequence, it still provides an unbiased estimate of the error variance for all the tests. It is traditional in formulating an ANOVA table to base the estimated error variance on the largest model fit to the data.

4.4.4   THE Anova FUNCTION

The Anova function in the **car** package, with an upper case A to distinguish it from anova, addresses hypotheses that are generally of more interest, by default reporting so-called *Type II tests*:

```
> Anova(prestige.mod.1)

Anova Table (Type II tests)

Response: prestige
```

```
              Sum Sq Df F value  Pr(>F)
education       1285  1   29.17 5.1e-07
log2(income)    1644  1   37.32 2.3e-08
type             469  2    5.32  0.0065
Residuals       4096 93
```

The hypotheses tested here compare the following pairs of models:

```
prestige ~ log2(income) + type versus
                   prestige ~ education + log2(income) + type
prestige ~ education + type versus
                   prestige ~ education + log2(income) + type
prestige ~ education + log2(income) versus
                   prestige ~ education + log2(income) + type
```

In each case, we get a test for adding one of the predictors to a model that includes all the others. The last of the three tests is identical to the third test from the sequential ANOVA, but the other two tests are different and are more likely to be sensible. Because the Type II tests for `log2(income)` and `education` are tests of terms that are each represented by a single coefficient, the reported F statistics are equal to the squares of the corresponding t statistics in the model summary.

Tests for models with factors and interactions are generally summarized in an ANOVA table. We recommend using the Type II tests computed by default by the `Anova` function: for example,

```
> prestige.mod.3 <- update(prestige.mod.1,
+        . ~ . + log2(income):type + education:type)
> Anova(prestige.mod.3)

Anova Table (Type II tests)

Response: prestige
                   Sum Sq Df F value  Pr(>F)
education            1209  1   29.44 4.9e-07
log2(income)         1691  1   41.17 6.6e-09
type                  469  2    5.71  0.0046
log2(income):type     290  2    3.53  0.0333
education:type        179  2    2.18  0.1195
Residuals            3655 89
```

Type II ANOVA obeys the *marginality principle* (Nelder, 1977), summarized in Table 4.1 for the example. All the tests compare two models. For example, the test for `log2(income)` compares a smaller model consisting of all terms that do not involve `log2(income)` with a model that includes all this plus `log2(income)`. The general principle is that the test for a *lower-order term*, for example, a *main effect* (i.e., a separate, partial effect), such as `log2(income)`, is never computed after fitting a *higher-order term*, such as an interaction, that *includes* the lower-order term—as `log2(income)`:

Table 4.1 Type II tests performed by the `Anova` function for the model `prestige ~ education*type + log2(income)*type`.

Sum of Squares for	after...	ignoring ...
education	log2(income), type, log2(income):type	education:type
log2(income)	education, type, education:type	log2(income):type
type	education, log2(income)	education:type, log2(income):type
education:type	education, log2(income), type, log2(income):type	
log2(income):type	education, log2(income), type, education:type	

`type` includes `log2(income)`. The error variance for all the tests is estimated from the full model—that is, the largest model fit to the data. As we mentioned in connection with the `anova` function, although it would also be correct to estimate the error variance for each test from the larger model for that test, using the largest model produces an unbiased estimate of σ^2 even when it includes extraneous terms.

If the regressors for different terms in a linear model are mutually orthogonal (i.e., uncorrelated), then Type I and Type II tests are identical. When the regressors are not orthogonal, then Type II tests address more generally sensible hypotheses than Type I tests.

UNBALANCED ANOVA

How to formulate hypotheses, contrasts, and sums of squares in unbalanced two-way and higher-way ANOVA is the subject of a great deal of controversy and confusion. For balanced data, with all cell counts equal, none of these difficulties arise. This is not the place to disentangle the issue, but we will nevertheless make the following brief points:

- The essential goal in ANOVA is to test sensible hypotheses about differences among cell means and averages of cell means. Sums of squares and tests should follow from the hypotheses.
- It is difficult to go wrong if we construct tests that conform to the principle of marginality, always ignoring higher-order relatives—for example, ignoring the A:B interaction when testing the A main effect. This approach produces Type II tests.
- Some people do test lower-order terms *after* their higher-order relatives—for example, the main effect of A after the B main effect *and* the A:B interaction. The main effect of A, in this scheme, represents the effect of A averaged over the levels of B. Whether or not this effect is really of interest is another matter and depends on context. The incremental *F* test for a term after everything else in the model is called a *Type III test*.

The Type I and Type II tests described previously are the same for any choice of contrasts for a factor, and therefore the same hypotheses are tested regardless of the contrasts. This is not so for Type III tests, and the hypotheses tested are complicated functions of the parameters and the counts in each cell of the table. If we choose to perform Type III tests, then we should use `contr.sum`, `contr.helmert`, or `contr.poly` to code the factors (see Section 4.6); in particular, we should not use the default `contr.treatment` with Type III tests.[22]

- These considerations also apply to the analysis of covariance. Imagine a regression model with one factor (A) and one quantitative predictor (or covariate, X). Suppose that we test the hypothesis that the main effect of A is zero in the model including the interactions between A and X. This tests that the intercepts for the different levels of A are the same. If the slopes vary across the levels of A, then the separation among the levels varies with the value of X, and assessing this separation at $X = 0$ is probably not sensible. To justify the use of Type III tests, we could express X as deviations from its mean, making the test for differences in intercepts a test for differences among the levels of A at the average score of X. Proceeding in this manner produces a sensible, but not necessarily interesting, test.

In light of these considerations, we obtain the ANOVA for Moore and Krupat's data (from Section 4.2.3). For Type II tests, we can use the default definitions for factor dummy regressors, implicitly employing `contr.-treatment`:

```
> Anova(moore.mod <- lm(conformity ~ fcategory*partner.status,
+     data=Moore))

Anova Table (Type II tests)

Response: conformity
                          Sum Sq Df F value Pr(>F)
fcategory                     12  2    0.28 0.7596
partner.status               212  1   10.12 0.0029
fcategory:partner.status     175  2    4.18 0.0226
Residuals                    818 39
```

To get sensible Type III tests, we should change the factor coding, which requires refitting the model; one approach is as follows:

```
> contrasts(Moore$fcategory) <-
+       contrasts(Moore$partner.status) <- "contr.sum"
> moore.mod.1 <- update(moore.mod)
> Anova(moore.mod.1, type="III")

Anova Table (Type III tests)
```

---

[22]* The contrasts produced by `contr.sum`, `contr.helmert`, and `contr.poly` for different factors are orthogonal in the row-basis of the model matrix, but those produced by `contr.treatment` are not.

```
Response: conformity
                          Sum Sq Df F value Pr(>F)
(Intercept)                 5753  1  274.36 <2e-16
fcategory                     36  2    0.86 0.4315
partner.status               240  1   11.42 0.0017
fcategory:partner.status     175  2    4.18 0.0226
Residuals                    818 39
```

In this instance, the Type II and Type III tests produce similar results.[23] The reader may wish to verify that repeating the analysis with Helmert contrasts (contr.helmert) gives the same Type III results, while the output using the default contr.treatment is different.

Before proceeding, we return the contrasts for fcategory and partner.status to their default values:

```
> contrasts(Moore$fcategory) <-
+       contrasts(Moore$partner.status) <- NULL
```

4.4.5   TESTING GENERAL LINEAR HYPOTHESES*

The *general linear hypothesis* is an alternative way of formulating model-comparison F tests without refitting the model. A matrix formulation of the linear models considered in this chapter is

$$E(y|X) = X\beta$$

or, equivalently,

$$y = X\beta + \varepsilon$$

where y is an $n \times 1$ vector containing the response; X is an $n \times (k+1)$ model matrix, the first column of which usually contains 1s; β is a $(k+1) \times 1$ parameter vector including the intercept; and ε is an $n \times 1$ vector of errors. Assuming that X is of full column rank, the least squares regression coefficients are

$$b = (X'X)^{-1} X'y$$

All the hypotheses described in this chapter, and others that we have not discussed, can be tested as general linear hypotheses of the form H_0: $L\beta = c$, where L is a $q \times (k+1)$ hypothesis matrix of rank q containing prespecified constants and c is a prespecified $q \times 1$ vector, most often containing 0s. Under H_0, the test statistic

$$F_0 = \frac{(Lb - c)' \left[L(X'X)^{-1} L'\right]^{-1} (Lb - c)}{q\widehat{\sigma}^2}$$

follows an F distribution with q and $n-(k+1)$ df; $\widehat{\sigma}^2$ is the estimated error variance.

Here are two nonstandard examples:

---

[23] The Type III ANOVA table produced by Anova also includes a test that the intercept is 0. This hypothesis is not usually of interest.

EXAMPLE: TRANSACTION DATA

In the transaction data (introduced in Section 4.3.6), there are two regressors, t1 and t2, which count the number of transactions of each of two types in a bank branch. Because the coefficients for these two regressors have the same units, minutes per transaction, we may wish to test that the coefficients for the two regressors are equal. Using the linearHypothesis function in the **car** package:

```
> summary(trans.mod)$coef

              Estimate Std. Error t value  Pr(>|t|)
(Intercept)   144.369  170.54410  0.8465 3.980e-01
t1              5.462    0.43327 12.6066 1.032e-28
t2              2.035    0.09434 21.5669 1.124e-59

> linearHypothesis(trans.mod, c(0, 1, -1))

Linear hypothesis test

Hypothesis:
t1 - t2 = 0

Model 1: restricted model
Model 2: time ~ t1 + t2

  Res.Df       RSS Df Sum of Sq    F   Pr(>F)
1    259 395855965
2    258 336801747  1  59054218 45.2 1.1e-10
```

In this case, the hypothesis matrix consists of a single row, $\mathbf{L} = (0, 1, -1)$, contrasting the t1 and t2 coefficients; and the right-hand-side vector for the hypothesis is implicitly $\mathbf{c} = (0)$. The *p* value for the test is very small, suggesting that the two types of transactions *do not* take the same number of minutes on average. We can also do the test using the sandwich estimator in place of the usual coefficient-variance estimator (Section 4.3.6):

```
> linearHypothesis(trans.mod, c(0, 1, -1), vcov=hccm)

Linear hypothesis test

Hypothesis:
t1 - t2 = 0

Model 1: restricted model
Model 2: time ~ t1 + t2

Note: Coefficient covariance matrix supplied.

  Res.Df Df    F  Pr(>F)
1    259
2    258  1 15.3 0.00012
```

Although the *F* statistic for the test is now much smaller, the hypothesis is still rejected, even without the assumption of constant variance.

EXAMPLE: DAVIS'S REGRESSION OF MEASURED ON REPORTED WEIGHT

In Section 4.2.1, we fit two models to Davis's data: `davis.mod` includes a bad observation, while `davis.mod.2` deletes the bad (12*th*) observation. The estimated coefficients for the two fits can be conveniently compared using the `compareCoefs` function in the **car** package:

```
> compareCoefs(davis.mod, davis.mod.2)

Call:
1:lm(formula = weight ~ repwt, data = Davis)
2:lm(formula = weight ~ repwt, data = Davis, subset = -12)
            Est. 1    SE 1 Est. 2    SE 2
(Intercept) 5.3363 3.0369 2.7338 0.8148
repwt       0.9278 0.0453 0.9584 0.0121
```

If individuals are unbiased reporters of their weight, then the intercept should be 0 and the slope 1; we can test these values simultaneously as a linear hypothesis:

```
> diag(2)   # order-2 identity matrix

     [,1] [,2]
[1,]    1    0
[2,]    0    1

> linearHypothesis(davis.mod, diag(2), c(0, 1))

Linear hypothesis test

Hypothesis:
(Intercept) = 0
repwt = 1

Model 1: restricted model
Model 2: weight ~ repwt

  Res.Df   RSS Df Sum of Sq    F Pr(>F)
1    183 13074
2    181 12828  2       246 1.74   0.18

> linearHypothesis(davis.mod.2, diag(2), c(0, 1))

Linear hypothesis test

Hypothesis:
(Intercept) = 0
repwt = 1

Model 1: restricted model
Model 2: weight ~ repwt

  Res.Df RSS Df Sum of Sq    F Pr(>F)
1    182 974
2    180 914  2      59.7 5.88 0.0034
```

The hypothesis matrix **L** is just an order-two identity matrix, constructed in R by `diag(2)`, while the right-hand-side vector is **c** = (0, 1)′. Even though the regression coefficients are closer to 0 and 1 when Observation 12 is omitted, the hypothesis of unbiased reporting is acceptable for the original data set but not for the corrected data because the estimated error variance is much smaller when the outlying Observation 12 is deleted, producing a more powerful test.

The `linearHypothesis` function also has a more convenient interface for specifying hypotheses using the names of coefficients. Here are alternative but equivalent ways of specifying the hypotheses considered above for the `Duncan` and `Davis` regressions:

```
> linearHypothesis(trans.mod, "t1 = t2")
> linearHypothesis(davis.mod, c("(Intercept) = 0", "repwt = 1"))
```

For a hypothesis such as this one, which includes the intercept, we must write `(Intercept)` (i.e., within parentheses), which is the name of the intercept in the coefficient vector.

4.4.6 NONLINEAR FUNCTIONS OF COEFFICIENTS*

In the second model fit to Davis's data in Section 4.2.1, the fitted line has a positive intercept $b_0 = 2.73$ and estimated slope $b_1 = 0.96$. At some point, this line crosses the unbiased-reporting line with intercept 0 and slope 1; for values of `weight` to the left of the crossing point, we estimate that people over-report their weight; for larger weights, we estimate that they underreport. We can find the crossing point by solving for `weight` in

$$
\begin{aligned}
0 + 1 \times \text{weight} &= b_0 + b_1 \text{weight} \\
\text{weight} &= b_0 / (1 - b_1) \\
&= 2.73 / (1 - 0.96) \\
&= 65.68
\end{aligned}
$$

The crossover weight is a *nonlinear* function of the coefficients, and so standard linear-model methods cannot be used to find the standard error of this quantity. The *delta method*, however, can be used to approximate the standard error. Given an approximately normally distributed estimator **b** of a vector of parameters β with estimated covariance matrix **V**, an estimator of any function $g(\beta)$ is $g(\mathbf{b})$, and its approximate variance is

$$
\text{Var}\left[g\left(\mathbf{b}\right)\right] = \dot{g}\left(\mathbf{b}\right)' \mathbf{V} \dot{g}\left(\mathbf{b}\right) \tag{4.4}
$$

where $\dot{g}(\mathbf{b})$ is the vector of partial derivatives of $g(\beta)$ with respect to the elements of β, evaluated at the estimates **b**. A function for this computation is available in the **car** package:

```
> deltaMethod(davis.mod.2, "(Intercept)/(1 - repwt)")

                        Estimate    SE
(Intercept)/(1 - repwt)    65.68  4.013
```

The first argument to `deltaMethod` is the regression-model object `davis-.mod.2`. The second argument is a quoted expression that when evaluated gives $g(\beta)$, using the names of the coefficients in the fitted-model object. The standard R function `D` is used internally by `deltaMethod` to differentiate this expression symbolically. The returned values are $g(\mathbf{b})$ and its standard error, computed as the square root of Equation 4.4.

As a second example, we return to the `Transact` data. In Section 4.4.5, we decided that there is strong evidence that the coefficients for `t1` and `t2` are not equal. We may be interested in estimating the *ratio* of these two coefficients and computing the standard error of the ratio. Using the delta method:

```
> (d1 <- deltaMethod(trans.mod, "t1/t2"))

      Estimate    SE
t1/t2    2.685 0.319
```

A 95% Wald confidence interval can then be calculated as

```
> c("2.5%" = d1$Estimate - 1.96*d1$SE,
+      "97.5%" = d1$Estimate + 1.96*d1$SE)

 2.5% 97.5%
2.059 3.310
```

The confidence interval for the ratio, and the justification for using the delta method in general, depend on the large-sample normality of the estimated regression coefficients. The method, therefore, may not be reliable.

We can compare the solution from the delta method with the solution from the bootstrap for this example by reusing the bootstrap samples that we computed earlier for the transaction regression (in Section 4.3.7):

```
> colnames(betahat.boot)

[1] "(Intercept)" "t1"          "t2"
> ratio <- betahat.boot[ , 2]/betahat.boot[ , 3] # t1/t3
> c(est=coef(trans.mod)[2]/coef(trans.mod)[3],
+    bootSE=sd(ratio), quantile(ratio, c(.025, .975)))

    est.T1      bootSE       2.5%        97.5
    2.6847      0.5494     1.8002      3.8808
```

The delta method is optimistic in this example, giving an estimated standard error that is too small and therefore a confidence interval that is too short. The problem here is that the assumption of constant error variance is doubtful; consequently, the estimated variances of the regression coefficients are too small, and so the estimated variance of their ratio is also too small.

The `deltaMethod` function has an optional argument, `vcov`, which can be set either to a function that, when applied to the model object, returns a coefficient covariance matrix or to a covariance matrix itself. If we use a heteroscedasticity-consistent estimate of the coefficient covariance matrix (provided by the `hccm` function in the **car** package, and discussed in Section 4.3.6), we get the following:

```
> deltaMethod(trans.mod, "t1/t2", vcov=hccm)

      Estimate     SE
t1/t2    2.685 0.5584
```

which gives an estimated standard error much closer to the bootstrap solution.

The second argument to deltaMethod is a quoted expression giving the function of parameters that is to be estimated. In all the examples in this section, we have not, strictly speaking, used the names of the *parameters*, but rather, we have used the names of the *corresponding regressors*. The convenience of using regressor names in place of parameter names extends to GLMs (discussed in the next chapter). We can, however, use the parameter names, if we wish—where b0 is the name of the intercept and the remaining parameters are named b1, b2, ...—in the same order as the parameters appear in the model. Thus, the call to deltaMethod for the transactions data could have been written as deltaMethod(trans.mod, "b1/b2"). This latter definition of parameter names is more general in that it applies to nonlinear models and other models in R where there isn't a simple one-to-one correspondence between parameters and regressors.

4.4.7   TESTING REGRESSION MODELS USING SIMULATION*

The Salaries data set in the **car** package provides the 2008–2009 nine-month academic salary for assistant professors, associate professors, and professors in a U.S. college:

```
> some(Salaries)

        rank discipline yrs.since.phd yrs.service    sex salary
66  AssocProf        B             9           8   Male 100522
128   AsstProf        A             2           0 Female  72500
180   AsstProf        B             3           3 Female  92000
199       Prof        B            34          33   Male 189409
284       Prof        A            45          43   Male 155865
287       Prof        A            28          27   Male 115800
301       Prof        A            39          36   Male  88600
347       Prof        B            41          27   Male 142023
350       Prof        B            27          28   Male 144309
385       Prof        A            27          21   Male 125192

> nrow(Salaries)

[1] 397
```

We have data on each faculty member's academic rank, yrs.since.phd, and sex. In addition, each individual's academic department was classified as either A or B, roughly corresponding to theoretical disciplines and applied disciplines, respectively. The data were collected in this form as part of the ongoing effort of the college's administration to monitor salary differences between male and female faculty members.

We start by changing the rank factor to have AsstProf as its baseline level:

```
> Salaries$rank <- relevel(Salaries$rank, ref="AsstProf")
```

Before looking at the salaries, we examine the numbers of male and female faculty in the college by `discipline` and `rank`:

```
> ftable(x1 <- xtabs(~ discipline + rank + sex, data=Salaries))
```

```
                      sex Female Male
discipline rank
A          AsstProf           6   18
           AssocProf          4   22
           Prof               8  123
B          AsstProf           5   38
           AssocProf          6   32
           Prof              10  125
```

We use the `xtabs` function to get a three-dimensional cross-classification and then employ the `ftable` function to flatten the output to a two-way table for printing. It is clear that the faculty is mostly male, but it is harder to see if the fraction of females varies by rank and discipline. We therefore compute the percentages of males and females in combinations of discipline and rank:

```
> round(100*ftable(prop.table(x1, margin=c(1, 2))), 1) # % m and f
```

```
                      sex Female Male
discipline rank
A          AsstProf          25.0 75.0
           AssocProf         15.4 84.6
           Prof               6.1 93.9
B          AsstProf          11.6 88.4
           AssocProf         15.8 84.2
           Prof               7.4 92.6
```

The `prop.table` function transforms the cell counts into proportions, based on the first (`discipline`) and second (`rank`) margins of the three-way table; we multiply the proportions by 100 to obtain percentages, rounding to one digit to the right of the decimal point. Assistant professors in Discipline A are 25% female. In all other cells, females comprise 6% to 16% of the faculty.

The data set we use has three factors and one numeric predictor. It is possible to view all the data in a single, very helpful graph. We make use of the `xyplot` function in the **lattice** package (Section 7.3.1) to produce the graph in Figure 4.13:

```
> library(lattice)
> xyplot(salary ~ yrs.since.phd | discipline:rank, group=sex,
+   data=Salaries, type=c("g", "p", "r"), auto.key=TRUE)
```

A formula determines the horizontal and vertical axes of the graph. The variables to the right of the | (vertical bar) define the different panels of the plot, and so we will have six panels, one for each combination of `discipline` and `rank`. The `groups` argument gives a grouping variable within each panel, using different symbols for males and females. The `type` argument specifies printing a grid (`"g"`), showing the individual points (`"p"`), and

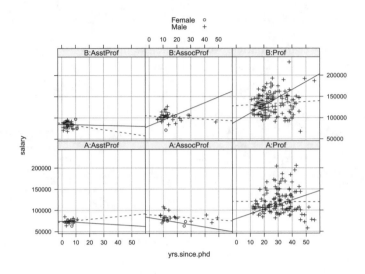

Figure 4.13   The college salary data.

displaying a least-squares regression line (`"r"`) for each group in each panel of the plot. Finally, the `auto.key` argument prints the legend at the top of the plot.

Surprisingly, after controlling for rank and discipline, `salary` appears to be more or less independent of `yrs.since.phd`. In some cases, the fitted lines even have *negative* slopes, implying that the larger the value of `yrs.since.phd`, the *lower* the `salary`. There are clear rank effects, however, with professors earning more on average than others, and professors' salaries are also much more variable. Differences by discipline are harder to discern because to examine these differences we would have to compare graphs in different rows, a more difficult task than comparing graphs in the same row.

Because the numeric variable `years.since.phd` doesn't seem to matter much, we can usefully summarize the data with parallel boxplots, as in Figure 4.14, using the `bwplot` (box-and-whisker `plot`) function in the **lattice** package:

```
> bwplot(salary ~ discipline:sex | rank, data=Salaries,
+     scales=list(rot=90), layout=c(3, 1))
```

The specification `rot=90` in the `scales` argument rotates the tick-mark labels for the horizontal and vertical axes by 90°. The panels in the graph are organized so that the comparisons of interest, between males and females of the same discipline and rank, are closest to each other. Relatively small differences between males and females are apparent in the graphs, with males generally a bit higher in salary than females. Discipline effects are clearer in this graph, as is the relatively large variation in male professors' salaries in both disciplines.

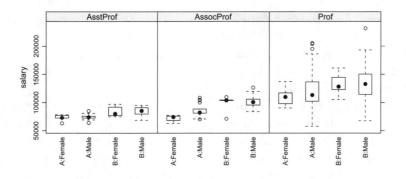

Figure 4.14 Boxplots for the college salary data.

We now turn to the problem of assessing the difference between males' and females' salaries. In the area of wage discrimination, it is traditional to assess differences using the following paradigm:

1. Fit a model, usually the linear-regression model, to the majority group, in this case the male faculty members. This model allows us to predict salary for male faculty members given their rank, discipline, and yrs.since.phd.

2. Predict salaries for the minority group, in this case the female faculty members, based on the model fit to the majority group. If no real distinction exists between the two groups, then predictions based on the majority group should be unbiased estimates of the actual salaries of the minority group.

3. Compute the average difference between the actual minority salaries and the predicted minority salaries.

Here are the computations:

```
> fselector <- Salaries$sex == "Female" # TRUE for females
> salmod <- lm(salary ~ rank*discipline + yrs.since.phd,
+     data=Salaries, subset=!fselector) # regression for males
> # predictions for females:
> femalePreds <- predict(salmod, newdata=Salaries[fselector, ])
> (meanDiff <- mean(Salaries$salary[fselector] - femalePreds))

[1] -4551
```

We first define a *selector variable* that has the value TRUE for females and FALSE for males. We then fit a regression to the males only, allowing for interactions between rank and discipline and an additive yrs.since.phd effect, which we expect will be small in light of the earlier graphical analysis. We use the generic function predict to get predictions from the fitted regression. The newdata argument tells the function to obtain predictions only for the females. If we had omitted the second argument, then predictions would have been returned for the data used in fitting the model, in this case the males only, which is not what we want. We finally compute the mean difference between the observed and predicted salaries for the females. The average female salary is therefore $4,551 less than the amount predicted from the fitted model for males.

A question of interest is whether or not this difference of $-$4,551$ is due to chance alone. Many of the usual ideas of significance testing are not obviously applicable here. First, the data form a complete population, not a sample, and so we are not inferring from a sample to a larger population. Nevertheless, because we are interested in drawing conclusions about the *social process* that generated the data, statistical inference is at least arguably sensible. Second, a sex effect can be added to the model in many ways, and these could all lead to different conclusions. Third, the assumptions of the linear-regression model are unlikely to hold; for example, we noted that professors are more variable than others in salary.

Here is a way to judge statistical significance based on simulation: We will compare the mean difference for the real minority group, the 39 females, with the mean difference we would have obtained had we nominated 39 of the faculty selected at random to be the "minority group." We will compute the mean difference between the actual and predicted salaries for these 39 "random females" and then repeat the process a large number of times, say $B = 999$:

```
> set.seed(8141976) # for reproducibility
> fnumber <- sum(fselector) # number of females
> n <- length(fselector) # number of observations
> B <- 999 # number of replications
> simDiff <- numeric(B) # initialize vector with B entries
> for (j in 1:B){
+     sel <- sample(1:n, fnumber) # sample of nominated 'females'
+     m2 <- update(salmod, subset=-sel) # refit regression model
+     simDiff[j] <- mean(Salaries$salary[sel]
+         - predict(m2, newdata=Salaries[sel, ])) #  mean diff.
+ }
```

We first compute the number of females and the number of faculty members. We employ a for loop (Section 8.3) to perform the calculation repeatedly. Within the loop, the sample function is used to assign fnumber randomly selected faculty members to be "females"; the regression is updated without the randomly chosen "females"; the predictions are obtained; and the average difference between actual and predicted salary is saved.

There are many ways to summarize the simulation; we have used a histogram (see Figure 4.15):

```
> (frac <- round(sum(meanDiff > simDiff)/(1 + B), 3))
```

```
0.102
```

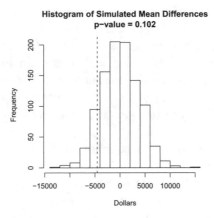

Figure 4.15 Histogram of simulated sex differences for the college salary data. The vertical line is drawn at the observed mean difference of −4551.

```
> hist(simDiff,
+    main=paste(
+        "Histogram of Simulated Mean Differences\np-value =",
+        frac),
+    xlab="Dollars")
> abline(v=meanDiff, lty="dashed")
```

The variable `frac` is the fraction of replications in which the simulated difference is less that the observed difference, and it gives the estimated p value. The escaped character `\n` in the histogram title, specified by the `main` argument, is the new-line character. We draw the histogram with a vertical line at the observed mean difference.[24]

The histogram looks more or less symmetric and is centered close to 0. The simulated p value is .102, suggesting only weak evidence against the hypothesis that salaries are determined by a process unrelated to sex.

This procedure can be criticized on several grounds, not the least of which is the manner in which "females" were randomly created. Most male faculty are professors, while the female faculty are more evenly spread among the ranks. Thus, the randomly generated "females" tend to be professors, which does not reflect the true state of affairs in the college. The reader is invited to repeat this analysis by changing the random mechanism used to generate "females" to ensure that each set of randomly generated "females" has the same number in each rank as do the actual females.

4.5 Model Selection

In linear-regression and generalized linear-regression models, the *model selection* problem is often stated as a *variable selection* problem. We have

---

[24] See Chapter 7 for more on graphics in R.

a response y and a set of predictors $\mathbf{x} = \{x_1, \ldots, x_m\}$, and we wish to divide $\mathbf{x}$ into two groups, $\mathbf{x} = (\mathbf{x}_A, \mathbf{x}_I)$, the *active* and *inactive* predictors, such that the distribution of $y|\mathbf{x}_A$ is the same as the distribution of $y|(\mathbf{x}_A, \mathbf{x}_I)$, so all the information about y is in the active predictors. Thinking about regression problems in this way is most clearly relevant when the aim is to use regression models for prediction. The literature on this problem is enormous, and the area on the interface between statistics and computer science called *machine learning* is largely dedicated to it.

General model selection can concern not just finding the active predictors $\mathbf{x}_A$ but also building the model itself, including defining regressors from the predictors and selecting distributions and other assumptions made in modeling. In this section, we discuss only the more limited variable selection problem: We assume that the model we have fit is appropriate for the data at hand, and our only remaining goal is to find the active variables $\mathbf{x}_A$ or, equivalently, to delete the inactive variables $\mathbf{x}_I$. In the context of linear regression, one common approach is as follows:

- Fit a sequence of models using standard fitting routines such as lm or glm, which differ only in the elements of $\mathbf{x}$ that are used to define the regressors. We call a model fit with only a subset of the regressors a *subset model*. If we have m predictors, then there are $2^m - 1$ possible subset models. For example, if $m = 10$, $2^m - 1 = 1,023$, while if $m = 20$, $2^m - 1$ is slightly more than 1 million.
- Select the subset model that optimizes some criterion of model quality.

If this paradigm is accepted, then all that remains is, first, to choose the subsets to examine, and, second, to choose a criterion to optimize.

THE step FUNCTION

The step function provides both a statistic to optimize and useful algorithms for examining numerous subset models. For selecting subsets to examine, step has three choices: "backward", in which we start with all the regressors in the model and continue to remove terms until removing another term makes the criterion of interest worse; "forward", in which we start with no regressors and continue to add terms until adding another term makes the criterion of interest worse; or "both", in which at each step we consider either an addition or a removal. The default is "backward", which we will illustrate first.

As an example, we will use the data set Highway1 in the **car** package, slightly modified from Weisberg (2005), with response log2(rate), the base-2 logarithm of the automobile accident rate per million vehicle miles on 39 segments of Minnesota highways in 1973. After extensive initial graphical analysis, a set of potential regressors includes log2(len), the base-2 logarithm of the length of the segment in miles; log2(ADT), the base-2 logarithm of the average daily traffic; log2(trks), the base-2 logarithm of the percentage of daily traffic due to trucks; slim, the speed limit on the segment; and four variables that describe the geometry of the roadway—lane, the number of lanes, lwid, the lane width in feet, shld, the shoulder width in feet, and itg, the number of intersections in the segment. The variable sigs1 is also included in the data frame, and is defined by sigs1 = (sigs × len + 1)/len, where sigs is the number of traffic signals in the segment; sigs1 is consequently the number of signals per mile, with a small start to avoid 0 values. The base-2 logarithm of sigs1 is used in this example. Finally, there is one factor, called hwy, which has four classes corresponding to the four funding sources for maintenance of the roadway. The example therefore has $m = 11$ predictors, of which 10 are numeric and one is a factor:

```
> summary(highway.mod <- lm(log2(rate) ~ log2(len) + log2(ADT) +
+          log2(trks) + log2(sigs1) + slim + shld + lane + acpt +
+          itg + lwid + hwy, data=Highway1))

Call:
lm(formula = log2(rate) ~ log2(len) + log2(ADT) + log2(trks) +
    log2(sigs1) + slim + shld + lane + acpt + itg +
    lwid + hwy, data = Highway1)

Residuals:
     Min       1Q    Median       3Q      Max
-0.64635 -0.14705 -0.00998  0.17645  0.60761

Coefficients:
             Estimate Std. Error t value Pr(>|t|)
(Intercept)   6.04734    2.62352    2.31    0.030
log2(len)    -0.21447    0.09999   -2.15    0.042
log2(ADT)    -0.15462    0.11189   -1.38    0.179
log2(trks)   -0.19756    0.23981   -0.82    0.418
log2(sigs1)   0.19232    0.07537    2.55    0.017
slim         -0.03933    0.02424   -1.62    0.117
shld          0.00429    0.04928    0.09    0.931
lane         -0.01606    0.08226   -0.20    0.847
acpt          0.00873    0.01169    0.75    0.462
itg           0.05154    0.35031    0.15    0.884
lwid          0.06077    0.19739    0.31    0.761
hwyMA        -0.55006    0.51572   -1.07    0.296
hwyMC        -0.34271    0.57682   -0.59    0.558
hwyPA        -0.75500    0.41844   -1.80    0.083

Residual standard error: 0.376 on 25 degrees of freedom
Multiple R-squared: 0.791,          Adjusted R-squared: 0.683
F-statistic: 7.29 on 13 and 25 DF,  p-value: 0.0000125
```

While $R^2 = .79$, few of the individual coefficients have small p values, a common symptom of fitting too elaborate a model.

Stepwise regression by *backward elimination* is carried out with the command

```
> highway.backward <-
+     step(highway.mod, scope=list(lower= ~ log2(len)))
```

We used all the default arguments to step, except that we set scope= list(lower=~ log2(len)), which has the effect of forcing log2(len) into all the models. As described in Weisberg (2005), this variable is included because of the way the data were collected, and so it must be among the active predictors.

The step command produces lots of output, and we display it in edited segments:

```
Start:  AIC=-65.61
log2(rate) ~ log2(len) + log2(ADT) + log2(trks) + log2(sigs1) +
    slim + shld + lane + acpt + itg + lwid + hwy

               Df Sum of Sq  RSS    AIC
- shld          1    0.001  3.54  -67.6
- itg           1    0.003  3.54  -67.6
- lane          1    0.005  3.54  -67.6
- lwid          1    0.013  3.55  -67.5
- acpt          1    0.079  3.62  -66.8
- log2(trks)    1    0.096  3.63  -66.6
<none>                      3.54  -65.6
- hwy           3    0.625  4.16  -65.3
- log2(ADT)     1    0.270  3.81  -64.7
- slim          1    0.373  3.91  -63.7
- log2(sigs1)   1    0.921  4.46  -58.6
```

This first segment of the output shows the result of dropping each predictor in turn from the current regression model. If the predictor is a factor, then step will drop as a group all the regressors created from the factor.[25] The output provides the name of the term that is dropped, the change in degrees of freedom, the sum of squares explained by the dropped term, the residual sum of squares for each subset-model, and finally the value of a criterion statistic to be used to compare models. The default criterion is the *Akaike information criterion*, or *AIC*.[26] Provided that at least one of the subset models has a value of AIC less than that for the model with all the predictors, marked <none> in the output, the predictor that corresponds to the smallest value of AIC is dropped, in this case shld.

The next section of output from step is similar to the first section, except that the now-current model has shld removed:

```
Step:  AIC=-67.6
log2(rate) ~ log2(len) + log2(ADT) + log2(trks) + log2(sigs1) +
    slim + lane + acpt + itg + lwid + hwy

               Df Sum of Sq   RSS      AIC
- itg           1   0.00276  3.5408  -69.569
- lane          1   0.00571  3.5437  -69.537
- lwid          1   0.01489  3.5529  -69.436
- acpt          1   0.09737  3.6354  -68.541
- log2(trks)    1   0.11580  3.6538  -68.344
```

---

[25]The step function described in this section will not violate the marginality principle and thus will not drop a low-order term if one of its higher-order relatives is included in the model. In the current example, however, the starting model is additive and therefore does not include terms related by marginality.

[26]The criterion can be changed with the argument k to step; for example, to use the *Bayesian information criterion* (*BIC*), we would set k to $\log_e(n)$. See the help page for step and the references in the Complementary Reading for details.

```
<none>                            3.5380  -67.600
- hwy            3    0.68361  4.2216  -66.710
- log2(ADT)      1    0.28417  3.8222  -66.587
- slim           1    0.70869  4.2467  -62.479
- log2(sigs1)    1    1.00199  4.5400  -59.875
```

In the second step, therefore, itg will be removed.

We continue in this fashion, at each step either deleting the predictor that corresponds to the model with the smallest AIC or stopping if all prospective deletions increase AIC. We omit several steps, showing only the final two:

```
Step:  AIC=-74.21
log2(rate) ~ log2(len) + log2(ADT) + log2(trks) + log2(sigs1) +
    slim + hwy

                Df Sum of Sq    RSS      AIC
- log2(trks)     1    0.14288  3.8097  -74.714
<none>                         3.6668  -74.205
- log2(ADT)      1    0.31064  3.9775  -73.034
- hwy            3    1.51292  5.1797  -66.733
- log2(sigs1)    1    1.15981  4.8266  -65.487
- slim           1    1.20713  4.8740  -65.107

Step:  AIC=-74.71
log2(rate) ~ log2(len) + log2(ADT) + log2(sigs1) + slim + hwy

                Df Sum of Sq    RSS      AIC
<none>                         3.8097  -74.714
- log2(ADT)      1    0.28821  4.0979  -73.870
- hwy            3    1.68565  5.4954  -66.427
- slim           1    1.15948  4.9692  -66.352
- log2(sigs1)    1    1.56367  5.3734  -63.302
```

The step function stops at this last step because deleting any of the four remaining predictors would *increase* the AIC. The backward-elimination algorithm examined only 49 of the possible 1,023 subset models before stopping. Because we made an assignment in the call to step shown above, highway.backward is the final model, selected by backward elimination to minimize the AIC:

```
> highway.backward

Call:
lm(formula = log2(rate) ~ log2(len) + log2(ADT) + log2(sigs1) +
    slim + hwy, data = Highway1)

Coefficients:
(Intercept)    log2(len)     log2(ADT)   log2(sigs1)        slim
     6.4554      -0.2616       -0.1269        0.2084     -0.0429
      hwyMA        hwyMC         hwyPA
    -0.3845      -0.1786       -0.7147
```

We can compare the fit of the full and subset models by looking at the corresponding fitted values, as in Figure 4.16:

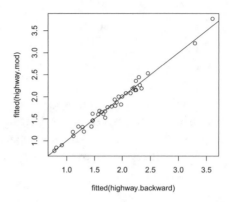

Figure 4.16   Comparison of fitted values for the Highway data with all the regressors and with the regressors selected by backward stepwise fitting.

```
> plot(fitted(highway.mod) ~ fitted(highway.backward))
> abline(0, 1)
> cor(fitted(highway.mod), fitted(highway.backward))
```

```
[1] 0.9898
```

The change in the fitted values is relatively small, and the two sets of fitted values have correlation .99; we conclude that the subset model and the full model provide essentially the same information about the value of the response given the predictors.

With *forward selection*, specifying `direction="forward"` in the `step` command, we start with the smallest model that we are willing to entertain:

```
> highway.mod0 <- update(highway.mod, . ~ log2(len))
```

and then tell `step` which terms to consider adding to the model using the `scope` argument. The `step` function employs `add1` to add predictors to the model one at a time:

```
> (highway.forward <- step(highway.mod0, direction="forward",
+    scope=list(lower = ~ log2(len),
+      upper = ~ log2(len) + log2(ADT) + log2(trks) +
+        log2(sigs1) + slim + shld + lane + acpt + itg + lwid + hwy),
+    trace=0))

Call:
lm(formula = log2(rate) ~ log2(len) + slim + acpt +
    log2(trks), data = Highway1)

Coefficients:
(Intercept)    log2(len)          slim          acpt    log2(trks)
     6.0110      -0.2357       -0.0460        0.0159       -0.3290
```

We used the argument `trace=0` to suppress printing the steps in full. The forward and backward algorithms suggest different subset models, but an examination of the fitted values for these models demonstrates their general predictive similarity: for example,

```
> R <- cor(cbind(fitted(highway.mod), fitted(highway.backward),
+       fitted(highway.forward)))
> rownames(R) <- colnames(R) <- c("original", "backward", "forward")
> R

          original backward forward
original    1.0000   0.9898  0.9379
backward    0.9898   1.0000  0.9153
forward     0.9379   0.9153  1.0000

> AIC(highway.mod)

[1] 47.07

> AIC(highway.backward)

[1] 37.96

> AIC(highway.forward)

[1] 43.73
```

As is common, backward elimination produces a lower value of AIC. That different subset models can have similar values of a criterion such as the AIC should give us pause in interpreting the output of automatic model selection methods, particularly methods, such as stepwise regression, that report a single best model.

ALL POSSIBLE REGRESSIONS

As an alternative to stepwise regression, the **leaps** package contains the regsubsets function for linear models, which will find the nbest subsets to optimize a criterion called Mallows' C_p statistic, which is closely related to the AIC. The regsubsets function works directly on regressors, not predictors, and so it treats each regressor for a factor or polynomial separately. Moreover, if the model includes interactions, the computing algorithm used pays no attention to the marginality principle, and so unacceptable models are examined. Finally, the computing method works only for linear models. Subject to these limitations, the output from regsubsets can be used as input to the **car** function subsets to produce a C_p plot.[27]

4.6 More on Factors

4.6.1 CODING FACTORS

As we have seen, a factor with d levels requires $d-1$ regressors. For example, a factor with two levels requires only one regressor, defined by replacing

---

[27]See ?subsets for an example and the Complementary Reading for further discussion.

the qualitative levels of the factor with numeric values, usually 0 for the first level and 1 for the second. This *dummy regressor* then replaces the factor in fitting the model. When the dummy regressor has the value 1, we know that the factor is at its second level; when it is 0, the factor is at its first level.

With more than two levels, the default method of defining dummy regressors in R is a straightforward generalization, in which the jth dummy regressor, for $j = 1, \ldots, d - 1$, has the value 1 for cases with the factor at its level $(j + 1)$ and 0 otherwise, as was illustrated in Section 4.2.3 for a factor named z. We call this approach the *drop-first-level* method, in which the first level of the factor becomes the baseline level, with which all the other levels are compared. R uses the function `contr.treatment` to create dummy regressors according to the drop-first-level method.

4.6.2 OTHER FACTOR CODINGS

The default method of coding factors is easy to use and intuitive; indeed, for most purposes the method of coding a factor is irrelevant to the analysis. Nevertheless, R allows us to change how factors are coded.

How R codes regressors for factors is controlled by the `contrasts` option:

```
> getOption("contrasts")

        unordered              ordered
  "contr.treatment"         "contr.poly"
```

Two values are provided by the `contrasts` option, one for unordered factors and the other for ordered factors, which have levels that are ordered from smallest to largest. Each entry corresponds to the name of a function that converts a factor into an appropriate set of contrasts; thus, the default function for defining contrasts for an unordered factor is `contr.treatment`.

We can see how the contrasts for a factor are coded by using the `contrasts` function:

```
> with(Prestige, contrasts(type))

      wc prof
bc     0    0
wc     1    0
prof   0    1
```

The result shows compactly the coding discussed in Section 4.6.1: The first level of `type` is coded 0 for both dummy regressors; the second level is coded 1 for the first and 0 for the second regressor; and the third level is coded 1 for the second and 0 for the first regressor. As previously explained, it is possible to change the baseline level using the `relevel` function:

```
> Prestige$type1 <- relevel(Prestige$type, ref="prof")
```

This command creates a new factor with `prof` as the baseline level:

```
> with(Prestige, contrasts(type1))
```

```
        bc wc
prof  0   0
bc    1   0
wc    0   1
```

The function `contr.SAS` is similar to `contr.treatment` except that it uses the *last* level as the baseline rather than the *first*. It is included in R to make many results match those from the SAS program:

```
> contrasts(Prestige$type) <- "contr.SAS"
> contrasts(Prestige$type)
```

```
        bc wc
bc    1   0
wc    0   1
prof  0   0
```

R includes two additional functions for coding unordered factors, `contr-.helmert` and `contr.sum`. The first of these uses *Helmert matrices*:

```
> contrasts(Prestige$type) <- "contr.helmert"
> contrasts(Prestige$type)
```

```
       [,1]  [,2]
bc     -1    -1
wc      1    -1
prof    0     2
```

Each of the Helmert regressors compares one level with the average of the preceding levels. If the number of observations at each level is equal, then the Helmert regressors are orthogonal in the model matrix, but they are not orthogonal in general. Helmert coding is currently rarely used, although it was the default method for coding factors in some older computer programs.

The final method available is called *deviation coding*, implemented in R via the function `contr.sum`:

```
> contrasts(Prestige$type) <- "contr.sum"
> contrasts(Prestige$type)
```

```
       [,1]  [,2]
bc      1     0
wc      0     1
prof   -1    -1
```

Deviation coding results from so-called *sigma* or *sum-to-zero* constraints on the coefficients. The coefficient for the last level, `prof`, is implicitly constrained equal to the negative of the sum of the coefficients for the other levels, and the redundant last coefficient is omitted from the model. Each coefficient compares the corresponding level of the factor with the average of all the levels. This coding corresponds to the treatment of factors in ANOVA models in many statistical textbooks. Although in unbalanced data the regressors produced for different factors by `contr.sum` and `contr.helmert` are correlated in the model matrix, they may nevertheless be used to compute correct

Type III tests, because the sets of regressors are orthogonal in the row-basis of the model matrix.

Finally, the **car** package includes the functions `contr.Treatment` and `contr.Sum`. These behave similarly to the standard `contr.treatment` and `contr.sum` functions but produce more descriptive contrast names:

```
> contrasts(Prestige$type) <- "contr.Treatment"
> contrasts(Prestige$type)

      [T.wc] [T.prof]
bc        0        0
wc        1        0
prof      0        1

> contrasts(Prestige$type) <- "contr.Sum"
> contrasts(Prestige$type)

      [S.bc] [S.wc]
bc        1        0
wc        0        1
prof     -1       -1
```

An alternative to changing the contrasts of individual factors is to reset the global `contrasts` option: for example,

```
> options(contrasts = c("contr.sum", "contr.poly"))
```

These contrast-generating functions would then be used by default for all subsequent model fits. In setting the `contrasts` option, we must specify contrasts for both unordered and ordered factors. Contrasts can also be set as an argument to the `lm` function (see Section 4.8.8).

4.6.3 ORDERED FACTORS AND ORTHOGONAL POLYNOMIALS

R has a built-in facility for working with factors that have ordered levels. The default contrast-generating function for ordered factors is `contr.poly`, which creates *orthogonal-polynomial contrasts*. Suppose, for example, that we treat the variable `fcategory` in the `Moore` data set as an ordered factor:

```
> Moore$fcategory1 <- ordered(Moore$fcategory)
> Moore$fcategory1

 [1] low    high   high   low    low    low    medium medium
 [9] low    low    medium high   low    medium high   high
[17] low    high   high   high   low    low    high   medium
[25] low    high   low    high   medium medium high   medium
[33] low    medium medium low    high   medium medium medium
[41] medium high   low    high   medium
Levels: low < medium < high

> round(contrasts(Moore$fcategory1), 2)
```

```
        .L   .Q
[1,] -0.71  0.41
[2,]  0.00 -0.82
[3,]  0.71  0.41
```

The column labeled .L represents a linear contrast and that labeled .Q, a quadratic contrast. The two contrasts are orthogonal when there are equal numbers of observations at the different levels of the factor, but not in general. Because the contrasts are orthogonal in the row-basis of the model matrix, however, they will produce correct Type III tests, even for unbalanced data. This approach is most appropriate when the categories are, in some sense, equally spaced, but in certain fields, it is traditional to use orthogonal contrasts for ordinal predictors.

Applied to the Moore data, we get the following result:

```
> summary(lm(conformity ~ partner.status*fcategory1, data=Moore))

Call:
lm(formula = conformity ~ partner.status * fcategory1,
    data = Moore)

Residuals:
   Min     1Q Median     3Q    Max
-8.625 -2.900 -0.273  2.727 11.375

Coefficients:
                            Estimate Std. Error t value Pr(>|t|)
(Intercept)                   12.051      0.728   16.56   <2e-16
partner.status1               -2.459      0.728   -3.38   0.0017
fcategory1.L                  -0.643      1.220   -0.53   0.6013
fcategory1.Q                   1.579      1.299    1.22   0.2314
partner.status1:fcategory1.L   3.277      1.220    2.69   0.0106
partner.status1:fcategory1.Q   1.289      1.299    0.99   0.3273

Residual standard error: 4.58 on 39 degrees of freedom
Multiple R-squared: 0.324,       Adjusted R-squared: 0.237
F-statistic: 3.73 on 5 and 39 DF,  p-value: 0.0074

> options(contrasts=c("contr.treatment",
+          "contr.poly")) # return to defaults
```

Using contr.sum with partner.status and contr.poly with fcategory1, the main-effect coefficients for fcategory1 represent linear and quadratic trends averaged across the levels of partner.status, while the interaction coefficients represent departures from the average trends. The linear component of the interaction is statistically significant, while the quadratic component is not significant.

When there is a discrete numeric predictor, we suggest using the poly function to generate *orthogonal-polynomial regressors*. To construct a simple example, suppose that we have a numeric variable representing the dosage of a drug in a clinical trial:

```
> dosage <- c(1, 4, 8, 1, 4, 8, 1, 4)
```

Because `dosage` has three distinct values—1, 4, and 8—we could treat it as a factor, coding regressors to represent it in a linear model. It wouldn't be appropriate to use `contr.poly` here to generate the regressors, however, because the levels of `dosage` aren't equally spaced; moreover, because the data are unbalanced, the regressors created by `contr.poly` would be correlated. The `poly` function will generate orthogonal-polynomial regressors for `dosage`:

```
> X <- poly(dosage, degree=2)

> round(X, 3)

          1       2
[1,] -0.375  0.261
[2,]  0.016 -0.456
[3,]  0.538  0.293
[4,] -0.375  0.261
[5,]  0.016 -0.456
[6,]  0.538  0.293
[7,] -0.375  0.261
[8,]  0.016 -0.456
. . .

> round(cor(X), 3)

  1 2
1 1 0
2 0 1
```

The second argument to `poly` specifies the degree of the polynomial—here, degree 2, a quadratic. The first column of X represents a linear trend in `dosage`, while the second column represents a quadratic trend net of the linear trend.

The `poly` function can also be used to generate raw—as opposed to orthogonal—polynomials:

```
> poly(dosage, degree=2, raw=TRUE)

     1  2
[1,] 1  1
[2,] 4 16
[3,] 8 64
[4,] 1  1
[5,] 4 16
[6,] 8 64
[7,] 1  1
[8,] 4 16
. . .
```

The first column is just `dosage` and the second the square of `dosage`. Used in a linear model, the two specifications—orthogonal and raw polynomials—are equivalent in the sense that they produce the same fit to the data, although, because they reduce collinearity, orthogonal polynomials tend to yield more accurate least-squares computations. We could also put `dosage + I(dosage^2)` directly in a model formula, but there are advantages in keeping the polynomial regressors together in the same term of a model—for example, for producing an ANOVA table for the model. If we want to put the regressor dosage^2 directly in the model, we have to protect it with the identity function, I, to ensure that the ^ operator is properly interpreted as exponentiation (see Section 4.8.1 on model formulas).

4.6.4 USER-SPECIFIED CONTRASTS*

In some instances, there are $d - 1$ specific comparisons among the d levels of a factor that are of interest. Recall, for example, the Baumann data set (p. 160), for a randomized experiment in which children were taught reading by one of three methods, a standard method (Basal) and two new methods (DTRA and Strat), with 22 subjects assigned to each condition. It appears natural here to test for differences between the standard method and the new methods and between the two new methods. These tests can be formulated in R with user-defined contrasts.

Here is the general idea: Suppose that the vector μ represents the population factor-level means in a one-way ANOVA, or the raveled factor-combination means for a two-way or higher classification. If there are d means, then there are $d-1$ df for the differences among them. Let the *contrast matrix* C be a $d \times (d - 1)$ matrix of rank $d - 1$, each of the columns of which sums to 0. Then,

$$\mu = [\mathbf{1}, C] \begin{bmatrix} \alpha \\ \gamma \end{bmatrix}$$

is a linear model for the factor-level means. In this equation, $\mathbf{1}$ is a $d \times 1$ vector of ones, α is the overall mean, and γ contains $d - 1$ parameters for the $d - 1$ contrasts specified by the columns of C. The trick is to formulate C so that the $(d - 1) \times 1$ parameter vector γ represents interesting contrasts among the level means. Because $[\mathbf{1}, C]$ is nonsingular (*Reader:* why?), we can solve for the parameters as a linear transformation of the means:

$$\begin{bmatrix} \alpha \\ \gamma \end{bmatrix} = [\mathbf{1}, C]^{-1} \mu$$

A very simple way to proceed (though not the only way) is to make the columns of C mutually orthogonal. Then, the rows of $[\mathbf{1}, C]^{-1}$ will be proportional to the corresponding columns of $[\mathbf{1}, C]$, and we can directly code the contrasts of interest among the means in the columns of C.

None of this requires that the factor have equal numbers of observations at its several levels, but if these counts are equal, as in the Baumann data set, then not only are the columns of C orthogonal, but the columns of the model matrix X constructed from C are orthogonal as well. Under these circumstances, we can partition the regression sum of squares for the model into 1-df components due to each contrast.

For the Baumann and Jones data, the two contrasts of interest are (1) Basal versus the average of DRTA and Strat and (2) DRTA versus Strat:

```
> C <- matrix(c(1,-0.5,-0.5,  0,1,-1), 3, 2)
> colnames(C) <- c("Basal vs. DRTA & Strat", "DRTA vs. Strat")
> C

     Basal vs. DRTA & Strat DRTA vs. Strat
[1,]                    1.0              0
[2,]                   -0.5              1
[3,]                   -0.5             -1
```

The columns of C correspond to these two comparisons, which we set as the contrasts for the factor group and refit the model:

```
> contrasts(Baumann$group) <- C
> summary(lm(post.test.3 ~ group, data=Baumann))

Call:
lm(formula = post.test.3 ~ group, data = Baumann)

Residuals:
   Min     1Q Median     3Q    Max
-16.73  -3.61   1.11   3.95  12.95

Coefficients:
                           Estimate Std. Error t value Pr(>|t|)
(Intercept)                  44.015      0.777   56.63   <2e-16
groupBasal vs. DRTA & Strat  -2.970      1.099   -2.70   0.0088
groupDRTA vs. Strat           1.227      0.952    1.29   0.2020

Residual standard error: 6.31 on 63 degrees of freedom
Multiple R-squared: 0.125,      Adjusted R-squared: 0.0967
F-statistic: 4.48 on 2 and 63 DF,  p-value: 0.0152
```

The t statistics for the contrasts test the two hypotheses of interest, and so we have strong evidence that the new methods are superior to the old but little evidence of a difference in efficacy between the two new methods. The overall F test, and other similar summaries, are unaffected by the choice of contrasts as long as we use $d - 1$ of them and the **C** matrix has full column rank $d - 1$.

User-specified contrasts may also be used for factors in more complex linear models, including multi-factor models with interactions.

4.7   Overparametrized Models*

4.7.1   NO INTERCEPT

The rule that a factor with d levels requires $d - 1$ regressors may not hold if the model formula does not include an intercept:

```
> summary(prestige.mod.4 <- update(prestige.mod.1, . ~ . - 1))

Call:
lm(formula = prestige ~ education + log2(income) +
    type - 1, data = na.omit(Prestige))
```

```
Residuals:
   Min     1Q Median     3Q    Max
 -13.51  -3.75   1.01   4.36  18.44

Coefficients:
              Estimate Std. Error t value Pr(>|t|)
education        3.284      0.608    5.40 5.1e-07
log2(income)     7.269      1.190    6.11 2.3e-08
typebc         -81.202     13.743   -5.91 5.6e-08
typewc         -82.641     13.788   -5.99 3.9e-08
typeprof       -74.451     15.118   -4.92 3.7e-06

Residual standard error: 6.64 on 93 degrees of freedom
Multiple R-squared: 0.983,          Adjusted R-squared: 0.983
F-statistic: 1.11e+03 on 5 and 93 DF,  p-value: <2e-16
```

The primary difference between this fit and `prestige.mod.1` (p. 163) is that there is now a separate intercept for each level of `type`. Summaries such as df, $\widehat{\sigma}$, and the estimates of the other coefficients and their standard errors are all identical.[28] The coefficients of the now three dummy regressors for `type` are the intercepts for the three groups, and in some instances, this can provide a simpler description of the model. The usefulness of tests for this parametrization is questionable, however. For example, the Type II F test for `type`, in

```
> Anova(prestige.mod.4)

Anova Table (Type II tests)

Response: prestige
             Sum Sq Df F value  Pr(>F)
education      1285  1    29.2 5.1e-07
log2(income)   1644  1    37.3 2.3e-08
type           3449  3    26.1 2.4e-12
Residuals      4096 93
```

has 3 df, rather than 2 df, and tests the probably uninteresting hypothesis that all three intercepts are equal to 0 rather than the more interesting hypothesis that they are all equal to *each other*. We suggest that you generally avoid leaving off the intercept in a linear model unless you have a specific reason for doing so, and then are very careful to interpret the coefficients and the results of the statistical tests correctly.

4.7.2 SINGULARITY

In some instances, we may end up trying to fit regressors that are exact linear combinations of each other in a model. This can happen by accident or due to confusion, for example, by including scores on subtests and the total score of all the subtests as predictors. In other instances, two predictors might

---

[28] The observant reader will notice, however, that the R^2s for the two models differ: When the intercept is suppressed, R calculates R^2 based on variation around 0 rather than around the mean of the response, producing a statistic that does not generally have a sensible interpretation.

be included accidently that are really the same quantity, such as height in centimeters and height in inches.

Probably the most common situation producing singularity that isn't simply an error in specifying the model is fitting a model with two or more factors, including main effects and all interactions among the factors, but with at least one of the cells in the cross-classification of the factors empty. Suppose, for example, that we have two factors, A and B, with a and b levels, respectively. Then the model y ~ A + B + A:B creates one regressor for the intercept, $a-1$ regressors for the main effects of A, $b-1$ regressors for the main effects of B, and $(a-1)(b-1)$ regressors for the A:B interactions—that is, $a \times b$ regressors in all. Furthermore, suppose that one cell in the A×B table is empty, so that there are only $(a \times b)-1$ rather than $a \times b$ observed cell means. The model now has one too many regressors—one more than there are observed cell means. It is only the last regressor that will cause a problem, however, and we should still be able to contrast the additive model y ~ A + B with the model that includes interactions, y ~ A + B + A:B, as long as we remove the redundant interaction regressor.

As an example, we return to the Moore and Krupat data in Moore, discussed in Section 4.2.3. We remove all seven observations with fcategory = high and partner.status = high to create an empty cell:

```
> deleted.cell <-
+       with(Moore, fcategory == "high" & partner.status=="high")
> mod.moore.3 <- update(mod.moore.1, subset = !deleted.cell)
> summary(mod.moore.3)

Call:
lm(formula = conformity ~ fcategory * partner.status,
    data = Moore, subset = !deleted.cell)

Residuals:
    Min     1Q  Median     3Q     Max
 -8.625 -2.900  -0.273  2.727  11.375

Coefficients: (1 not defined because of singularities)
                                         Estimate Std. Error t value
(Intercept)                                  8.90       1.48    6.00
fcategorymedium                             -1.65       2.77   -0.60
fcategoryhigh                                3.72       2.22    1.68
partner.statushigh                           8.50       2.57    3.31
fcategorymedium:partner.statushigh          -1.48       3.75   -0.39
fcategoryhigh:partner.statushigh              NA         NA      NA
                                         Pr(>|t|)
(Intercept)                               9.5e-07
fcategorymedium                            0.5559
fcategoryhigh                              0.1033
partner.statushigh                         0.0023
fcategorymedium:partner.statushigh         0.6963
fcategoryhigh:partner.statushigh               NA

Residual standard error: 4.69 on 33 degrees of freedom
Multiple R-squared: 0.35,       Adjusted R-squared: 0.272
F-statistic: 4.45 on 4 and 33 DF,  p-value: 0.00551
```

With the empty cell, there is only 1 *df* remaining for the interaction, rather than 2 *df*, although the output still shows two coefficients. The second inter-action coefficient, however, is given a value of NA, as lm recognizes that this coefficient, which is said to be *aliased*, cannot be estimated. Interpretation of the remaining coefficients with empty cells present depends on the contrasts used to define the factors and the order of terms in the model, and is therefore not straightforward. Some functions, such as coef, applied to a model with a singularity return a coefficient vector with the NAs included. Others, such as anova and Anova, correctly recognize the singularity and do the right thing, adjusting degrees of freedom for the redundant coefficients:

```
> Anova(mod.moore.3)

Anova Table (Type II tests)

Response: conformity
                        Sum Sq Df F value  Pr(>F)
fcategory                  128  2    2.91 0.06883
partner.status             382  1   17.39 0.00021
fcategory:partner.status     3  1    0.16 0.69633
Residuals                  725 33
```

These are the correct Type II tests. With empty cells, Type III tests, however, are very hard to justify, and they are consequently not produced by Anova.

4.8 The Arguments of the lm Function

The lm function has several additional useful arguments, and some of the arguments that we discussed have uses that were not mentioned. The args function prints out the arguments to lm:

```
> args(lm)

function (formula, data, subset, weights, na.action, method = "qr",
    model = TRUE, x = FALSE, y = FALSE, qr = TRUE, singular.ok = TRUE,
    contrasts = NULL, offset, ...)
NULL
```

We will describe each of these arguments in turn.

4.8.1 formula

A formula for lm consists of a left-hand side, specifying the response variable, and a right-hand side, specifying the terms in the model; the two sides of the formula are separated by a tilde (~). We read the formula a ~ b as "a is modeled as b," or "a is regressed on b."

The left-hand side of the formula can be any valid R expression that evaluates to a numeric vector of the appropriate length. On the left side of the formula, the arithmetic operators, -, +, *, /, and ^, have their usual meanings, and we can call whatever functions are appropriate to our purpose. For example, with reference to Moore and Krupat's data, we could replace the number of conforming responses by the percentage of conforming responses,

```
> lm(100*conformity/40 ~ partner.status*fcategory, data=Moore)
```

or (using the `logit` function in the **car** package) by the log-odds of conformity,

```
> lm(logit(conformity/40) ~ partner.status*fcategory, data=Moore)
```

The right-hand side of the model formula may include factors and expressions that evaluate to numeric vectors and matrices. Because several operators have special meaning in formulas, arithmetic expressions that use them have to be *protected*. Expressions are protected automatically when they are inside function calls: For example, the + in the term `log(a + b)` has its usual arithmetic meaning on the right-hand side of a model formula, even though a + b does not when it is unprotected.

The *identity function* I may be used to protect arithmetic expressions in model formulas. For example, to regress `prestige` on the sum of `education` and `income` in Duncan's data set, thus implicitly forcing the coefficients of these two predictors to be equal, we may write,

```
> lm(prestige ~ I(income + education), data=Duncan)
```

We have already described most of the special operators that appear on the right of linear-model formulas. In Table 4.2 (adapted from Chambers, 1992, p. 29), A and B represent elements in a linear model: numeric vectors, matrices, factors, or expressions (such as a + b or a*b) composed from these.

Table 4.2 Expressions used in R formulas.

Expression	Interpretation	Example
A + B	include both A and B	income + education
A - B	exclude B from A	a*b*c - a:b:c
A:B	all interactions of A and B	type:education
A*B	A crossed with B, i.e., A + B + A:B	type*education
B %in% A	B nested within A	education %in% type
A/B	A + B %in% A	type/education
A^k	all effects crossed up to order k	(a + b + c)^2

The last three operators, `%in%`, `/`, and `^`, are new to us:

- `%in%` is actually a synonym for `:` but is typically used differently, to create nested terms rather than for interactions.
- `/` is a shorthand for nesting, in the same sense as `*` is a shorthand for crossing. As the table indicates, `A/B` is equivalent to `A + B %in% A` and hence to `A + B:A`. To see how this works, consider the following contrived example:

```
> (a <- factor(rep(LETTERS[1:3], each=3)))

[1] A A A B B B C C C
Levels: A B C

> (x <- rep(1:3, 3))

[1] 1 2 3 1 2 3 1 2 3

> model.matrix(~ a/x)

  (Intercept) aB aC aA:x aB:x aC:x
1           1  0  0    1    0    0
2           1  0  0    2    0    0
3           1  0  0    3    0    0
4           1  1  0    0    1    0
5           1  1  0    0    2    0
6           1  1  0    0    3    0
7           1  0  1    0    0    1
8           1  0  1    0    0    2
9           1  0  1    0    0    3

. . .

> model.matrix(~ x:a)

  (Intercept) x:aA x:aB x:aC
1           1    1    0    0
2           1    2    0    0
3           1    3    0    0
4           1    0    1    0
5           1    0    2    0
6           1    0    3    0
7           1    0    0    1
8           1    0    0    2
9           1    0    0    3

. . .
```

Thus, `a/x` fits an intercept; two dummy variables for a, with a = "A" as the baseline level; and a separate slope for x within each of the levels of a. In contrast, `x:a`, or equivalently `x %in% a` (or, indeed, `a:x` or `a %in% x`), fits a common intercept and a separate slope for x within each level of a.

- The `^` operator builds crossed effects up to the order given in the exponent. Thus, the example in the table, `(a + b + c)^2`, expands to all main effects and pairwise interactions among a, b, and c: that is, `a + b + c + a:b + a:c + b:c`. This is equivalent to another example in the table, `a*b*c - a:b:c`.

The intercept, represented by `1` in model formulas, is included in the model unless it is explicitly excluded, by specifying `-1` or `0` in the formula.

4.8.2 `data`

The `data` argument ordinarily specifies a data frame for use in fitting the model. If the `data` argument is omitted, then data are retrieved from the global environment, and so objects will be found in the normal manner along the search path, such as in an attached data frame. We find explicitly setting the `data` argument to be a sound general practice (as explained in Section 2.2.2).

4.8.3 `subset`

The `subset` argument is used to fit a model to a subset of observations. Several forms are possible:

- A logical vector, as in

```
> lm(weight ~ repwt, data=Davis,
+        subset = sex == "F")   # fit only to women
```

- A numeric vector of observation indices

```
> lm(weight ~ repwt, data=Davis,
+        subset=c(1:99, 141))   # use only obs. 1 to 99 and 141
```

- A numeric vector with negative entries, indicating the observations to be *omitted* from the fitted model

```
> lm(prestige ~ income + education, data=Duncan,
+        subset=-c(6, 16)) # exclude obs. 6 and 16
```

- A character vector containing the row names of the observations to be included, an option for which it is hard to provide a compelling example.

4.8.4 `weights`

If we loosen the constant-variance assumption in Equation 4.2 (p. 150) to

$$\mathrm{Var}(y|x_1, \ldots, x_k) = \sigma^2/w$$

for known weights $w > 0$, then we have a weighted-least-squares problem. The `weights` argument takes a numeric vector of nonnegative values of length equal to the number of observations and produces a weighted-least-squares fit.

4.8.5 `na.action`

The `na.action` option is initially set to `"na.omit"`, deleting observations with missing values for any of the variables appearing in the model. The function `na.exclude` is similar to `na.omit`, but it saves information about the deleted observations. This information may be used by functions that perform computations on linear-model objects. When quantities such as residuals are calculated, `na.exclude` causes entries corresponding to observations with missing data to be NA, rather than simply absent from the result. Filling out results with NAs can be advantageous because it preserves the number of observations in the data set; for example, when plotting residuals against a predictor, we need do nothing special to ensure that both variables have the same number of entries.

A third `na.action` option is `na.fail`, which stops all calculations and reports an error if any missing data are encountered. Although we will not pursue the possibility here, you can handle missing data in other ways by writing your own missing-data function.

Because we usually fit more than one model to the data, it is generally advantageous to handle missing data *outside* of lm, to ensure that all models are fit to the same subset of valid observations (see Section 2.2.3). To do otherwise is to invite inconsistency. This is true, incidentally, not only in R but also in other statistical software.

4.8.6 method, model, x, y, qr*

These are technical arguments, relating to how the computations are performed and what information is stored in the returned linear-model object; see ?lm.

4.8.7 singular.ok*

Under normal circumstances, R builds a full-rank model matrix, removing redundant dummy regressors, for example. Under some circumstances, however—perfect collinearity, for example, or when there is an empty cell in an ANOVA—the model matrix may be of deficient rank, and not all the coefficients in the linear model will be estimable. If singular.ok is TRUE, which is the default, then R will fit the model anyway, setting the aliased coefficients of the redundant regressors to NA (see Section 4.7.2).

4.8.8 contrasts

This argument allows us to specify contrasts for factors in a linear model, in the form of a list with named elements: for example,

```
> lm(conformity ~ partner.status*fcategory, data=Moore,
+       contrasts=list(partner.status=contr.sum, fcategory=contr.poly))
```

4.8.9 offset

An *offset* is a term added to the right-hand side of a model with no associated parameter to be estimated—it implicitly has a fixed coefficient of 1. In a linear model, specifying a variable as an offset is equivalent to subtracting that variable from the response. Offsets are more useful in GLMs (discussed in Chapter 5) than in linear models.

4.9 Using lm Objects

One of the mystifying features to neophytes of a command-line program such as R is that there are no visual cues to indicate what should be done next or even what *can* be done next. Suppose, for example, that we want to get predictions based on a fitted model, or to examine residuals, or to look at the correlation matrix of the estimated coefficients—well, you get the idea.

R has many functions that we can use to extract information from a linear-model object beyond those, such as `print` and `summary`, that we have seen so far. We can find out many of these functions using the `hints` function from the **hints** package:

```
> library(hints)
> hints(prestige.mod)

. . .

Functions for lm in package stats:

add1                    Add or Drop All Possible Single Terms
                        to a Model
alias                   Find Aliases (Dependencies) in a Model
anova.lm                ANOVA for Linear Model Fits
confint                 Confidence intervals for regression
                        coefficients
cooks.distance.lm       Regression Deletion Diagnostics
formula.lm              Accessing Linear Model Fits
hatvalues.lm            Regression Deletion Diagnostics
influence.lm            Regression Diagnostics
logLik                  Extract Log-Likelihood
model.matrix.lm         Construct Design Matrices
plot.lm                 Plot Diagnostics for an lm Object
predict.lm              Predict method for Linear Model Fits
print.lm                Fitting Linear Models
residuals.lm            Accessing Linear Model Fits
rstandard.lm            Regression Deletion Diagnostics
rstudent.lm             Regression Deletion Diagnostics
summary.lm              Summarizing Linear Model Fits
vcov                    Calculate Variance-Covariance Matrix
                        for a Fitted Model Object
influence.measures      Regression Deletion Diagnostics
lm                      Fitting Linear Models
lm.influence            Regression Diagnostics
model.matrix            Construct Design Matrices
. . .
```

We have shown only a few of the available functions with methods for `"lm"` objects, some of which are located in the **stats** package, which is part of the standard R distribution and is loaded when R starts up. There are additional methods in the **car**, **alr3**, and **MASS** packages, and in many others.

4.10 Complementary Reading and References

- The material in this chapter is covered in detail in Fox (2008, Part II) and in Weisberg (2005, chaps. 2–6).
- Model selection, briefly introduced in Section 4.5, is discussed in Fox (2008, sec. 13.2.2) and Weisberg (2005, chap. 10). The stepwise methods presented in the *Companion* may be viewed as rather old-fashioned, with newer methodology such as penalized fitting and tree methods now common, particularly in the related field of data mining. For these latter methods, see Berk (2008) and Hastie et al. (2009).

Fitting Generalized Linear Models 5

I n an article on the history of statistics, Efron (2003) traces the important trends in statistical analysis. At the beginning of the twentieth century, statistical methodology and ideas were largely discipline specific, with methods for economics, agronomy, psychology, and so on. The first half of the century saw rapid change from an applications-oriented field to a field dominated by mathematical theory, perhaps best symbolized by the rise of methods that relied on the centrality of the normal distribution, until midcentury, when most of the basic theory was worked out. The ascendence of the computer in the second half of the century meant that practical problems could be solved even if they lacked simple analytical solutions. In the past 40 years or so, statistics has become a synthesis of theory, computation, and practical applications.

According to Efron (2003), one of the central advances in statistics during the second half of the twentieth century was the development of *generalized linear models* (GLMs) and their most important special case, *logistic regression*. The basic ideas appeared, almost fully formed, in a single paper by Nelder and Wedderburn (1972). The fundamental breakthrough was the extension of the elegant and well-understood linear model to problems in which the response is categorical or discrete rather than a continuous numeric variable. Although GLMs also permit continuous responses, including normal (called *Gaussian* in the GLM literature) responses, the categorical-response problem remains the most important application of GLMs. Their use is now routine, made possible by the confluence of the general theory laid out by Nelder and Wedderburn, progress in computation, and the need to solve real-world data analysis problems.

This chapter explains how GLMs are implemented in R. We also discuss statistical models, such as the multinomial and proportional-odds logit models for *polytomous* (multicategory) responses, which, while not GLMs in the strict sense, are closely related to GLMs.

5.1   The Structure of GLMs

The structure of a GLM is very similar to that of the linear models discussed in Chapter 4. In particular, we have a response variable y and m predictors, and we are interested in understanding how the mean of y varies as the values of the predictors change.

A GLM consists of three components:

1. A *random component*, specifying the conditional distribution of the response variable, y, given the predictors. Nelder and Wedderburn (1972) considered conditional distributions that are from an *exponential family*. Both binomial and Poisson distributions are in the class of exponential families, and so problems with categorical or discrete responses can be studied with GLMs. Other, less frequently used, exponential families are the gamma and the inverse-Gaussian distributions for positively skewed continuous data. Since the initial introduction of GLMs, the class of error distributions has been enlarged, as we will discuss later. The linear models in Chapter 4 don't require the specification of the random component, but if we assume that the response has a Gaussian (i.e., normal) distribution, then the linear models are a special case of the GLMs.

2. As in linear models, the predictors in a GLM are translated into a set of k regressor variables, $\mathbf{x} = (x_1, \ldots, x_k)'$, possibly using dummy regressors, polynomials, regression splines, transformations, and so on.[1] In a GLM, the response depends on the predictors only through a linear function of the regressors, called the *linear predictor*,

$$\eta(\mathbf{x}) = \beta_0 + \beta_1 x_1 + \cdots + \beta_k x_k$$

3. In a linear model, the connection between the conditional mean $E(y|\mathbf{x})$ and the linear predictor $\eta(\mathbf{x})$ is direct,

$$E(y|\mathbf{x}) = \eta(\mathbf{x}) = \beta_0 + \beta_1 x_1 + \cdots + \beta_k x_k$$

and so the mean is equal to a linear combination of the regressors. This direct relationship is not appropriate for all GLMs because $\eta(\mathbf{x})$ can take on any value in $(-\infty, +\infty)$, whereas the mean of a binary (i.e., 0/1) random variable, for example, must be in the interval $(0, 1)$. We therefore introduce an invertible *link function* that translates from the scale of the mean response to the scale of the linear predictor. As is standard in GLMs, we write $\mu(\mathbf{x}) = E(y|\mathbf{x})$ for the conditional mean of the response. Then we have

$$g[\mu(\mathbf{x})] = \eta(\mathbf{x})$$

[1] If you are unfamiliar with vector notation, simply think of $\mathbf{x}$ as the collection of regressors.

Table 5.1 Standard link functions and their inverses: μ is the expected value of the response; η is the linear predictor.

Link	$\eta = g(\mu)$	$\mu = g^{-1}(\eta)$	Inverse Link
identity	μ	η	identity
log	$\log_e \mu$	e^{η}	exponential
inverse	μ^{-1}	η^{-1}	inverse
inverse-square	μ^{-2}	$\eta^{-1/2}$	inverse square-root
square-root	$\sqrt{\mu}$	η^2	square
logit	$\log_e \dfrac{\mu}{1-\mu}$	$\dfrac{1}{1+e^{-\eta}}$	logistic
probit	$\Phi(\mu)$	$\Phi^{-1}(\eta)$	normal quantile
complementary log-log	$\log_e[-\log_e(1-\mu)]$	$1 - \exp[-\exp(\eta)]$	—

Table 5.2 Canonical or default link, response range, and conditional variance function for generalized-linear-model families. ϕ is the dispersion parameter, equal to one in the cases where it is not shown; $\mu = \mu(\mathbf{x})$ is the conditional mean of y given the values of the predictors; in the binomial family, N is the number of trials.

Family	Default Link	Range of y	Var$(y\|\mathbf{x})$
gaussian	identity	$(-\infty, +\infty)$	ϕ
binomial	logit	$\dfrac{0, 1, ..., N}{N}$	$\dfrac{\mu(1-\mu)}{N}$
poisson	log	$0, 1, 2, ...$	μ
Gamma	inverse	$(0, \infty)$	$\phi\mu^2$
inverse.gaussian	1/mu^2	$(0, \infty)$	$\phi\mu^3$

Reversing this relationship produces the *inverse-link function*, $g^{-1}[\eta(\mathbf{x})] = \mu(\mathbf{x})$. The inverse of the link function is sometimes called the *mean function* (or the *kernel mean function*).[2]

Standard link functions and their inverses are shown in Table 5.1. The identity link function simply maps the linear predictor to itself, and so it is generally appropriate only for a distribution like the normal that supports positive and negative values. The next four link functions can be used only with responses that are nonnegative, like the gamma distribution or the Poisson. The remaining three links require the mean to be constrained to $(0, 1)$, as is appropriate for dichotomous or binomial data.

GLMs are typically fit to data by the method of maximum likelihood, using the iteratively weighted least squares procedure outlined in Section 5.12. Denote the maximum-likelihood estimates of the regression parameters as

---

[2]The math in this last result can be daunting, so here is an explanation in words: A nonlinear transformation of the mean, given by the expression $g[\mu(\mathbf{x})]$, can be modeled as a linear combination of the regressors, given by $\eta(\mathbf{x})$.

$b_0, b_1, ..., b_k$ and the estimated value of the linear predictor as $\widehat{\eta}(\mathbf{x}) = b_0 + b_1 x_1 + \cdots + b_k x_k$. The estimated mean of the response is $\widehat{\mu}(\mathbf{x}) = g^{-1}[\widehat{\eta}(\mathbf{x})]$.

The variance of distributions in an exponential family is the product of a positive *dispersion* (or *scale*) parameter ϕ, and a function of the the mean given the linear predictor:

$$\text{Var}(y|\mathbf{x}) = \phi \times V[\mu(\mathbf{x})]$$

The variances for the several exponential families are shown in the last column of Table 5.2. For the binomial and Poisson distributions, the dispersion parameter $\phi = 1$, and so the variance depends only on μ. For the Gaussian distribution, $V[\mu(\mathbf{x})] = 1$, and the variance depends only on the dispersion parameter ϕ. For Gaussian data, it is usual to replace ϕ by σ^2, as we have done for linear models in Chapter 4. Only the Gaussian family has constant variance, and in all other GLMs, the conditional variance of y at $\mathbf{x}$ depends on $\mu(\mathbf{x})$.

The *deviance*, based on the maximized value of the log-likelihood, provides a measure of the fit of a GLM to the data, much as the residual sum of squares does for a linear model. We write $p[y; \mu(\mathbf{x}), \phi]$ for the probability-mass or probability-density function of a single response y given the predictors $\mathbf{x}$. Then the value of the log-likelihood evaluated at the maximum-likelihood estimates of the regression coefficients for fixed dispersion is

$$\log_e L_0 = \sum \log_e p[y_i; \widehat{\mu}(\mathbf{x}_i), \phi]$$

where the sum is over the n independent observations in the data.

Similarly, imagine fitting another model, called a *saturated model*, with one parameter for each of the n observations; under the saturated model, the estimated value of the mean response for each observation is just its observed value. Consequently, the log-likelihood for the saturated model is

$$\log_e L_1 = \sum \log_e p(y_i; y_i, \phi)$$

The *residual deviance* is defined as twice the difference between these log-likelihoods,

$$D(\mathbf{y}; \widehat{\boldsymbol{\mu}}) = 2(\log_e L_1 - \log_e L_0)$$

Because the saturated model must fit the data at least as well as any other model, the deviance is never negative. The larger the deviance, the less well the model of interest matches the data. In families with a known value of the dispersion parameter ϕ, such as the binomial and Poisson families, the deviance provides a basis for testing lack of fit of the model and for other tests that compare different specifications of the linear predictor. If ϕ is estimated from the data, then the *scaled deviance* $D(\mathbf{y}; \widehat{\boldsymbol{\mu}})/\widehat{\phi}$ is the basis for hypothesis tests. The degrees of freedom associated with the residual deviance are equal to the number of observations n minus the number of estimated regression parameters, including the intercept if it is in the linear predictor.

Table 5.3 Family generators and corresponding link functions for the glm function. Default links are shown as • other possible links as ○.

family	identity	inverse	log	logit	probit	cloglog	sqrt	1/mu^2
gaussian	•	○	○					
binomial			○	•	○	○		
poisson	○		•				○	
Gamma	○	•	○					
inverse.gaussian	○	○	○					•
quasi	•	○	○	○	○	○	○	○
quasibinomial				•	○	○		
quasipoisson	○		•				○	

5.2   The glm Function in R

Most GLMs in R are fit with the glm function. The most important arguments of glm are formula, family, data, and subset: As for the lm function discussed in Chapter 4, the response variable and predictors are given in the model formula, and the data and subset arguments determine the data to which the model is fit. The family argument is new to glm, and it supplies a *family-generator function*, which provides the random component of the model; additional optional arguments (usually just a link argument—see below) to the family-generator function specify the link function for the model.

The family-generator functions for the five standard exponential families are given in Table 5.2. All family names start with lowercase letters, except for Gamma, which is capitalized to avoid confusion with the gamma function in R. Each family has its own *canonical link*, which is used by default if a link isn't given explicitly; in most cases, the canonical link is a reasonable choice. Also shown in the table are the range of the response and the variance function for each family.

Table 5.3 displays the links available for each family-generator function. Nondefault links are selected via a link argument to the family-generator functions: for example, binomial(link=probit). The quasi, quasibinomial, and quasipoisson family generators do not correspond to exponential families; these family generators are described in Section 5.10. If no family argument is supplied to glm, then the gaussian family with the identity link is assumed, resulting in a fit identical to that of lm, albeit computed less efficiently—like using a sledgehammer to set a tack.

5.3   GLMs for Binary-Response Data

We begin by considering data in which each case provides a *binary response*, say "success" or "failure"; the cases are independent; and the probability of success $\mu(\mathbf{x})$ is the same for all cases with the same values $\mathbf{x}$ of the regressors. In R, the response may be either a variable or an R expression that evaluates

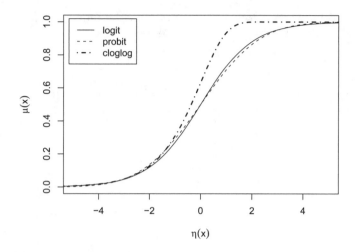

Figure 5.1 Comparison of logit, probit, and complementary log-log links. The probit link is rescaled to match the variance of the logistic distribution, $\pi^2/3$.

to 0 (failure) or 1 (success); a logical variable or expression (with TRUE representing success and FALSE, failure); or a factor, in which case the first category is taken to represent failure and the others success. We will consider the more general binomial responses, where the response is the *number* of successes in one or more trials, in the next section.

When the response is binary, we think of the mean function, $\mu(\mathbf{x})$, as the conditional probability that the response is a success given the values $\mathbf{x}$ of the regressors. The most common link function used with binary-response data is the logit link, for which

$$\log_e\left[\frac{\mu(\mathbf{x})}{1-\mu(\mathbf{x})}\right] = \eta(\mathbf{x}) \tag{5.1}$$

The quantity on the left of Equation 5.1 is called the *logit* or the *log-odds*, where the *odds* is the probability of success divided by the probability of failure. Solving for $\mu(\mathbf{x})$ gives the mean function,

$$\mu(\mathbf{x}) = \frac{1}{1+\exp\left[-\eta(\mathbf{x})\right]}$$

Other link functions, which are used less often, include the probit and the complementary log-log links. These three links are drawn as functions of the linear predictor $\eta(\mathbf{x})$ in Figure 5.1. The logit and probit links are very similar, except in the extreme tails, which aren't well resolved in a graph of the link functions, while the complementary log-log has a different shape and is asymmetric, approaching $\mu(\mathbf{x}) = 1$ more abruptly than $\mu(\mathbf{x}) = 0$.

The binomial model with the logit link is often called the *logistic-regression model* because the inverse of the logit link (see Table 5.1) is the logistic function. The name *logit regression* or *logit model* is also used.

Table 5.4 Variables in the `Mroz` data set.

Variable	Description	Remarks
lfp	wife's labor-force participation	factor: no, yes
k5	number of children ages 5 and younger	0–3, few 3's
k618	number of children ages 6 to 18	0–8, few > 5
age	wife's age in years	30–60, single years
wc	wife's college attendance	factor: no, yes
hc	husband's college attendance	factor, no, yes
lwg	log of wife's estimated wage rate	see text
inc	family income excluding wife's income	$1,000s

To illustrate logistic regression, we turn to an example from Long (1997), which draws on data from the 1976 U.S. Panel Study of Income Dynamics, and in which the response variable is married women's labor-force participation. The data were originally used in a different context by Mroz (1987), and the same data appear in Berndt (1991) as an exercise in logistic regression. The data are in the data frame `Mroz` in the **car** package; printing 10 of the $n = 753$ observations at random:

```
> library(car)
> some(Mroz)   # sample 10 rows

    lfp k5 k618 age  wc  hc     lwg   inc
43  yes  1    2  31 yes yes  0.9450 22.50
127 yes  0    3  45 yes yes -0.9606 23.67
194 yes  0    3  31  no  no  1.4971 18.00
232 yes  0    0  52  no  no  1.2504 10.40
277 yes  0    3  36  no yes  1.6032 16.40
351 yes  0    0  46  no  no  1.3069 28.00
362 yes  0    0  54 yes  no  2.1893 18.22
408 yes  1    3  36  no  no  3.2189 21.00
415 yes  0    3  36 yes yes  0.5263 32.00
607  no  1    1  44  no  no  0.9905  9.80

> nrow(Mroz)

[1] 753
```

The definitions of the variables in the `Mroz` data set are shown in Table 5.4. With the exception of `lwg`, these variables are straightforward. The log of each woman's estimated wage rate, `lwg`, is based on her actual earnings if she is in the labor force; if the woman is not in the labor force, then this variable is imputed (i.e., filled in) as the predicted value from a regression of log wages on the other predictors for women in the labor force. As we will see later (in Section 6.6.3), this definition of expected earnings creates a problem for the logistic regression.

5.3.1 FITTING THE BINARY LOGISTIC-REGRESSION MODEL

The variable `lfp` is a factor with two levels, and if we use this variable as the response, then the first level, `no`, corresponds to failure (0) and the second level, `yes`, to success (1).

```
> mroz.mod <- glm(lfp ~ k5 + k618 + age + wc + hc + lwg + inc,
+     family=binomial, data=Mroz)
```

The only features that differentiate this command from fitting a linear model are the change of function from lm to glm and the addition of the family argument. The family argument is set to the family-generator function binomial. The first argument to glm, the model formula, specifies the linear predictor for the logistic regression, not the mean function directly, as it did in linear regression. Because the link function is not given explicitly, the default logit link is used; the command is therefore equivalent to

```
> mroz.mod <- glm(lfp ~ k5 + k618 + age + wc + hc + lwg + inc,
+     family=binomial(link=logit), data=Mroz)
```

The model summary for a logistic regression is very similar to that for a linear regression:

```
> summary(mroz.mod)

Call:
glm(formula = lfp ~ k5 + k618 + age + wc + hc + lwg +
    inc, family = binomial, data = Mroz)

Deviance Residuals:
   Min      1Q   Median      3Q      Max
-2.106  -1.090    0.598    0.971    2.189

Coefficients:
            Estimate Std. Error z value Pr(>|z|)
(Intercept)  3.18214    0.64438    4.94  7.9e-07
k5          -1.46291    0.19700   -7.43  1.1e-13
k618        -0.06457    0.06800   -0.95  0.34234
age         -0.06287    0.01278   -4.92  8.7e-07
wcyes        0.80727    0.22998    3.51  0.00045
hcyes        0.11173    0.20604    0.54  0.58762
lwg          0.60469    0.15082    4.01  6.1e-05
inc         -0.03445    0.00821   -4.20  2.7e-05

(Dispersion parameter for binomial family taken to be 1)

    Null deviance: 1029.75  on 752  degrees of freedom
Residual deviance:  905.27  on 745  degrees of freedom
AIC: 921.3

Number of Fisher Scoring iterations: 4
```

The Wald tests, given by the ratio of the coefficient estimates to their standard errors, are now labeled as z values because the large-sample reference distribution for the tests is the normal distribution, not the t distribution as in a linear model. The dispersion parameter, $\phi = 1$, for the binomial family is noted in the output. Additional output includes the null deviance and degrees of freedom, which are for a model with all parameters apart from the intercept set to 0; the residual deviance and degrees of freedom for the model actually fit to the data; and the AIC, an alternative measure of fit sometimes used for model selection (see Section 4.5). Finally, the number of iterations required to obtain the maximum-likelihood estimates is printed.[3]

5.3.2 PARAMETER ESTIMATES FOR LOGISTIC REGRESSION

The estimated logistic-regression model is given by

$$\log_e \left[\frac{\widehat{\mu}(\mathbf{x})}{1 - \widehat{\mu}(\mathbf{x})} \right] = b_0 + b_1 x_1 + \cdots + b_k x_k$$

If we exponentiate both sides of this equation, we get

$$\frac{\widehat{\mu}(\mathbf{x})}{1 - \widehat{\mu}(\mathbf{x})} = \exp(b_0) \times \exp(b_1 x_1) \times \cdots \times \exp(b_k x_k)$$

where the left-hand side of the equation, $\widehat{\mu}(\mathbf{x}) / [1 - \widehat{\mu}(\mathbf{x})]$, gives the *fitted odds* of success—that is, the fitted probability of success divided by the fitted probability of failure. Exponentiating the model removes the logarithms and changes it from a model that is additive in the log-odds scale to one that is multiplicative in the odds scale. For example, increasing the age of a woman by 1 year, holding the other predictors constant, *multiplies* the odds of her being in the workforce by $\exp(b_3) = \exp(-0.06287) = 0.9391$—that is, reduces the odds of her working by 6%. The exponentials of the coefficient estimates are generally called *risk factors* (or *odds ratios*), and they can be viewed all at once, along with their confidence intervals, by the command

```
> round(exp(cbind(Estimate=coef(mroz.mod), confint(mroz.mod))), 2)
```

	Estimate	2.5 %	97.5 %
(Intercept)	24.10	6.94	87.03
k5	0.23	0.16	0.34
k618	0.94	0.82	1.07
age	0.94	0.92	0.96
wcyes	2.24	1.43	3.54
hcyes	1.12	0.75	1.68
lwg	1.83	1.37	2.48
inc	0.97	0.95	0.98

Compared with a woman who did not attend college, for example, a college-educated woman with all other predictors the same has odds of working about 2.24 times higher, with 95% confidence interval 1.43 to 3.54.

The confint function provides confidence intervals for GLMs based on profiling the log-likelihood rather than on the Wald statistics used for linear models (Venables and Ripley, 2002, sec. 8.4). Confidence intervals for GLMs based on the log-likelihood take longer to compute but tend to be more accurate than those based on the Wald statistic. Even before exponentiation, the log-likelihood-based confidence intervals need not be symmetric about the estimated coefficients.

---

[3] The iterative algorithm employed by glm to maximize the likelihood is described in Section 5.12.

5.3.3 ANALYSIS OF DEVIANCE FOR LOGISTIC REGRESSION

MODEL COMPARISONS AND SEQUENTIAL TESTS

As is true for linear models (see Section 4.4.2), the `anova` function can be used to compare two or more nested GLMs that differ by one or more terms. For example, we will remove the two variables that count the number of children, to test the hypothesis that labor-force participation does not depend on the number of children versus the alternative that it depends jointly on the number of young children and the number of older children:

```
> mroz.mod.2 <- update(mroz.mod, . ~ . - k5 - k618)
> anova(mroz.mod.2, mroz.mod, test="Chisq")

Analysis of Deviance Table

Model 1: lfp ~ age + wc + hc + lwg + inc
Model 2: lfp ~ k5 + k618 + age + wc + hc + lwg + inc
  Resid. Df Resid.    Dev Df Deviance  P(>|Chi|)
1       747           972
2       745           905  2     66.5    3.7e-15
```

The test statistic is the change in deviance between the two fitted models, and the p value is computed by comparing this value with the chi-square distribution with df equal to the change in the degrees of freedom for the two models. For the example, the change in deviance is 66.5 with 2 df, reflecting the two regressors removed from the model; when compared with the $\chi^2(2)$ distribution, we get a p value that is effectively 0. That the probability of a woman's participation in the labor force depends on the number of children she has is, of course, unsurprising. Because this test is based on deviances rather than variances, the output is called an *analysis of deviance* table.

Applied to GLMs, the `anova` function does not by default compute any significance tests. To obtain likelihood ratio chi-square tests for binary-regression models and other GLMs, we have to include the argument `test= "Chisq"`. For GLMs with a dispersion parameter estimated from the data (discussed, for example, in Section 5.10.4), specifying `test="F"` produces F tests in the analysis-of-deviance table.

As with linear models (see Section 4.4.3), the `anova` function can be used to compute a Type I or sequential analysis-of-deviance table, and as in linear models, these tables are rarely useful. We instead recommend using the Type II tests described in the next section.

TYPE II TESTS AND THE Anova FUNCTION

The `Anova` function in the **car** package can be used for GLMs as well as for linear models:

```
> Anova(mroz.mod)

Analysis of Deviance Table (Type II tests)
```

```
Response: lfp
      LR Chisq Df  Pr(>Chisq)
k5        66.5  1     3.5e-16
k618       0.9  1     0.34204
age       25.6  1     4.2e-07
wc        12.7  1     0.00036
hc         0.3  1     0.58749
lwg       17.0  1     3.7e-05
inc       19.5  1     1.0e-05
```

Each line of the analysis-of-deviance table provides a likelihood ratio test based on the change in deviance when comparing the two models. These tests are analogous to the corresponding Type II tests for a linear model (Section 4.4.4). For an additive model in which all terms have 1 *df*—as is the case in the current example—the Type II likelihood ratio statistics test the same hypotheses tested by the Wald statistics in the `summary` output for the model. Unlike in linear models, however, the Wald tests are not *identical* to the corresponding likelihood ratio tests. Although they are asymptotically equivalent, in some circumstances—but not in our example—the two approaches to testing can produce quite different significance levels. The likelihood ratio test is generally more reliable than the Wald test.

The `Anova` function is considerably more flexible than is described here, including options to compute Type II Wald tests that are equivalent to the *z* tests from the `summary` output; to compute *F* tests for models with an estimated dispersion parameter; and to compute Type III tests (details are provided in Section 5.10.1).

5.3.4 FITTED VALUES

As for linear models, the `predict` function is used to get predicted values for GLMs. By default, `predict` returns the estimated linear predictor for each observation: for example,

```
> head(predict(mroz.mod))  # first 6 values

       1        2        3        4        5        6
 0.06334  0.69382 -0.17411  0.67230  0.67772  0.38872
```

These are the predicted log-odds of success for the first 6 cases. To get the fitted probabilities (i.e., the fitted values on the scale of the response) rather than fitted logits, we use the argument `type="response"`:

```
> head(predict(mroz.mod, type="response"))

      1      2      3      4      5      6
 0.5158 0.6668 0.4566 0.6620 0.6632 0.5960
```

Fitted values on the scale of the response can also be obtained with the `fitted` function.

Table 5.5   Voter turnout by perceived closeness of the election and intensity of partisan preference, for the 1956 U.S. presidential election. Frequency counts are shown in the body of the table. *Source:* Campbell et al. (1960, Table 5-3).

Perceived Closeness	Intensity of Preference	Turnout		Logit
		Voted	Did Not Vote	$\log_e \left(\dfrac{\text{Voted}}{\text{Did Not Vote}} \right)$
One-Sided	Weak	91	39	0.847
	Medium	121	49	0.904
	Strong	64	24	0.981
Close	Weak	214	87	0.900
	Medium	284	76	1.318
	Strong	201	25	2.084

5.4   Binomial Data

For binomial-response data, the response variable is the number of successes in a fixed number N of independent trials, each with the same probability of success. Binary regression is a limiting case of binomial regression with all the $N = 1$.

For binomial data, it is necessary to specify not only the number of successes but also the number of trials for each of the n binomial observations. We can do this in R by setting the response variable in the model formula to a matrix with two columns, the first giving the number of successes y and the second, the number of failures, $N - y$ (as opposed to the number of trials). Alternatively for binomial data, the response can be the *proportion* (rather than the *number*) of successes for each observation, y/N, in which case the number of trials, N, is specified by the weights argument to glm (an unfortunate choice of argument name that invites confusion with other uses of weights in GLMs—see Section 5.11.1).

Regardless of how the model is specified, glm considers the response in a binomial GLM to be y/N, the fraction of successes. In this scaling, the mean of the response, $\mu(\mathbf{x})$, has the same interpretation as in binary regression and represents the probability of success on one trial when the regressors are equal to $\mathbf{x}$.

Consider, for example, the data given in Table 5.5, from *The American Voter* (Campbell et al., 1960), a classic study of voting in the 1956 U.S. presidential election. The body of the table, in the center panel, shows the frequency counts. The rows correspond to the six possible combinations of the two predictor factors, and the two columns correspond to the response. Here, y is the number who voted, and $N - y$ is the number who did not vote.

For small data sets like this one, typing data directly into R is not particularly difficult:

```
> closeness <- factor(rep(c("one.sided", "close"), c(3, 3)),
+     levels=c("one.sided", "close"))
> preference <- factor(rep(c("weak", "medium", "strong"), 2),
+     levels=c("weak", "medium", "strong"))
> voted <- c(91, 121, 64, 214, 284, 201)
> did.not.vote <- c(39, 49, 24, 87, 76, 25)
> logit.turnout <- log(voted/did.not.vote)
> Campbell <- data.frame(closeness, preference, voted, did.not.vote,
+       logit=logit.turnout)
```

We use the `rep` command to simplify entering data that follow a pattern (see Section 2.1.1) and then collect the data into a data frame. We verify that the data are correct by comparing the data frame with Table 5.5:

```
> Campbell

  closeness preference voted did.not.vote  logit
1 one.sided       weak    91           39 0.8473
2 one.sided     medium   121           49 0.9040
3 one.sided     strong    64           24 0.9808
4     close       weak   214           87 0.9001
5     close     medium   284           76 1.3182
6     close     strong   201           25 2.0844
```

The final variable in the data frame, and the last column of Table 5.5, show the sample logit, $\log_e(\text{Voted/Did Not Vote})$, for each combination of categories of the predictors. These logits are computed and saved so that they can be graphed in Figure 5.2, much as one would graph cell means in a two-way ANOVA when there are two factors as predictors and the response variable is quantitative. Voter turnout appears to increase with intensity of preference but much more dramatically when the election is perceived to be close than when it is perceived to be one-sided.

Figure 5.2 was drawn using the following commands:

```
> oldpar <- par(mar=c(5.1, 4.1, 4.1, 4.1)) # adjust margins
> with(Campbell,
+     interaction.plot(preference, closeness, logit,
+         type="b", pch=c(1, 16), cex=2,
+         ylab="log(Voted/Did Not Vote)"))
> probabilityAxis(side="right", at=seq(0.7, 0.875, by=0.025),
+     axis.title="Proportion(Voted)")  # right y-axis
> par(oldpar) # restore default margins
```

We use the `par` function to set global graphical parameters, in this case allowing extra room at the right for an additional axis. By assigning the result of `par` to a variable, we can call `par` again to reset the margins to their original values. An alternative is simply to close the plot device window before creating a new graph.[4] The `interaction.plot` function (which we previously encountered in Section 4.2.3) does most of the work. It is designed to work with two factors: The first is put on the horizontal axis, and the second defines

---

[4]See Chapter 7 on graphics in R for more details.

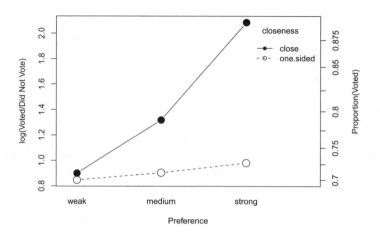

Figure 5.2 Voter turnout by perceived closeness of the election and intensity of partisan preference.

a grouping variable. The mean value of the third variable is plotted for each combination of the two factors. In this case, there is no mean to compute—there is only one observed logit per combination—so we changed the label on the *y*-axis to reflect this fact. The argument `type="b"` asks `interaction.plot` to plot both lines and points; `cex=2` (character expansion) draws the points double-size; and `pch=c(1, 16)` specifies the plotting characters `1` (an open circle) and `16` (a filled circle) for the two levels of `closeness`. We used the `probabilityAxis` function from the **car** package to draw a right-side probability axis, which is a *nonlinear* transformation of the scale of the linear predictor, the logit scale, shown at the left.

We proceed to fit a logistic-regression model to the *American Voter* data that is analogous to a two-way ANOVA model for a numeric response:

```
> campbell.mod <- glm(cbind(voted, did.not.vote) ~
+       closeness*preference, family=binomial, data=Campbell)
> summary(campbell.mod)

Call:
glm(formula = cbind(voted, did.not.vote) ~ closeness *
    preference, family = binomial, data = Campbell)

Deviance Residuals:
[1]  0   0   0   0   0   0

Coefficients:
                                  Estimate Std. Error z value
(Intercept)                         0.8473     0.1914    4.43
closenessclose                      0.0528     0.2298    0.23
preferencemedium                    0.0567     0.2555    0.22
preferencestrong                    0.1335     0.3065    0.44
closenessclose:preferencemedium     0.3615     0.3133    1.15
closenessclose:preferencestrong     1.0508     0.3938    2.67
                                  Pr(>|z|)
```

```
(Intercept)                            9.6e-06
closenessclose                         0.8184
preferencemedium                       0.8245
preferencestrong                       0.6630
closenessclose:preferencemedium        0.2485
closenessclose:preferencestrong        0.0076


(Dispersion parameter for binomial family taken to be 1)

    Null deviance: 3.4832e+01  on 5  degrees of freedom
Residual deviance: 7.4163e-14  on 0  degrees of freedom
AIC: 44.09

Number of Fisher Scoring iterations: 3
```

The data consist of only six combinations of the factors, and we have fit a model that has six parameters: an intercept, three main-effect parameters, and two interaction parameters. This is, therefore, a saturated model, which fits the data exactly, with all cell fitted log-odds equal to the observed values,

```
> predict(campbell.mod, type="link")

     1      2      3      4      5      6
0.8473 0.9040 0.9808 0.9001 1.3182 2.0844
```

and all residuals equal to 0. Consequently, the residual deviance is also 0 within rounding error.

The no-interaction model corresponds to parallel profiles of logits in the population. We can test for interaction either with the anova function, comparing the saturated and no-interaction models, or with the Anova function:

```
> campbell.mod.2 <- update(campbell.mod,
+       . ~ . - closeness:preference) # no interactions
> anova(campbell.mod.2, campbell.mod, test="Chisq")

Analysis of Deviance Table

Model 1: cbind(voted, did.not.vote) ~ closeness + preference
Model 2: cbind(voted, did.not.vote) ~ closeness * preference
  Resid. Df Resid. Dev Df Deviance P(>|Chi|)
1         2       7.12
2         0       0.00  2     7.12     0.028

> Anova(campbell.mod)

Analysis of Deviance Table (Type II tests)

Response: cbind(voted, did.not.vote)
                    LR Chisq Df Pr(>Chisq)
closeness               8.29  1      0.004
preference             19.11  2    7.1e-05
closeness:preference    7.12  2      0.028
```

The test for interaction is the same for both commands. The alternative hypothesis for this test is the saturated model with 0 residual deviance, and so the likelihood ratio test statistic could also be computed as the residual deviance for the fit of the no-interaction model:

```
> c(df=df.residual(campbell.mod.2), Test=deviance(campbell.mod.2))

    df   Test
2.000 7.119
```

This last approach doesn't automatically provide a significance level for the
test, but this could be obtained from the `pchisq` function.

The `Anova` command also provides Type II tests for the main effects, but
if we judge the interaction to be different from zero, then these tests, which
ignore the interaction, should not be interpreted.[5]

Rather than fitting a *binomial* logit model to the contingency table, we
could alternatively have fit a *binary* logit model to the 1,275 individual observations comprising Campbell et al.'s data. Let's generate the data in that form.
Manipulating data frames in this manner is often complicated, even in relatively small examples like this one:

```
> Campbell.long <- data.frame(close=NULL, prefer=NULL,
+     turn=NULL) # initialize an empty data frame
> for (j in 1:6) { # loop over combinations of factors
+   x1 <- with(Campbell,
+     data.frame(close=closeness[j],
+       prefer=preference[j],
+       turn=rep("did.not.vote", did.not.vote[j])))# non-voters rows
+   x2 <- with(Campbell,
+     data.frame(close=closeness[j],
+       prefer=preference[j],
+       turn=rep("voted", voted[j])))# rows for voters
+   Campbell.long <- rbind(Campbell.long, x1, x2) # build up rows
+ }
> some(Campbell.long) # sample rows

          close prefer          turn
123   one.sided   weak         voted
213   one.sided medium         voted
252   one.sided medium         voted
435       close   weak did.not.vote
460       close   weak did.not.vote
499       close   weak         voted
679       close   weak         voted
961       close medium         voted
1018      close medium         voted
1252      close strong         voted

> nrow(Campbell.long)

[1] 1275
```

We abbreviated the names of the original predictors to distinguish the variables in the new data set from those in `Campbell`, and now check that we
have correctly generated the data by rebuilding the contingency table for the
three variables:

---

[5]Had we specified Type III tests on the `Anova` command and used `contr.sum` to generate contrasts
for the factors (see Section 4.4.4), we could have interpreted each of the main-effects tests as an
average over the levels of the other factor. These tests, however, would be of dubious interest in light
of the interaction.

```
> ftable(xtabs(~ close + prefer + turn, data=Campbell.long))

                turn did.not.vote voted
close       prefer
one.sided   weak                39    91
            medium              49   121
            strong              24    64
close       weak                87   214
            medium              76   284
            strong              25   201
```

The `xtabs` function creates the three-way contingency table, and then `ftable` flattens the table for printing.

We proceed to fit a binary logistic-regression model to the newly generated `Campbell.long` data:

```
> campbell.mod.long <- glm(turn ~ close*prefer,
+       family=binomial, data=Campbell.long)
> summary(campbell.mod.long)

Call:
glm(formula = turn ~ close * prefer, family = binomial,
    data = Campbell.long)

Deviance Residuals:
   Min     1Q  Median     3Q     Max
-2.098  0.484   0.689  0.825   0.845

Coefficients:
                          Estimate Std. Error z value Pr(>|z|)
(Intercept)                 0.8473     0.1914    4.43  9.6e-06
closeclose                  0.0528     0.2298    0.23   0.8184
prefermedium                0.0567     0.2555    0.22   0.8245
preferstrong                0.1335     0.3065    0.44   0.6630
closeclose:prefermedium     0.3615     0.3133    1.15   0.2485
closeclose:preferstrong     1.0508     0.3938    2.67   0.0076

(Dispersion parameter for binomial family taken to be 1)

    Null deviance: 1391.3  on 1274  degrees of freedom
Residual deviance: 1356.4  on 1269  degrees of freedom
AIC: 1368

Number of Fisher Scoring iterations: 4

> Anova(campbell.mod.long)

Analysis of Deviance Table (Type II tests)

Response: turn
             LR Chisq Df Pr(>Chisq)
close            8.29  1      0.004
prefer          19.11  2    7.1e-05
close:prefer     7.12  2      0.028
```

As is apparent from this example, the two approaches give identical coefficient estimates and standard errors, and identical values of tests based on *differences* in residual deviance. The residual deviance itself, however, is different for the two models, because the binomial-logit model `campbell.mod` is fit to six cells while the binary-logit model `campbell.mod.long` is fit to 1,275 individual observations. The saturated model fit to the data summarized in the six cells is not the saturated model fit to the 1,275 individual observations.

When, as here, the predictors are discrete and thus divide the data into groups, there is an advantage in fitting the binomial-logit model: The residual deviance for any unsaturated model, such as the no-interaction model in the example, can be interpreted as a test of *lack of fit*. We can equivalently test lack of fit for a binary-logit model with discrete predictors by formulating a model with all the interactions among the predictors treated as factors—in the example, the model with the `closeness:preference` interactions and the main effects marginal to them—and using that as a point of comparison.

5.5   Poisson GLMs for Count Data

Poisson GLMs arise in two distinct contexts. The first, covered in this section, is more straightforward, in which the conditional distribution of the response variable given the predictors follows a Poisson distribution. The second, presented in the next section, is the use of loglinear models for analyzing the associations in contingency tables. In most instances, the cell counts in contingency tables have multinomial, not Poisson, conditional distributions, but it turns out that with appropriate interpretation of parameters, the multinomial maximum-likelihood estimators can be obtained *as if* the counts were Poisson random variables. Thus, the same Poisson-GLM approach can be used for fitting Poisson-regression models and loglinear models for contingency tables.

The default link for the `poisson` family generator is the log link; all the models discussed in this section and the next use the log link.

Recall Ornstein's data (Ornstein, 1976) on interlocking director and top executive positions in 248 major Canadian firms (introduced in Chapter 3):

```
> some(Ornstein)
```

	assets	sector	nation	interlocks
41	7564	FIN	US	22
79	3561	MIN	US	8
112	1601	WOD	CAN	25
123	1427	HLD	CAN	1
175	586	TRN	CAN	10
179	558	AGR	CAN	14
188	516	TRN	CAN	5
217	359	AGR	US	0
218	358	AGR	US	0
237	245	MIN	CAN	11

```
> nrow(Ornstein)
```

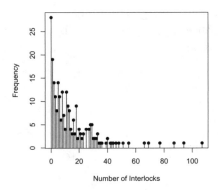

Figure 5.3 Distribution of number of interlocks maintained by 248 large Canadian corporations.

[1] 248

Ornstein performed a least-squares regression of the response interlocks, the number of interlocks maintained by each firm, on the firm's assets in millions of dollars; sector of operation, a factor with eight levels; and nation of control, a factor with four levels. Because the response variable interlocks is a count, a Poisson GLM might be preferable.[6] Indeed, the marginal distribution of number of interlocks, in Figure 5.3, shows many 0 counts and a substantial positive skew. To construct this graph, we first use the xtabs function to find the frequency distribution of interlocks:

```
(tab <- xtabs(~ interlocks, data=Ornstein))

  0   1   2   3   4   5   6   7   8   9  10  11  12  13  14  15
 28  19  14  11   8  14  11   6  12   7   4  12   9   8   4   3
 . . .
 94 107
  1   1
```

The numbers on top of the frequencies are the different values of interlocks: Thus, there are 28 firms with 0 interlocks, 19 with 1 interlock, 14 with 2 interlocks, and so on. The graph is produced by plotting the counts in tab against the category labels converted into numbers:

```
> x <- as.numeric(names(tab)) # distinct values of interlocks
> plot(x, tab, type="h", xlab="Number of Interlocks",
+       ylab="Frequency")
> points(x, tab, pch=16)
```

Specifying type="h" in the call to plot produces the histogram-like vertical lines, while the points function adds the filled circles (pch=16) at the top of the lines.

---

[6]Actually, Ornstein used both assets and the log of assets in a least-squares regression. Poisson regression was essentially unknown to sociologists at the time, and so we don't mean to imply criticism of Ornstein's work.

Using `glm` to fit a Poisson-regression model is very simple. Preliminary examination of the data suggests the use of `log2(assets)` in place of `assets` in the regression:

```
> mod.ornstein <- glm(interlocks ~ log2(assets) + nation + sector,
+     family=poisson, data=Ornstein)
> summary(mod.ornstein)

Call:
glm(formula = interlocks ~ log2(assets) + nation +
    sector, family = poisson, data = Ornstein)

Deviance Residuals:
   Min      1Q  Median      3Q     Max
-6.711  -2.316  -0.459   1.282   6.285

Coefficients:
              Estimate Std. Error z value Pr(>|z|)
(Intercept)    -0.8394     0.1366   -6.14  8.1e-10
log2(assets)    0.3129     0.0118   26.58  < 2e-16
nationOTH      -0.1070     0.0744   -1.44  0.15030
nationUK       -0.3872     0.0895   -4.33  1.5e-05
nationUS       -0.7724     0.0496  -15.56  < 2e-16
sectorBNK      -0.1665     0.0958   -1.74  0.08204
sectorCON      -0.4893     0.2132   -2.29  0.02174
sectorFIN      -0.1116     0.0757   -1.47  0.14046
sectorHLD      -0.0149     0.1192   -0.13  0.90051
sectorMAN       0.1219     0.0761    1.60  0.10949
sectorMER       0.0616     0.0867    0.71  0.47760
sectorMIN       0.2498     0.0689    3.63  0.00029
sectorTRN       0.1518     0.0789    1.92  0.05445
sectorWOD       0.4983     0.0756    6.59  4.4e-11

(Dispersion parameter for poisson family taken to be 1)

    Null deviance: 3737.0  on 247   degrees of freedom
Residual deviance: 1547.1  on 234   degrees of freedom
AIC: 2473

Number of Fisher Scoring iterations: 5

> Anova(mod.ornstein)

Analysis of Deviance Table (Type II tests)

Response: interlocks
             LR Chisq Df Pr(>Chisq)
log2(assets)      731  1      <2e-16
nation            276  3      <2e-16
sector            103  9      <2e-16
```

The Type II analysis of deviance, produced by the `Anova` function in the **car** package, shows that all three predictors have highly statistically significant effects.

The coefficients of the model are interpreted as effects on the log-count scale (the scale of the linear predictor), and consequently exponentiating the coefficients produces multiplicative effects on the count scale (the scale of the response):

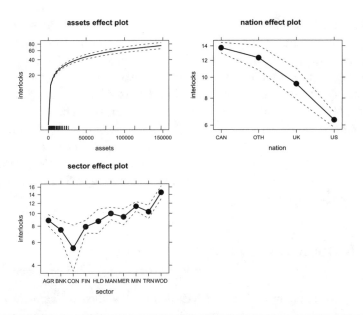

Figure 5.4 Effect plots for the terms in the Poisson-regression model fit to Ornstein's interlocking-directorate data. The broken lines show point-wise 95% confidence envelopes around the fitted effects.

```
> exp(coef(mod.ornstein))
```

(Intercept)	log2(assets)	nationOTH	nationUK	nationUS
0.431978	1.367410	0.898532	0.678941	0.461908
sectorBNK	sectorCON	sectorFIN	sectorHLD	sectorMAN
0.846612	0.613065	0.894394	0.985203	1.129602
sectorMER	sectorMIN	sectorTRN	sectorWOD	
1.063510	1.283828	1.163938	1.645846	

We thus estimate, for example, that doubling assets (i.e., increasing the log_2 of assets by 1), holding the other predictors constant, multiplies the expected number of interlocks by 1.37 (i.e., increases expected interlocks by 37%). Likewise, when compared to a similar Canadian firm, which is the baseline level for the factor nation, a U.S. firm on average maintains only 46% as many interlocks.

We can also use the **effects** package (introduced for linear models in Section 4.3.3) to visualize the terms in a GLM, such as a Poisson regression. For the model fit to Ornstein's data:

```
> library(effects)
> plot(allEffects(mod.ornstein, default.levels=50), ask=FALSE)
```

By default, the vertical axes in these graphs are on the scale of the linear predictor, which is the log-count scale for Ornstein's Poisson regression. The axis tick marks are labeled on the scale of the response, however—number of interlocks, in our example. Also by default, the range of the vertical axis is different in the several graphs, a feature of the graphs to which we should attend in assessing the relative impact of the predictors on `inter-locks`.[7] The argument `default.levels=50` produces a smoother plot, setting `assets` to 50 distinct values across its range rather than the default 10; the rug-plot at the bottom of the effect display for `assets` shows the marginal distribution of the predictor. The levels of the factor `sector` are ordered alphabetically; the effect plot for this factor would be easier to read if we rearranged the levels so that they were in the same order as the effects, as happened accidentally for the factor `nation`. The plot for `assets` is curved because the model used `log2(assets)` as the regressor. About 95% of the values of `assets` are less than 20,000 (corresponding to $20 billion), so the right portion of this plot may be suspect.

5.6 Loglinear Models for Contingency Tables

A path-breaking paper by Birch (1963) defined the class of *loglinear models* for contingency tables, and in the early years following the publication of Birch's paper, specialized software was developed for fitting these models. The publication of Nelder and Wedderburn (1972), however, made it clear that Poisson regression could be used to fit loglinear models. Comprehensive treatments of the subject are listed in the Complementary Reading at the end of the chapter.

5.6.1 TWO-DIMENSIONAL TABLES

A *contingency table* is an array of counts in two or more dimensions. The most familiar is the two-dimensional (or two-way) contingency table, and as an example, we will use a cross-classification of all the PhDs awarded in the mathematical sciences in the United States in 2008–2009 (from Phipps et al., 2009, Supp. Table IV), which is found in the data frame `AMSsurvey` in the **car** package. There are several variables in `AMSsurvey`:

- `type` of institution, a factor in which Levels `I(Pu)` and `I(Pr)` are math departments in high-quality public and private universities, Levels `II` and `III` are math departments in progressively lower-quality universities, Level `IV` represents statistics and biostatistics departments, and Level `Va` refers to applied mathematics departments.
- `sex` of the degree recipient, with levels `Female` and `Male`.
- `citizen`, the citizenship of the degree recipient, a factor with levels `US` and `Non-US`.
- `count`, the number of individuals for each combination of `type`, `sex`, and `citizen`—and, consequently, for each combination of `type` and

---

[7]We could set common scales for the vertical axes by, for example, specifying the argument `ylim=log(c(1, 80))` to `plot`, but then the graphs for `nation` and `sector` would be considerably compressed.

class. The data in AMSsurvey have one row for each of the cells in the table, thus $6 \times 2 \times 2 = 24$ rows in all.

```
> head(AMSsurvey)   # first 6 rows

    type      sex citizen count
1 I(Pu)    Male        US   132
2 I(Pu)  Female        US    35
3 I(Pr)    Male        US    87
4 I(Pr)  Female        US    20
5    II    Male        US    96
6    II  Female        US    47

> nrow(AMSsurvey)

[1] 24
```

The most common approach to tables of counts is to test (many) two-dimensional tables for independence. To examine the association between sex and citizen, for instance, we can create a two-way table by summing over the levels of the third variable, type:

```
> (tab.sex.citizen <- xtabs(count ~ sex + citizen, data=AMSsurvey))

        citizen
sex      Non-US  US
  Female    260 202
  Male      501 467
```

For example, 260 female PhD recipients were non-U.S. citizens in this period.

The usual analysis of a two-dimensional table such as this consists of a test of independence of the row and column classifications:

```
> chisq.test(tab.sex.citizen,
+       correct=FALSE) # suppress Yates correction

        Pearson's Chi-squared test

data:  tab.sex.citizen
X-squared = 2.567, df = 1, p-value = 0.1091
```

The test statistic is the uncorrected Pearson's X^2, defined by the familiar formula

$$X^2 = \sum \frac{(O - E)^2}{E}$$

where the sum is over all cells of the table, O are the observed cell counts, and E are the estimated expected cell counts computed under the assumption that the null hypothesis of independence is true. Approximate significance levels are determined by comparing the value of X^2 to a χ^2 distribution with degrees of freedom depending on the number of cells and the number of parameters estimated under the null hypothesis. For an $r \times c$ table, the degrees of freedom for the test of independence are $(r-1)(c-1)$—here, $(2-1)(2-1) = 1\ df$. The chisq.test function can also estimate the significance level using a simulation, an approach that is preferred when the cell counts are small. Using the default argument `correct=TRUE` would produce a corrected version of X^2 that is also more accurate in small samples.

The p value close to .1 suggests at best weak evidence that the proportion of women is different for citizens and non-citizens, or, equivalently, that the proportion of non-citizens is different for males and females.

A loglinear model can also be fit to the two-way contingency table by assuming that the cell counts are independent Poisson random variables. First, we need to change the two-way table into a data frame:

```
> (AMS2 <- as.data.frame(tab.sex.citizen))

    sex citizen Freq
1 Female  Non-US  260
2   Male  Non-US  501
3 Female      US  202
4   Male      US  467
```

The model of independence is then given by

```
> (phd.mod.indep <- glm(Freq ~ sex + citizen, family=poisson,
+      data=AMS2))

Call:  glm(formula = Freq ~ sex + citizen, family = poisson,
    data = AMS2)

Coefficients:
(Intercept)     sexMale     citizenUS
      5.505       0.740        -0.129

Degrees of Freedom: 3 Total (i.e. Null);  1 Residual
Null Deviance:              191
Residual Deviance: 2.57          AIC: 39.2
```

Recall that the residual deviance is the difference in deviance between the model that we fit to the data—here, the model of independence—and a saturated model, which, in this case adds the term `sex:citizen`, representing the association—the departure from independence—between the two variables.[8] The residual deviance of 2.57 for the independence model is a lack-of-fit test for this model or, equivalently, a test that the association between `sex` and `citizen` is zero. Like Pearson's X^2, the residual deviance is compared with the χ^2 distribution with degrees of freedom equal to the residual df for the model. The significance level for this test is not automatically reported because the residual deviance is a lack-of-fit test only for cross-classified data with one row in the data set for each cell. We can compute the significance level as

```
> pchisq(2.57, df=1, lower.tail=FALSE)

[1] 0.1089
```

---

[8]It is traditional in loglinear models to call terms such as `sex:citizen` "interactions," even though they represent not interaction in the usual sense of the word—that is, a change in the partial relationship between two variables across different levels of a third variable—but rather the association between a pair of variables.

The test based on the deviance is a likelihood ratio test of the hypothesis of independence, while Pearson's X^2 is a *score test* of the same hypothesis. The two tests are asymptotically equivalent, but in small samples, Pearson's chi-square can give more accurate inferences. In general, however, the change in deviance is preferred because it is more useful for comparing models other than the saturated model. To compute Pearson's X^2 for any GLM fit, use

```
> sum(residuals(phd.mod.indep, type="pearson")^2)

[1] 2.567
```

5.6.2 THREE-DIMENSIONAL CONTINGENCY TABLES

The AMSsurvey data comprise a three-dimensional table, the first dimension representing the type of institution; the second, the sex of the degree recipient; and the third, citizenship status (citizen). In the preceding section, we collapsed the data over type to analyze a two-way table for sex and citizen. With three dimensions, there is a much richer set of models that can be fit to the data. The saturated model consists of an intercept, all possible main effects, all two-factor interactions or associations, and the three-factor interaction.[9] The formula for the saturated model is

```
count ~ type + sex + citizen
        + type:sex + type:citizen + sex:citizen
        + type:sex:citizen
```

or, equivalently and more compactly,

```
count ~ type*sex*citizen
```

Additional models are obtained from the saturated model by deleting terms, subject to the constraints of the marginality principle. The Anova function can be used to test all Type II hypotheses, which conform to the principle of marginality:

```
> phd.mod.all <- glm(count ~ type*sex*citizen, # saturated model
+       family=poisson, data=AMSsurvey)
> Anova(phd.mod.all)

Analysis of Deviance Table (Type II tests)

Response: count
                 LR Chisq Df Pr(>Chisq)
type                233.3  5   < 2e-16
sex                 183.0  1   < 2e-16
citizen               5.9  1   0.01494
type:sex             69.1  5   1.6e-13
type:citizen         24.0  5   0.00021
sex:citizen           0.5  1   0.46346
type:sex:citizen      1.4  5   0.92220
```

---

[9]As in the case of two-way tables, the terms *main effect* and *interaction* can be misleading: The "main effects" pertain to the marginal distributions of the three variables and the "two-way interactions" to the partial associations between pairs of variables. The "three-way interaction" represents interaction in the more usual sense, in that the presence of this term in the model implies that the partial association between each pair of variables varies over the levels of the third variable.

As usual, when there are higher-order terms such as interactions in a model, we read the analysis-of-deviance table from bottom to top. The *p* values for the three-factor interaction and for the `sex:citizen` interaction are very large, and so these terms can probably be ignored. The *p* values for the remaining two-factor interactions are small, suggesting that these interactions are nonzero. The tests for the main effects are generally irrelevant in loglinear models and are usually ignored—they pertain to the marginal distributions of the factors. The model with two interactions can be shown to be a model of *conditional independence*: Given the level of institution `type`, the variable common to the two interactions, `sex` and `citizen` are independent (see Agresti, 2007, sec. 3.1.2).

We update the saturated model, removing the nonsignificant interactions:

```
> summary(phd.mod.1 <- update(phd.mod.all,
+      . ~ .- sex:citizen - type:sex:citizen))

Call:
glm(formula = count ~ type + sex + citizen + type:sex +
    type:citizen, family = poisson, data = AMSsurvey)

Deviance Residuals:
     Min       1Q    Median        3Q       Max
-0.60314  -0.22365  -0.00152   0.22934   0.58670

Coefficients:
                      Estimate Std. Error z value Pr(>|z|)
(Intercept)            3.4409     0.1373   25.06  < 2e-16
typeI(Pr)             -0.3417     0.2143   -1.59  0.11091
typeII                 0.4264     0.1811    2.35  0.01856
typeIII                0.2019     0.1948    1.04  0.30000
typeIV                 1.1893     0.1634    7.28  3.4e-13
typeVa                -0.9713     0.2664   -3.65  0.00027
sexMale                1.4095     0.1394   10.11  < 2e-16
citizenUS              0.0491     0.1108    0.44  0.65774
typeI(Pr):sexMale     -0.1041     0.2184   -0.48  0.63346
typeII:sexMale        -0.7638     0.1875   -4.07  4.6e-05
typeIII:sexMale       -1.0670     0.2086   -5.11  3.2e-07
typeIV:sexMale        -1.2157     0.1758   -6.91  4.7e-12
typeVa:sexMale        -0.5404     0.2721   -1.99  0.04701
typeI(Pr):citizenUS   -0.0207     0.1767   -0.12  0.90698
typeII:citizenUS      -0.0207     0.1627   -0.13  0.89866
typeIII:citizenUS     -0.2014     0.1892   -1.06  0.28709
typeIV:citizenUS      -0.6457     0.1571   -4.11  4.0e-05
typeVa:citizenUS       0.1332     0.2411    0.55  0.58048

(Dispersion parameter for poisson family taken to be 1)

    Null deviance: 521.4440  on 23  degrees of freedom
Residual deviance:   1.9568  on  6  degrees of freedom
AIC: 175.3

Number of Fisher Scoring iterations: 4
```

This model reproduces the data quite well, as reflected in a lack-of-fit test with a very large *p* value:

```
> pchisq(1.9568, df=6, lower.tail=FALSE)
```

```
[1] 0.9236
```

Examining the coefficient estimates, the fraction of male doctorates are similar in Type I(Pu) and Type I(Pr), because the coefficient for Type I(Pr) that compares these two groups is small with a relatively large p value. The other coefficients in the type by sex interaction are all negative and large relative to their standard errors, so male doctorates are less frequent in institutions other than Type I(Pu) and Type I(Pr). Similarly, U.S. citizens are less frequent in Type IV, statistics and biostatistics programs, than in the other types.

5.6.3 SAMPLING PLANS FOR LOGLINEAR MODELS

An interesting characteristic of the AMSsurvey data is that the 2008–2009 doctorate recipients were simply classified according to the three variables. Assuming that the counts in each of the cells has a Poisson distribution leads immediately to the Poisson-regression model that we used.

Not all contingency tables are constructed in this way, however. Consider this thought experiment: We will collect data to learn about the characteristics of customers who use human tellers in banks to make transactions. We will study the transactions between the tellers and the customers, classifying each transaction by the factor age of the customer, A, with, say, three age groups; the factor gender, B, either male or female; and the factor C, whether or not the transaction was simple enough to be done at an ATM rather than with a human teller. Each of the following sampling plans leads to a different distribution for the counts, but Poisson regression can legitimately be used to estimate parameters and perform tests in all these cases:

Poisson sampling Go to the bank for a fixed period of time, observe the transactions, and classify them according to the three variables. In this case, even the sample size n is random. Poisson-regression models are appropriate here, and all parameters are potentially of interest.

Multinomial sampling Fix the sample size n in advance, and sample as long as necessary to get n transactions. This scheme differs from the first sampling plan only slightly: The counts are no longer independent Poisson random variables, because their sum is constrained to equal the fixed sample size n, and so the counts follow a multinomial distribution. Poisson regression can be used, but the overall mean parameter (i.e., the intercept of the Poisson-regression model) is determined by the sampling plan.

Product-multinomial sampling We will sample equal numbers of men and women. In this case, the intercept and the main effect of B, which reflects the marginal distribution of B, are fixed by the design.

Fix two variables Sample a fixed number in each age × sex combination to get a different multinomial sampling scheme. All models fit to the data must include the terms `1 + A + B + A:B = A*B`, because these are all fixed by the sampling design.

Retrospective sampling Suppose that complex transactions are rare, and so we decide to sample $n/2$ complex transactions first, and then $n/2$ simple ones. This scheme differs from the earlier sampling plans because the factor `C` is effectively a response variable, and we have guaranteed that we will have an equal number of observations in each of the response categories. All models must include `1 + C`. The terms `A:C`, `B:C`, and `A:B:C` tell us whether and how the response is related to the predictors, and all these terms are estimable. This type of sampling is usually called *case-control sampling* or *retrospective sampling* and is very commonly used in medical studies of rare diseases.

5.6.4 RESPONSE VARIABLES

In the `AMSsurvey` data, none of the three classification variables can reasonably be considered response variables. In other loglinear models, however, any—or all—the classification variables could be considered to be responses. When there are response variables, the interesting terms in a loglinear model are typically the interactions or associations between the predictors and the responses. All models will generally include the highest-order interaction among the predictor factors, the interactions among the responses, and all lower-order terms by the marginality principle.

An example is provided by the *American Voter* data in Table 5.5 (p. 240), to which we previously fit a logistic-regression model in which `turnout` was the response. We can also view these data as forming a three-way contingency table and fit loglinear models to the table. The three dimensions of the table are `closeness`, with two levels; `preference`, with three levels; and the response `turnout`, with two levels. In this case, then, there are two predictors and a single response. The data here were drawn from a national survey; ignoring the complexity of the sampling design of the survey, we will treat the data as if they arose from a Poisson or simple multinomial sampling plan.[10] We recall the data frame `Campbell` that we created in Section 5.4:

```
> Campbell

  closeness preference voted did.not.vote  logit
1 one.sided       weak    91           39 0.8473
2 one.sided     medium   121           49 0.9040
3 one.sided     strong    64           24 0.9808
4     close       weak   214           87 0.9001
5     close     medium   284           76 1.3182
6     close     strong   201           25 2.0844
```

[10]Complex survey data can be properly analyzed in R using the **survey** package, which, among its many facilities, has a function for fitting GLMs. We do not, however, have the original data set from which our contingency table was constructed.

To turn this data set into a form that can be used to fit a loglinear model, we need to stack the variables `voted` and `did.not.vote` into one column to create the response factor, an operation that can be performed conveniently with the `melt` function in the **reshape** package (which, as its name implies, provides facilities for rearranging data):

```
> library(reshape)
> (Campbell1 <- melt(Campbell,
+       id.vars=c("closeness", "preference"),
+       measure.var=c("voted", "did.not.vote"),
+       variable_name="turnout"))

   closeness preference       turnout value
1  one.sided       weak         voted    91
2  one.sided     medium         voted   121
3  one.sided     strong         voted    64
4      close       weak         voted   214
5      close     medium         voted   284
6      close     strong         voted   201
7  one.sided       weak  did.not.vote    39
8  one.sided     medium  did.not.vote    49
9  one.sided     strong  did.not.vote    24
10     close       weak  did.not.vote    87
11     close     medium  did.not.vote    76
12     close     strong  did.not.vote    25
```

The first argument in the call to `melt` is the name of a data frame, and the second argument gives the names of the *ID variables* that are duplicated in each row of the new data frame. The *measure variables* are stacked into a column and given the variable name `value`. The new data frame has one row for each of the 12 cells in the $2 \times 3 \times 2$ contingency table.

Because we are interested in finding the important interactions with the response, we start by fitting the saturated model and examining tests for various terms:

```
> mod.loglin <- glm(value ~ closeness*preference*turnout,
+       family=poisson, data=Campbell1)
> Anova(mod.loglin)

Analysis of Deviance Table (Type II tests)

Response: value
                               LR Chisq Df Pr(>Chisq)
closeness                           201  1    < 2e-16
preference                           56  2    6.8e-13
turnout                             376  1    < 2e-16
closeness:preference                  1  2      0.540
closeness:turnout                     8  1      0.004
preference:turnout                   19  2    7.1e-05
closeness:preference:turnout          7  2      0.028
```

The only terms of interest are those that include the response variable `turnout`, and all three of these terms, including the highest-order term `closeness:preference:turnout`, have small *p* values.

As long as a loglinear model with a dichotomous response variable includes the highest-order interaction among the predictors, here `close-ness:preference`, and obeys the principle of marginality, the loglinear model is equivalent to a logistic-regression model. All the parameter estimates in the logistic regression also appear in the loglinear model, but they are labeled differently. For example, the `closeness` main effect in the logistic regression corresponds to the `closeness:turnout` term in the loglinear model; similarly, the `closeness:preference` interaction in the logistic regression corresponds to `closeness:preference:turnout` in the loglinear model. Likelihood ratio tests for corresponding terms are identical for the logistic-regression and loglinear models, as the reader can verify for the example (cf., page 243). The only important difference is that the residual deviance for the loglinear model provides a goodness-of-fit test for that model, but it is not a goodness-of-fit test for the logistic regression.[11]

5.6.5   PREPARING DATA FOR FITTING A LOGLINEAR MODEL

Data to which we want to fit a loglinear model often arrive in the form of a data frame with one observation for each response, rather than one observation for each cell in the table. For example, in the `Salaries` data in the **car** package (introduced in Section 4.4.7), we have one row for each of the 397 faculty members in the data set:

```
> some(Salaries)
```

	rank	discipline	yrs.since.phd	yrs.service	sex	salary
1	Prof	B	19	18	Male	139750
14	AsstProf	B	2	0	Male	78000
61	AssocProf	B	9	8	Male	90304
70	Prof	B	28	36	Male	91412
152	AsstProf	B	4	4	Male	92000
154	AssocProf	B	12	10	Female	103994
157	AssocProf	B	12	18	Male	113341
182	Prof	B	18	5	Male	141136
291	Prof	A	33	7	Male	174500
370	Prof	A	33	31	Male	134690

```
> nrow(Salaries)
```

```
[1] 397
```

Suppose that we want to study the three-way contingency table of `rank` by `discipline` by `sex`, perhaps to determine whether the prevalence of women varies by discipline and rank:

---

[11]These conclusions extend to polytomous (i.e., multi-category) responses, where loglinear models that fit the highest-order interaction among the predictors are equivalent to multinomial-logit models (described in Section 5.7).

```
> ftable(tab1 <- xtabs(~ rank + discipline + sex, data=Salaries))
                     sex Female Male
rank       discipline
AsstProf   A                 6   18
           B                 5   38
AssocProf  A                 4   22
           B                 6   32
Prof       A                 8  123
           B                10  125
```

We created the three-way table with xtabs, saved the result in the variable tab1, and as before applied ftable to flatten the table for printing.

We turn the table into a data frame with one row for each cell to use with glm:

```
> (Salaries1 <- data.frame(tab1))
        rank discipline    sex Freq
1   AsstProf          A Female    6
2  AssocProf          A Female    4
3       Prof          A Female    8
4   AsstProf          B Female    5
5  AssocProf          B Female    6
6       Prof          B Female   10
7   AsstProf          A   Male   18
8  AssocProf          A   Male   22
9       Prof          A   Male  123
10  AsstProf          B   Male   38
11 AssocProf          B   Male   32
12      Prof          B   Male  125
```

The response count is given the name Freq.

5.7   Multinomial Response Data

The data frame Womenlf in the **car** package contains data drawn from a social survey of the Canadian population conducted in 1977. The data are for $n = 263$ married women between the ages of 21 and 30:

```
> some(Womenlf)
        partic hincome children   region
12    fulltime      13  present  Ontario
65    not.work      11  present  Prairie
78    not.work       7  present Atlantic
86    fulltime      27   absent       BC
98    fulltime      15   absent  Ontario
139   not.work      28  present  Ontario
151   fulltime      13   absent       BC
159   fulltime      22   absent  Ontario
171   fulltime       7  present  Prairie
186   parttime      15  present       BC

> nrow(Womenlf)

[1] 263
```

The following variables are included in this data set:

- `partic`: labor-force participation, a factor with levels `not.work`, `parttime`, and `fulltime`.
- `hincome`: husband's income, in thousands of dollars.
- `children`: presence of children in the household, a factor with levels `absent` and `present`.
- `region`: a factor with levels `Atlantic`, `Quebec`, `Ontario`, `Prairie`, and `BC`. (We have listed the levels of `partic` in their natural order and those of `region` from east to west, but the levels are in alphabetical order in the data frame.)

If husband's income were recoded as a factor with a relatively small number of levels, we could view these data as a four-way contingency table. There is one response variable, `partic`, which has three possibly ordered categories. Assuming Poisson sampling or its equivalent, we could then analyze the data using appropriate loglinear models with one response. In particular, we would fit models conforming to the principle of marginality that always include the highest-order interactions among the three predictors and then examine the interesting interactions (i.e., associations) between the predictors and the response variable.

Just as a contingency table with a single binomial-response variable is more conveniently modeled using a binomial-regression model than an equivalent loglinear model, a contingency table with a single multinomial response can be modeled with a multinomial-regression model that generalizes the binomial model. Moreover, multinomial-regression models can also be fit to data that include continuous numeric predictors.

In the *multinomial-logit model*, one of the m response categories is selected as a baseline, and we effectively fit logistic-regression models comparing each of the remaining categories with that baseline. As usual, R selects the first category to be the baseline. Suppose we let $\eta_j(\mathbf{x})$ be the linear predictor for the comparison of category j with the baseline, $j = 2, \ldots, m$; assuming that an intercept is included in the model,

$$\eta_j(\mathbf{x}) = \beta_{0j} + \beta_{1j}x_1 + \cdots + \beta_{kj}$$

Then, for $j = 2, \ldots, m$,

$$\log_e\left[\frac{\Pr(\text{response is category } j|\mathbf{x})}{\Pr(\text{response is baseline category } 1|\mathbf{x})}\right] = \eta_j(\mathbf{x})$$

In terms of probabilities, if $\mu_j(\mathbf{x}) = \Pr(\text{response is category } j|\mathbf{x})$,

$$\mu_j(\mathbf{x}) = \frac{\exp\left[\eta_j(\mathbf{x})\right]}{1 + \sum_{\ell=2}^{m} \exp\left[\eta_\ell(\mathbf{x})\right]} \quad \text{for } j = 2, ..., m \tag{5.2}$$

$$\mu_1(\mathbf{x}) = 1 - \sum_{\ell=2}^{m} \mu_\ell(\mathbf{x}) \quad \text{for } j = 1$$

The log-odds between *any* pair of response categories j and $j' \neq 1$ is

$$\log_e \frac{\mu_j(\mathbf{x})}{\mu_{j'}(\mathbf{x})} = \log_e \left[\frac{\mu_j(\mathbf{x})/\mu_1(\mathbf{x})}{\mu_{j'}(\mathbf{x})/\mu_1(\mathbf{x})} \right]$$

$$= \log_e \frac{\mu_j(\mathbf{x})}{\mu_1(\mathbf{x})} - \log_e \frac{\mu_{j'}(\mathbf{x})}{\mu_1(\mathbf{x})}$$

$$= \eta_j(\mathbf{x}) - \eta_{j'}(\mathbf{x})$$

$$= (\beta_{0j} - \beta_{0j'}) + (\beta_{1j} - \beta_{1j'})x_1 + \cdots + (\beta_{kj} - \beta_{kj'})x_k$$

Thus, the logistic-regression coefficients for the log-odds of membership in category j versus j' are given by the *differences* in the corresponding parameters of the multinomial-logit model.

The multinomial-logit model is not a traditional GLM and cannot be fit by the `glm` function. Instead, we use the `multinom` function in the **nnet** package (Venables and Ripley, 2002), one of the recommended packages that are part of the standard R distribution.[12] Just as `glm` can fit regression models to both binomial and binary data, `multinom` can fit models in which the observations represent counts in the several response categories, as one would have in a contingency table, or individual responses, as in our example.

We begin our analysis of the Canadian women's labor-force data by recoding the response so that the baseline level is `not.work`, and then fitting a multinomial-logit model with the predictors `hincome`, `children`, and `region`:

```
> library(nnet)
> Womenlf$partic <- factor(Womenlf$partic,
+     levels=c("not.work", "parttime", "fulltime"))
> mod.multinom <- multinom(partic ~ hincome + children + region,
+     data=Womenlf)

# weights:  24 (14 variable)
initial  value 288.935032
iter  10 value 208.509124
iter  20 value 207.732802
final  value 207.732796
converged
```

As a side effect, the call to `multinom` prints a summary of the iteration history required to find the estimates. A Type II analysis of deviance for this model, computed by the `Anova` function in the **car** package, shows that husband's income and presence of children both have highly statistically significant effects but that the `region` term is nonsignificant:

```
> Anova(mod.multinom)

Analysis of Deviance Table (Type II tests)

Response: partic
```

---

[12]There are other packages that also can fit multinomial-logit models. Of particular note is the **VGAM** package, which fits a wide variety of regression models for categorical and other data.

```
          LR Chisq Df  Pr(>Chisq)
hincome       14.6  2     0.00066
children      65.2  2       7e-15
region         7.4  8     0.49245
```

We simplify the model by removing the `region` effects and summarize the resulting model:

```
> mod.multinom.1 <- update(mod.multinom, . ~ . - region)

> summary(mod.multinom.1, Wald=TRUE)

Call:
multinom(formula = partic ~ hincome + children, data = Womenlf)

Coefficients:
          (Intercept)    hincome childrenpresent
parttime       -1.432   0.006894         0.02146
fulltime        1.983  -0.097232        -2.55861

Std. Errors:
          (Intercept) hincome childrenpresent
parttime       0.5925 0.02345          0.4690
fulltime       0.4842 0.02810          0.3622

Value/SE (Wald statistics):
          (Intercept) hincome childrenpresent
parttime       -2.418  0.2939         0.04574
fulltime        4.095 -3.4607        -7.06407

Residual Deviance: 422.9
AIC: 434.9
```

The printed output produced by `summary` for the multinomial-logit model is organized differently than the model summary for a GLM: The estimates, standard errors, and Wald tests, obtained with the argument `Wald=TRUE`, are displayed in separate tables. The first row of each table corresponds to the comparison between `parttime` and the baseline level `not.working`, and the second row to the comparison between `fulltime` and `not.working`. Examining the Wald statistics, the coefficients for the logit of `parttime` versus `not.work` are, apart from the regression constant, small and nonsignificant, while the coefficients for the logit of `fulltime` versus `not.work` are much larger and highly statistically significant. Apparently, husband's income and presence of children primarily influenced the women's decision to work full-time, as opposed to the decision to work part-time or not to work outside the home.

Because there are several response categories, and because the parametrization of the multinomial-logit model entails a comparison with an arbitrarily selected baseline, interpreting estimated coefficients can be challenging. A useful way to visualize the fitted model is with effect displays (which we applied to a GLM in Section 5.5 and to linear models in Section 4.3.3). In the current example, the high-order terms are husband's income and presence of children, and the effect plots, computed using the **effects** package, show how

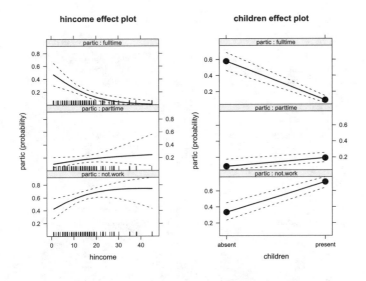

Figure 5.5   Effect plots for the multinomial-logit model `mod.multinom.1` fit to the Canadian women's labor force data.

the fitted probabilities for the three response categories vary with each predictor when the other predictor is fixed to a typical value (see Figure 5.5). The fitted probabilities $\mu_j(\mathbf{x})$ are calculated according to Equation 5.2, separately for each level of `partic`. Pointwise confidence intervals on the probability scale are computed by the delta method (as described in Fox and Andersen, 2006).

```
> library(effects)
> plot(allEffects(mod.multinom.1), ask=FALSE)
```

Alternatively, we can show how the response depends simultaneously on `hincome` and `children`, generating Figure 5.6 (along with a warning that the `hincome:children` interaction term is not in the model):

```
> plot(effect("hincome*children", mod.multinom.1))
```

```
Warning message:
In analyze.model(term, mod, xlevels, default.levels) :
  hincome:children does not appear in the model
```

The probability of full-time work decreases with `hincome` and decreases when `children` are present, while the pattern is the opposite for `not-.working`. Part-time work is intermediate and is not strongly related to the two predictors.

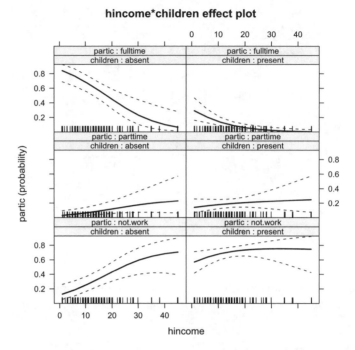

Figure 5.6 Fitted probabilities of working full-time, part-time, and not working outside the home by husband's income and presence of children, from the multinomial-logit model fit to the Canadian women's labor-force data.

5.8   Nested Dichotomies

The method of *nested dichotomies* provides an alternative to the multinomial-logit model when a single response variable has more than two categories. Nested dichotomies are constructed by successive binary divisions of the levels of the response factor.

Employing the `recode` function in the **car** package, we define two nested dichotomies to represent the three categories of labor force participation: (1) working versus not working outside the home; and (2) for those working at least part-time, working part-time versus full-time:

```
> Womenlf$working <- with(Womenlf,
+     recode(partic, " 'not.work' = 'no'; else = 'yes' "))
> Womenlf$fulltime <- with(Womenlf,recode (partic,
+     " 'fulltime' = 'yes'; 'parttime' = 'no'; 'not.work' = NA "))
```

The first of these new variables, `working`, simply compares the `not.work` category to a combination of the two working categories:

```
> xtabs(~ partic + working, data=Womenlf)
```

```
          working
partic      no yes
  not.work 155   0
  parttime   0  42
  fulltime   0  66
```

The second new variable—comparing part-time with full-time work—excludes those who are not working:

```
> xtabs(~ partic + fulltime, data=Womenlf)

          fulltime
partic      no yes
  not.work   0   0
  parttime  42   0
  fulltime   0  66
```

If the response had more than three levels, we would continue to subdivide compound levels such as working until only elementary levels (here, not.work, parttime, and fulltime) remain. In general, we require $m - 1$ nested dichotomies to represent the m levels of the response factor. In the current example, we therefore use two dichotomies for the three levels of partic. We will fit two binary logistic-regression models, the first with working as the response and the second with fulltime as the response. Because the second model considers only a subset of the cases, the combined models for the nested dichotomies are not equivalent to the multinomial model that we fit in the preceding section.

Because of their method of construction, models fit to different dichotomies are statistically independent. This means, for example, that we can add deviances and residual *df* over the models and can combine the models to get fitted probabilities for the several categories of the polytomy.

For our example, the two models for the nested dichotomies are as follows:

```
> mod.working <- glm(working ~ hincome + children + region,
+     family=binomial, data=Womenlf)
> summary(mod.working)

Call:
glm(formula = working ~ hincome + children + region,
    family = binomial, data = Womenlf)

Deviance Residuals:
   Min     1Q  Median      3Q     Max
-1.793  -0.883  -0.728   0.956   2.007

Coefficients:
                 Estimate Std. Error z value Pr(>|z|)
(Intercept)        1.2677     0.5530    2.29    0.022
hincome           -0.0453     0.0206   -2.20    0.028
childrenpresent   -1.6043     0.3019   -5.31  1.1e-07
regionBC           0.3420     0.5850    0.58    0.559
regionOntario      0.1878     0.4676    0.40    0.688
regionPrairie      0.4719     0.5568    0.85    0.397
regionQuebec      -0.1731     0.4996   -0.35    0.729
```

```
(Dispersion parameter for binomial family taken to be 1)

    Null deviance: 356.15  on 262   degrees of freedom
Residual deviance: 317.30  on 256   degrees of freedom
AIC: 331.3

Number of Fisher Scoring iterations: 4

> mod.fulltime <- update(mod.working, fulltime ~ .)
> summary(mod.fulltime)

Call:
glm(formula = fulltime ~ hincome + children + region,
    family = binomial, data = Womenlf)

Deviance Residuals:
   Min      1Q  Median      3Q     Max
-2.520  -0.805   0.358   0.720   1.996

Coefficients:
                  Estimate Std. Error z value Pr(>|z|)
(Intercept)        3.7616     1.0572    3.56  0.00037
hincome           -0.1048     0.0403   -2.60  0.00938
childrenpresent   -2.7478     0.5689   -4.83  1.4e-06
regionBC          -1.1825     1.0276   -1.15  0.24986
regionOntario     -0.1488     0.8470   -0.18  0.86059
regionPrairie     -0.3917     0.9631   -0.41  0.68420
regionQuebec       0.1484     0.9330    0.16  0.87361

(Dispersion parameter for binomial family taken to be 1)

    Null deviance: 144.34  on 107   degrees of freedom
Residual deviance: 101.84  on 101   degrees of freedom
  (155 observations deleted due to missingness)
AIC: 115.8

Number of Fisher Scoring iterations: 5

> Anova(mod.working)

Analysis of Deviance Table (Type II tests)

Response: working
         LR Chisq Df Pr(>Chisq)
hincome      5.13  1      0.024
children    30.55  1    3.3e-08
region       2.43  4      0.657

> Anova(mod.fulltime)

Analysis of Deviance Table (Type II tests)

Response: fulltime
         LR Chisq Df Pr(>Chisq)
hincome       7.8  1     0.0051
children     31.9  1    1.6e-08
region        2.7  4     0.6176
```

The results are broadly similar for the two dichotomies: Working outside the home and working full-time among those working outside the home both decline with husband's income and presence of children. In both cases, there is no evidence of region effects. We could, if we wished, manually add the corresponding likelihood ratio chi-square statistics and *df* (e.g., for the region effects) across the two analysis-of-deviance tables.

The **effects** package won't handle a set of binary-logit models fit to nested dichotomies, but we can graph the fitted models by constructing a plot step by step. We begin by refitting the models, eliminating the nonsignificant region terms:

```
> mod.working.1 <- update(mod.working, . ~ . - region)
> mod.fulltime.1 <- update(mod.fulltime, . ~ . - region)
```

The predictor hincome ranges from 1 to 45, and the predictor children has the values absent or present. For drawing graphs, we need fitted values for combinations of the predictors covering their ranges; we use the expand.grid function to produce combinations of hincome and children:

```
> (Predictors <- expand.grid(hincome=1:45,
+                    children=c("absent", "present")))

   hincome children
1        1   absent
2        2   absent
3        3   absent
4        4   absent
5        5   absent
. . .
86      41  present
87      42  present
88      43  present
89      44  present
90      45  present
```

We then employ the predict function, with its newdata argument set to the data frame Predictors, to obtain fitted values for all combinations of the two predictors:

```
> p.work <- predict(mod.working.1, newdata=Predictors,
+             type="response")
> p.fulltime <- predict(mod.fulltime.1, newdata=Predictors,
+                 type="response")
> p.full <- p.work*p.fulltime
> p.part <- p.work*(1 - p.fulltime)
> p.not <- 1 - p.work
```

Recall that specifying the argument type="response" to predict yields fitted values on the probability scale, and that the default, type="link", produces fitted values on the logit scale. The fitted values for the fulltime dichotomy are conditional on working outside the home; we multiply by the

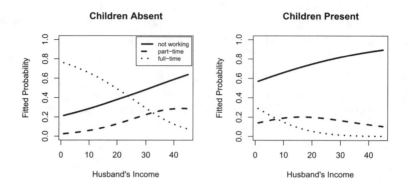

Figure 5.7 Fitted probabilities from binary-logit models fit to nested dichotomies for the Canadian women's labor force data.

probability of working to produce *unconditional* fitted probabilities of working full-time. The unconditional probability of working part-time is found similarly; and the probability of not working outside the home is calculated as the complement of the probability of working.

So as not to clutter the graph, we use the mfrow plot parameter to create two panels: one for children absent and the other for children present. The result is shown in Figure 5.7:[13]

```
> par(mfrow=c(1, 2))   # 1 row and 2 columns of panels
> plot(c(1, 45), c(0, 1),
+     type="n", xlab="Husband's Income", ylab="Fitted Probability",
+     main="Children Absent")
> lines(1:45, p.not[1:45], lty="solid", lwd=3)    # not working
> lines(1:45, p.part[1:45], lty="dashed", lwd=3)  # part-time
> lines(1:45, p.full[1:45], lty="dotted", lwd=3)  # full-time
> legend("topright", lty=1:3, lwd=3, cex=0.75, inset=0.01,
+     legend=c("not working", "part-time", "full-time"))
> plot(c(1, 45), c(0, 1),
+     type="n", xlab="Husband's Income", ylab="Fitted Probability",
+     main="Children Present")
> lines(1:45, p.not[46:90], lty="solid", lwd=3)
> lines(1:45, p.part[46:90], lty="dashed", lwd=3)
> lines(1:45, p.full[46:90], lty="dotted", lwd=3)
```

The legend in the graph is positioned using the "topright" argument, and inset=0.01 insets the legend by 1% from the edges of the plot.

Even though there are only three categories in the polytomy, there is more than one way of forming nested dichotomies. For example, we could define the alternative dichotomies: {full-time versus part-time and not working} and {part-time versus not working}. Models for alternative sets of nested dichotomies are *not* equivalent, and so this approach should only be used when there is a substantively compelling resolution of the polytomy into a *specific*

---

[13]General strategies for constructing complex graphs are described in Chapter 7.

set of nested dichotomies. In some areas, notably education, *continuation-ratio logits* (e.g., Agresti, 2002, sec. 7.4.3) are commonly used—for example, {less than high school versus some high school or more}, {incomplete high school versus high school graduate or more}, {high school graduate versus some post secondary or more}, and so on.

5.9 Proportional-Odds Model

Models for multinomial responses are potentially very complex: If we have k regressor variables and m response categories, we will end up with $(k + 1)(m - 1)$ estimated coefficients. Simpler models can be very helpful if they fit the data well. There are several statistical models for ordinal responses, developed, for example, in Agresti (2010), Clogg and Shihadeh (1994), and Powers and Xie (2000). The nested dichotomies discussed in the preceding section can also be useful when the response categories are ordered, as in the case of educational attainment. The most common model for an ordinal response, however, is the *proportional-odds logistic-regression model*.

The proportional-odds model can be derived from a linear regression with a *latent response variable* ξ, that is, a continuous response variable that isn't directly observable. To fix ideas, think of ξ as the achievement level of a student in a particular class. Suppose, further, that if ξ were observable it could be expressed as a linear combination of the regressors $x_1, \ldots, x_k$ plus an error term,

$$\xi = \alpha + \beta_1 x_1 + \cdots + \beta_k x_k + \varepsilon$$

If ξ were observable and we knew the distribution of the errors ε, then we could estimate the regression coefficients using standard methods. Rather than observing ξ, however, we instead observe another variable, y, derived from ξ. In our imaginary example, the observable variable might be the grade the student received in the course. Grade is an *ordinal variable* consisting of the ordered categories F, D, C, B, and A, from lowest to highest, corresponding consecutively to $y = 1, 2, 3, 4, 5$. In general, y is an ordinal variable with m levels $1, \ldots, m$, such that

$$y = \begin{cases} \text{level } 1 & \text{if } -\infty < \xi \leq \alpha_1 \\ \text{level } 2 & \text{if } \alpha_1 < \xi \leq \alpha_2 \\ \quad \vdots & \\ \text{level } m-1 & \text{if } \alpha_{m-2} < \xi \leq \alpha_{m-1} \\ \text{level } m & \text{if } \alpha_{m-1} < \xi \leq \infty \end{cases}$$

where $\alpha_1 < \ldots < \alpha_{m-1}$ are the *thresholds* between each level of y and the next. Thus y is a crudely measured version of ξ. The dissection of ξ into m levels introduces $m - 1$ additional parameters into the model.

The cumulative probability distribution of y is given by

$$\begin{aligned}
\Pr(y \leq j|\mathbf{x}) &= \Pr(\xi \leq \alpha_j|\mathbf{x}) \\
&= \Pr(\alpha + \beta_1 x_1 + \cdots + \beta_k x_k + \varepsilon \leq \alpha_j|\mathbf{x}) \\
&= \Pr(\varepsilon_i \leq \alpha_j - \alpha - \beta_1 x_1 - \cdots - \beta_k x_k|\mathbf{x})
\end{aligned}$$

for $j = 1, 2, ..., m - 1$. In our example, $m = 5$.

The next step depends on a distributional assumption concerning the errors ε. If we assume that the errors follow a standard logistic distribution, then we get the *proportional-odds logistic-regression model*,

$$\begin{aligned}
\text{logit}[\Pr(y > j|\mathbf{x})] &= \log_e \frac{\Pr(y > j|\mathbf{x})}{\Pr(y \leq j|\mathbf{x})} \\
&= (\alpha - \alpha_j) + \beta_1 x_1 + \cdots + \beta_k x_k
\end{aligned}$$

for $j = 1, 2, ..., m - 1$. If we instead assume a standard-normal distribution for ε, then we get the *ordered probit model*,

$$\Phi^{-1}[\Pr(y > j|\mathbf{x})] = (\alpha - \alpha_j) + \beta_1 x_1 + \cdots + \beta_k x_k$$

where, as before, Φ^{-1} is the quantile function of the standard-normal distribution. As we mentioned in Section 5.3, the logistic and normal distributions are very similar symmetric and unimodal distributions, although the logistic distribution has somewhat heavier tails. As a consequence, in most applications the proportional-odds and the ordered probit models produce similar results; we will discuss only the proportional-odds model here.

Because the equations for logit[$\Pr(y > j|\mathbf{x})$] for different values of j differ only in their intercepts, the regression curves for the cumulative probabilities $\Pr(Y_i > j|\mathbf{x})$ are parallel, as illustrated in Figure 5.8; in this graph, the cumulative probabilities are plotted for a four-category response against an imagined linear predictor $\eta = \alpha + \beta_1 x_1 + \cdots + \beta_k x_k$. The designation *proportional odds* follows from the constant difference between the cumulative log-odds (logits) for different categories of the observable response y, which translates into a constant ratio of odds.

Assuming that the errors follow a standard logistic distribution fixes the scale of the latent response ξ but not its origin, and so the general intercept α is not identified independently of the thresholds α_j. Setting $\alpha = 0$ to fix the origin of ξ, the negatives of the category boundaries (i.e., the $-\alpha_j$) become the intercepts for the logistic-regression equations.

An attractive feature of the proportional-odds model is that it uses a single linear predictor rather than $m - 1$ linear predictors, as in the multinomial-logit and nested-dichotomies models, reducing the number of parameters to just $m - 1$ thresholds and k regression coefficients. Of course, the proportional-odds model is therefore more restrictive than the other two models and may not fit the data well. Because the proportional-odds model is not a specialization of either the nested-dichotomies model or the multinomial-logit model,

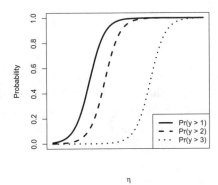

Figure 5.8 The proportional-odds model: Cumulative probabilities, Pr(y > j), plotted against the linear predictor, η, for a four-category ordered response.

we can't use likelihood ratio tests to compare these models, but comparisons based on the AIC can be informative.

There is also a score test (as far as we know, unavailable in R) of the proportional-odds assumption. Venables and Ripley (2002, sec. 7.3) suggest a test in the form of a likelihood ratio test that compares the deviances for the proportional-odds and multinomial-logit models, and which, in our experience, usually produces results similar to the score test for proportional odds. A more strictly correct test of the assumption of proportional odds is to compare the proportional-odds model to a model for the cumulative logits that does *not* constrain the regressions to be parallel.[14]

The proportional-odds model may be fit in R using the `polr` function in the **MASS** package (Venables and Ripley, 2002).[15] For the women's labor-force data, we may proceed as follows:

```
> library(MASS) # actually previously loaded by library(car)
> mod.polr <- polr(partic ~ hincome + children, data=Womenlf)
> summary(mod.polr)

Call:
polr(formula = partic ~ hincome + children, data = Womenlf)

Coefficients:
                 Value Std. Error t value
hincome        -0.0539    0.01949  -2.766
childrenpresent -1.9720    0.28695  -6.872

Intercepts:
                Value   Std. Error t value
```

---

[14]The `vglm` function in the **VGAM** packages fits a wide variety of models, including both the proportional-odds model and a similar model for cumulative logits that doesn't impose the assumption of parallel regressions. We had trouble, however, using `vglm` to fit this model to the data in our example.

[15]The `polr` function can also be used to fit some other similar models for an ordered response, including the ordered probit model.

```
not.work|parttime -1.852   0.386      -4.794
parttime|fulltime -0.941   0.370      -2.544

Residual Deviance: 441.66
AIC: 449.66
```

The AIC for the proportional-odds model (449.7) is quite a bit larger than for the multinomial-logit model fit earlier (434.9), casting doubt on the assumption of proportional odds. A rough analysis of deviance yields a p value of .00008, suggesting the inadequacy of the proportional-odds model:

```
> pchisq(deviance(mod.polr) - deviance(mod.multinom.1),
+       df = 6 - 4, lower.tail=FALSE)

[1] 8.351e-05
```

The fit of the proportional-odds model, shown in Figure 5.9, is also quite different from that of the multinomial-logit model (Figure 5.6) and the nested-dichotomies model (Figure 5.7):

```
> plot(effect("hincome*children", mod.polr))

Warning message:
In analyze.model(term, mod, xlevels, default.levels) :
  hincome:children does not appear in the model
```

Alternative displays are shown in Figure 5.10, using *stacked-area plots*, and in Figure 5.11, by plotting the estimated latent response:

```
> plot(effect("hincome*children", mod.polr), style="stacked")

> plot(effect("hincome*children", mod.polr, latent=TRUE))
```

5.10   Extensions

5.10.1   MORE ON THE Anova FUNCTION

The primary use of the Anova function is to calculate Type II likelihood ratio tests of hypotheses about the terms in a model. The function is more general, however, and for GLMs, it can be used to calculate Wald or F tests, specified via the test argument, and can perform Type III tests, specified by the type argument.

Likelihood ratio tests and F tests require fitting more than one model to the data, while Wald tests do not. Moreover, the F tests computed by Anova base the estimated dispersion on Pearson's X^2 by default and, therefore, are not the same as likelihood ratio tests, even when the dispersion is fixed, as in the binomial and Poisson models. As we have explained before, the Pearson statistic is the sum of squared Pearson residuals from the GLM.

For terms with 1 *df* in an additive model, the Wald chi-square statistics provided by Anova are simply the squares of the corresponding zs printed by the summary function.

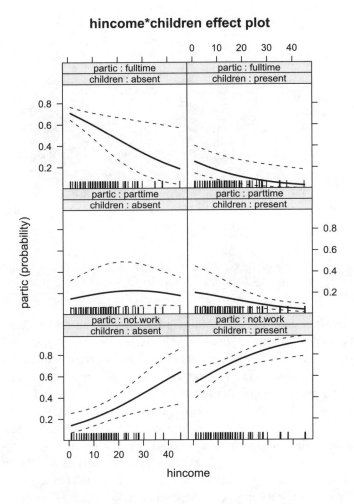

hincome*children effect plot

Figure 5.9 Estimated probabilities of working full-time, working part-time, and not working outside the home by husband's income and presence of children, from the proportional-odds model fit to the Canadian women's labor-force data. The broken lines, showing 95% pointwise confidence envelopes around the fitted probabilities, are based on standard errors computed by the delta method (Fox and Andersen, 2006).

5.10.2 GAMMA MODELS

GLMs with errors from a gamma distribution are used much less often than are binomial, Poisson, or normal models. A gamma distribution can be appropriate for a strictly positive random variable.[16] Like the normal distribution, the gamma distribution has two parameters, which can be taken to be a mean parameter μ and a positive *shape parameter* α. Unlike the normal

---

[16]The inverse-Gaussian family is also appropriate for continuous positive data, but its applications are rare.

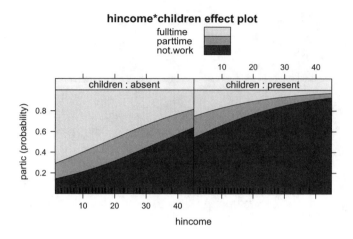

Figure 5.10 Estimated probabilities, shown as stacked areas, from the proportional-odds model fit to the Canadian women's labor-force data.

distribution, in a gamma distribution the shape of the corresponding density function changes with the parameters, as shown in Figure 5.12 for fixed $\mu = 1$ and varying α. For $\alpha \leq 1$ the density has a pole at the origin, while for $\alpha > 1$ it is unimodal but skewed. The skewness decreases as α increases. Because the variance of a gamma distribution is μ^2/α, the shape parameter is the inverse of the dispersion parameter ϕ in the usual notation for a GLM. A characteristic of the gamma distribution is that the coefficient of variation, the ratio of the standard deviation to the mean, is constant and is equal to $\sqrt{\alpha}$.

An example for which gamma errors are likely to be useful is the `Trans-act` data, introduced in Section 4.3.6. Errors in these data probably increase with the size of the response, and the gamma assumption of constant coefficient of variation is reasonable, as suggested by Cunningham and Heathcote (1989) for these data:

```
> trans.gamma <- glm(time ~ t1 + t2, family=Gamma(link=identity),
+                    data=Transact)
> summary(trans.gamma)

Call:
glm(formula = time ~ t1 + t2, family = Gamma(link = identity),
    data = Transact)

Deviance Residuals:
     Min         1Q     Median         3Q        Max
-0.46866   -0.10718    0.00159    0.08656    0.67933

Coefficients:
            Estimate Std. Error t value Pr(>|t|)
(Intercept)  152.951     51.800    2.95   0.0034
t1             5.706      0.426   13.41   <2e-16
t2             2.007      0.058   34.61   <2e-16

(Dispersion parameter for Gamma family taken to be 0.02939)
```

hincome*children effect plot

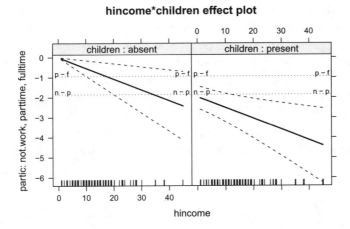

Figure 5.11 The estimated latent response from the proportional-odds model fit to the Canadian women's labor-force data. The dotted horizontal lines are the estimated thresholds between adjacent levels of the observed response.

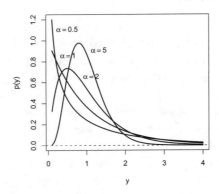

Figure 5.12 Gamma densities for various values of the shape parameter, α, with $\mu = 1$ fixed.

```
   Null deviance: 92.603  on 260  degrees of freedom
Residual deviance:  7.477  on 258  degrees of freedom
AIC: 4322

Number of Fisher Scoring iterations: 4
```

The canonical link for the Gamma family is the `inverse` link (see Table 5.2, p. 231), and if we were to use that link, we would then model the mean for `time` as $E(\texttt{time}|\texttt{t1},\texttt{t2}) = 1/(\beta_0 + \beta_1\texttt{t1} + \beta_2\texttt{t2})$. Using the identity link in this example, the coefficients of the gamma-regression model will have the same interpretations as the coefficients of the linear model that we fit by least squares in Section 4.3.6: The intercept is the amount of time required independent of the transactions; the coefficient of `t1` is the typical time required for each Type 1 transaction; and the coefficient of `t2` is the typical time required for each Type 2 transaction. The inverse scale loses this simple interpretation of the coefficients. In general, however, using the identity link with the gamma family is problematic because it can lead to negative fitted values for a strictly positive response, a problem that doesn't occur for our example.

The estimate of the shape parameter, which is the inverse of the dispersion parameter in the GLM, is returned by the `gamma.shape` function:

```
> gamma.shape(trans.gamma)


Alpha: 35.073
SE:     3.056
```

The large estimated shape implies that the error distribution is nearly symmetric.

5.10.3   QUASI-LIKELIHOOD ESTIMATION

The likelihood functions for exponential families depend only on the mean and variance of the conditional distribution of y. The essential idea of *quasi-likelihood estimation* is to use the same maximizing function for any distribution that matches the first two moments (i.e., the mean and variance) of an exponential-family distribution. It can be shown (McCullagh and Nelder, 1989, chap. 9) that most of the desirable properties of maximum-likelihood estimates for exponential families—including asymptotic normality, asymptotic unbiasedness, and the usual covariance matrix for the estimates—are shared by estimates from distributions that match the first two moments of an exponential family.

This is a familiar idea: When we apply least-squares regression to a model with nonnormal errors, for example, the resulting estimates are unbiased, are asymptotically normal, and have the usual covariance matrix, as long as the assumptions of linearity, constant error variance, and independence hold. Moreover, when the errors are nonnormal, the least-squares estimates are not in general maximum-likelihood estimates but are still maximally efficient among linear unbiased estimators (by the Gauss-Markov theorem), though no longer necessarily among *all* unbiased estimators.

In R, quasi-likelihood estimation for GLMs is achieved by specifying the `quasi` family generator, with `link` and `variance` as arguments. These arguments default to `"identity"` and `"constant"`, respectively, a combination that yields linear least-squares estimates. Of course, there would be no reason to compute the least-squares estimates in this convoluted manner. There are also the special families `quasipoisson` and `quasibinomial` for quasi-likelihood estimation of overdispersed Poisson and binomial GLMs, which we will discuss in the next section.

5.10.4 OVERDISPERSED BINOMIAL AND POISSON MODELS

The term *overdispersion* means that the observed conditional variance of the response is larger than the variation implied by the distribution used in fitting the model. Overdispersion can be symptomatic of several different problems:

1. Observations on different individuals with the same values of the regressors **x** do not have exactly the same distribution; that is, there are unaccounted-for individual differences that produce additional variation. This situation is often termed *unmodeled heterogeneity*.

2. Observations may be correlated or clustered, while the specified variance function wrongly assumes uncorrelated data.

3. The specified mean function is wrong, and this misspecification "leaks" into the estimated variance function.

The first two problems are addressed in this section. The third problem will be discussed in Chapter 6.

One approach to overdispersion is to estimate a scale parameter ϕ rather than use the assumed value $\phi = 1$ for the Poisson or binomial distributions. The usual estimator of the dispersion parameter is $\widehat{\phi} = X^2/df$, the value of Pearson's X^2 divided by the residual df. Estimating the dispersion has no effect on the coefficient estimates, but it inflates all their standard errors by the factor $\sqrt{\widehat{\phi}}$.

QUASI-LIKELIHOOD AND ESTIMATING ϕ

As an example, the model `ornstein.mod` fit to Ornstein's interlocking-directorate data in Section 5.5 has residual deviance 1547.1 with 234 df. The large value of the deviance when compared with its degrees of freedom indicates possible overdispersion.[17] The estimator of ϕ is

```
> (phihat <- sum(residuals(mod.ornstein, type="pearson")^2)/
+        df.residual(mod.ornstein))

[1] 6.399
```

Standard errors and Wald tests adjusted for overdispersion may be obtained by the command

```
> summary(mod.ornstein, dispersion=phihat)

Call:
glm(formula = interlocks ~ log2(assets) + nation +
    sector, family = poisson, data = Ornstein)
```

---

[17] This is so for both Poisson data and binomial data with binomial denominators larger than 1—that is, binomial rather than binary data.

```
Deviance Residuals:
   Min     1Q   Median      3Q      Max
 -6.711  -2.316  -0.459    1.282    6.285

Coefficients:
             Estimate Std. Error z value Pr(>|z|)
(Intercept)   -0.8394     0.3456   -2.43   0.0152
log2(assets)   0.3129     0.0298   10.51  < 2e-16
nationOTH     -0.1070     0.1881   -0.57   0.5696
nationUK      -0.3872     0.2264   -1.71   0.0872
nationUS      -0.7724     0.1256   -6.15  7.7e-10
sectorBNK     -0.1665     0.2422   -0.69   0.4918
sectorCON     -0.4893     0.5393   -0.91   0.3643
sectorFIN     -0.1116     0.1915   -0.58   0.5601
sectorHLD     -0.0149     0.3016   -0.05   0.9606
sectorMAN      0.1219     0.1926    0.63   0.5269
sectorMER      0.0616     0.2193    0.28   0.7789
sectorMIN      0.2498     0.1742    1.43   0.1516
sectorTRN      0.1518     0.1997    0.76   0.4471
sectorWOD      0.4983     0.1912    2.61   0.0092


(Dispersion parameter for poisson family taken to be 6.399)

    Null deviance: 3737.0  on 247   degrees of freedom
Residual deviance: 1547.1  on 234   degrees of freedom
AIC: 2473

Number of Fisher Scoring iterations: 5
```

The `Anova` function in the **car** package uses this estimate of ϕ to get tests if we specify `test="F"`:

```
> Anova(mod.ornstein, test="F")

Analysis of Deviance Table (Type II tests)

Response: interlocks
               SS  Df       F  Pr(>F)
log2(assets)  731   1  114.28 < 2e-16
nation        276   3   14.38 1.2e-08
sector        103   9    1.78   0.072
Residuals    1497 234
```

The estimated dispersion, $\widehat{\phi} = 6.399$, is substantially greater than 1, producing much larger standard errors and thus smaller test statistics than were obtained from the standard Poisson-regression model (fit to the `Ornstein` data in Section 5.5). An identical analysis would also be produced using the `quasipoisson` family:

```
> mod.ornstein.q <- update(mod.ornstein, family=quasipoisson)
```

NEGATIVE-BINOMIAL REGRESSION

An alternative strategy for overdispersed count data is to model between-individual variability. One useful approach leads to fitting negative-binomial regression models for data that might otherwise be modeled with a Poisson distribution. We introduce a random subject effect S that has a different value for each subject and assume that the conditional distribution of the response given the predictors and the subject effect $(y|\mathbf{x}, S)$ is a Poisson distribution with mean $S \times \mu(\mathbf{x})$. The new feature is that the marginal distribution of S is a gamma distribution with mean parameter θ and shape parameter α.[18] It then follows (e.g., Venables and Ripley, 2002, sec. 7.4) that $E(y|\mathbf{x}) = \mu(\mathbf{x})$ and $\text{Var}(y|\mathbf{x}) = \mu(\mathbf{x}) + \mu(\mathbf{x})^2/\theta$. The second term in the variance provides the overdispersion. If θ is small relative to $\mu(\mathbf{x})$, then the overdispersion can be substantial. As $\theta \to \infty$, the negative-binomial model approaches the Poisson.

The negative-binomial distribution only fits into the framework of GLMs when the value of θ is assumed to be known. We can then fit negative-binomial regression models with the `negative.binomial` family generator in the **MASS** package. The default link is the log link, as for the Poisson family, and therefore the regression coefficients have the same interpretation as in Poisson regression.

For example, setting $\theta = 1.5$, we have

```
> mod.ornstein.nb <- update(mod.ornstein,
+       family=negative.binomial(1.5))
```

To select a value for θ, we could choose a grid of reasonable values and then select the one that minimizes the AIC:

```
> thetas <- seq(0.5, 2.5, by=0.5)
> aics <- rep(0, 5) # allocate vector
> for (i in seq(along=thetas)) aics[i] <- AIC(update(mod.ornstein.nb,
+           family=negative.binomial(thetas[i])))
> rbind(thetas, aics)

         [,1]  [,2]   [,3] [,4]   [,5]
thetas    0.5     1    1.5    2    2.5
aics   1772.9  1691 1673.8 1676 1686.3
```

The minimum AIC is at about $\theta = 1.5$, the value we used above:

```
> summary(mod.ornstein.nb)

Call:
glm(formula = interlocks ~ log2(assets) + nation +
    sector, family = negative.binomial(1.5), data = Ornstein)

Deviance Residuals:
   Min      1Q  Median      3Q     Max
-2.731  -0.957  -0.181   0.414   2.329

Coefficients:
             Estimate Std. Error t value Pr(>|t|)
(Intercept)   -0.8271     0.3718   -2.22    0.027
```

---

[18] In Section 5.10.2, we used the symbol μ for the mean of a gamma distribution, but doing so here would confuse the mean of the marginal distribution of the random effect S with the mean function for the conditional distribution of $y|\mathbf{x}, S$. This notation is also consistent with the labeling of output in the `glm.nb` function.

```
log2(assets)     0.3164        0.0352      8.98   < 2e-16
nationOTH       -0.1043        0.2257     -0.46     0.645
nationUK        -0.3889        0.2308     -1.68     0.093
nationUS        -0.7884        0.1292     -6.10   4.3e-09
sectorBNK       -0.4106        0.3708     -1.11     0.269
sectorCON       -0.7619        0.4453     -1.71     0.088
sectorFIN       -0.1036        0.2472     -0.42     0.676
sectorHLD       -0.2126        0.3428     -0.62     0.536
sectorMAN        0.0766        0.1818      0.42     0.674
sectorMER        0.0787        0.2276      0.35     0.730
sectorMIN        0.2395        0.1844      1.30     0.195
sectorTRN        0.1015        0.2428      0.42     0.676
sectorWOD        0.3904        0.2280      1.71     0.088
```

```
(Dispersion parameter for Negative Binomial(1.5) family taken
    to be 0.8906)
```

```
    Null deviance: 487.78   on 247   degrees of freedom
Residual deviance: 279.50   on 234   degrees of freedom
AIC: 1674
```

```
Number of Fisher Scoring iterations: 5
```

An alternative is to estimate θ along with the regression coefficients. The resulting model, which is not a traditional GLM, can be fit with the `glm.nb` function in the **MASS** package, for which the default link is again the log link:

```
> summary(glm.nb(interlocks ~ log2(assets) + nation + sector,
+       data=Ornstein))
```

```
Call:
glm.nb(formula = interlocks ~ log2(assets) + nation +
    sector, data = Ornstein, init.theta = 1.639034209,
    link = log)
```

```
Deviance Residuals:
   Min     1Q  Median     3Q     Max
-2.809  -0.990  -0.189   0.430   2.408
```

```
Coefficients:
               Estimate Std. Error z value Pr(>|z|)
(Intercept)     -0.8254     0.3798   -2.17     0.030
log2(assets)     0.3162     0.0359    8.80   < 2e-16
nationOTH       -0.1045     0.2300   -0.45     0.649
nationUK        -0.3894     0.2357   -1.65     0.099
nationUS        -0.7882     0.1320   -5.97   2.4e-09
sectorBNK       -0.4085     0.3773   -1.08     0.279
sectorCON       -0.7570     0.4571   -1.66     0.098
sectorFIN       -0.1035     0.2518   -0.41     0.681
sectorHLD       -0.2110     0.3498   -0.60     0.546
sectorMAN        0.0768     0.1860    0.41     0.680
sectorMER        0.0776     0.2325    0.33     0.738
sectorMIN        0.2399     0.1884    1.27     0.203
sectorTRN        0.1013     0.2475    0.41     0.682
sectorWOD        0.3908     0.2325    1.68     0.093
```

```
(Dispersion parameter for Negative Binomial(1.639)
```

```
    family taken to be 1)

    Null deviance: 521.58  on 247   degrees of freedom
Residual deviance: 296.52  on 234   degrees of freedom
AIC: 1675

Number of Fisher Scoring iterations: 1


            Theta:   1.639
        Std. Err.:   0.192

 2 x log-likelihood:   -1645.257
```

The estimate $\widehat{\theta} = 1.639$ is very close to the value 1.5 that we picked by grid search.

5.10.5 "ROLLING YOUR OWN" GLM*

To supplement the flexibility provided by the standard and quasi family generators, it is also possible to add family generators, link functions, and variance functions to R—assuming, of course, that you have the necessary statistical knowledge and programming prowess. In the previous section, for example, we used the family generator negative.binomial, added by Venables and Ripley's **MASS** package, to fit a negative-binomial GLM.

5.11 Arguments to glm

The glm function in R takes the following arguments:

```
> args(glm)

function (formula, family = gaussian, data, weights, subset,
    na.action, start = NULL, etastart, mustart, offset,
    control = glm.control(...), model = TRUE,
    method = "glm.fit", x = FALSE, y = TRUE, contrasts = NULL,
    ...)
```

We have already discussed in some detail the use of the formula and family arguments. The data, subset, na.action, and contrasts arguments work as in lm (see Section 4.8).

Here are a few comments on the other arguments to glm:

5.11.1 weights

The weights argument is used to specify *prior weights*, which are a vector of n positive numbers. Leaving off this argument effectively sets all the prior weights to 1. For Gaussian GLMs, the weights argument is used for weighted-least-squares regression, and this argument can serve a similar purpose for gamma GLMs. For a Poisson GLM, the weights have no obvious elementary use. As we mentioned in Section 5.4, the weights argument may also be used to specify binomial denominators (i.e., total counts) in a binomial GLM.

The IWLS computing algorithm used by `glm` (Section 5.12) produces a set of *working weights*, which are different from the prior weights. The `weights` function applied to a fitted `glm` object retrieves the *prior* weights.

5.11.2   start

This argument supplies start values for the coefficients in the linear predictor. One of the remarkable features of GLMs is that the automatic algorithm that is used to find starting values is almost always effective, and the user therefore need not provide starting values.

5.11.3   offset

An offset allows for a regressor in a GLM that has a fixed coefficient of 1. The most common use for offsets is in Poisson models. Suppose, for example, that for a single individual with regressors $\mathbf{x}$, the number of visits made to the doctor in a fixed time period has a Poisson distribution with mean $\mu(\mathbf{x})$. We don't observe each individual, however, but rather observe the total number of doctor visits y among the N people who share the predictors $\mathbf{x}$. From a basic property of the Poisson distribution, $y|(N, \mathbf{x})$ has a Poisson distribution with mean $N \times \exp[\eta(\mathbf{x})]$. If we fit a model with the log link,

$$
\begin{aligned}
\mu(\mathbf{x}) &= N \exp[\eta(\mathbf{x})] \\
\log_e[\mu(\mathbf{x})] &= \eta(\mathbf{x}) + \log_e N
\end{aligned}
$$

and we would therefore want to fit a Poisson regression with the linear predictor $\eta(\mathbf{x}) + \log_e N$. This is accomplished by setting the argument `offset=log(N)`.

5.11.4   control

This argument allows the user to set several technical options, in the form of a list, controlling the IWLS fitting algorithm (described in the next section): `epsilon`, the convergence criterion (which defaults to `0.0001`), representing the maximum relative change in the deviance before a solution is declared and iteration stops; `maxit`, the maximum number of iterations (default, `10`); and `trace` (default, `FALSE`), which if `TRUE` causes a record of the IWLS iterations to be printed. These control options can also be specified directly as arguments to `glm`. The ability to control the IWLS fitting process is sometimes useful—for example, when convergence problems are encountered.

5.11.5   model, method, x, y

As for linear models, these are technical arguments.

5.12   Fitting GLMs by Iterated Weighted Least Squares*

Maximum-likelihood estimates for GLMs in R are obtained by IWLS, also called *iteratively reweighted least squares* (IRLS). It occasionally helps to know some of the details.

IWLS proceeds by forming a quadratic local approximation to the log-likelihood function; maximizing this approximate log-likelihood is a linear weighted-least-squares problem. Suppose that the vector $\boldsymbol{\beta}^{(t)}$ contains the current estimates of the regression parameters of the GLM at iteration t. Using the subscript i for the ith observation, we calculate the current values of the linear predictor, $\eta_i^{(t)} = \mathbf{x}_i'\boldsymbol{\beta}^{(t)}$; the fitted values, $\mu_i^{(t)} = g^{-1}(\eta_i^{(t)})$; the variance function, $v_i^{(t)} = \text{Var}(\mu_i^{(t)})/\phi$; the *working response*,[19]

$$z_i^{(t)} = \eta_i^{(t)} + (y_i - \mu_i^{(t)})\left(\frac{\partial \eta_i}{\partial \mu_i}\right)^{(t)}$$

and the *working weights*,

$$w_i^{(t)} = \frac{1}{c_i v_i^{(t)}\left[\left(\dfrac{\partial \eta_i}{\partial \mu_i}\right)^{(t)}\right]^2}$$

where the c_i are fixed constants (e.g., in the binomial family, $c_i = n_i^{-1}$). Then we perform a weighted-least-squares regression of $z^{(t)}$ on the xs in the linear predictor, minimizing the weighted sum of squares $\sum_{i=1}^{n} w_i(z_i - \mathbf{x}_i'\boldsymbol{\beta})^2$, where $\mathbf{x}_i'$ is the ith row of the model matrix $\mathbf{X}$ of the regressors, obtaining new estimates of the regression parameters, $\boldsymbol{\beta}^{(t+1)}$. This process is initiated with suitable starting values $\boldsymbol{\beta}^{(0)}$ and continues until the coefficients stabilize at the maximum-likelihood estimates $\widehat{\boldsymbol{\beta}}$.

The estimated asymptotic covariance matrix of $\widehat{\boldsymbol{\beta}}$ is obtained from the last iteration of the IWLS procedure as

$$\widehat{\text{Var}}(\widehat{\boldsymbol{\beta}}) = \widehat{\phi}(\mathbf{X}'\mathbf{W}\mathbf{X})^{-1}$$

where $\mathbf{W} = \text{diag}\{w_i\}$ and (if ϕ is to be estimated from the data) $\widehat{\phi}$ is the Pearson statistic divided by the residual *df* for the model.

---

[19]The values

$$z_i^{(t)} - \eta_i^{(t)} = (y_i - \mu_i^{(t)})\left(\frac{\partial \eta_i}{\partial \mu_i}\right)^{(t)}$$

are called *working residuals* and play a role in diagnostics for GLMs (see Section 6.6).

Binomial logistic regression provides a relatively simple illustration; we have (after algebraic manipulation)

$$\mu_i^{(t)} = [1 + \exp(-\eta_i^{(t)})]^{-1}$$

$$v_i^{(t)} = \mu_i^{(t)}(1 - \mu_i^{(t)})$$

$$\left(\frac{\partial \eta_i}{\partial \mu_i}\right)^{(t)} = \frac{1}{\mu_i^{(t)}(1 - \mu_i^{(t)})}$$

$$z_i^{(t)} = \eta_i^{(t)} + (y_i - \mu_i^{(t)})/v_i^{(t)}$$

$$w_i^{(t)} = N_i v_i$$

where N_i is the number of trials associated with the ith observation, and $\phi = 1$ for the binomial.

5.13   Complementary Reading and References

- The structure of GLMs, introduced in Section 5.1, is amplified in Fox (2008, sec. 15.1) and Weisberg (2005, sec. 12.4). The canonical reference for GLMs is McCullagh and Nelder (1989).
- Logistic regression, covered in Sections 5.3 to 5.4, is discussed in Fox (2008, chap. 14) and Weisberg (2005, sec. 12.1–12.3).
- Poisson-regression models, and the related loglinear models for contingency tables, are discussed in Fox (2008, sec. 15.2). More complete treatments can be found in books by Agresti (2007), Simonoff (2003), and Fienberg (1980), among others.
- The material in Sections 5.7 to 5.9 on models for polytomous responses is discussed in Fox (2008, sec. 14.2).
- Many of these topics are also covered in Long (1997).

Diagnosing Problems in Linear and Generalized Linear Models 6

R *egression diagnostics* are methods for determining whether a fitted regression model adequately represents the data. We use the term *regression* broadly in this chapter to include methods for both linear and generalized linear models, and many of the methods described here are also appropriate for other regression models. Because most of the methods for diagnosing problems in linear models extend naturally to generalized linear models, we deal at greater length with linear-model diagnostics, briefly introducing the extensions to GLMs.

Linear models fit by least squares make strong and sometimes unrealistic assumptions about the structure of the data. When these assumptions are violated, least-squares estimates can behave badly and may even completely misrepresent the data. Regression diagnostics can reveal such problems and often point the way toward solutions.

Section 6.1 describes various kinds of residuals in linear models, and Section 6.2 introduces basic scatterplots of residuals, along with related plots that are used to assess the fit of a model to data. The remaining sections are specialized to particular problems, describing methods for diagnosis and at least touching on possible remedies. Section 6.3 introduces methods for detecting unusual data, including outliers, high-leverage points, and influential observations. Section 6.4 returns to the topic of transformations of the response and predictors (discussed previously in Section 3.4) to correct problems such as nonnormally distributed errors and nonlinearity. Section 6.5 deals with nonconstant error variance. Section 6.6 describes the extension of diagnostic methods to GLMs such as logistic and Poisson regression. Finally, diagnosing collinearity in regression models is the subject of Section 6.7.

All the methods discussed in this chapter either are available in standard R functions or are implemented in the **car** package. A few functions that were once in earlier versions of the **car** package are now a standard part of R.

One goal of the **car** package is to make diagnostics for linear models and GLMs readily available in R. It is our experience that diagnostic methods are much more likely to be used when they are *convenient*. For example, added-variable plots (described in Section 6.3.3) are constructed by regressing a particular regressor and the response on all the other regressors, computing the residuals from these auxiliary regressions, and plotting one set of residuals against the other. This is not hard to do in R, although the steps are somewhat more complicated when there are factors, interactions, or polynomial or regression spline terms in the model. The `avPlots` function in the **car** package constructs all the added-variable plots for a linear model or GLM and adds enhancements such as a least-squares line and point identification.

6.1   Residuals

Residuals of one sort or another are the basis of most diagnostic methods. Suppose that we specify and fit a linear model assuming constant error variance σ^2. The *ordinary residuals* are given by the differences between the responses and the fitted values:

$$e_i = y_i - \widehat{y}_i, \ i = 1, \ldots, n \qquad (6.1)$$

In OLS regression, the residual sum of squares is equal to $\sum e_i^2$. If the regression model includes an intercept, then $\sum e_i = 0$. The ordinary residuals are uncorrelated with the fitted values or indeed any linear combination of the regressors, and so patterns in the plots of ordinary residuals versus linear combinations of the regressors can occur only if one or more assumptions of the model are inappropriate.

If the regression model is correct, then the ordinary residuals are random variables with mean 0 and with variance given by

$$\text{Var}(e_i) = \sigma^2(1 - h_i) \qquad (6.2)$$

The quantity h_i is called a *leverage* or *hat-value*. In linear models with fixed predictors, h_i is a nonrandom value constrained to be between 0 and 1, depending on the location of the predictors for a particular observation relative to the other observations.[1] Large values of h_i correspond to observations with relatively unusual $\mathbf{x}_i$ values, whereas a small h_i value corresponds to observations close to the center of the regressor space (see Section 6.3.2).

Ordinary residuals for observations with large h_i have smaller variances. To correct for the nonconstant variance of the residuals, we can divide them by an estimate of their standard deviation. Letting $\widehat{\sigma}^2$ represent the estimate of σ^2, the *standardized residuals* are

$$e_{Si} = \frac{e_i}{\widehat{\sigma}\sqrt{1 - h_i}} \qquad (6.3)$$

---

[1]In a model with an intercept, the minimum hat-value is $1/n$.

While the e_{Si} have constant variance, they are no longer uncorrelated with the fitted values or linear combinations of the regressors, so using standardized residuals in plots is not an obvious improvement.

Studentized residuals are given by

$$e_{Ti} = \frac{e_i}{\widehat{\sigma}_{(-i)}\sqrt{1 - h_i}} \tag{6.4}$$

where $\widehat{\sigma}^2_{(-i)}$ is the estimate of σ^2 computed from the regression without the ith observation. Like the standardized residuals, the Studentized residuals have constant variance. In addition, if the original errors are normally distributed, then e_{Ti} follows a t distribution with $n - k - 2$ df and can be used to test for outliers (see Section 6.3). One can show that

$$\widehat{\sigma}^2_{(-i)} = \frac{\widehat{\sigma}^2(n - k - 1 - e^2_{Si})}{n - k - 2} \tag{6.5}$$

and so computing the Studentized residuals doesn't really require refitting the regression without the ith observation.

If the model is fit by WLS regression with known positive weights w_i, then the ordinary residuals are replaced by the *Pearson residuals*:

$$e_{Pi} = \sqrt{w_i}e_i \tag{6.6}$$

In WLS estimation, the residual sum of squares is $\sum e^2_{Pi}$. If we construe OLS regression to have implicit weights of $w_i = 1$ for all i, then Equation 6.1 is simply a special case of Equation 6.6, and we will generally use the term *Pearson residuals* to cover both of these cases. The standardized and Studentized residuals are unaffected by weights because the weights cancel out in the numerator and denominator of their formulas.

The generic R function `residuals` can compute various kinds of residuals. The default for a linear model is to return the ordinary residuals even if weights are present. Setting the argument `type="pearson"` (with a lowercase p) returns the Pearson residuals, which produces correctly weighted residuals if weights are present and ordinary residuals if there are no weights. Pearson residuals are the default when `residuals` is used with a GLM. The functions `rstandard` and `rstudent` return the standardized and Studentized residuals, respectively. The function `hatvalues` returns the hat-values.

6.2 Basic Diagnostic Plots

The **car** package includes a number of functions that produce plots of residuals and related quantities. The variety of plots reflects the fact that no one diagnostic graph is appropriate for all purposes.

6.2.1   PLOTTING RESIDUALS

Plots of residuals versus fitted values and versus each of the predictors in turn are the most basic diagnostic graphs. If a linear model is correctly specified, then the Pearson residuals are independent of the fitted values and the predictors, and these graphs should be *null plots*, with no systematic features—in the sense that the conditional distribution of the residuals (on the vertical axis of the graph) should not change with the fitted values or with a predictor (on the horizontal axis). The presence of systematic features generally implies a failure of one or more assumptions of the model. Of interest in these plots are nonlinear trends, trends in variation across the graph, and isolated points.

Plotting residuals against fitted values and predictors is useful for revealing problems but less useful for determining the exact nature of the problem. Consequently, we will employ other diagnostic graphs to suggest improvements to a model.

Consider, for example, a modification of the model used in Section 4.2.2 for the Canadian occupational-prestige data:

```
> prestige.mod.2 <- lm(prestige ~ education + income + type,
+      data=Prestige)
```

In Section 3.4.7, we had suggested replacing income by its logarithm, and we followed that advice in Section 4.2.2. Here, we naively use income without transformation, in part to demonstrate what happens when a predictor needs transformation.[2]

The standard residual plots for this model are given by the residualPlots function in the **car** package:

```
> residualPlots(prestige.mod.2)
```

	Test stat	Pr(>|t|)
education	-0.684	0.496
income	-2.886	0.005
type	NA	NA
Tukey test	-2.610	0.009

This command produces scatterplots of the Pearson residuals versus each of the predictors and versus the fitted values (Figure 6.1).

The most common diagnostic graph in linear regression is the plot of residuals versus the fitted values, shown at the bottom right of Figure 6.1. The plot has a curved general trend, suggesting that the model we fit is not adequate to describe the data. The plot of residuals versus education at the top left, however, resembles a null plot, in which no particular pattern is apparent. A null plot is consistent with an adequate model, but as is the case here, one null plot is insufficient to provide evidence of an adequate model, and indeed one nonnull plot is enough to suggest that the specified model does not match the data. The plot of residuals versus income at the top right is also curved, as

---

[2]Our experience in statistical consulting suggests that this kind of naivete is common.

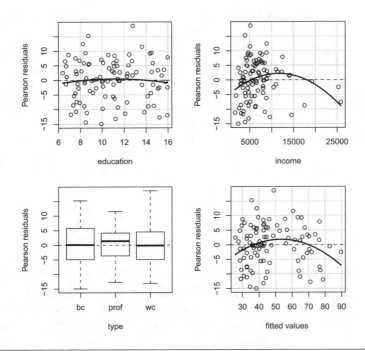

Figure 6.1 Basic residual plots for the regression of `prestige` on `education`, `income`, and `type` in the `Prestige` data set.

might have been anticipated in light of the results in Section 3.4.7. The residual plot for a factor such as `type`, at the bottom left, is a set of boxplots of the residuals at the various levels of the factor. In a null plot, the boxes should all have about the same center and spread, as is more or less the case here.

To help examine these residual plots, a *lack-of-fit test* is computed for each numeric predictor, and a curve is added to the graph. The lack-of-fit test for `education`, for example, is the t test for the regressor (`education`)^2 added to the model, for which the corresponding p value rounds to .50, indicating no lack-of-fit of this type. For `income`, the lack-of-fit test has the p value .005, clearly confirming the nonlinear pattern visible in the graph. The lines shown on the plot are the fitted quadratic regressions of the Pearson residuals on the numeric predictors.

For the plot of residuals versus fitted values, the test—called *Tukey's test for nonadditivity* (Tukey, 1949)—is obtained by adding the squares of the fitted values to the model and refitting. The significance level for Tukey's test is obtained by comparing the statistic with the standard-normal distribution. The test confirms the visible impression of curvature in the residual plot, further reinforcing the conclusion that the fitted model is not adequate.

The `residualPlots` function shares many arguments with other graphics functions in the **car** package; see `?residualPlots` for details. In `residualPlots`, all arguments other than the first are optional. The argument `id.n` could be set to a positive number to identify automatically the `id.n` most unusual cases, which by default are the cases with the largest (absolute) residuals (see Section 3.5). There are additional arguments to control the layout of the plots and the type of residual plotted. For example, setting `type="rstudent"` would plot Studentized residuals rather than Pearson residuals. Setting `smooth=TRUE`, `quadratic=FALSE` would display a lowess smooth rather than a quadratic curve on each plot, although the test statistics always correspond to the fitting quadratics.

If you want only the plot of residuals against fitted values, you can use

```
> residualPlots(prestige.mod.2, ~ 1, fitted=TRUE)
```

whereas the plot against `education` only can be obtained with

```
> residualPlots(prestige.mod.2, ~ education, fitted=FALSE)
```

The second argument to `residualPlots`—and to other functions in the **car** package that can produce graphs with several panels—is a *one-sided formula* that specifies the predictors against which to plot residuals. The formula `~ .` is the default, to plot against *all* the available predictors; `~ 1` plots against *none* of the predictors, and in the current context produces a plot against fitted values only; `~ . - income` plots against all predictors but `income`. Because the fitted values are not part of the formula that defined the model, there is a separate `fitted` argument, which is set to `TRUE` (the default) to include a plot of residuals against fitted values and `FALSE` to exclude it.

We could of course draw residual plots using `plot` or `scatterplot`, but we would have to be careful if there are missing data. In the current example, the value of `type` is missing for a few of the cases, and so the regression was computed using only the complete cases. Consequently, the vector of residuals is shorter than the vector of values for, say, `income`. We can circumvent this problem by setting `option(na.action=na.exclude)` (as explained in Section 4.8.5). Then the residual vector will include a value for each observation in the original data set, equal to `NA` for observations with missing values on one or more variables in the model.

6.2.2 MARGINAL MODEL PLOTS

A variation on the basic residual plot is the *marginal model plot*, proposed by Cook and Weisberg (1997):

```
> marginalModelPlots(prestige.mod.2)
```

These plots (shown in Figure 6.2) all have the response variable, in this case `prestige`, on the vertical axis, while the horizontal axis is given in turn by each of the numeric predictors in the model and the fitted values. The plots of the response versus individual predictors display the conditional distribution of the response given each predictor, ignoring the other predictors; these are

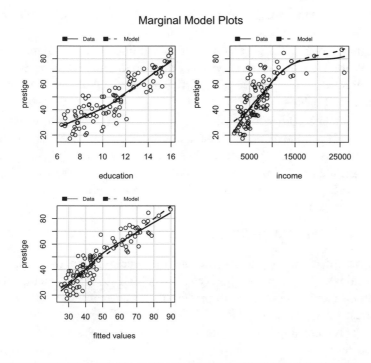

Figure 6.2 Marginal-model plots for the regression of `prestige` on education, `income`, and `type` in the `Prestige` data set.

marginal plots in the sense that they show the marginal relationship between the response and each predictor. The plot versus fitted values is a little different in that it displays the conditional distribution of the response given the fit of the model.

We can estimate a regression function for each of the marginal plots by fitting a smoother to the points in the plot. The `marginalModelPlots` function uses a `lowess` smooth, as shown by the solid line on the plot.

Now imagine a second graph that replaces the vertical axis with the fitted values from the model. If the model is appropriate for the data, then, under fairly mild conditions, the smooth fit to this second plot should also estimate the conditional expectation of the response given the predictor on the horizontal axis. The second smooth is also drawn on the marginal model plot, as a dashed line. If the model fits the data well, then the two smooths should match on each of the marginal model plots; if any pair of smooths fails to match, then we have evidence that the model does not fit the data well.

An interesting feature of the marginal model plots in Figure 6.2 is that even though the model that we fit to the `Prestige` data specifies linear *partial* relationships between `prestige` and each of education and `income`, it is able to reproduce nonlinear *marginal* relationships for these two predictors. Indeed, the model, as represented by the dashed lines, does a fairly good job of matching the marginal relationships represented by the solid lines, although the systematic failures discovered in the residual plots are discernable here as well.

Marginal model plots can be used with any fitting or modeling method that produces fitted values, and so they can be applied to some problems where the definition of residuals is unclear. In particular, marginal model plots generalize nicely to GLMs.

The `marginalModelPlots` function has an `SD` argument, which if set to `TRUE` adds estimated standard deviation lines to the graph. The plots can therefore be used to check both the regression function, as illustrated here, and the assumptions about variance. Other arguments to the `marginal-ModelPlots` function are similar to those for `residualPlots`.

6.2.3   ADDED-VARIABLE PLOTS

The marginal model plots of the previous section display the *marginal* relationships—both directly observed and implied by the model—between the response and each regressor *ignoring* the other regressors in the model. In contrast, *added-variable plots*, also called *partial-regression plots*, display the *partial* relationship between the response and a regressor, *adjusted for* all the other regressors.

Suppose that we have a regression problem with response y and regressors $x_1, \ldots, x_k$.[3] To draw the added-variable plot for one of the regressors—say the first, x_1—we must conduct the following two auxiliary regressions:

1. Regress y on all the regressors excluding x_1. The residuals from this regression are *the part of y that is not explained by all the regressors except x_1*.

2. Regress x_1 on the other regressors and again obtain the residuals. These residuals represent the *part of x_1 that is not explained by the other regressors*; put another way, the residuals are the part of x_1 that remains when we condition on the other regressors.

The added-variable plot for x_1 is simply a scatterplot with the residuals from Step 1 on the vertical axis and the residuals from Step 2 on the horizontal axis.

The `avPlots` function in the **car** package works both for linear models and GLMs. It has arguments for controlling which plots are drawn, point labeling, and plot layout, and these arguments are the same as for the `residualPlots` function (described in Section 6.2.1).

Added-variable plots for the Canadian occupational-prestige regression (in Figure 6.3) are produced by the following command:

```
> avPlots(prestige.mod.2, id.n=2, id.cex=0.6)
```

---

[3]Although it is not usually of interest, when there is an intercept in the model, it is also possible to construct an added-variable plot for the constant regressor, x_0, which is equal to 1 for every observation.

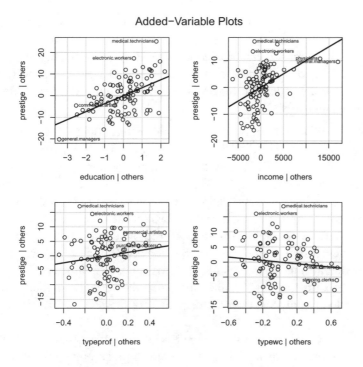

Figure 6.3 Added-variable plots for the regression of `prestige` on education, income, and `type` in the `Prestige` data set.

The argument `id.n=2` will result in identifying up to four points in each graph, the two that are farthest from the mean on the horizontal axis and the two with the largest absolute residuals from the fitted line. Because the case labels in the `Prestige` data set are very long, we used `id.cex=0.6` to reduce the printed labels to 60% of their default size.

The added-variable plot has several interesting and useful properties:

- The least-squares line on the added-variable plot for the regressor x_j has slope b_j, equal to the partial slope for x_j in the full regression. Thus, for example, the slope in the added-variable plot for `education` is $b_1 = 3.67$, and the slope in the added-variable plot for `income` is $b_2 = 0.00101$. (The income slope is small because the unit of income— $1 of annual income—is small.)
- The residuals from the least-squares line in the added-variable plot are the same as the residuals e_i from the regression of the response on *all* of the regressors.
- Because the positions on the horizontal axis of the added-variable plot show values of x_j conditional on the other regressors, points far to the left or right represent observations for which the value of x_j is unusual given the values of the other regressors. Likewise, the variation of the variable on the horizontal axis is the conditional variation of x_j, and the

added-variable plot therefore allows us to visualize the precision of the estimation of b_j.

- For factors, an added-variable plot is produced for each of the contrasts that are used to define the factor, and thus, if we change the way the contrasts are coded for a factor, the corresponding added-variable plots will change as well.

The added-variable plot allows us to visualize the effect of each regressor after adjusting for all the other regressors in the model. In Figure 6.3, the plot for `income` has a positive slope, but the slope appears to be influenced by two high-income occupations (physicians and general managers), which pull down the regression line at the right. There don't seem to be any particularly noteworthy points in the added-variable plots for the other regressors.

Although added-variable plots are useful for studying the impact of observations on regression coefficients (see Section 6.3.3), they can prove misleading when diagnosing other sorts of problems, such as nonlinearity. A further disadvantage of the added-variable plot is that the variables on both axes are sets of residuals, and so neither the response nor the regressors are displayed directly.

Sall (1990) and Cook and Weisberg (1991) generalize added-variable plots to terms with more than 1 df, such as a factor or polynomial regressors. Following Sall, we call these graphs *leverage plots*. For terms with 1 df, the leverage plots are very similar to added-variable plots, except that the slope in the plot is always equal to 1, not to the corresponding regression coefficient. Although leverage plots can be misleading in certain circumstances,[4] they can be useful for locating groups of cases that are jointly high-leverage or influential. Leverage, influence, and related ideas are explored in the next section. There is a `leveragePlots` function in the **car** package, which works only for linear models.

6.3   Unusual Data

Unusual data can wreak havoc with least-squares estimates but may prove interesting in their own right. Unusual data in regression include outliers, high-leverage points, and influential observations.

6.3.1   OUTLIERS AND STUDENTIZED RESIDUALS

Regression outliers are y values that are unusual *conditional on* the values of the predictors. An illuminating way to search for outliers is via the *mean-shift outlier model*:

$$y_i = \alpha + \beta_1 x_{i1} + \cdots + \beta_k x_{ik} + \gamma d_i + \varepsilon_i$$

[4]For example, if a particular observation causes one dummy-regressor coefficient to get larger and another smaller, these changes can cancel each other out in the leverage plot for the corresponding factor, even though a different pattern of results for the factor would be produced by removing the observation.

where d_i is a dummy regressor coded 1 for observation i and 0 for all other observations. If $\gamma \neq 0$, then the conditional expectation of the ith observation has the same dependence on $x_1, \ldots, x_k$ as the other observations, but its intercept is shifted from α to $\alpha + \gamma$. The t statistic for testing the null hypothesis $H_0: \gamma = 0$ against a two-sided alternative has $n - k - 2$ df if the errors are normally distributed and is the appropriate test for a single mean-shift outlier at observation i. Remarkably, this t statistic turns out to be identical to the ith Studentized residual, e_{Ti} (Equation 6.4, p. 287), and so we can get the test statistics for the n different null hypotheses, H_{0i}: case i is not a mean-shift outlier, $i = 1, \ldots, n$, at minimal computational cost.

Our attention is generally drawn to the largest absolute Studentized residual, and this presents a problem: Even if the Studentized residuals were independent, which they are not, there would be an issue of simultaneous inference entailed by picking the largest of n test statistics. The dependence of the Studentized residuals complicates the issue. We can deal with this problem (a) by a *Bonferroni adjustment* of the p value for the largest absolute Studentized residual, multiplying the usual two-tail p by the sample size, n, or (b) by constructing a quantile-comparison plot of the Studentized residuals with a confidence envelope that takes their dependence into account.

We reconsider Duncan's occupational-prestige data (introduced in Section 1.2), regressing `prestige` on occupational `income` and `education` levels:

```
> mod.duncan <- lm(prestige ~ income + education, data=Duncan)
```

The generic `qqPlot` function in the **car** package has a method for linear models, plotting Studentized residuals against the corresponding quantiles of $t(n-k-2)$. By default, `qqPlot` generates a 95% pointwise confidence envelope for the Studentized residuals, using a parametric version of the bootstrap, as suggested by Atkinson (1985):[5]

```
> qqPlot(mod.duncan, id.n=3)

[1] "minister"    "reporter"    "contractor"
```

The resulting plot is shown in Figure 6.4. Setting the argument `id.n=3`, the `qqPlot` function returns the names of the three observations with the largest absolute Studentized residuals (see Section 3.5 on point identification); in this case, only one observation, `minister`, strays slightly outside of the confidence envelope. If you repeat this command, your plot may look a little different from ours because the envelope is computed by simulation. The distribution of the Studentized residuals looks heavy-tailed compared to the reference t distribution: Perhaps a method of robust regression would be more appropriate for these data.[6]

---

[5]Bootstrap methods in R are described in the online appendix to the book.
[6]R functions for robust and resistant regression are described in Section 4.3.7 and in the online appendix to the text.

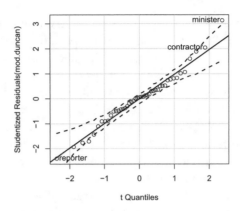

Figure 6.4   Quantile-comparison plot of Studentized residuals from Duncan's occupational-prestige regression, showing the pointwise 95% simulated confidence envelope.

The `outlierTest` function in the **car** package locates the largest Studentized residual in absolute value and computes the Bonferroni-corrected *t* test:

```
> outlierTest(mod.duncan)

No Studentized residuals with Bonferonni p < 0.05
Largest |rstudent|:
         rstudent unadjusted p-value Bonferonni p
minister    3.135           0.003177       0.1430
```

The Bonferroni-adjusted *p* value is not statistically significant, and so it isn't surprising that the largest Studentized residual in a sample of size $n = 45$ is as large as 3.135.

6.3.2   LEVERAGE: HAT-VALUES

Observations that are relatively far from the center of the regressor space, taking account of the correlational pattern among the regressors, have potentially greater influence on the least-squares regression coefficients; such points are said to have *high leverage*. The most common measures of leverage are the h_i, or *hat-values*.[7] The h_i are bounded between 0 and 1 (in models with an intercept, they are bounded between $1/n$ and 1), and their sum, $\sum h_i$, is always equal to the number of coefficients in the model, including the intercept. Problems in which there are a few very large h_i can be troublesome: In particular, large-sample normality of some linear combinations of the regressors is likely to fail, and high-leverage observations may exert undue influence on the results (see below).

---

[7]* The name *hat-values* comes from the relationship between the observed vector of responses and the fitted values. The vector of fitted values is given by $\widehat{\mathbf{y}} = \mathbf{Xb} = \mathbf{X}(\mathbf{X'X})^{-1}\mathbf{X'y} = \mathbf{Hy}$, where $\mathbf{H} = \{h_{ij}\} = \mathbf{X}(\mathbf{X'X})^{-1}\mathbf{X'}$, called the *hat-matrix*, projects $\mathbf{y}$ into the subspace spanned by the columns of the model matrix $\mathbf{X}$. Because $\mathbf{H} = \mathbf{H'H}$, the hat-values h_i are simply the diagonal entries of the hat-matrix.

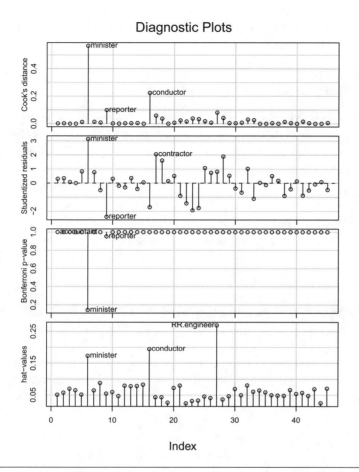

Figure 6.5 Index plots of diagnostic statistics for Duncan's occupational-prestige regression.

The `hatvalues` function works for both linear models and GLMs. One way of examining the hat-values and other individual-observation diagnostic statistics is to construct *index plots*, graphing the statistics against the corresponding observation indices.

For example, the following command uses the **car** function `influenceIndexPlot` to produce Figure 6.5, which includes index plots of Studentized residuals, the corresponding Bonferroni p values for outlier testing, the hat-values, and Cook's distances (discussed in the next section) for Duncan's occupational-prestige regression:

```
> influenceIndexPlot(mod.duncan, id.n=3)
```

The occupations railroad engineer (`RR.engineer`), `conductor`, and `minister` stand out from the rest in the plot of hat-values, indicating that their regressor values are unusual relative to the other occupations. In the plot of p values for the outlier tests, cases for which the Bonferroni bound is bigger than 1 are set equal to 1, and here only one case (`minister`) has a Bonferroni p value much less than 1.

6.3.3 INFLUENCE MEASURES

An observation that is both outlying and has high leverage exerts *influence* on the regression coefficients, in the sense that if the observation is removed, the coefficients change considerably. As usual, let **b** be the estimated value of the coefficient vector $\boldsymbol{\beta}$, and as new notation, define $\mathbf{b}_{(-i)}$ to be the estimate of $\boldsymbol{\beta}$ but now computed without the ith case.[8] Then the difference $\mathbf{b}_{(-i)} - \mathbf{b}$ directly measures the influence of the ith observation on the estimate of $\boldsymbol{\beta}$. If this difference is small, then the influence of observation i is small, whereas if the difference is large, then its influence is large.

COOK'S DISTANCE

It is convenient to summarize the size of the difference $\mathbf{b}_{(-i)} - \mathbf{b}$ by a single number, and this can be done in several ways. The most common summary measure of influence is *Cook's distance* (Cook, 1977), D_i, which is just a weighted sum of squares of the differences between the individual elements of the coefficient vectors.[9] Interestingly, Cook's distance can be computed from diagnostic statistics that we have already encountered:

$$D_i = \frac{e_{Si}^2}{k+1} \times \frac{h_i}{1 - h_i}$$

where e_{Si}^2 is the squared standardized residual (Equation 6.3, p. 286) and h_i is the hat-value for observation i. The first factor may be thought of as a measure of outlyingness and the second as a measure of leverage. Observations for which D_i is large are potentially influential cases. If any noteworthy D_i are apparent, then it is prudent to remove the corresponding cases temporarily from the data, refit the regression, and see how the results change. Because an influential observation can affect the fit of the model at other observations, it is best to remove observations one at a time, refitting the model at each step and reexamining the resulting Cook's distances.

The generic function `cooks.distance` has methods for linear models and GLMs. Cook's distances are also plotted, along with Studentized residuals and hat-values, by the `influenceIndexPlot` function, as illustrated for Duncan's regression in Figure 6.5. The occupation `minister` is the most influential according to Cook's distance, and we therefore see what happens when we delete this case and refit the model:

---

[8] If vector notation is unfamiliar, simply think of **b** as the collection of estimated regression coefficients, $b_0, b_1, \ldots, b_k$.

[9] * In matrix notation,

$$D_i = \frac{\left(\mathbf{b}_{(-i)} - \mathbf{b}\right)' \mathbf{X}'\mathbf{X} \left(\mathbf{b}_{(-i)} - \mathbf{b}\right)}{(k+1)\hat{\sigma}^2}.$$

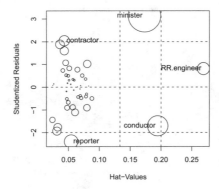

Figure 6.6 Plot of hat-values, Studentized residuals, and Cook's distances for Duncan's occupational-prestige regression. The size of the circles is proportional to Cook's D_i.

```
> mod.duncan.2 <- update(mod.duncan,
+       subset= rownames(Duncan) != "minister")
> compareCoefs(mod.duncan, mod.duncan.2)

Call:
1:lm(formula = prestige ~ income + education, data = Duncan)
2:lm(formula = prestige ~ income + education, data = Duncan,
      subset = rownames(Duncan) != "minister")
            Est. 1    SE 1  Est. 2    SE 2
(Intercept) -6.0647  4.2719 -6.6275  3.8875
income       0.5987  0.1197  0.7316  0.1167
education    0.5458  0.0983  0.4330  0.0963
```

The `compareCoefs` function displays the estimates from one or more fitted models in a compact table. Removing `minister` increases the coefficient for `income` by about 20% and decreases the coefficient for `education` by about the same amount. Standard errors are much less affected. In other problems, removing an observation can change significant results to insignificant ones, and vice-versa.

The `influencePlot` function in the **car** package provides an alternative to index plots of diagnostic statistics:

```
> influencePlot(mod.duncan, id.n=3)

            StudRes     Hat   CookD
minister      3.135 0.17306  0.7526
reporter     -2.397 0.05439  0.3146
conductor    -1.704 0.19454  0.4729
contractor    2.044 0.04326  0.2419
RR.engineer   0.809 0.26909  0.2845
```

This command produces a *bubble-plot*, shown in Figure 6.6, which combines the display of Studentized residuals, hat-values, and Cook's distances, with the

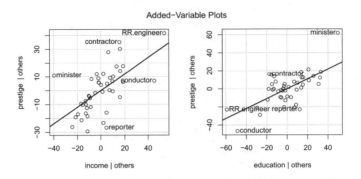

Figure 6.7 Added-variable plots for Duncan's occupational-prestige regression.

areas of the circles proportional to Cook's D_i.[10] As usual the id.n argument is used to label points. In this case, the id.n points with the largest hat-values, Cook's distances, or absolute Studentized residuals will be flagged, so more than id.n points in all may be labeled.

We invite the reader to continue the analysis by examining the influence diagnostics for Duncan's regression after the observation minister has been removed.

ADDED-VARIABLE PLOTS AS INFLUENCE DIAGNOSTICS

Added-variable plots (Section 6.2.3) are a useful diagnostic for finding potentially jointly influential points, which will correspond to sets of points that are out of line with the rest of the data and are at the extreme left or right of the horizontal axis. Figure 6.7, for example, shows the added-variable plots for income and education in Duncan's regression:

```
> avPlots(mod.duncan, id.n=3)
```

The observations minister, conductor, and RR.engineer (railroad engineer) have high leverage on both coefficients. The cases minister and conductor also work together to decrease the income slope and increase the education slope; RR.engineer, on the other hand, is more in line with the rest of the data. Removing *both* minister and conductor changes the regression coefficients dramatically—much more so than deleting minister alone:

```
> mod.duncan.3 <- update(mod.duncan,
+     subset = !(rownames(Duncan) %in% c("minister", "conductor")))
> compareCoefs(mod.duncan, mod.duncan.2, mod.duncan.3, se=FALSE)
```

[10]In Chapter 8, we describe how to write a similar function as a preliminary example of programming in R.

```
Call:
1:lm(formula = prestige ~ income + education, data = Duncan)
2:lm(formula = prestige ~ income + education, data = Duncan,
      subset = rownames(Duncan) != "minister")
3:lm(formula = prestige ~ income + education, data = Duncan,
      subset = !(rownames(Duncan) %in% c("minister", "conductor")))
            Est. 1 Est. 2 Est. 3
(Intercept) -6.065 -6.628 -6.409
income       0.599  0.732  0.867
education    0.546  0.433  0.332
```

INFLUENCE SEPARATELY FOR EACH COEFFICIENT

Rather than summarizing influence by looking at all coefficients simultaneously, we could create $k + 1$ measures of influence by looking at individual differences:

$$\text{dfbeta}_{ij} = b_{(-i)j} - b_j \text{ for } j = 0, \dots, k$$

where b_j is the coefficient computed using all the data and $b_{(-i)j}$ is the same coefficient computed with case i omitted. As with D_i, computation of dfbeta$_{ij}$ can be accomplished efficiently without having to refit the model. The dfbeta$_{ij}$ are expressed in the metric (units of measurement) of the coefficient b_j. A standardized version, dfbetas$_{ij}$, divides dfbeta$_{ij}$ by an estimate of the standard error of b_j computed with observation i removed.

The dfbeta function in R takes a linear-model or GLM object as its argument and returns all values of dfbeta$_{ij}$; similarly dfbetas computes the dfbetas$_{ij}$, as in the following example for Duncan's regression:

```
> dfbs.duncan <- dfbetas(mod.duncan)
> head(dfbs.duncan)  # first few rows

           (Intercept)      income  education
accountant  -0.0225344  6.662e-04   0.0359439
pilot       -0.0254350  5.088e-02  -0.0081183
architect   -0.0091867  6.484e-03   0.0056193
author      -0.0000472 -6.018e-05   0.0001398
chemist     -0.0658168  1.700e-02   0.0867771
minister     0.1449367 -1.221e+00   1.2630190
```

We could examine each column of the dfbetas matrix separately (e.g., via an index plot), but because we are not really interested here in influence on the regression intercept and because there are just two slope coefficients, we instead plot influence on the income coefficient against influence on the education coefficient (Figure 6.8):

```
> plot(dfbs.duncan[ , c("income", "education")])  # for b1 and b2
> identify(dfbs.duncan[ , "income"], dfbs.duncan[ , "education"],
+     rownames(Duncan))

[1] "minister"    "conductor"    "RR.engineer"
```

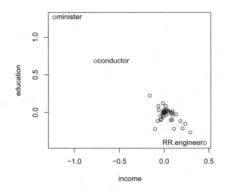

Figure 6.8 dfbetas$_{ij}$ values for the `income` and `education` coefficients in Duncan's occupational-prestige regression. Three points were identified interactively.

The negative relationship between the dfbetas$_{ij}$ values for the two regressors reflects the *positive* correlation of the regressors themselves. Two pairs of values stand out: Consistent with our earlier remarks, observations `minister` and `conductor` make the `income` coefficient smaller and the `education` coefficient larger. We also identified the occupation `RR.engineer` in the plot.

6.4   Transformations After Fitting a Regression Model

Suspected outliers and possibly cases with high leverage should be studied individually to decide whether or not they should be included in an analysis. Influential cases can cause changes in the conclusions of an analysis and also require special treatment. Other systematic features in residual plots—for example, curvature or apparent nonconstant variance—require action on the part of the analyst to modify the structure of the model to match the data more closely. Apparently distinct problems can also interact: For example, if the errors have a skewed distribution, then apparent outliers may be produced in the direction of the skew. Transforming the response to make the errors less skewed can solve this problem. Similarly, properly modeling a nonlinear relationship may bring apparently outlying observations in line with the rest of the data.

Transformations were introduced in Section 3.4 in the context of examining data and with the understanding that regression modeling is often easier and more effective when the predictors behave as if they were normal random variables. Transformations can also be used *after* fitting a model, to improve a model that does not adequately represent the data. The methodology in these two contexts is very similar.

6.4.1 TRANSFORMING THE RESPONSE

NONNORMAL ERRORS

Departures from the assumption of normally distributed errors are probably the most difficult problem to diagnose. The only data available for studying the error distribution are the residuals. Even for an otherwise correctly specified model, the residuals can have substantially different variances, can be strongly correlated, and tend to behave more like a normal sample than do the original errors, a property that has been called *supernormality* (Gnanadesikan, 1977).

A quantile-comparison plot of Studentized residuals against the t distribution (as described in Section 6.3.1) is useful in drawing our attention to the tail behavior of the residuals, possibly revealing heavy-tailed or skewed distributions. A nonparametric density estimate, however, does a better job of conveying a general sense of the shape of the residual distribution.

In Section 5.5, we fit a Poisson regression to Ornstein's data on interlocking directorates among Canadian corporations, regressing the number of interlocks maintained by each firm on the firm's assets, nation of control, and sector of operation. Because number of interlocks is a count, the Poisson model is a natural starting point, but the original source used a least-squares regression similar to the following:

```
> mod.ornstein <- lm(interlocks + 1 ~ log(assets) + nation + sector,
+       data=Ornstein)
```

We put `interlocks + 1` on the left-hand side of the model formula because there are some 0 values in `interlocks` and we will shortly consider power transformations of the response variable.

Quantile-comparison and density plots of the Studentized residuals for Ornstein's regression are produced by the following R commands (Figure 6.9):

```
> par(mfrow=c(1,2))
> qqPlot(mod.ornstein, id.n=0)
> plot(density(rstudent(mod.ornstein)))
```

Both tails of the distribution of Studentized residuals are heavier than they should be, but the upper tail is even heavier than the lower one, and consequently, the distribution is positively skewed. A positive skew in the distribution of the residuals can often be corrected by transforming y down the ladder of powers. The next section describes a systematic method for selecting a normalizing transformation of y.

BOX-COX TRANSFORMATIONS

The goal of fitting a model that exhibits linearity, constant variance, and normality can in principle require three different response transformations, but experience suggests that one transformation is often effective for all of these tasks. The most common method for selecting a transformation of the response in regression was introduced by Box and Cox (1964). If the response

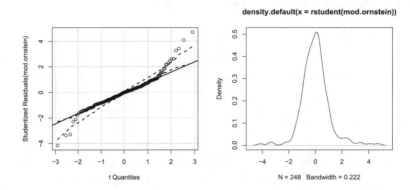

Figure 6.9 Quantile-comparison plot and nonparametric density estimate for the distribution of the Studentized residuals from Ornstein's interlocking-directorate regression.

y is a strictly positive variable, then the Box-Cox power transformations (introduced in Section 3.4.2), implemented in the `bcPower` function in the **car** package, are often effective:

$$T_{\text{BC}}(y, \lambda) = y^{(\lambda)} = \begin{cases} \dfrac{y^\lambda - 1}{\lambda} & \text{when } \lambda \neq 0 \\ \log_e y & \text{when } \lambda = 0 \end{cases} \tag{6.7}$$

If y is not strictly positive, then the Yeo-Johnson family, computed by the `yjPower` function, can be used in place of the Box-Cox family; alternatively, we can add a start to y to make all the values positive (as explained in Section 3.4.2).

Box and Cox proposed selecting the value of λ by analogy to the method of maximum likelihood, so that the residuals from the linear regression of $T_{\text{BC}}(y, \lambda)$ on the predictors are as close to normally distributed as possible.[11] The **car** package provides two functions for estimating λ. The first, `box-Cox`, is a slight generalization of the `boxcox` function in the **MASS** package (Venables and Ripley, 2002).[12] The second is the `powerTransform` function introduced in a related context in Section 3.4.7.

For Ornstein's least-squares regression, for example,

```
> boxCox(mod.ornstein, lambda = seq(0, 0.6, by=0.1))
```

This command produces the graph of the *profile log-likelihood* function for λ in Figure 6.10. The best estimate of λ is the value that maximizes the profile

---

[11]* If $T_{\text{BC}}(y, \lambda_0) | \mathbf{x}$ is normally distributed, then $T_{\text{BC}}(y, \lambda_1) | \mathbf{x}$ cannot be normally distributed for $\lambda_1 \neq \lambda_0$, and so the distribution changes for every value of λ. The method Box and Cox proposed ignores this fact to get a maximum-likelihood-like estimate that turns out to have properties similar to those of maximum-likelihood estimates.

[12] `boxCox` adds the argument `family`. If set to the default `family="bcPower"`, then the function is identical to the original `boxcox`. If set to `family="yjPower"`, then the Yeo-Johnson power transformations are used.

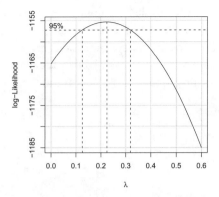

Figure 6.10 Profile log-likelihood for the transformation parameter λ in the Box-Cox model applied to Ornstein's interlocking-directorate regression.

likelihood, which in this example is $\lambda \approx 0.2$. An approximate 95% confidence interval for λ is the set of all λs for which the value of the profile log-likelihood is within 1.92 of the maximum—from about 0.1 to 0.3.[13] It is usual to round the estimate of λ to a familiar value, such as $-1, -1/2, 0, 1/3, 1/2, 1,$ or 2. In this case, we would round to the cube-root transformation, $\lambda = 1/3$. Because the response variable `interlocks` is a count, however, we might prefer the log transformation ($\lambda = 0$) or the square-root transformation ($\lambda = 1/2$).

In the call to `boxCox`, we used only the linear-model object `mod.-ornstein` and the optional argument `lambda`, setting the range of powers to be searched to λ in $[0, 0.6]$. We did this to provide more detail in the plot, and the default of `lambda = seq(-2, 2, by=0.1)` is usually recommended for an initial profile log-likelihood plot. If the maximum-likelihood estimate of λ turns out to lie outside this range, then the range can always be extended, although transformations outside $[-2, 2]$ are rarely helpful.

The function `powerTransform` in the **car** package performs calculations that are similar to those of the `boxCox` function when applied to an `lm` object, but it produces numeric rather than graphical output:

```
> summary(p1 <- powerTransform(mod.ornstein))

bcPower Transformation to Normality

    Est.Power Std.Err. Wald Lower Bound Wald Upper Bound
Y1     0.2227   0.0493           0.126           0.3193

Likelihood ratio tests about transformation parameters
                         LRT df        pval
LR test, lambda = (0)  19.76  1   8.794e-06
LR test, lambda = (1) 243.40  1   0.000e+00
```

The maximum-likelihood estimate of the transformation parameter is $\widehat{\lambda} = 0.22$, with the 95% confidence interval for λ running from 0.13 to 0.32—quite

---

[13] The value 1.92 is $\frac{1}{2}\chi^2_{.95}(1) = \frac{1}{2}1.96^2$.

a sharp estimate that even excludes the cube-root transformation, $\lambda = 1/3$. The significance levels for the tests that $\lambda = 0$ and for $\lambda = 1$ are very small, suggesting that neither of these transformations is appropriate for the data.

The result returned by powerTransform, which we stored in p1, can be used to add the transformed values to the data frame:

```
> Ornstein1 <- transform(Ornstein,
+     y1=bcPower(interlocks + 1, coef(p1)),
+     y1round=bcPower(interlocks + 1, coef(p1, round=TRUE)))
> mod.ornstein.trans <- update(mod.ornstein, y1round ~ .,
+     data=Ornstein1)
```

This command saves the transformed values with λ rounded to the convenient value in the confidence interval that is closest to the point estimate. If none of the convenient values are in the interval, then no rounding is done.

CONSTRUCTED-VARIABLE PLOT FOR THE BOX-COX TRANSFORMATION

Atkinson (1985) suggests an approximate score test and diagnostic plot for the Box-Cox transformation of y, based on the *constructed variable*

$$g_i = y_i \left[\log_e \left(\frac{y_i}{\widetilde{y}} \right) - 1 \right]$$

where $\widetilde{y}$ is the geometric mean of y; that is,

$$\widetilde{y} = (y_1 \times y_2 \times \cdots \times y_n)^{1/n} = \exp \left(\frac{1}{n} \sum \log_e y_i \right)$$

The constructed variable is added as a regressor, and the t statistic for this variable is the approximate score statistic for the transformation. Although the score test isn't terribly interesting in light of the ready availability of likelihood ratio tests for the transformation parameter, an added-variable plot for the constructed variable in the auxiliary regression—called a *constructed-variable plot*—shows leverage and influence on the decision to transform y.

The boxCoxVariable function in the **car** package facilitates the computation of the constructed variable. Thus, for Ornstein's regression:

```
> mod.ornstein.cv <- update(mod.ornstein,
+     . ~ . + boxCoxVariable(interlocks + 1))
> summary(
+    mod.ornstein.cv)$coef["boxCoxVariable(interlocks + 1)", ,
+                     drop=FALSE]

                              Estimate Std. Error t value
boxCoxVariable(interlocks + 1)   0.6161    0.02421   25.45
                              Pr(>|t|)
boxCoxVariable(interlocks + 1) 3.176e-69

> avPlots(mod.ornstein.cv, "boxCoxVariable(interlocks + 1)")
```

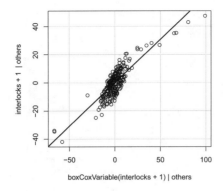

Figure 6.11   Constructed-variable plot for the Box-Cox transformation of *y* in Ornstein's interlocking-directorate regression.

We are only interested in the *t* test and added-variable plot for the constructed variable, so we printed only the row of the coefficient table for that variable. The argument `drop=FALSE` told R to print the result as a matrix, keeping the labels, rather than as a vector (see Section 2.3.4). The constructed-variable plot is obtained using `avPlots`, with the second argument specifying the constructed variable. The resulting constructed-variable plot is shown in Figure 6.11. The *t* statistic for the constructed variable demonstrates that there is very strong evidence of the need to transform *y*, agreeing with the preferred likelihood ratio test. The constructed-variable plot suggests that this evidence is spread through the data rather than being dependent on a small fraction of the observations.

INVERSE RESPONSE PLOTS

An alternative—or, better, a complement—to the Box-Cox method for transforming the response is the *inverse response plot*, proposed by Cook and Weisberg (1994). While this method produces a transformation toward linearity rather than normality, the results are often similar in cases where the Box-Cox method can be applied. The inverse response plot provides both a numeric estimate and a useful graphical summary; moreover, the inverse response plot can be used even if transformations outside a power family are needed.

The inverse response plot is a special case of the inverse transformation plots introduced in Section 3.4.6. In the current context, we plot the response on the horizontal axis and the fitted values on the vertical axis. To illustrate, we introduce an example that is of historical interest, because it was first used by Box and Cox (1964). Box and Cox's data are from an industrial experiment to study the strength of wool yarn under various conditions. Three predictors were varied in the experiment: `len`, the length of each sample of yarn in millimeters; `amp`, the amplitude of the loading cycle in minutes; and `load`, the amount of weight used in grams. The response, `cycles`, was the number

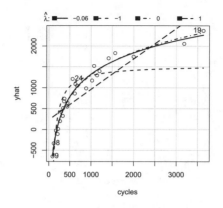

Figure 6.12   Inverse response plot for an additive-regression model fit to Box and Cox's `Wool` data.

of cycles until the sample failed. Data were collected using a $3 \times 3 \times 3$ design, with each of the predictors at three levels. We fit a linear model with main effects only:

```
> (wool.mod <- lm(cycles ~ len + amp + load, data=Wool))

Call:
lm(formula = cycles ~ len + amp + load, data = Wool)

Coefficients:
(Intercept)           len           amp          load
     4521.4          13.2        -535.8         -62.2
```

The inverse response plot for the model is drawn by the following command (and appears in Figure 6.12):

```
> inverseResponsePlot(wool.mod, id.n=4)

    lambda       RSS
1 -0.06052    503066
2 -1.00000   3457493
3  0.00000    518855
4  1.00000   3995722
```

Four lines are shown on the inverse response plot, each of which is from the nonlinear regression of $\widehat{y}$ on $T_{\mathrm{BC}}(y, \lambda)$, for $\lambda = -1, 0, 1$ and for the value of λ that best fits the points in the plot. A linearizing transformation of the response would correspond to a value of λ that matches the data well. In the example, the linearizing transformation producing the smallest residual sum of squares, $\lambda = -0.06$, is essentially the log-transform. As can be seen on the graph, the optimal transformation and log-transform produce essentially the same fitted line, while the other default choices are quite a bit worse. The printed output from the function gives the residual sums of squares for the four fitted lines.

As an alternative approach, the Box-Cox method can be used to find a normalizing transformation, as in the original analysis of these data by Box and Cox (1964):

```
> summary(powerTransform(wool.mod))

bcPower Transformation to Normality

   Est.Power Std.Err. Wald Lower Bound Wald Upper Bound
Y1   -0.0592   0.0611         -0.1789           0.0606

Likelihood ratio tests about transformation parameters
                          LRT df    pval
LR test, lambda = (0)  0.9213  1 0.3371
LR test, lambda = (1) 84.0757  1 0.0000
```

Both methods therefore suggest that the log-transform is appropriate here. The reader is invited to explore these data further. Without transformation, inclusion of higher-order terms in the predictors is required, but in the log-transformed scale, there is a very simple model that closely matches the data.

One advantage of the inverse response plot is that we can visualize the leverage and influence of individual observations on the choice of a transformation; separated points tend to be influential. In Figure 6.12, we marked the four points with the largest residuals from the line for $\lambda = 1$. All these points are very well fit by the log-transformed curve and are in the same pattern as the rest of the data; there are no observations that appear to be overly influential in determining the transformation.

For the Ornstein data described earlier in this section, the inverse response plot (not shown) is not successful in selecting a transformation of the response. For these data, the problem is lack of normality, and the inverse response plots transform for linearity, not directly for normality.

6.4.2 PREDICTOR TRANSFORMATIONS

In some instances, predictor transformations resolve problems with a fitted model. Often, these transformations can, and should, be done *before* fitting models to the data (as outlined in Section 3.4). Even well-behaved predictors, however, aren't necessarily linearly related to the response, and graphical diagnostic methods are available that can help select a transformation *after* fitting a model. Moreover, some kinds of nonlinearity can't be fixed by transforming a predictor, and other strategies, such as polynomial regression or regression splines, may be entertained.

COMPONENT-PLUS-RESIDUAL AND CERES PLOTS

Component-plus-residual plots, also called *partial-residual plots*, are a simple graphical device that can be effective in detecting the need to transform a predictor, say x_j, to a new variable $T(x_j)$, for some transformation T. The plot has x_{ij} on the horizontal axis and the *partial residuals*, $e_{\text{Partial},ij} = e_i + b_j x_{ij}$, on

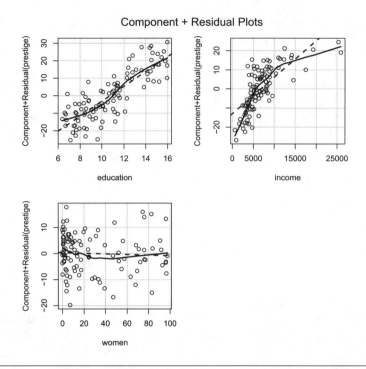

Figure 6.13 Component-plus-residual plots of `order=2` for the Canadian occupational-prestige regression.

the vertical axis. Cook (1993) shows that if the regressions of x_j on the other xs are approximately linear, then the regression function in the component-plus-residual plot provides a visualization of T. Alternatively, if the regressions of x_j on the other xs resemble polynomials, then a modification of the component-plus-residual plot due to Mallows (1986) can be used.

The `crPlots` function in the **car** package constructs component-plus-residual plots for linear models and GLMs. By way of example, we return to the Canadian occupational-prestige regression (from Section 6.2.1). A scatterplot matrix of the three predictors, `education`, `income`, and `women` (Figure 3.13, p. 126), suggests that the predictors are not all linearly related to each other, but no more complicated than quadratic regressions should provide reasonable approximations. Consequently, we draw the component-plus-residual plots specifying `order=2`, permitting quadratic relationships among the predictors:

```
> prestige.mod.3 <- update(prestige.mod.2, ~ . - type + women)
> crPlots(prestige.mod.3, order=2)
```

The component-plus-residual plots for the three predictors appear in Figure 6.13. The broken line on each panel is the *partial fit*, $b_j x_j$, assuming linearity in the partial relationship between y and x_j. The solid line is a `lowess` smooth, and it should suggest a transformation if one is appropriate, for example, via the bulging rule (see Section 3.4.6). Alternatively, the smooth might suggest a quadratic or cubic partial regression or, in more complex cases, the use of a regression spline.

For the Canadian occupational-prestige regression, the component-plus-residual plot for `income` is the most clearly curved, and transforming this variable first and refitting the model is therefore appropriate. In contrast, the component-plus-residual plot for `education` is only slightly nonlinear, and the partial relationship is not simple (in the sense of Section 3.4.6). Finally, the component-plus-residual plot for `women` looks mildly quadratic (although the lack-of-fit test computed by the `residualPlots` command does not suggest a significant quadratic effect), with `prestige` first declining and then rising as `women` increases.

Trial-and-error experimentation moving `income` down the ladder of powers and roots suggests that a log transformation of this predictor produces a reasonable fit to the data:

```
> prestige.mod.4 <- update(prestige.mod.3,
+        . ~ . + log2(income) - income)
```

which is the model we fit in Section 4.2.2. The component-plus-residual plot for `women` in the revised model (not shown) is broadly similar to the plot for `women` in Figure 6.13 (and the lack-of-fit test computed in `residualPlots` has a p value of .025) and suggests a quadratic regression:

```
> prestige.mod.5 <- update(prestige.mod.4,
+        . ~ . - women + poly(women, 2))
> summary(prestige.mod.5)$coef
```

	Estimate	Std. Error	t value	Pr(>|t|)
(Intercept)	-110.60	13.9817	-7.910	4.160e-12
education	3.77	0.3475	10.850	1.985e-18
log2(income)	9.36	1.2992	7.204	1.262e-10
poly(women, 2)1	15.09	9.3357	1.616	1.093e-01
poly(women, 2)2	15.87	6.9704	2.277	2.499e-02

The quadratic term for `women` is statistically significant but not overwhelmingly so.

If the regressions among the predictors are strongly nonlinear and not well described by polynomials, then the component-plus-residual plots may not be effective in recovering nonlinear partial relationships between the response and the predictors. For this situation, Cook (1993) provides another generalization of component-plus-residual plots, called *CERES plots* (for *C*ombining conditional *E*xpectations and *RES*iduals). CERES plots use nonparametric-regression smoothers rather than polynomial regressions to adjust for nonlinear relationships among the predictors. The `ceresPlots` function in the **car** package implements Cook's approach.

Experience suggests that nonlinear relationships among the predictors create problems for component-plus-residual plots only when these relationships are very strong. In such cases, a component-plus-residual plot can appear nonlinear even when the true partial regression is linear—a phenomenon termed *leakage*. For the Canadian occupational-prestige regression, higher-order component-plus-residual plots (in Figure 6.13) and CERES plots are nearly identical to the standard component-plus-residual plots, as the reader may verify.

THE BOX-TIDWELL METHOD FOR CHOOSING PREDICTOR TRANSFORMATIONS

As in transforming the response, transformations of the predictors in regression can be estimated by maximum likelihood. This possibility was suggested by Box and Tidwell (1962), who introduced the model for strictly positive predictors,

$$y = \beta_0 + \beta_1 T_{BC}(x_1, \gamma_1) + \cdots + \beta_k T_{BC}(x_k, \gamma_k) + \varepsilon$$

where $T_{BC}(x_j, \gamma_j)$ is a Box-Cox power transformation (Equation 6.7, p. 304) and the errors ε_i are assumed to be independent and normally distributed with common variance σ^2. Of course, we do not necessarily want to transform *all* the predictors, and in some contexts—such as when dummy regressors are present in the model—it does not even make sense to do so.

The Box-Tidwell regression model is a nonlinear model, which in principle can be fit by nonlinear least-squares.[14] Box and Tidwell describe an approximate computational approach, implemented in the `boxTidwell` function in the **car** package. We apply this function to the Canadian occupational-prestige regression, estimating power transformation parameters for `income` and `education`[15] but specifying a quadratic partial regression for `women`:

```
> boxTidwell(prestige ~ income + education,
+       other.x = ~ poly(women, 2), data=Prestige)

          Score Statistic p-value MLE of lambda
income              -5.301  0.0000       -0.0378
education            2.406  0.0161        2.1928

iterations =  12
```

The one-sided formula for the argument `other.x` indicates the terms in the model that are *not* to be transformed—here the quadratic in `women`. The score tests for the power transformations of `income` and `education` suggest that both predictors need to be transformed; the maximum-likelihood estimates of the transformation parameters are $\widehat{\gamma}_1 = -0.04$ for `income` (effectively, the log transformation of `income`) and $\widehat{\gamma}_2 = 2.2$ for `education` (effectively, the square of `education`).

Constructed variables for the Box-Tidwell transformations of the predictors are given by $x_j \log_e x_j$. These can be easily computed and added to the regression model to produce approximate score tests and constructed-variable plots.

---

[14]Nonlinear least squares is taken up in the online appendix to this *Companion*.

[15]The component-plus-residual plot for `education` in the preceding section reveals that the curvature of the partial relationship of `prestige` to `education`, which is in any event small, appears to change direction—that is, though monotone is not simple—and so a power transformation is not altogether appropriate here.

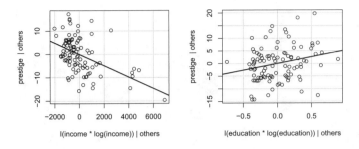

Figure 6.14 Constructed-variable plots for the Box-Tidwell transformation of `income` and `education` in the Canadian occupational-prestige regression.

Indeed, these constructed variables are the basis for Box and Tidwell's computational approach to fitting the model and yield the score statistics printed by the `boxTidwell` function.

To obtain constructed-variable plots (Figure 6.14) for `income` and `education` in the Canadian occupational-prestige regression:[16]

```
> mod.prestige.cv <- lm(prestige ~ income + education
+       + poly(women, 2)
+       + I(income * log(income)) + I(education * log(education)),
+       data=Prestige)
> summary(
+       mod.prestige.cv)$coef["I(income * log(income))", ,
+                       drop=FALSE]

                          Estimate Std. Error t value  Pr(>|t|)
I(income * log(income))  -0.00243   0.0004584  -5.301 7.459e-07

> summary(
+       mod.prestige.cv)$coef["I(education * log(education))", ,
+                       drop=FALSE]

                              Estimate Std. Error t value
I(education * log(education))    5.298      2.202   2.406
                              Pr(>|t|)
I(education * log(education))  0.01808
```

The *identity function* `I()` was used to protect the multiplication operator (`*`), which would otherwise be interpreted specially within a model formula, inappropriately generating main effects and an interaction (see Section 4.8).

The constructed-variable plot for `income` reveals some high-leverage points in determining the transformation of this predictor, but even when these points are removed, there is still substantial evidence for the transformation in the rest of the data.

---

[16]The observant reader will notice that the *t* values for the constructed-value regression are the same as the score statistics reported by `boxTidwell` but that there are small differences in the *p* values. These differences occur because `boxTidwell` uses the standard-normal distribution for the score test, while the standard summary for a linear model uses the *t* distribution.

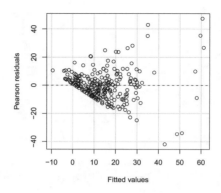

Figure 6.15   Plot of Pearson residuals against fitted values for Ornstein's interlocking-directorate regression.

6.5   Nonconstant Error Variance

One of the assumptions of the standard linear model is that the error variance is fully known apart from an unknown constant, σ^2. It is, however, possible that the error variance depends on one or more of the predictors, on the magnitude of the response, or systematically on some other variable.

To detect nonconstant variance as a function of a variable z, we would like to plot the Pearson residuals, or perhaps their absolute values, versus z. Nonconstant variance would be diagnosed if the variability of the residuals in the graph increased from left to right, decreased from left or right, or displayed another systematic pattern, such as large variation in the middle of the range of z and smaller variation at the edges.

In multiple regression, there are many potential plotting directions. Because obtaining a two-dimensional graph entails projecting the predictors from many dimensions onto one horizontal axis, however, we can never be sure if a plot showing nonconstant spread really reflects nonconstant error variance or some other problem, such as unmodeled nonlinearity (see Cook, 1998, sec. 1.2.1).

For Ornstein's interlocking-directorate regression, for example, we can obtain a plot of residuals against fitted values from the `residualPlots` function in the **car** package (introduced in Section 6.2.1), producing Figure 6.15:

```
> residualPlots(mod.ornstein, ~ 1, fitted=TRUE, id.n=0,
+     quadratic=FALSE, tests=FALSE)
```

The obvious fan-shaped array of points in this plot indicates that residual variance appears to increase as a function of the fitted values—that is, with the estimated magnitude of the response. In Section 5.5, we modeled these data using Poisson regression, for which the variance does increase with the mean, and so reproducing that pattern here is unsurprising. A less desirable

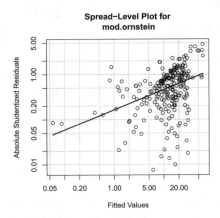

Figure 6.16   Spread-level plot of Studentized residuals against fitted values, for Ornstein's interlocking-directorate regression.

alternative to a regression model that is specifically designed for count data is to try to stabilize the error variance in Ornstein's least-squares regression by transforming the response, as described in the next section.

6.5.1   SPREAD-LEVEL PLOTS

Another diagnostic for nonconstant error variance uses an adaptation of the spread-level plots (Tukey, 1977; introduced in Section 3.4.5), graphing the log of the absolute Studentized residuals against the log of the fitted values. This approach also produces a suggested spread-stabilizing power transformation of y. The `spreadLevelPlot` function in the **car** package has a method for linear models:

```
> spreadLevelPlot(mod.ornstein)

Suggested power transformation:   0.554

Warning message:
In spreadLevelPlot.lm(mod.ornstein) :
    16 negative fitted values removed
```

The linear-regression model fit to Ornstein's data doesn't constrain the fitted values to be positive, even though the response variable `interlocks + 1` is positive. The `spreadLevelPlot` function removes negative fitted values, as indicated in the warning message, before computing logs. The spread-level plot, shown in Figure 6.16, has an obvious tilt to it. The suggested transformation, $\lambda = 0.55$, is not quite as strong as the normalizing transformation estimated by the Box-Cox method, $\widehat{\lambda} = 0.22$ (Section 6.4.1).

6.5.2   SCORE TESTS FOR NONCONSTANT ERROR VARIANCE

Breusch and Pagan (1979) and Cook and Weisberg (1983) suggest a score test for nonconstant error variance in a linear model. The idea is that either the variance is constant or it depends on the mean,

$$\text{Var}(\varepsilon_i) = \sigma^2 g[\text{E}(y|\mathbf{x})]$$

or on a linear combination of regressors $z_1, \ldots, z_p$,

$$\text{Var}(\varepsilon_i) = \sigma^2 g(\gamma_1 z_{i1} + \cdots + \gamma_p z_{ip})$$

In typical applications, the zs are the same as the regressors in the linear model (i.e., the xs), but other choices of zs are possible. For example, in an industrial experiment, variability might differ among the factories that produce a product, and a set of dummy regressors for factory would be candidates for the zs.

The `ncvTest` function in the **car** package implements this score test. We apply `ncvTest` to test for the dependence of spread on level (the default) in Ornstein's regression and for a more general dependence of spread on the predictors in the regression, given in a one-sided formula as the optional second argument to `ncvTest`:

```
> ncvTest(mod.ornstein)

Non-constant Variance Score Test
Variance formula: ~ fitted.values
Chisquare = 205.9    Df = 1      p = 1.070e-46

> ncvTest(mod.ornstein,~log(assets)+nation+sector, data=Ornstein)

Non-constant Variance Score Test
Variance formula: ~ log(assets) + nation + sector
Chisquare = 290.9    Df = 13     p = 1.953e-54
```

Both tests are highly statistically significant, and the difference between the two suggests that the relationship of spread to level does not entirely account for the pattern of nonconstant error variance in these data. It was necessary to supply the `data` argument in the second command because the `ncvTest` function does not assume that the predictors of the error variance are included in the linear-model object.

6.5.3   OTHER APPROACHES TO NONCONSTANT ERROR VARIANCE

We have suggested transformation as a strategy for stabilizing error variance, but other approaches are available. In particular, if the error variance is proportional to a variable z, then we can fit the model using WLS, with the weights given by $1/z$. In Ornstein's regression, for example, we might take the error variance to increase with the log(`assets`) of the firm, in which case the correct weights would be the inverses of these values:

```
> mod.ornstein.wts <- update(mod.ornstein, weights = 1/log(assets))
```

Still another approach is to rely on the unbiasedness of the least-squares regression coefficients, even when the error variance is misspecified, and then to use a sandwich estimate of the coefficient variances (see Section 4.3.6) to correct the standard errors of the estimated coefficients. These corrections may also be used in the `linearHypothesis`, `deltaMethod`, and `Anova` functions in the **car** package.

6.6 Diagnostics for Generalized Linear Models

Most of the diagnostics of the preceding sections extend straightforwardly to GLMs. These extensions typically take advantage of the computation of maximum-likelihood estimates for GLMs by IRLS (see Section 5.12), which in effect approximates the true log-likelihood by a WLS problem. At the convergence of the IWLS algorithm, diagnostics are formed as if the WLS problem were the problem of interest, and so the exact diagnostics for the WLS fit are approximate diagnostics for the original GLM. Seminal work on the extension of linear least-squares diagnostics to GLMs was done by Pregibon (1981), Landwehr et al. (1980), Wang (1985, 1987), and Williams (1987).

The following functions, some in standard R and some in the **car** package, have methods for GLMs: `rstudent`, `hatvalues`, `cooks.distance`, `dfbeta`, `dfbetas`, `outlierTest`, `avPlots`, `residualPlots`, `marginalModelPlots`, `crPlots`, and `ceresPlots`. We will illustrate the use of these functions selectively, rather than exhaustively repeating all the topics covered for linear models in the previous sections of the chapter.

6.6.1 RESIDUALS AND RESIDUAL PLOTS

One of the major philosophical, though not necessarily practical, differences between linear-model diagnostics and GLM diagnostics is in the definition of residuals. In linear models, the ordinary residual is the difference $\widehat{y} - y$, which is meant to mimic the statistical error $\varepsilon = E(y|\eta) - y$. Apart from Gaussian or normal linear models, there is no additive error in the definition of a GLM, and so the idea of a residual has a much less firm footing.

Residuals for GLMs are generally defined in analogy to linear models. Here are the various types of GLM residuals that are available in R:

- *Response residuals* are simply the differences between the observed response and its estimated expected value: $y_i - \widehat{\mu}_i$. These differences correspond to the ordinary residuals in the linear model. Apart from the Gaussian or normal case, the response residuals are not used in diagnostics, however, because they ignore the nonconstant variance that is part of a GLM.

- *Pearson residuals* are casewise components of the Pearson goodness-of-fit statistic for the model:

$$e_{Pi} = \frac{y_i - \widehat{\mu}_i}{\sqrt{\widehat{\mathrm{Var}(y_i|\mathbf{x})/\widehat{\phi}}}}$$

Formulas for Var($y|\mathbf{x}$) are given in the last column of Table 5.2 (p. 231). This definition of e_{Pi} corresponds exactly to the Pearson residuals defined in Equation 6.6 (p. 287) for WLS regression. These are a basic set of residuals for use with a GLM because of their direct analogy to linear models. For a model named m1, the command residuals(m1, type="pearson") returns the Pearson residuals.

- *Standardized Pearson residuals* correct for conditional response variation and for the leverage of the observations:

$$e_{PSi} = \frac{y_i - \widehat{\mu}_i}{\sqrt{\widehat{\mathrm{Var}(y_i|\mathbf{x})}(1 - h_i)}}$$

To compute the e_{PSi}, we need to define the hat-values h_i for GLMs. The h_i are taken from the final iteration of the IWLS procedure for fitting the model and have the usual interpretation, except that, unlike in a linear model, the hat-values in a GLM depend on y as well as on the configuration of the xs.

- *Deviance residuals*, e_{Di}, are the square roots of the casewise components of the residual deviance, attaching the sign of $y_i - \widehat{\mu}_i$. In the linear model, the deviance residuals reduce to the Pearson residuals. The deviance residuals are often the preferred form of residual for GLMs, and are returned by the command residuals(m1, type="deviance").

- *Standardized deviance residuals* are

$$e_{DSi} = \frac{e_{Di}}{\sqrt{\widehat{\phi}(1 - h_i)}}$$

- The ith Studentized residual in linear models is the scaled difference between the response and the fitted value computed without case i. Because of the special structure of the linear model, these differences can be computed without actually refitting the model by removing case i, but this is not the case for GLMs. While computing n regressions to get the Studentized residuals is not impossible, it is not a desirable option when the sample size is large. An approximation proposed by Williams (1987) is therefore used instead:

$$e_{Ti} = \mathrm{sign}(y_i - \widehat{\mu}_i)\sqrt{(1 - h_i)e_{DSi}^2 + h_i e_{PSi}^2}$$

The approximate Studentized residuals are computed when the function rstudent is applied to a GLM. A Bonferroni outlier test using the standard-normal distribution may be based on the largest absolute Studentized residual.

As an example, we return to the Canadian women's labor-force participation data, described in Section 5.7. We define a binary rather than a polytomous response, with categories working or not working outside the home, and fit a logistic-regression model to the data:

```
> mod.working <- glm(partic != "not.work" ~ hincome + children,
+        family=binomial, data=Womenlf)
> summary(mod.working)

Call:
glm(formula = partic != "not.work" ~ hincome + children,
    family = binomial, data = Womenlf)

Deviance Residuals:
   Min     1Q  Median      3Q     Max
-1.677  -0.865  -0.777   0.929   1.997

Coefficients:
                Estimate Std. Error z value Pr(>|z|)
(Intercept)       1.3358     0.3838    3.48   0.0005
hincome          -0.0423     0.0198   -2.14   0.0324
childrenpresent  -1.5756     0.2923   -5.39   7e-08

(Dispersion parameter for binomial family taken to be 1)

    Null deviance: 356.15  on 262  degrees of freedom
Residual deviance: 319.73  on 260  degrees of freedom
AIC: 325.7

Number of Fisher Scoring iterations: 4
```

The expression `partic != "not.work"` creates a logical vector, which serves as the binary-response variable in the model.

The `residualPlots` function provides the basic plots of residuals versus the predictors and versus the linear predictor:

```
> residualPlots(mod.working, layout=c(1, 3))

          Test stat Pr(>|t|)
hincome      1.226    0.268
children        NA       NA
```

We used the `layout` argument to reformat the graph to have one row and three columns. The function plots Pearson residuals versus each of the predictors in turn. Instead of plotting residuals against fitted values, however, `residualPlots` plots residuals against the estimated linear predictor, $\widehat{\eta}(\mathbf{x})$. Each panel in the graph by default includes a smooth fit rather than a quadratic fit; a lack-of-fit test is provided only for the numeric predictor `hincome` and not for the factor `children` or for the estimated linear predictor.

In binary regression, the plots of Pearson residuals or deviance residuals are strongly patterned—particularly the plot against the linear predictor, where the residuals can take on only two values, depending on whether the response is equal to 0 or 1. In the plot versus `hincome`, we have a little more variety in

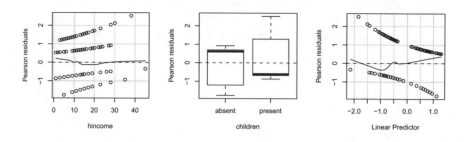

Figure 6.17 Residual plots for the binary logistic regression fit to the Canadian women's labor-force participation data.

the possible residuals: `children` can take on two values, and so the residuals can take on four values for each value of `hincome`. Even in this extreme case, however, a correct model requires that the conditional mean function in any residual plot be constant as we move across the plot. The fitted smooth helps us learn about the conditional mean function, and neither of the smooths shown is especially curved. The lack-of-fit test for `hincome` has a large significance level, confirming our view that this plot does not indicate lack of fit. The residuals for `children` are shown as a boxplot because `children` is a factor. The boxplots for `children` are difficult to interpret because of the discreteness in the distribution of the residuals.

6.6.2 INFLUENCE MEASURES

An approximation to Cook's distance for GLMs is

$$D_i = \frac{e_{PSi}^2}{k+1} \times \frac{h_i}{1 - h_i}$$

These values are returned by the `cooks.distance` function. Approximate values of dfbeta_{ij} and dfbetas_{ij} may be obtained directly from the final iteration of the IWLS procedure.

Figure 6.18 shows index plots of Cook's distances and hat-values, produced by the following command:

```
> influenceIndexPlot(mod.working, vars=c("Cook", "hat"), id.n=3)
```

Setting `vars=c("Cook", "hat")` limited the graphs to these two diagnostics. Cases 76 and 77 have the largest Cook distances, although even these are quite small. We remove both Cases 76 and 77 as a check:

```
> compareCoefs(mod.working, update(mod.working, subset=-c(76, 77)))

Call:
1:glm(formula = partic != "not.work" ~ hincome + children,
    family = binomial, data = Womenlf)
2:glm(formula = partic != "not.work" ~ hincome + children,
    family = binomial, data = Womenlf, subset = -c(76, 77))
```

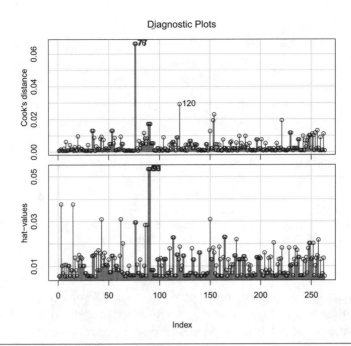

Figure 6.18   Index plots of diagnostic statistics for the logistic regression fit to the Canadian women's labor-force participation data.

```
                 Est. 1    SE 1   Est. 2    SE 2
(Intercept)      1.3358  0.3838   1.6090  0.4052
hincome         -0.0423  0.0198  -0.0603  0.0212
childrenpresent -1.5756  0.2923  -1.6476  0.2978
```

The reader can verify that removing just one of the two observations does not alter the results much, but removing *both* observations changes the coefficient of husband's income by more than 40%, about one standard error. Apparently, the two cases mask each other, and removing them both is required to produce a meaningful change in the coefficient for `hincome`. Cases 76 and 77 are women working outside the home even though both have children and high-income husbands.

6.6.3   GRAPHICAL METHODS: ADDED-VARIABLE AND COMPONENT-PLUS-RESIDUAL PLOTS

We are aware of two extensions of added-variable plots to GLMs. Suppose that the focal regressor is x_j. Wang (1985) proceeds by refitting the model with x_j removed, extracting the working residuals from this fit. Then x_j is regressed on the other xs by WLS, using the weights from the last IWLS step and obtaining residuals. Finally, the two sets of residuals are plotted against each other. The Arc regression software developed by Cook and Weisberg (1999) employs a similar procedure, except that weights are not used in the least-squares regression of x_j on the other xs. The `avPlots` function in

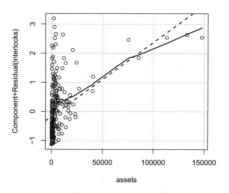

Figure 6.19   Component-plus-residual plot for `assets` in the Poisson regression fit to Ornstein's interlocking-directorate data.

the **car** package implements both approaches, with Wang's procedure as the default. Added-variable plots for binary-regression models can be uninformative because of the extreme discreteness of the response variable.

Component-plus-residual and CERES plots also extend straightforwardly to GLMs. Nonparametric smoothing of the resulting scatterplots can be important for interpretation, especially in models for binary responses, where the discreteness of the response makes the plots difficult to examine. Similar, if less striking, effects can occur for binomial and Poisson data.

For an illustrative component-plus-residual plot, we reconsider Ornstein's interlocking-directorate Poisson regression (from Section 5.5), but now we fit a model that uses `assets` as a predictor rather than the log of `assets`:

```
> mod.ornstein.pois <- glm(interlocks ~ assets + nation + sector,
+     family=poisson, data=Ornstein)
> crPlots(mod.ornstein.pois, "assets")
```

The component-plus-residual plot for `assets` is shown in Figure 6.19. This plot is difficult to interpret because of the extreme positive skew in `assets`, but it appears as if the `assets` slope is a good deal steeper at the left than at the right. The bulging rule, therefore, points toward transforming `assets` down the ladder of powers, and indeed the log-rule in Section 3.4.1 suggests replacing `assets` by its logarithm *before* fitting the regression in the first place (which, of course, is what we did originally):

```
> mod.ornstein.pois.2 <- update(mod.ornstein.pois,
+     . ~ log2(assets) + nation + sector)
> crPlots(mod.ornstein.pois.2, "log2(assets)")
```

The linearity of the follow-up component-plus-residual plot in Figure 6.20 confirms that the log-transform is a much better scale for `assets`.

The other diagnostics described in Section 6.4 for selecting a predictor transformation lead to the log-transform as well. For example, the Box-Tidwell

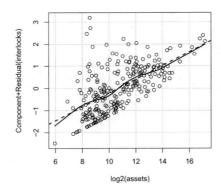

Figure 6.20 Component-plus-residual plot for the log of `assets` in the respecified Poisson regression for Ornstein's data.

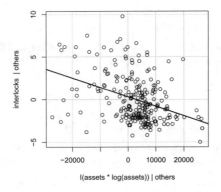

Figure 6.21 Constructed-variable plot for the power transformation of `assets` in Ornstein's interlocking-directorate Poisson regression.

constructed-variable plot for the power transformation of a predictor (introduced in Section 6.4.2) also extends directly to GLMs, augmenting the model with the constructed variable $x_j \log_e x_j$. We can use this method with Ornstein's Poisson regression:

```
> mod.ornstein.pois.cv <- update(mod.ornstein.pois,
+      . ~ . + I(assets*log(assets)))
> avPlots(mod.ornstein.pois.cv, "I(assets * log(assets))", id.n=0)
> summary(
+      mod.ornstein.pois.cv)$coef["I(assets * log(assets))", ,
+                          drop=FALSE]

                        Estimate Std. Error z value  Pr(>|z|)
I(assets * log(assets)) -2.177e-05  1.413e-06  -15.41 1.409e-53
```

Only the z test statistic for the constructed variable `I(assets * log(assets))` is of interest, and it leaves little doubt about the need for transforming `assets`. The constructed-variable plot in Figure 6.21 supports the transformation.

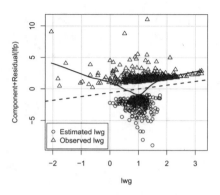

Figure 6.22 Component-plus-residual plot for `lwg` in the binary logistic regression for Mroz's women's labor force participation data.

An estimate of the transformation parameter can be obtained from the coefficient of `assets` in the *original* Poisson regression (2.09×10^{-5}) and the coefficient of the constructed variable (-2.18×10^{-5}):[17]

$$\widetilde{\lambda} = 1 + \frac{-2.18 \times 10^{-5}}{2.09 \times 10^{-5}} = -0.043$$

that is, essentially the log transformation, $\lambda = 0$.

We conclude with a reexamination of the binary logistic-regression model fit to Mroz's women's labor force participation data (introduced in Section 5.3). One of the predictors in this model—the log of the woman's expected wage rate (`lwg`)—has an odd definition: For women in the labor force, for whom the response `lfp = "yes"`, `lwg` is the log of the *actual* wage rate, while for women not in the labor force, for whom `lfp = "no"`, `lwg` is the log of the *predicted* wage rate from the regression of wages on the other predictors.

To obtain a component-plus-residual plot for `lwg` (Figure 6.22):

```
> mod.mroz <- glm(lfp ~ k5 + k618 + age + wc + hc + lwg + inc,
+       family=binomial, data=Mroz)
> crPlots(mod.mroz, "lwg", pch=as.numeric(Mroz$lfp))
> legend("bottomleft",c("Estimated lwg", "Observed lwg"),
+       pch=1:2, inset=0.01)
```

The peculiar split in the plot reflects the binary-response variable, with the lower cluster of points corresponding to `lfp = "no"` and the upper cluster to `lfp = "yes"`. It is apparent that `lwg` is much less variable when `lfp = "no"`, inducing an artifactually curvilinear relationship between `lwg` and `lfp`: We expect fitted values (such as the values of `lwg` when `lfp = "no"`) to be more homogeneous than observed values, because fitted values lack a residual component of variation.

We leave it to the reader to construct component-plus-residual or CERES plots for the other predictors in the model.

---

[17]Essentially the same calculation is the basis of Box and Tidwell's iterative procedure for finding transformations in linear least-squares regression (Section 6.4.2).

6.7   Collinearity and Variance Inflation Factors

When there are strong linear relationships among the predictors in a regression analysis, the precision of the estimated regression coefficients in linear models declines compared with what it would have been were the predictors uncorrelated with each other. Other important aspects of regression analysis beyond coefficients, such as prediction, are much less affected by collinearity (as discussed in Weisberg, 2005, sec. 10.1).

The estimated sampling variance of the jth regression coefficient may be written as

$$\widehat{\text{Var}}(b_j) = \frac{\widehat{\sigma}^2}{(n-1)s_j^2} \times \frac{1}{1 - R_j^2}$$

where $\widehat{\sigma}^2$ is the estimated error variance, s_j^2 is the sample variance of x_j, and $1/(1 - R_j^2)$, called the *variance inflation factor* (VIF$_j$) for b_j, is a function of the multiple correlation R_j from the regression of x_j on the other xs. The VIF is the simplest and most direct measure of the harm produced by collinearity: The square root of the VIF indicates how much the confidence interval for β_j is expanded relative to similar uncorrelated data, were it possible for such data to exist. If we wish to explicate the collinear relationships among the predictors, then we can examine the coefficients from the regression of each predictor with a large VIF on the other predictors.

The VIF is not applicable, however, to sets of related regressors for multiple-degree-of-freedom effects, such as polynomial regressors or contrasts constructed to represent a factor. Fox and Monette (1992) generalize the notion of variance inflation by considering the relative size of the joint confidence region for the coefficients associated with a related set of regressors. The resulting measure is called a *generalized variance inflation factor* (or GVIF).[18] If there are p regressors in a term, then GVIF$^{1/2p}$ is a one-dimensional expression of the decrease in the precision of estimation due to collinearity—analogous to taking the square root of the usual VIF. When $p = 1$, the GVIF reduces to the usual VIF.

The `vif` function in the **car** package calculates VIFs for the terms in a linear model. When each term has one degree of freedom, the usual VIF is returned, otherwise the GVIF is calculated.

As a first example, consider the data on the 1980 U.S. Census undercount in the data frame `Ericksen` (Ericksen et al., 1989):

---

[18]* Let $\mathbf{R}_{11}$ represent the correlation matrix among the regressors in the set in question; $\mathbf{R}_{22}$, the correlation matrix among the other regressors in the model; and $\mathbf{R}$, the correlation matrix among all the regressors in the model. Fox and Monette show that the squared area, volume, or hyper-volume of the joint confidence region for the coefficients in either set is expanded by the GVIF,

$$\text{GVIF} = \frac{\det \mathbf{R}_{11} \det \mathbf{R}_{22}}{\det \mathbf{R}}$$

relative to similar data in which the two sets of regressors are uncorrelated with each other. This measure is independent of the bases selected to span the subspaces of the two sets of regressors and so is independent, for example, of the contrast-coding scheme employed for a factor.

```
> head(Ericksen)
```

```
             minority crime poverty language highschool housing
Alabama          26.1    49    18.9      0.2       43.5     7.6
Alaska            5.7    62    10.7      1.7       17.5    23.6
Arizona          18.9    81    13.2      3.2       27.6     8.1
Arkansas         16.9    38    19.0      0.2       44.5     7.0
California.R     24.3    73    10.4      5.0       26.0    11.8
Colorado         15.2    73    10.1      1.2       21.4     9.2
             city conventional undercount
Alabama      state            0      -0.04
Alaska       state          100       3.35
Arizona      state           18       2.48
Arkansas     state            0      -0.74
California.R state            4       3.60
Colorado     state           19       1.34
```

These variables describe 66 areas of the United States, including 16 major cities, the 38 states without major cities, and the remainders of the 12 states that contain the 16 major cities. The following variables are included:

- minority: Percentage of residents who are black or Hispanic.
- crime: Number of serious crimes per 1,000 residents.
- poverty: Percentage of residents who are poor.
- language: Percentage having difficulty speaking or writing English.
- highschool: Percentage of those 25 years of age or older who have *not* finished high school.
- housing: Percentage of dwellings in small, multi-unit buildings.
- city: A factor with levels state and city.
- conventional: Percentage of households counted by personal enumeration (rather than by a mail-back questionnaire with follow-up).
- undercount: The estimated percent undercount (with negative values indicating an estimated *over*count).

We regress the Census undercount on the other variables:

```
> mod.census <- lm(undercount ~ ., data=Ericksen)
> summary(mod.census)

Call:
lm(formula = undercount ~ ., data = Ericksen)

Residuals:
    Min      1Q  Median      3Q     Max
-2.8356 -0.8033 -0.0553  0.7050  4.2467

Coefficients:
            Estimate Std. Error t value Pr(>|t|)
(Intercept) -0.61141    1.72084   -0.36  0.72368
minority     0.07983    0.02261    3.53  0.00083
crime        0.03012    0.01300    2.32  0.02412
poverty     -0.17837    0.08492   -2.10  0.04012
language     0.21512    0.09221    2.33  0.02320
highschool   0.06129    0.04477    1.37  0.17642
```

```
housing       -0.03496    0.02463   -1.42  0.16126
citystate     -1.15998    0.77064   -1.51  0.13779
conventional   0.03699    0.00925    4.00  0.00019

Residual standard error: 1.43 on 57 degrees of freedom
Multiple R-squared: 0.708,        Adjusted R-squared: 0.667
F-statistic: 17.2 on 8 and 57 DF,  p-value: 1.04e-12
```

We included the data argument to lm, so we may use a period (.) on the right-hand side of the model formula to represent all the variables in the data frame with the exception of the response—here, undercount.

Checking for collinearity, we see that three coefficients—for minority, poverty, and highschool—have VIFs exceeding 4, indicating that confidence intervals for these coefficients are more than twice as wide as they would be for uncorrelated predictors:

```
> vif(mod.census)

    minority        crime      poverty     language    highschool
       5.009        3.344        4.625        1.636         4.619
     housing         city conventional
       1.872        3.538        1.691
```

To illustrate the computation of GVIFs, we return to Ornstein's interlocking-directorate regression, where it turns out that collinearity is relatively slight:

```
> vif(mod.ornstein)

            GVIF Df GVIF^(1/(2*Df))
log(assets) 1.909  1          1.382
nation      1.443  3          1.063
sector      2.597  9          1.054
```

The vif function can also be applied to GLMs, such as the Poisson-regression model fit to Ornstein's data:[19]

```
> vif(mod.ornstein.pois.2)

             GVIF Df GVIF^(1/(2*Df))
log2(assets) 2.617  1          1.618
nation       1.620  3          1.084
sector       3.718  9          1.076
```

Other, more complex, approaches to collinearity include principal-components analysis of the predictors or standardized predictors and singular-value decomposition of the model matrix or the mean-centered model matrix. These, too, are simple to implement in R: See the princomp, prcomp, svd, and eigen functions (the last two of which are discussed in Section 8.2).

---

[19]Thanks to a contribution from Henric Nilsson.

6.8   Complementary Reading and References

- Residuals and residual plotting for linear models are discussed in Weisberg (2005, sec. 8.1–8.2). Marginal model plots, introduced in Section 6.2.2, are described in Weisberg (2005, sec. 8.4). Added-variable plots are discussed in Weisberg (2005, sec. 3.1). Outliers and influence are taken up in Weisberg (2005, chap. 9).
- Diagnostics for unusual and influential data are described in Fox (2008, chap. 11); for nonnormality, nonconstant error variance, and nonlinearity in Fox (2008, chap. 12); and for collinearity in Fox (2008, chap. 13). A general treatment of residuals in models without additive errors, which expands on the discussion in Section 6.6.1, is given by Cox and Snell (1968). Diagnostics for GLMs are taken up in Fox (2008, sec. 15.4).
- For further information on various aspects of regression diagnostics, see Cook and Weisberg (1982, 1994, 1997, 1999), Fox (1991), Cook (1998), and Atkinson (1985).

Drawing Graphs 7

One of the strengths of R is its ability to produce high-quality statistical graphs. R's strength in graphics reflects the origin of S at Bell Labs, long a center for innovation in statistical graphics.

We find it helpful to make a distinction between *analytical graphics* and *presentation graphics* (see, e.g., Weisberg, 2004). Much of this *Companion* has described various analytical graphs, which are plots designed for discovery, to help the analyst better understand data. These graphs should be easy to draw and interpret, and they quite likely will be discarded when the analyst moves on to the next graph. The **car** package includes a number of functions for this very purpose, such as scatterplot, scatterplot-Matrix, residualPlots, and avPlots (see, in particular, Chapters 3 and 6). A desirable feature of analytical graphs is the ability of the analyst to interact with them, by identifying points, removing points to see how a model fit to the data changes, and so on. Standard R graphs allow only limited interaction, for example, via the identify function, a limitation that we view as a deficiency in the current R system (but see the discussion of other graphics packages for R in Section 7.3).

Presentation graphs have a different goal and are more likely to be published in reports, in journals, online, and in books, and then examined by others. While in some instances presentation graphs are nothing more than well-selected analytical graphs, they can be much more elaborate, with more attention paid to color, line types, legends, and the like, where representing the data with clarity and simplicity is the overall goal. Although the default graphs produced by R are often aesthetic and useful, they may not meet the requirements of a publisher. R has a great deal of flexibility for creating presentation graphs, and that is the principal topic of this chapter.

Standard R graphics are based on a simple metaphor: Creating a standard R graph is like drawing with a pen, in ink, on a sheet of paper. We typically create a simple graph with a function such as plot, and build more elaborate graphs by adding to the simple graph, using functions such as lines, points, and legend. Apart from resizing the graphics window in the usual manner by dragging a side or corner with the mouse, once we put something in the graph we can't remove it—although we can draw over it. In most cases, if we want to change a graph, we must redraw it. This metaphor works well for creating presentation graphs, because the user can exert control over every step of the drawing process; it works less well when ease of use is paramount, as in data-analytic graphics.

There are many other useful and sophisticated kinds of graphs that are readily available in R. Frequently, there is a `plot` method to produce a standard graph or set of graphs for objects of a given class—try the `plot` command with a data frame or a linear-model object as the argument, for example. In some cases `plot` will produce useful analytical graphs (e.g., when applied to a linear model), and in others it will produce presentation graphs (e.g., when applied to a *regression tree* computed with the **rpart** package).

Because R is an open system, it is no surprise that other metaphors for statistical graphics have also been created, the most important of which is the **lattice** package, and we will briefly introduce some of these in Section 7.3.

This chapter, and the following chapter on programming, deal with general matters, and we have employed many of the techniques described here in the earlier parts of this *Companion*. Rather than introducing this material near the beginning of the book, however, we preferred to regard the previous examples of R graphs as background and motivation.

7.1   A General Approach to R Graphics

For the most part, the discussion in this chapter is confined to two-dimensional coordinate plots, and a logical first step in drawing such a graph is to define a coordinate system. Sometimes that first step will include drawing axes and axis labels on the graph, along with a rectangular frame enclosing the plotting region and possibly other elements such as points and lines; sometimes, however, these elements will be omitted or added in separate steps to assert greater control over what is plotted. The guts of the graph generally consist of plotted points, lines, text, and, occasionally, shapes and arrows. Such elements are added as required to the plot. The current section describes, in a general way, how to perform these tasks.

7.1.1   DEFINING A COORDINATE SYSTEM: `plot`

The `plot` function is generic:[1] There are really many `plot` functions, and the function that is actually used depends on the arguments that are passed to `plot`. If the first argument is a numeric vector—for example, as in the command `plot(x, y)`—then the default method function `plot.default` is invoked. If the first argument is a linear-model object (i.e., an object of class `"lm"`), then the method `plot.lm` is used rather than the default method.

---

[1] See Sections 1.4 and 8.7 for an explanation of how generic functions and their methods work in R.

If the first argument is a formula—for example, `plot(y ~ x)`—then the method `plot.formula` is used. This last method simply calls `plot.-default` with arguments decoded to correspond to the arguments for the default method.

The default `plot` method can be employed to make a variety of point and line graphs; `plot` can also be used to define a coordinate space, which is our main reason for discussing it here. The list of arguments to `plot.default` is a point of departure for understanding how to use the traditional R graphics system:

```
> args(plot.default)
function (x, y = NULL, type = "p", xlim = NULL, ylim = NULL,
    log = "", main = NULL, sub = NULL, xlab = NULL, ylab = NULL,
    ann = par("ann"), axes = TRUE, frame.plot = axes,
    panel.first = NULL, panel.last = NULL, asp = NA, ...)
NULL
```

To see in full detail what the arguments mean, consult the documentation for `plot.default`;[2] the following points are of immediate interest, however:

- The first two arguments, `x` and `y`, can provide the horizontal and vertical coordinates of the points or lines to be plotted, respectively, and also define a data-coordinate system for the graph. The argument `x` is required. In constructing a complex graph, a good initial step is often to use `x` and `y` to establish the ranges for the axes. If we want horizontal coordinates to range from `xmin` to `xmax` and vertical coordinates to range from `ymin` to `ymax`, then the initial command

  ```
  > plot(c(xmin, xmax), c(ymin, ymax),
  +     type="n", xlab="", ylab="")
  ```

  is sufficient to set up the coordinate space for the plot, as we will explain in more detail shortly.
- The argument `type`, naturally enough, determines the type of graph to be drawn, of which there are several: The default type, `"p"`, plots points at the coordinates specified by `x` and `y`. The character used to draw the points is given by the argument `pch`, which can designate a vector of characters of the same length as `x` and `y`, which may therefore differ for different points. Specifying `type="l"` (the letter "el") produces a line graph, and specifying `type="n"`, as in the command above, sets up the plotting region to accommodate the data but plots nothing. Other types of graphs include `"b"`, both points and lines; `"o"`, points and lines overlaid; `"h"`, histogram-like vertical lines; and `"s"` and `"S"`, stairstep-like lines, starting horizontally and vertically, respectively.

---

[2]In general, in this chapter we will not discuss all the arguments of the graphics functions that we describe. Details are available in the documentation for the various graphics functions. With a little patience and trial and error, we believe that most readers of this book will be able to master the subtleties of R documentation.

- The arguments $xlim$ and $ylim$ may be used to define the limits of the horizontal and vertical axes; these arguments are usually unnecessary because R will pick reasonable limits from x and y, but they provide an additional measure of control over the graph. For example, extending the limits of an axis can provide room for explanatory text, and contracting the limits can cause some data to be omitted from the graph. If we are drawing several graphs, we may want all of them to have the same range for one or both axes, and this can also be accomplished with the arguments $xlim$ and $ylim$.
- The log argument makes it easy to define logarithmic axes: $log="x"$ produces a logged horizontal axis; $log="y"$, a logged vertical axis; and $log="xy"$ (or $log="yx"$), logged axes for both variables. Base-10 logarithms are used, and the conversion from data values to their logs is automatic.
- $xlab$ and $ylab$ take character string or expression arguments, which are used to label the axes;[3] similarly, the argument $main$ may be used to place a title above the plot, or the $title$ function may be called subsequently to add main or axis titles. The default axis label, NULL, is potentially misleading, in that by default $plot$ constructs labels from the arguments x and y. To suppress the axis labels, either specify empty labels—e.g., $xlab=" "$—or set $ann=FALSE$.
- Setting $axes=FALSE$ and $frame.plot=FALSE$ suppresses the drawing of axes and a box, respectively, around the plotting region. A frame can subsequently be added by the box function, and axes can be added using the $axis$ function.
- The argument col may be used to specify the color (or colors) for the points and lines drawn on the plot. (Color specification in R is described in Section 7.1.4.)
- cex (for character expansion) specifies the relative size of the points in the graph; the default size is $cex=1$; cex may be a vector, indicating the size of each point individually.
- The arguments lty and lwd select the type and width of lines drawn on the graph. (See Section 7.1.3 for more information on drawing lines.)

For example, the following command sets up the blank plot in Figure 7.1, with axes and a frame but without axis labels:

```
> plot(c(0, 1), c(0, 1), type="n", xlab="", ylab="")
```

7.1.2   GRAPHICS PARAMETERS: par

Many of the arguments to $plot$, such as pch and col, get defaults from the par function if they are not set directly in the call to $plot$. The par

---

[3]An expression can be used to produce mathematical notation in labels, such as superscripts, subscripts, and Greek letters. The ability of R to typeset mathematics in graphs is both useful and unusual. For details, see ?plotmath and Murrell and Ihaka (2000); also see Figures 7.11 (p. 342) and 7.13 (p. 345) for examples.

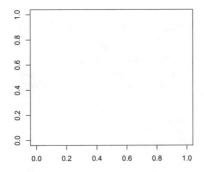

Figure 7.1 Empty plot, produced by `plot(c(0, 1), c(0, 1), type="n", xlab="", ylab="")`

function is used to set and retrieve a variety of graphics parameters and thus is similar to the `options` function, which sets global defaults for R—for instance,

```
> par("col")
```

```
[1] "black"
```

Consequently, unless their color is changed explicitly, all points and lines in a standard R graph will be drawn in black. To change the general default plotting color to red, for example, we could enter the command `par(col="red")`.

To print the current values of all the plotting parameters, call `par` with no arguments. Here is a listing of all the graphics parameters:

```
> names(par())
```

```
 [1] "xlog"      "ylog"      "adj"       "ann"       "ask"
 [6] "bg"        "bty"       "cex"       "cex.axis"  "cex.lab"
[11] "cex.main"  "cex.sub"   "cin"       "col"       "col.axis"
[16] "col.lab"   "col.main"  "col.sub"   "cra"       "crt"
[21] "csi"       "cxy"       "din"       "err"       "family"
[26] "fg"        "fig"       "fin"       "font"      "font.axis"
[31] "font.lab"  "font.main" "font.sub"  "lab"       "las"
[36] "lend"      "lheight"   "ljoin"     "lmitre"    "lty"
[41] "lwd"       "mai"       "mar"       "mex"       "mfcol"
[46] "mfg"       "mfrow"     "mgp"       "mkh"       "new"
[51] "oma"       "omd"       "omi"       "pch"       "pin"
[56] "plt"       "ps"        "pty"       "smo"       "srt"
[61] "tck"       "tcl"       "usr"       "xaxp"      "xaxs"
[66] "xaxt"      "xpd"       "yaxp"      "yaxs"      "yaxt"
```

Table 7.1 presents brief descriptions of some of the plotting parameters that can be set by `par`; many of these can also be used as arguments to `plot` and other graphics functions, but some, in particular the parameters that concern the layout of the plot window (e.g., `mfrow`), can only be set using `par`, and others (e.g., `usr`) only return information and cannot be set by the user. For complete details on the plotting parameters available in R, see `?par`.

Table 7.1   Some plotting parameters set by par. Parameters marked with a
* concern the layout of the graphics window and can only be set using par,
not as arguments to higher-level graphics functions such as plot; parameters marked with a + return information only.

Parameter	Default Value	Purpose
adj	0.5	text-string justification: 0 = left, 0.5 = centered, 1 = right
ann	TRUE	annotate graph
cex	1	relative character expansion
col	"black"	default color
las	0	orientation of axis labels: 0 = parallel to axis, 1 = horizontal
lty	"solid"	default line type
lwd	1	default line width
mar*	c(5.1,4.1,4.1,2.1)	plot margins in lines of text: bottom, left, top, right
mfcol*, mfrow*	c(1,1)	plot array, filled by columns or rows: number of rows, columns
new	FALSE	if FALSE, next high-level plotting function clears plot
pch	1	plotting symbol: number or character
pin+	current values	size of plot in inches: width, height
pty	"m"	type of plotting region: "m" maximal; "s" square
srt	0	rotation of character strings, in degrees
usr+	current values	user coordinates, range of data: x-min, x-max, y-min, y-max

It is sometimes helpful to be able to change plotting parameters in par
temporarily for a particular graph or set of graphs and then to change them
back to their previous values after the plot is drawn. For example,

```
> oldpar <- par(lwd=2)
> plot(x, y, type="l")
> par(oldpar)
```

draws lines at twice their normal thickness. The original setting of
par("lwd") is saved in the variable oldpar, and after the plot is drawn,
lwd is reset to its original value. Alternatively, and usually more simply, closing the current graphics device window returns the graphical parameters to
their default values.

7.1.3   ADDING GRAPHICAL ELEMENTS: axis, points, lines, text, **ETCETERA**

Having defined a coordinate system, we will typically want to add graphical
elements, such as points and lines, to the plot. Several functions useful for this
purpose are described in this section.

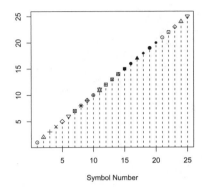

Figure 7.2 Plotting symbols (plotting characters, pch) by number.

points AND lines

As you might expect, `points` and `lines` add points and lines to the current plot; either function can be used to plot points, lines, or both, but their default behavior is implied by their names. The argument pch is used to select the plotting character (symbol), as the following example (which produces Figure 7.2) illustrates:

```
> plot(1:25, pch=1:25, xlab="Symbol Number", ylab="")
> lines(1:25, type="h", lty="dashed")
```

The `plot` command graphs the symbols numbered 1 through 25; because the y argument to `plot` isn't given, an *index plot* is produced, with the values of x on the *vertical* axis plotted against their indices—in this case, also the numbers from 1 through 25. Finally, the `lines` function draws broken vertical lines (selected by `lty="dashed"`; see Figure 7.2) up to the symbols; because `lines` is given only one vector of coordinates, these too are interpreted as vertical coordinates, to be plotted against their indices as horizontal coordinates. Specifying `type="h"` draws spikes (or histogram-like lines) up to the points.

One can also plot arbitrary characters, as the following example (shown in Figure 7.3) illustrates:

```
> head(letters) # first 6 lowercase letters

[1] "a" "b" "c" "d" "e" "f"

> plot(1:26, xlab="letters", ylab="", pch=letters,
+     axes=FALSE, frame.plot=TRUE)
```

Once again, `ylab=""` suppresses the vertical axis label, `axes=FALSE` suppresses tick marks and axes, and `frame.plot=TRUE` adds a box around the plotting region, which is equivalent to entering the separate command `box()` after the `plot` command.

letters

Figure 7.3   Plotting characters—the lowercase letters.

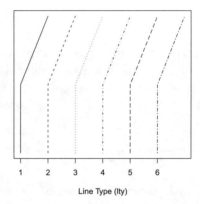

Line Type (lty)

Figure 7.4   Line types (`lty`), by number.

As shown in Figure 7.4, several different line types are available in R plots:

```
> plot(c(1, 7), c(0, 1), type="n", axes=FALSE,
+     xlab="Line Type (lty)", ylab="", frame.plot=TRUE)
> axis(1, at=1:6)  # x-axis
> for (lty in 1:6)
+     lines(c(lty, lty, lty + 1), c(0, 0.5, 1), lty=lty)
```

The `lines` function connects the points whose coordinates are given by its first two arguments, `x` and `y`. If a coordinate is `NA`, then the line drawn will be discontinuous. Line type (`lty`) may be specified by number (as here) or by name, such as `"solid"`, `"dashed"`, and so on. Line width is similarly given by the `lwd` parameter, which defaults to `1`. The exact effect varies according to the graphics device used to display the plot, but the general unit seems to be pixels: Thus, for example, `lwd=2` specifies a line 2 pixels wide. We used a `for` loop (see Section 8.3.2) to generate the six lines shown in Figure 7.4.

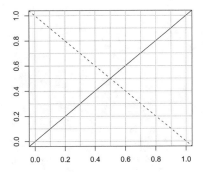

Figure 7.5   Lines created by the `abline` function.

abline

The `abline` function can be used to add straight lines to a graph.[4] We describe several of its capabilities here; for details and other options, see `?abline`.

- Called with a simple-regression-model object as its argument—for example, `abline(lm(y ~ x))`—`abline` draws the regression line. If there's a single coefficient in the model, as in `abline(lm(y ~ x - 1))`, `abline` draws the regression line through the origin.
- Called with two numbers as arguments, as in `abline(a, b)`, or with a two-element numeric vector as its argument, as in `abline(c(a, b))`, `abline` draws a line with intercept a and slope b.
- Called with the argument h or v, each of which can be set to a single number or a numeric vector, `abline` draws horizontal or vertical lines at the specified y or x values.

Figure 7.5, created by the following commands, illustrates the use of `abline`:

```
> plot(c(0, 1), c(0, 1), type="n", xlab="", ylab="")
> abline(0, 1)
> abline(c(1, -1), lty="dashed")
> abline(h=seq(0, 1, by=0.1), v=seq(0, 1, by=0.1), col="gray")
```

axis AND grid

In the `plot` command (on p. 336) for drawing Figure 7.4, the argument `axes=FALSE` suppressed both the horizontal and the vertical axis tick marks and tick labels. We used the `axis` function to draw a customized horizontal (bottom) axis but let the plot stand with no vertical (left) axis labels. The first argument to `axis` indicates the position of the axis: 1 corresponds to

---

[4]When logarithmic axes are used, `abline` can also draw the curved image of a straight line on the original scale.

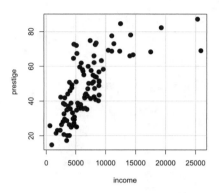

Figure 7.6   Grid of horizontal and vertical lines created by the `grid` function.

the bottom of the graph; 2, to the left side; 3, to the top; and 4, to the right side. The `at` argument controls the location of tick marks. There are several other arguments as well. Of particular note is the `labels` argument: If `labels=TRUE`, then numerical labels are used for the tick marks; otherwise, `labels` takes a vector of character strings (e.g., `c("male", "female")`) to provide tick labels.

The `grid` function can be used to add a grid of horizontal and vertical lines, typically at the default axis tick mark positions (see `?grid` for details); for example:

```
> library(car)  # for data
> plot(prestige ~ income, type="n", data=Prestige)
> grid(lty="solid")
> with(Prestige, points(income, prestige, pch=16, cex=1.5))
```

The resulting graph is shown in Figure 7.6. In the call to `grid`, we specified `lty="solid"` in preference to the default dotted lines. We were careful to plot the points *after* the grid, suppressing the points in the initial call to `plot`. We invite the reader to see what happens if the points are plotted *before* the grid.

text AND locator

The `text` function places character strings—as opposed to individual characters—on a plot; the function has several arguments that determine the position, size, and font that are used. For example, the following commands produce Figure 7.7a:

```
> plot(c(0, 1), c(0, 1), axes=FALSE, type="n", xlab="", ylab="",
+       frame.plot=TRUE, main="(a)")
> text(x=c(0.2, 0.5), y=c(0.2, 0.7),
+      c("example text", "another string"))
```

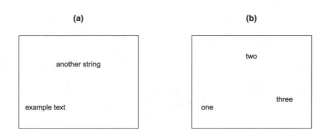

Figure 7.7 Plotting character strings with `text`.

We sometimes find it helpful to use the `locator` function along with `text` to position text with the mouse; `locator` returns a list with vectors of *x* and *y* coordinates corresponding to the position of the mouse cursor when the left button is clicked. Figure 7.7b was constructed as follows:

```
> plot(c(0, 1), c(0, 1), axes=FALSE, type="n", xlab="", ylab="",
+     frame.plot=TRUE, main="(b)")
> text(locator(), c("one", "two", "three"))
```

To position each of the three text strings, we moved the mouse cursor to a point in the plot and clicked the left button. Called with no arguments, `locator()` returns pairs of coordinates corresponding to left clicks until the right mouse button is pressed and *Stop* is selected from the resulting pop-up context menu (under Windows) or the esc key is pressed (under Mac OS X). Alternatively, we can indicate in advance the number of points to be returned as an argument to `locator`—`locator(3)` in the current example—in which case, control returns to the R command prompt after the specified number of left clicks.

Another useful argument to `text`, not used in these examples, is `adj`, which controls the horizontal justification of text: 0 specifies left justification; 0.5, centering (the initial default, given by `par`); and 1, right justification. If two values are given, `adj=c(x, y)`, then the second value controls vertical justification.

Sometimes we want to add text outside the plotting area. The function `mtext` can be used for this purpose; `mtext` is similar to `text`, except that it writes in the margins of the plot. Alternatively, specifying the argument `xpd=TRUE` to `text` or setting the global graphics option `par(xpd=TRUE)` also allows us to write outside the normal plotting region.

arrows AND segments

As their names suggest, the `arrows` and `segments` functions may be used to add arrows and line segments to a plot. For example, the following commands produced Figures 7.8a and b:

```
> plot(c(1, 5), c(0, 1), axes=FALSE, type="n",
+     xlab="", ylab="", main="(a) arrows")
> arrows(x0=1:5, y0=rep(0.1, 5),
```

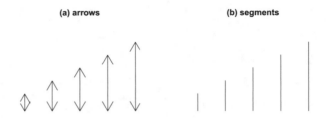

Figure 7.8   The arrows and segments functions.

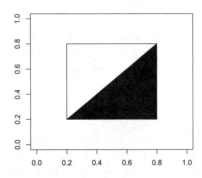

Figure 7.9   Filled and unfilled triangles produced by polygon.

```
+       x1=1:5, y1=seq(0.3, 0.9, len=5), code=3)
> plot(c(1, 5), c(0, 1), axes=FALSE, type="n",
+       xlab="", ylab="", main="(b) segments")
> segments(x0=1:5, y0=rep(0.1, 5),
+       x1=1:5, y1=seq(0.3, 0.9, len=5))
```

The argument code=3 to arrows produces double-headed arrows.

The arrows drawn by the arrows function are rather crude, and other packages provide more visually pleasing alternatives; see, for example, the p.arrows function in the **sfsmisc** package.

polygon

Another self-descriptive function is polygon, which takes as its first two arguments vectors defining the *x* and *y* coordinates of the vertices of a polygon; for example, to draw Figure 7.9:

```
> plot(c(0, 1), c(0, 1), type="n", xlab="", ylab="")
> polygon(c(0.2, 0.8, 0.8), c(0.2, 0.2, 0.8), col="black")
> polygon(c(0.2, 0.2, 0.8), c(0.2, 0.8, 0.8))
```

The col argument, if specified, gives the color to be used in filling the polygon (see the discussion of colors in Section 7.1.4).

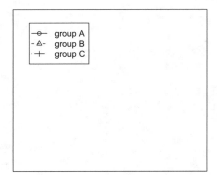

Figure 7.10   Using the `legend` function.

legend

The `legend` function may be used to add a legend to a graph; an illustration is provided in Figure 7.10:

```
> plot(c(1, 5), c(0, 1), axes=FALSE, type="n",
+     xlab="", ylab="", frame.plot=TRUE)
> legend(locator(1), legend=c("group A", "group B", "group C"),
+     lty=c(1, 2, 4), pch=1:3)
```

We used `locator` to position the legend. We find that this is often easier than computing where the legend should be placed. Alternatively, we can place the legend by specifying its location to be one of `"topleft"`, `"topcenter"`, `"topright"`, `"bottomleft"`, `"bottomcenter"`, or `"bottomright"`. If we use one of the corners, the argument `inset=0.02` will inset the legend by 2% of the size of the plot.

curve

The `curve` function can be used to graph an R function or expression, given as `curve`'s first argument, or to add a curve representing a function or expression to an existing graph. The second and third arguments of `curve`, `from` and `to`, define the domain over which the function is to be evaluated; the argument n, which defaults to `101`, sets the number of points at which the function is to be evaluated; and the argument `add`, which defaults to `FALSE`, determines whether `curve` produces a new plot or adds a curve to an existing plot.

If the first argument to `curve` is a function, then it should be a function of one argument; if it is an expression, then the expression should be a function (in the mathematical sense) of a variable named x. For example, the left-hand panel of Figure 7.11 is produced by the following command, in which the built-in variable `pi` is the mathematical constant π:

```
> curve(x*cos(25/x), 0.01, pi, n=1000)
```

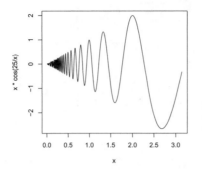
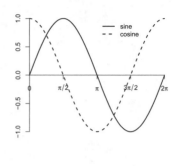

Figure 7.11   Graphs produced by the `curve` function.

The next command, in which the expression is a function of a variable named y rather than x, produces an error:

```
> curve(y*cos(25/y), 0.01, pi, n=1000)
```

```
Error in curve(y * cos(25/y), 0.01, pi, n = 1000) :
  'expr' must be a function or an expression containing 'x'
```

The graph in the right-hand panel of Figure 7.11 results from the following commands:

```
> curve(sin, 0, 2*pi, ann=FALSE, axes=FALSE, lwd=2)
> axis(1, pos=0, at=c(0, pi/2, pi, 3*pi/2, 2*pi),
+     labels=c(0, expression(pi/2), expression(pi),
+          expression(3*pi/2), expression(2*pi)))
> axis(2, pos=0)
> curve(cos, add=TRUE, lty="dashed", lwd=2)
> legend(pi, 1, lty=1:2, lwd=2, legend=c("sine", "cosine"), bty="n")
```

The `pos` argument to the `axis` function, set to 0 for both the horizontal and the vertical axes, places the axes at the origin. The argument `bty="n"` to `legend` suppresses the box that is normally drawn around a legend.

7.1.4   SPECIFYING COLORS

Using different colors can be an effective means of distinguishing graphical elements such as lines or points. Although we are limited to monochrome graphs in this book and in most print publications, the specification of colors in R graphs is nevertheless straightforward to describe. If you are producing graphics for others, keep in mind that some people have trouble distinguishing various colors, particularly red and green. Colors should be used for clarity rather than to provide "eye candy."

Plotting functions such as `lines` and `points` specify color via a `col` argument; this argument is vectorized, allowing us to select a separate color for each point. R provides three principal ways of specifying a color. The most basic, although rarely directly used, is by setting *RGB* (*Red, Green, Blue*) values. For example, the `rainbow` function creates a spectrum of RGB colors, in this case of 10 colors:

```
> rainbow(10)

 [1] "#FF0000FF" "#FF9900FF" "#CCFF00FF" "#33FF00FF" "#00FF66FF"
 [6] "#00FFFFFF" "#0066FFFF" "#3300FFFF" "#CC00FFFF" "#FF0099FF"
```

Similarly, the `gray` function creates gray levels from black [`gray(0)`] to white [`gray(1)`]:

```
> gray(0:9/9)

 [1] "#000000" "#1C1C1C" "#393939" "#555555" "#717171" "#8E8E8E"
 [7] "#AAAAAA" "#C6C6C6" "#E3E3E3" "#FFFFFF"
```

The color codes are represented as hexadecimal (base 16) numbers, of the form `"#RRGGBB"` or `"#RRGGBBTT"`, where each pair of hex digits *RR*, *GG*, and *BB* encodes the intensity of one of the three additive primary colors— from `00` (i.e., 0 in decimal) to `FF` (i.e., 255 in decimal).[5] The hex digits *TT*, if present, represent *transparency*, varying from `00`, completely transparent, to `FF`, completely opaque; if the `TT` digits are absent, then the value `FF` is implied. Ignoring transparency, there are over 16 million possible colors.

Specifying colors by name is more convenient, and the names that R recognizes are returned by the `colors` function:

```
> colors()[1:10]

 [1] "white"         "aliceblue"      "antiquewhite"
 [4] "antiquewhite1" "antiquewhite2"  "antiquewhite3"
 [7] "antiquewhite4" "aquamarine"     "aquamarine1"
[10] "aquamarine2"
```

We have shown only the first 10 of over 600 prespecified color names available. The full set of color definitions appears in the editable file rgb.txt, which resides in the R etc subdirectory.

The third and simplest way of specifying a color is by number. What the numbers mean depends on the value returned by the `palette` function:[6]

```
> palette()

[1] "black"   "red"    "green3"  "blue"   "cyan"   "magenta" "yellow"
[8] "gray"
```

Thus, `col=c(4, 2, 1)` would first use `"blue"`, then `"red"`, and finally `"black"`. We can enter the following command to see the default palette (the result of which is not shown because we are restricted to using monochrome graphs):

---

[5] Just as decimal digits run from 0 through 9, hexadecimal digits run from 0 through 9, A, B, C, D, E, F, representing the decimal numbers 0 through 15. The first hex digit in each pair is the 16s place and the second is the ones place of the number. Thus, e.g., the hex number `#39` corresponds to the decimal number $3 \times 16 + 9 \times 1 = 57$.

[6] At one time, the eighth color in the standard R palette was `"white"`. Why was that a bad idea?

```
> pie(rep(1, 8), col=1:8)
```

R permits us to change the value returned by `palette` and, thus, to change the meaning of the color numbers. For example, we used

```
> palette(rep("black", 8))
```

to write this *Companion*, so that all plots are rendered in black and white.[7] If you prefer the colors produced by `rainbow`, you could set

```
> palette(rainbow(10))
```

In this last example, we changed both the palette colors and the number of colors. The choice

```
> library(colorspace)
> palette(rainbow_hcl(10))
```

uses a palette suggested by Zeileis et al. (2009) and implemented in the **colorspace** package.

Changing the palette is session-specific and is forgotten when we exit from R. If you want a custom palette to be used at the beginning of each R session, you can add a `palette` command to your R profile (as described in the Preface).

To get a sense of how all this works, try each of the following commands:

```
> pie(rep(1, 100), col=rainbow(100), labels=rep("", 100))
> pie(rep(1, 100), col=rainbow_hcl(100), labels=rep("", 100))
> pie(rep(1, 100), col=gray(0:100/100), labels=rep("", 100))
```

The graph produced by the last command appears in Figure 7.12.

7.2   Putting It Together: Explaining Nearest-Neighbor Kernel Regression

Most of the analytic and presentation graphs that you will want to create are easily produced in R. The principal aim of this chapter is to show you how to construct the small proportion of graphs that require custom work. Such graphs are diverse by definition, and it would be futile to try to cover their construction exhaustively. Instead, we will develop an example that uses many of the functions introduced in the preceding section.

We describe step by step how to construct the diagram in Figure 7.13, which is designed to provide a graphical explanation of *nearest-neighbor kernel regression*, a method of nonparametric regression. Nearest-neighbor

---

[7]More correctly, all plots that refer to colors by number are black and white. We could still get other colors by referring to them by name or by their RGB values. Moreover, some graphics functions select colors independently of the color palette.

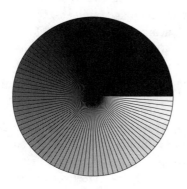

Figure 7.12 The 101 colors produced by `gray(0:100/100)`, starting with `gray(0)` (black) and ending with `gray(1)` (white).

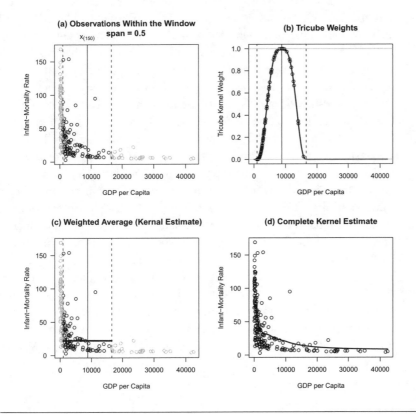

Figure 7.13 A four-panel diagram explaining nearest-neighbor kernel regression.

kernel regression is very similar to *lowess*, which is used by the `scatterplot` function in the **car** package to smooth scatterplots (see Section 3.2.1).

Whereas `lowess` uses locally linear (robust) weighted regression, kernel regression uses locally weighted averaging.

The end product of nearest-neighbor kernel regression is the estimated regression function shown in Figure 7.13d. In this graph, x is the GDP per capita and y the infant mortality rate of each of 190 nations of the world, from the UN data set in the **car** package.[8] The estimated regression function is obtained as follows:

- Select the *grid* of points at which to estimate the regression function, either by selecting a number (say 100) of equally spaced values that cover the range of x or by using the observed values of x. We follow the latter course and let x_0 be a value from among $x_1, x_2, \ldots, x_n$, at which we will compute the corresponding fitted value $\widehat{y}_0$. The fitted regression simply joins the points $(x_i, \widehat{y}_i)$, after arranging the x values in ascending order.

- Given x_0, the estimate $\widehat{y}_0$ is computed as a weighted average of the y_i corresponding to the m closest x_i to the focal value x_0, called the *nearest neighbors* of x_0. We set $m = [n \times s]$ for a prespecified fraction s of the data, called the *span*, where the square brackets represent rounding to the nearest integer. The span is a *tuning parameter* that can be set by the user, with larger values producing a smoother estimate of the regression function. To draw Figure 7.13, we set $s = 0.5$, and thus, $m = 0.5 \times 190 = 95$ points contribute to each local average.[9]

  The identification of the m nearest neighbors of x_0 is illustrated in Figure 7.13a for $x_0 = x_{(150)}$, the 150th ordered value of GDP, with the dashed vertical lines in the graph defining a *window* centered on $x_{(150)}$ that includes its 95 nearest neighbors. Selecting $x_0 = x_{(150)}$ for this example is entirely arbitrary, and we could have used any other x value in the grid. The size of the window is potentially different for each choice of x_0, but it always includes the same fraction of the data. In contrast, *fixed-bandwidth kernel regression* fixes the size of the window but lets the number of points used in the average vary.

- The scaled distances between each of the xs and the focal x_0 are $z_i = |x_i - x_0|/h_0$, where h_0 is the distance between x_0 and the most remote of its m nearest neighbors. Then, the weights, w_i, to be used depend on a *kernel function*, as in kernel-density estimation (discussed in Section 3.1.2). We use the *tricube kernel function*, setting $w_i = K_T(z_i)$, where

$$K_T(z) = \begin{cases} (1 - z^3)^3 & \text{for } z < 1 \\ 0 & \text{for } z \geq 1 \end{cases}$$

---

[8] We previously encountered the scatterplot for these two variables in Figure 3.15 (p. 129).

[9] For values of x_0 in the middle of the range of x, typically about half the nearest neighbors are smaller than x_0 and about half are larger than x_0, but for x_0 near the minimum (or maximum) of x, almost all the nearest neighbors will be larger (or smaller) than x_0, and this *edge effect* will introduce *boundary bias* into the estimated regression function. By fitting a local-regression line rather than a local average, the `lowess` function reduces bias near the boundaries. Modifying Figure 7.13 to illustrate nearest-neighbor local-linear regression rather than kernel regression is not hard: Simply fit a WLS regression, and compute a fitted value at each focal x. We leave this modification as an exercise for the reader.

The tricube weights, shown in Figure 7.13b, take on the maximum value of 1 at the focal x_0 in the center of the window and fall to 0 at the boundaries of the window.

- The y values associated with the m nearest neighbors of x_0 are then averaged, using the tricube weights, to obtain the fitted value

$$\widehat{y}_0 = \frac{\sum_{i=1}^{n} w_i y_i}{\sum_{i=1}^{n} w_i}$$

This step is illustrated in Figure 7.13c, in which a thick horizontal line is drawn at $\widehat{y}_{(150)}$.

- The whole process is repeated for all values of x on the selected grid, and the fitted points are joined to produce Figure 7.13d, completing the kernel regression.

To draw Figure 7.13, we first need to divide the graph into four panels:

```
> oldpar <- par(mfrow=c(2, 2), las=1) # 2-by-2 array of graphs
```

We are already familiar with using `par(mfrow=c(rows, cols))` and `par(mfcol=c(rows, cols))`, defining an array of panels to be filled either rowwise, as in the current example, or column-wise. We also included the additional argument `las=1` to `par`, which makes all axis tick labels, including those on the vertical axis, parallel to the horizontal axis, as is required in some journals. Finally, as suggested in Section 7.1.1, we saved the original value of `par` and will restore it when we finish the graph.

After removing the missing data from the UN data frame in the **car** package, where the data for the graph reside, we order the data by x values (i.e., gdp), being careful also to sort the y values (infant) in the same order:

```
> UN <- na.omit(UN)  # remove missing data
> gdp <- UN$gdp
> infant <- UN$infant.mortality
> ord <- order(gdp)       # order data by gdp
> gdp <- gdp[ord]         # sort gdp
> infant <- infant[ord] # sort infant into corresponding order
```

We turn our attention to Panel a of Figure 7.13:

```
> x0 <- gdp[150]         # focal x
> dist <- abs(gdp - x0)   # distance from focal x
> h <- sort(dist)[95]     # distance to most remote point
>                         #   in neighborhood for span=0.5
> pick <- dist <= h       # observations within window
```

Thus, x0 holds the focal x value, $x_{(150)}$; `dist` is the vector of distances between the xs and x_0; h is the distance to the most remote point in the neighborhood for span 0.5 and $n = 190$; and `pick` is a logical vector equal to TRUE for observations within the window and FALSE otherwise.

We draw the first graph using the `plot` function to define the axes and a coordinate space:

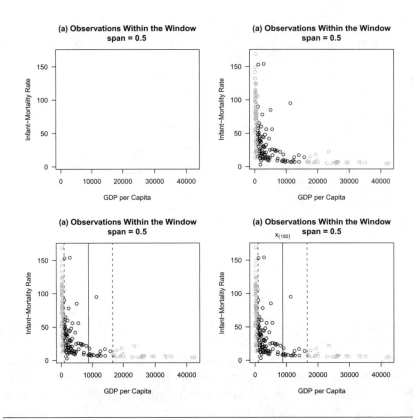

Figure 7.14   Building up Panel a of Figure 7.13 step by step.

```
> plot(gdp, infant, xlab="GDP per Capita",
+      ylab="Infant-Mortality Rate", type="n",
+      main="(a) Observations Within the Window\nspan = 0.5")
```

The \n in the main argument produces a new-line. The result of this command is shown in the upper-left panel of Figure 7.14. In the upper-right panel, we add points to the plot, using black for points within the window and light gray for those outside the window:

```
> points(gdp[pick], infant[pick], col="black")
> points(gdp[!pick], infant[!pick], col=gray(0.75))
```

Next, in the lower-left panel, we add a solid vertical line at the focal $x_0 = x_{(150)}$ and broken lines at the boundaries of the window:

```
> abline(v=x0)     # focal x
> abline(v=c(x0 - h, x0 + h), lty="dashed")  # window
```

Finally, in the lower-right panel, we use the text function to display the focal value $x_{(150)}$ at the top of the panel:

```
> text(x0, par("usr")[4] + 10, expression(x[(150)]), xpd=TRUE)
```

The second argument to text, giving the vertical coordinate, makes use of par("usr") to find the *user coordinates* of the boundaries of the plotting region. The command par("usr") returns a vector of the form c(x1, x2, y1, y2), and here we pick the fourth element, y2, which is the maximum vertical coordinate in the plotting region. Adding 10—one fifth of the distance between the vertical tick marks—to this value positions the text a bit above the plotting region, which is our aim. The argument xpd=TRUE permits drawing outside the normal plotting region. The text itself is given as an expression, allowing us to incorporate mathematical notation in the graph, here the subscript (150), to typeset the text as $x_{(150)}$.

Panel b of Figure 7.13 is also built up step by step. We begin by setting up the coordinate space and axes, drawing vertical lines at the focal x_0 and at the boundaries of the window, and horizontal gray lines at 0 and 1:

```
> plot(range(gdp), c(0, 1),
+     xlab="GDP per Capita", ylab="Tricube Kernel Weight",
+     type="n", main="(b) Tricube Weights")
> abline(v=x0)
> abline(v=c(x0 - h, x0 + h), lty="dashed")
> abline(h=c(0, 1), col="gray")
```

We then write a function to compute tricube weights:[10]

```
> tricube <- function(x, x0, h) {
+     z <- abs(x - x0)/h
+     ifelse(z < 1, (1 - z^3)^3, 0)
+ }
```

To complete Panel b, we draw the tricube weight function, showing points representing the weights for observations that fall within the window:

```
> tc <- function(x) tricube(x, x0, h) # to use with curve
> curve(tc, min(gdp), max(gdp), n=1000, lwd=2, add=TRUE)
> points(gdp[pick], tricube(gdp, x0, h)[pick], col="gray20")
```

The function tc is needed for curve, which requires a function of a single argument (see Section 7.1.3). The remaining two arguments to tricube are set to the value of x0 and h that we created earlier in the global environment.

Panel c is similar to Panel a, except that we draw a horizontal line at the locally weighted average value of *y*:

```
> plot(gdp, infant, xlab="GDP per Capita",
+     ylab="Infant-Mortality Rate", type="n",
+     main="(c) Weighted Average (Kernel Estimate)")
> points(gdp[pick], infant[pick], col="black")
> points(gdp[!pick], infant[!pick], col=gray(0.75))
> abline(v=x0)
> abline(v=c(x0 - h, x0 + h), lty=2)
> yhat <- weighted.mean(infant,
+                 w=tricube(gdp, x0, h))  # kernel estimate
> lines(c(x0 - h, x0 + h), c(yhat, yhat),
+     lwd=3) # draw thick horizontal line at yhat
```

---

[10]The ifelse command is described in Section 8.3.1.

Were we producing graphs for a computer presentation, we would have added color to the horizontal line in the last step, for example, `col="red"`, for clarity.

Finally, to draw Panel d, we repeat the calculation of $\widehat{y}$, using a `for` loop to set the focal x_0 to each value of `gdp` in turn:[11]

```
> plot(gdp, infant, xlab="GDP per Capita",
+       ylab="Infant-Mortality Rate",
+       main="(d) Complete Kernel Estimate")
> yhat <- numeric(length(gdp)) # initialize to vector of 0s
> for (i in 1:length(gdp)){    # kernel estimate at each x
+       x0 <- gdp[i]                 # focal value
+       dist <- abs(gdp - x0)        # distances
+       h <- sort(dist)[95]          # distance to most remote neighbor
+       yhat[i] <- weighted.mean(infant, w=tricube(gdp, x0, h))
+       }
> lines(gdp, yhat, lwd=2) # draw kernel-regression line
> par(oldpar)                  # restore original value of par
```

7.2.1   FINER CONTROL OVER PLOT LAYOUT

More complex arrangements than are possible with `mfrow` and `mfcol` can be defined using the `layout` function or the `fig` argument to par: See `?layout` and `?par`. We illustrate here with `fig`, producing Figure 7.15, a graph meant to demonstrate different kinds of nonlinearity:

```
> par(oma=c(0, 0, 1, 0), mar=c(2, 3, 3, 2)) # set margins
> par(fig=c(0, 0.5, 0.5, 1)) # top-left panel
> x <- seq(0, 1, length=200)
> Ey <- rev(1 - x^2)  # expected value of y; reverse values
> y <- Ey + 0.1*rnorm(200)  # add errors
> plot(x, y, axes=FALSE, frame=TRUE, main="(a) monotone, simple",
+       cex.main=1, xlab="", ylab="", col="gray", cex=0.75)
> lines(x, Ey, lwd=2)
> mtext("x", side=1, adj=1)  # text in bottom margin
> mtext("y ", side=2, at=max(y), las=1)  # text in left margin
> par(fig=c(0.5, 1, 0.5, 1)) # top-right panel
> par(new=TRUE)
> x <- seq(0.02, 0.99, length=200)
> Ey <- log(x/(1 - x))
> y <- Ey + 0.5*rnorm(200)
> plot(x, y, axes=FALSE, frame=TRUE,
+       main="(b) monotone, not simple",
+       cex.main=1, xlab="", ylab="", col="gray", cex=0.75)
> lines(x, Ey, lwd=2)
> mtext("x", side=1, adj=1)
> mtext("y ", side=2, at=max(y), las=1)
> par(fig=c(0.25, 0.75, 0, 0.5)) # bottom panel
> par(new=TRUE)
> x <- seq(0.2, 1, length=200)
> Ey <- (x - 0.5)^2
> y <- Ey + 0.04*rnorm(200)
> plot(x, y, axes=FALSE, frame=TRUE,
```

---

[11] `for` loops are described in Section 8.3.2.

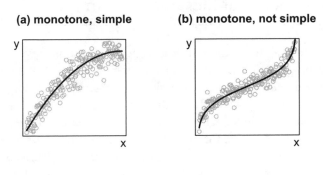

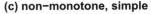

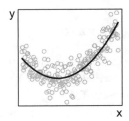

Figure 7.15 Using the `fig` graphical parameter for finer control over plot layout.

```
+      main="(c) non-monotone, simple",
+      cex.main=1, xlab="", ylab="", col="gray", cex=0.75)
> lines(x, Ey, lwd=2)
> mtext("x", side=1, adj=1)
> mtext("y ", side=2, at=max(y), las=1)
> title("Nonlinear Relationships", outer=TRUE)
```

The first `par` command leaves room in the top outer margin for the graph title, which is given in the `title` command at the end, and establishes the margins for each panel. The order of margins both for `oma` (the outer margins) and for `mar` (the margins for each panel) are c(*bottom, left, top, right*), and in each case the units for the margins are lines of text. The `fig` argument to `par` establishes the boundaries of each panel, expressed as fractions of the display region of the plotting device, in the order c(*x-minimum, x-maximum, y-minimum, y-maximum*), measured from the bottom-left of the device. Thus, the first panel, defined by the command `par(fig=c(0, 0.5, 0.5, 1))`, extends from the left margin to the horizontal middle and from the vertical middle to the top of the plotting device. Each subsequent panel begins with the command `par(new=TRUE)` so as not to clear the plotting device, as would normally occur when a high-level plotting function such as `plot` is invoked. We use the `mtext` command to position the axis labels just where we want them in the margins of each panel; in the `mtext` commands, `side=1` refers to the left margin and `side=2` to the bottom margin of the current panel.

7.3   Lattice and Other Graphics Packages in R

This section introduces the **lattice** package and mentions several other packages that provide alternative graphics systems for R and that are especially noteworthy in our opinion. Many of the more than 2,500 packages on CRAN make graphs of various sorts, and it is certainly not our object to take on the Herculean task of cataloging what's available to R users in the realm of statistical graphics. A search for the keyword `graphics` at `www.rseek.org` produces a wide variety of places to go on the Internet to learn about R graphics. Another source is the *CRAN Graphics Task View* at `http://cran. r-project.org/web/views/Graphics.html`.

7.3.1   THE LATTICE PACKAGE

Probably the most important current alternative to basic R graphics is provided by the **lattice** package, which is part of the standard R distribution. The **lattice** package is a descendant of the **trellis** library in S, originally written by Richard Becker and William Cleveland (Becker and Cleveland, 1996). The implementation of **lattice** graphics in R is completely independent of the S original, however, and is extensively documented in Sarkar (2008).

We used **lattice** graphics without much comment earlier in this *Companion*, in particular in the effect displays first introduced in Section 4.3.3. We also used **lattice** to produce separate graphs for different subgroups of data in Figures 4.13 and 4.14. The first of these, Figure 4.13 (p. 204), was generated by the following command:

```
> library(lattice)
> xyplot(salary ~ yrs.since.phd | discipline:rank, groups=sex,
+     data=Salaries, type=c("g", "p", "r"), auto.key=TRUE)
```

This is a typical **lattice** command: A formula is used to determine the horizontal and vertical axes of each *panel* in the graph, here with `salary` on the vertical axis and `yrs.since.phd` on the horizontal. The graph in each panel includes only a subset of the data, determined by the values of the variables to the right of the vertical bar (`|`), which is read as *given*. In the example, we get a separate panel for each combination of the factors `discipline` and `rank`. The `groups` argument allows more conditioning within a panel, using separate colors, symbols, and lines for each level of the grouping variable—`sex`, in this example. The familiar `data` argument is used, as in statistical-modeling functions, to supply a data frame containing the data for the graph. The `type` argument specifies the characteristics of each panel, in this case printing a background grid (`"g"`), showing the individual points (`"p"`), and displaying a least-squares regression line (`"r"`) for each group in each panel of the plot. Other useful options for `type` include `"smooth"` for a lowess smooth with default smoothing parameter and `"l"` for joining the points with lines. The latter will produce surprising, and probably undesirable,

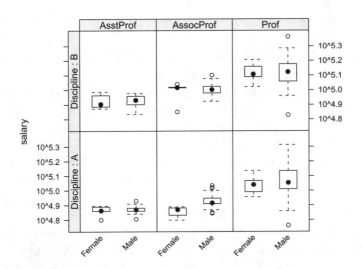

Figure 7.16 Boxplots of `log(salary)` by rank, sex, and discipline.

results unless the data within group are ordered according to the variable on the horizontal axis. The `auto.key` argument prints the legend at the top of the plot. If there is a grouping variable, then the regression lines and smooths are plotted separately for each level of the grouping variable; otherwise, they are plotted for all points in the panel.

The boxplots in Figure 4.14 (p. 205) were similarly generated using the **lattice** function `bwplot`. Graphs such as this one can be made more elaborate: for example,

```
> library(latticeExtra)
> useOuterStrips(
+    bwplot(salary ~ sex | rank + discipline, data=Salaries,
+      scales=list(x=list(rot=45), y=list(log=10, rot=0) )),
+    strip.left=strip.custom(strip.names=TRUE,
+      var.name="Discipline")
+ )
```

The result is shown in Figure 7.16. The conditioning is a little different from Figure 4.14, with each panel containing parallel boxplots by `sex` for each combination of `rank` and `discipline`. The `scales` argument is a list that specifies the characteristics of the scales on the axes. For the horizontal or x-axis, we specified a list with one argument to rotate the level labels by 45°. For the vertical or y-axis, we specified two arguments: to rotate the labels to horizontal and to use a base-10 logarithmic scale. We also applied the `useOuterStrips` function from the **latticeExtra** package (Sarkar and Andrews, 2010)[12] to get the levels for the second conditioning variable,

---

[12]While the **lattice** package is part of the standard R distribution, the **latticeExtra** package must be obtained from CRAN.

discipline, printed at the left. The `strip.custom` function allowed us to change the row labels to `Discipline:A` and `Discipline:B` rather than the less informative `A` and `B`.

Graphs produced with **lattice** are based on a different metaphor from standard R graphics, in that a plot is usually specified in a single call to a graphics function, rather than by adding to a graph in a series of independently executed commands. As a result, the command to create a customized **lattice** graph can be very complex. The key arguments include those for *panel functions*, which determine what goes into each panel; *strip functions*, as we used above, to determine what goes into the labeling strips; and *scale functions*, which control the axis scales. Both the **lattice** and the **latticeExtra** packages contain many prewritten panel functions likely to suit the needs of most users, or you can write your own panel functions.

In addition to scatterplots produced by `xyplot` and boxplots produced by `bwplot`, as we have illustrated here, **lattice** includes 13 other high-level plotting functions, for dot plots, histograms, various three-dimensional plots, and more, and the **latticeExtra** package adds several more high-level functions. The book by Sarkar (2008) is very helpful, providing dozens of examples of **lattice** graphs.

The **lattice** package is based on a lower-level, object-oriented graphics system provided by the **grid** package, which is described by Murrell (2006, Part II). Functions in the **grid** package create and manipulate editable graphics objects, thus relaxing the indelible-ink-on-paper metaphor underlying basic R graphics and permitting fine control over the layout and details of a graph. Its power notwithstanding, it is fair to say that the learning curve for **grid** graphics is steep.

7.3.2   MAPS

R has several packages for drawing maps, including the **maps** package (Becker et al., 2010).[13] Predefined maps are available for the world and for several countries, including the United States. Viewing data on maps can often be illuminating. As a brief example, the data frame `Depredations` in the **car** package contains data from Harper et al. (2008) on incidents of wolves killing farm animals, called *depredations*, in Minnesota for the period 1979–1998:

```
> head(Depredations)

  longitude latitude number early late
1     -94.5     46.1      1     0    1
2     -93.0     46.6      2     0    2
3     -94.6     48.5      1     1    0
4     -92.9     46.6      2     0    2
5     -95.9     48.8      1     0    1
6     -92.7     47.1      1     0    1
```

---

[13] The **maps** package is not part of the standard R distribution, so you must obtain it from CRAN.

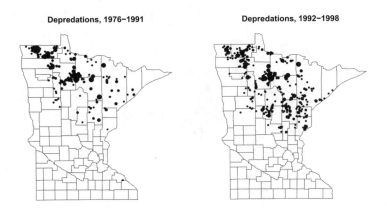

Figure 7.17 Wolf depredations in Minnesota. The areas of the dots are proportional to the number of depredations.

The data include the longitude and latitude of the farms where depredations occurred and the number of depredations at each farm for the whole period (1979–1998), and separately for the earlier period (1991 or before) and for the later period (after 1991). Management of wolf-livestock interactions is a significant public policy question, and maps can help us understand the geographic distribution of the incidents.

```
> library(maps)
> par(mfrow=c(1, 2))
> map("county", "minnesota", col=gray(0.4))
> with(Depredations, points(longitude, latitude,
+       cex=sqrt(early), pch=20))
> title("Depredations, 1976-1991", cex.main=1.5)
> map("county", "minnesota", col=grey(0.4))
> with(Depredations,points(longitude, latitude,
+       cex=sqrt(late), pch=20))
> title("Depredations, 1992-1998", cex.main=1.5)
```

To draw separate maps for the early and late periods, we set up the graphics device with the `mfrow` graphics parameter. The `map` function was used to draw the map, in this case a map of county boundaries in the state of Minnesota. The coordinates for the map are the usual longitude and latitude, and the `points` function is employed to add points to the plot, with areas proportional to the number of depredations at each location. We used `title` to add a title to each panel, with the argument `cex.main` to increase the size of the title. The maps tell us where in the state the wolf-livestock interactions occur and where the farms with the largest number of depredations can be found. The range of depredations has expanded to the south and east between time periods. There is also an apparent outlier in the data—one depredation in the southeast of the state in the early period.

Choropleth maps, which color geographic units according to the values of one or more variables, can be drawn using **lattice** graphics with the `mapplot` function in the **latticeExtra** package. These graphs are of little value without

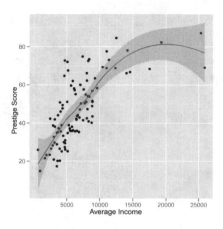

Figure 7.18 Scatterplot of `prestige` by `income` for the Canadian occupational-prestige data, produced by the ggplot2 function `qplot`.

color, so we don't provide an example here. See the examples on the help page for `mapplot`.

7.3.3   OTHER NOTABLE GRAPHICS PACKAGES

The **plotrix** package (Lemon, 2006) provides a number of tools that can be used to simplify adding features to a graph created with `plot` or related functions. We saw in Figure 3.11b (p. 122) an example of the use of the `plotCI` function to add error bars to a graph. Plots of coefficient estimates and their standard errors, for example, are easily displayed using this function. Type `help(package=plotrix)` for an index of the functions that are available, and see the individual help pages and the examples for more information on the various functions in the package.

The **ggplot2** package, inspired by Leland Wilkinson's *The Grammar of Graphics* (Wilkinson, 2005), is another graphics system based on the **grid** package and is oriented toward the production of fine, publication-quality graphs. Details are available in Wickham (2009). An illustrative scatterplot for the Canadian occupational-prestige data produced by the following **ggplot2** command is shown in Figure 7.18:

```
> library(ggplot2)
> qplot(income, prestige, xlab="Average Income",
+     ylab="Prestige Score",
+     geom=c("point", "smooth"), data=Prestige)
```

The nonparametric-regression smooth on the plot is produced by lowess, while the band around the smooth represents not conditional variation but a pointwise confidence envelope.

The **rgl** package (Adler and Murdoch, 2010) interfaces R with the OpenGL three-dimensional graphics system (`www.opengl.org`), providing a foundation for building three-dimensional dynamic statistical graphs. The possibilities are literally impossible to convey adequately on the static pages of a book, especially without color. A monochrome picture of an **rgl** graph, created by the `scatter3d` function in the **car** package, appeared in Figure 3.12 (on p. 125).

The **iplots** (Urbanek and Wichtrey, 2010) and **playwith** (Andrews, 2010) packages introduce interactive graphical capabilities to R, the former via the **RGtk2** package, which links R to the GTK+ GUI toolkit, and the latter via the **rJava** package, which links R to the Java computing platform.

The **rggobi** package (Cook and Swayne, 2009) provides a bridge from R to the GGobi system, which produces high-interaction dynamic graphics for visualizing multivariate data.

7.4 Graphics Devices

Graphics devices in R send graphs to windows, to files, or to printers. Drawing graphs on the computer screen first almost always makes sense, and it is easy enough to save the contents of a graphics window, to print the graph, or to copy it to the clipboard and then paste it into some other application.

When we use a higher-level graphics function such as `plot`, a graphics device corresponding to a new graphics window is opened if none is currently open. If a graphics device window is already open, then the graph will be drawn in the existing window, generally after erasing the current contents of the window.

The contents of a graphics window can be saved in a file under both Windows and Mac OS X by selecting *File → Save as* in the menu bar of the graphics window and then selecting the format in which to save the file. A graph can be copied to the clipboard in the normal manner (e.g., by Ctrl-c in Windows) when its window has the focus (which can be achieved by clicking the mouse in the window), and it can be pasted into another application, such as a graphics editor or word-processing program. Graphs can be printed by selecting *File → Print*, although printing from another program gives more control over the size and orientation of the plot.

In some cases, we may wish to skip the on-screen version of a plot and instead send a graph directly to a file, an operation that is performed in R by using a suitable graphics device: for example,

```
> pdf("mygraph.pdf")
> hist(rnorm(100))
> dev.off()
```

The first command calls the `pdf` function to open a graphics device of type PDF (Portable Document Format), which will create the graph as a PDF file in the working directory. The graph is then drawn by the second command, and finally the `dev.off` function is called to close the device and the file. All graphical output is sent to the PDF device until we invoke the `dev.off` command. The completed graph, in `mygraph.pdf`, can be used like any other PDF file. The command ?Devices gives a list of available graphics devices, and, for example, ?pdf explains the arguments that can be used to set up the PDF device.

Three useful mechanisms are available for viewing multiple graphs. One approach is the procedure that we employed in most of this *Companion*: drawing several graphs in the same window, using par(mfrow=c(*rows, columns*)), for example, to divide a graphics device window into panels.

A second approach makes use of the graphics history mechanism. Under Windows, we activate the graphics history by selecting *History → Recording* from the graphics device menus; subsequently, the PageUp and Page-Down keys can be used to scroll through the graphs. Under Mac OS X, we can scroll through graphs with the command-← and command-→ key combinations when a graphics device window has the focus.

The final method is to open more than one graphics window, and for this we must open additional windows directly, not rely on a call to plot or a similar high-level graphics function to open the windows. A new graphics window can be created directly in the Windows version of R by the windows function and under Mac OS X by the quartz function. If multiple devices are open, then only one is *active* and all others are inactive. New graphs are written to the active graphics device. The function dev.list returns a vector of all graphics devices in use; dev.cur returns the number of the currently active device; and dev.set sets the active device.

7.5   Complementary Reading and References

- Murrell (2006) is the definitive reference both for standard graphics in R and for the **grid** graphics system, on which the **lattice** and **ggplot2** packages are based; Sarkar (2008) and Becker and Cleveland (1996) provide references for lattice/trellis graphics; and Wickham (2009) documents the **ggplot2** package.
- There is a very large general literature on statistical graphics. Some influential treatments of the subject include Tukey (1977), Tufte (1983), Cleveland (1993, 1994), and Wilkinson (2005).

Writing Programs 8

Most of this *Companion* discusses the use of existing R functions and packages for working with linear models and GLMs. On occasion, you may want to perform a computation that the designers of R and contributed packages did not anticipate. These situations include the following:

- Data sets are frequently encountered that must be modified before they can be used by `lm` or `glm`. For example, you may need to change values of -99 to the missing value indicator `NA`, or you may regularly want to recode a variable with values 0 and 1 to the more informative labels `Male` and `Female`. Writing functions for these kinds of data management operations, and others that are more complicated, can automate the process of preparing similar data sets.
- Output from some existing R functions must be rearranged for publication. Writing a function to format the output automatically in the required form can save having to retype it.
- A graph is to be drawn that requires first performing several computations to produce the right data to plot and then using a sequence of graphics commands to complete the plot. A function written once can automate these tasks.
- A simulation is required to investigate robustness or estimator error, or otherwise to explore the data. Writing a function to perform the simulation can make it easier to vary factors such as parameter values, estimators, and sample sizes.
- A nonstandard model that doesn't fit into the usual frameworks can be fit by writing a special-purpose function that uses one of the available function optimizers in R.

This list is hardly exhaustive, but it does illustrate that writing functions can be useful in a variety of situations.

The goal of this chapter is to provide you with the basics of writing R functions to meet immediate needs in routine and not so routine data analysis. Although this brief introduction is probably not enough for you to write polished programs for general use, it is nevertheless worth cultivating good programming habits, and the line between programs written for one's own use and those written for others is often blurred. Recommendations for further reading on R programming are given at the end of the chapter.

8.1   Defining Functions

R is largely a functional programming language, which implies that writing programs in R entails defining functions. To begin, take a look again at Figure 6.6 (p. 299). This is a scatterplot of Studentized residuals versus hat-values from a linear model, produced by the `influencePlot` function in the **car** package. The points are plotted as circles with areas proportional to Cook's distances. Imagine that you want to draw this graph routinely for linear models and GLMs, but you don't have the `influencePlot` function available. Writing your own function for this purpose would make sense. Figure 8.1 shows a function that will draw a similar graph. So that you can conveniently correct errors and have a permanent copy of the finished function, a programming editor should be used to write the function (as explained in Section 1.1.7), rather than entering it directly at the command prompt.

Functions are defined using the `function` special form. In Figure 8.1, the function is named `inflPlot`. The *body* of the function appears between the initial curly brace { and the terminal } and consists of a sequence of R commands. Most functions are intended to return a value, and in R whatever is computed in the last command in the function is the object that is returned. In `inflPlot`, the last command is a *compound command*, enclosed in braces, returning different results depending on the value of the local variable `identify`, which is an argument to the function: If the argument `identify` is `TRUE`, then `inflPlot` returns the indices of noteworthy points; otherwise, it returns a `NULL` value invisibly, which means that the value is not printed. We have used the `return` function to clarify what is returned in each case, but in this function these are the alternative values that would be returned in any event. The main purpose of the `inflPlot` function is to draw a plot, and this is done in the body of the function as a *side effect*.[1]

The *formal arguments* of the `inflPlot` function, which are given as arguments to `function`, are named `model`, `scale`, `col`, `identify`, `labels`, and `. . . .` The equals sign (=) is used optionally to assign a *default value* to an argument in the function definition. For example, `scale=10` assigns the default value of `10` to the argument `scale`. In this illustrative function, all the arguments except the first, `model`, and the last, `. . .`, have been given default values; thus, if values for these arguments are not provided when the function is called, then the defaults are used. Because there is no default for `model`, the argument must be provided whenever the function

---

[1]*All* R functions return values, even if the value returned is NULL or invisible (or, as here, both NULL *and* invisible). The most common *side effects* in R—that is, effects produced by functions other than returned values—are the creation of printed output and graphs.

```
inflPlot <- function(model, scale=10, col=c(1, 2),
    identify=TRUE, labels=names(rstud), ... ) {
    # Plot hatvalues, Studentized residuals, and Cook's distances
    #   for a linear or generalized linear model
    # Arguments:
    #   model: an lm or glm model object
    #   scale: a scaling factor for the circles representing Cook's D
    #   col: colors for non-noteworthy and noteworthy points
    #   identify points: label noteworthy points (TRUE or FALSE)
    #   labels: for identified points
    hatval <- hatvalues(model)
    rstud <- rstudent(model)
    cook <- sqrt(cooks.distance(model))
    scale <- scale/max(cook, na.rm=TRUE)
    p <- length(coef(model))
    n <- sum(!is.na(rstud))
    cutoff <- sqrt(4/(n - p))
    plot(hatval, rstud, xlab="Hat-Values", ylab="Studentized Residuals",
        cex=scale*cook, col=ifelse(cook > cutoff, col[2], col[1]), ...)
    abline(v = c(2, 3)*p/n, lty = "dashed")
    bonf <- qt(.025/n, df = n - p - 1, lower.tail=FALSE)
    abline(h=c(-bonf, -2, 0, 2, bonf), lty="dashed")
    if (identify) {
        noteworthy <- cook > cutoff | abs(rstud) > bonf | hatval > 2*p/n
        pos <- ifelse(hatval - mean(range(hatval, na.rm=TRUE)) <= 0, 4, 2)
        text(hatval[noteworthy], rstud[noteworthy], labels[noteworthy],
            pos = pos[noteworthy])
        return(which(noteworthy))
    }
    else return(invisible(NULL))
}
```

Figure 8.1   Code for the `inflPlot` function.

is called. The argument . . . (the ellipses) is special and will be discussed shortly.

When the function is called, its formal arguments are set equal to *real arguments*, either supplied explicitly or given by default.[2] For example:

```
> inflPlot(lm(prestige ~ income + education, data=Duncan))
> m1 <- lm(prestige ~ income + education, data=Duncan)
> inflPlot(m1)
> inflPlot(model=m1)
> inflPlot(m1, scale=10, col=c(1, 2), identify=TRUE,
+     labels=names(rstud))
```

All these commands produce the same plot (not shown). In the first command, the first formal argument is replaced by the linear-model object returned by the command `lm(prestige~income + education, data=Duncan)`,

---

[2]It is possible to call a function without supplying values for all its arguments, even arguments that do not have defaults. First, arguments are evaluated only when they are first used in a function (a process called *lazy evaluation*, described later), and therefore if an argument is never used, it need not have a value. Second, the programmer can use the `missing` function to test whether an argument has been specified and proceed accordingly, avoiding the evaluation of an argument not given in the function call.

and all the remaining arguments are replaced by their default values. Before the second `inflPlot` command, an object named `m1` is created that is the result of fitting the same linear model as in the first command. This object is supplied as the `model` argument in the second `inflPlot` command. The third `inflPlot` command explicitly assigns the argument `model=m1`, while the first two commands relied on matching the `model` argument by its position in the sequence of formal arguments. It is common in R commands to use positional matching for the first two or three arguments, and matching by name for the remaining arguments. Matching by name is always required when the arguments are supplied in a different order from the order given in the function definition. Named arguments may be abbreviated as long as the abbreviation is unique. For example, because no other argument to `inflPlot` begins with the letter *s*, the argument `scale` may be abbreviated to `scal`, `sca`, `sc`, or `s`. The final `inflPlot` command explicitly sets the remaining arguments to their default values.

The formal ellipses argument . . . is special in that it may be matched by any number of real arguments when the function is called, and it is commonly used to soak up extra arguments to be passed to other functions. In `inflPlot`, the inclusion of . . . allows adding arguments that are passed to the `plot` function without specifying those arguments in the definition of `inflPlot`. When `inflPlot` is called without additional arguments, then none are passed to `plot`.[3]

Along with function arguments, variables defined within the body of a function are local to the function: They exist only while the function executes and do not interfere with variables of the same name in the global environment; for example:

```
> squareit <- function(x) {
+    y <- x^2
+    y
+ }
> y <- 3
> squareit(x=y)

[1] 9

> y

[1] 3
```

The value of `y` is unchanged in the global environment even though the local variable `y` in the `squareit` function took on a different value.

---

[3]A relatively subtle point is that . . . can be used only for arguments that aren't explicitly specified in the `plot` command in `inflPlot`. For example, were we to attempt to change the axis labels by the command `inflPlot(m1, xlab="Leverages", ylab="Stud. Res.")`, relying on . . . to absorb the `xlab` and `ylab` arguments, an error would be produced, because `plot` would then be called with duplicate `xlab` and `ylab` arguments. Duplicate arguments aren't permitted in a function call. If we really thought it worthwhile to allow the user to change the axis labels, we could explicitly provide `xlab` and `ylab` arguments to `inflPlot`, with the current labels as defaults, and pass these arguments explicitly to `plot`.

Although formal arguments are associated with real arguments when a function is called, an argument is not *evaluated* until its first use. At that point, the argument is evaluated in the environment from which the function was called. In contrast, default values for arguments, if they exist, are evaluated in the environment of the function itself. This process of *lazy evaluation* frequently proves efficient and convenient. The default value of one argument can depend on another argument or even on a value computed in the body of the function. In `inflPlot`, for example, the default value of `labels` references the local variable `rstud`. Lazy evaluation can trip up the unwary programmer, however.[4]

Reviewing the `inflPlot` function in Figure 8.1 line by line may be helpful, even though most of the R commands used in the function are self-explanatory:

- The first few lines of the function, which begin with the character #, are comments, used in the program code to explain what the function does and what the arguments mean. This is generally a good practice if you plan to save the function.
- The next three lines use the R functions `hatvalues`, `rstudent`, and `cooks.distance` to extract the hat-values, Studentized residuals, and Cook's distances from the `model` that was passed as an argument to `inflPlot`.
- The value of `scale` is used to determine the sizes of the points to be drawn, and it is computed to be the default size given as an argument divided by the square root of the maximum value of Cook's distance.
- The argument `na.rm=TRUE` is required in the `max` function or the scale factor would be `NA` if missing values are present.
- As explained in Chapter 7, the graph is drawn by first calling `plot` and then other functions to add features to the plot. The axis labels will be `Hat-Values` and `Studentized Residuals`, the size of the plotted points is given by `scale*cook`, and the color of the points depends on whether or not `cook > cutoff`.
- The `abline` function is used in `inflPlot` to add vertical and horizontal reference lines to the plot—the former at twice and three times the average hat-value and the latter at Studentized residuals of -2, 0, and 2 and at the Bonferroni cutoffs for a two-sided outlier test at the .05 level. The argument `lty="dashed"` specifies broken lines.
- If the argument `identify` is TRUE, then points with noteworthy values of Cook's D, Studentized residuals, or hat-values are labeled with their observation names, taken by default from `names(studres)`, the names of the Studentized residuals, which are the row names of the data frame given as an argument to `lm` or `glm`. The label is positioned to the left of the point if its hat-value is greater than the midrange of the

---

[4]Environments in R are discussed in Section 8.9.

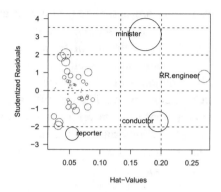

Figure 8.2   A graph produced by the `inflPlot` function.

hat-values (i.e., the average of the minimum and maximum values), and to the right otherwise.

We try out `inflPlot` on Duncan's occupational-prestige regression:

```
> library(car)   # for Duncan data
> inflPlot(lm(prestige ~ income + education, data=Duncan),
+      ylim=c(-3, 4), las=1, col=gray(c(0.5, 0)))

    minister     reporter    conductor RR.engineer
           6            9           16          27
```

The resulting graph appears in Figure 8.2. We set `col=gray(c(0.5, 0))`, which corresponds to medium gray and black, because the default colors in R—black and red—would not reproduce properly in the book; specifying `ylim=c(-3, 4)` expands the range of the vertical axis, and `las=1` makes all tick mark labels horizontal. These are specified here to illustrate the use of arguments passed down to `plot` via . . . .

8.2   Working With Matrices*

R incorporates extensive facilities for matrix and linear algebra. This section concentrates on basic matrix operations.

We begin by defining some matrices via the `matrix` function; `matrix` fills matrices by columns, unless the argument `byrow` is set to `TRUE`:

```
> (A <- matrix(c(1, 2, -4, 3, 5, 0), nrow=2, ncol=3))

     [,1] [,2] [,3]
[1,]    1   -4    5
[2,]    2    3    0
```

```
> (B <- matrix(1:6, 2, 3))

     [,1] [,2] [,3]
[1,]    1    3    5
[2,]    2    4    6

> (C <- matrix(c(2, -2, 0, 1, -1, 1, 4, 4, -4), 3, 3, byrow=TRUE))

     [,1] [,2] [,3]
[1,]    2   -2    0
[2,]    1   -1    1
[3,]    4    4   -4
```

8.2.1 BASIC MATRIX ARITHMETIC

Matrix addition, subtraction, negation, and the product of a matrix and a scalar (i.e., single number) use the usual arithmetic operators; addition and subtraction require matrices of the same order:

```
> A + B

     [,1] [,2] [,3]
[1,]    2   -1   10
[2,]    4    7    6

> A - B

     [,1] [,2] [,3]
[1,]    0   -7    0
[2,]    0   -1   -6

> A + C  # A and C not of the same order!

Error in A + C : non-conformable arrays

> 2*A

     [,1] [,2] [,3]
[1,]    2   -8   10
[2,]    4    6    0

> -A

     [,1] [,2] [,3]
[1,]   -1    4   -5
[2,]   -2   -3    0
```

Using * to multiply two matrices of the same order forms their element-wise product. The standard matrix product is computed with the inner-product operator, %*%, which requires that the matrices be conformable for multiplication:

```
> A %*% C

     [,1] [,2] [,3]
[1,]   18   22  -24
[2,]    7   -7    3
```

In matrix products, vectors are treated as row or column vectors, as required:

```
> (a <- rep(1, 3))

[1] 1 1 1

> (b <- c(1, 5, 3))

[1] 1 5 3

> C %*% a

     [,1]
[1,]    0
[2,]    1
[3,]    4

> a %*% C

     [,1] [,2] [,3]
[1,]    7    1   -3

> a %*% b

     [,1]
[1,]    9
```

The last of these examples illustrates that the inner product of two vectors of the same length, a %*% b, is a scalar—actually a 1×1 matrix in R.

The outer product of two vectors may be obtained via the outer function:

```
> outer(a, b)

     [,1] [,2] [,3]
[1,]    1    5    3
[2,]    1    5    3
[3,]    1    5    3
```

The outer function may also be used with operations other than multiplication; an optional third argument, which defaults to "*", specifies the function to be applied to pairs of elements from the first two arguments.

The function t returns the transpose of a matrix:

```
> t(B)

     [,1] [,2]
[1,]    1    2
[2,]    3    4
[3,]    5    6
```

8.2.2   MATRIX INVERSION AND THE SOLUTION OF LINEAR SIMULTANEOUS EQUATIONS

The solve function computes the inverse of a square, nonsingular matrix:

```
> solve(C)
```

```
      [,1] [,2]  [,3]
[1,]   0.0  0.5 0.125
[2,] -0.5  0.5 0.125
[3,] -0.5  1.0 0.000

> solve(C) %*% C   # check

      [,1] [,2] [,3]
[1,]    1    0    0
[2,]    0    1    0
[3,]    0    0    1
```

The fractions function in the **MASS** package may be used to display numbers as rational fractions, which is often convenient when working with simple matrix examples:

```
> library(MASS)
> fractions(solve(C))

      [,1] [,2] [,3]
[1,]    0  1/2  1/8
[2,] -1/2  1/2  1/8
[3,] -1/2    1    0
```

The solve function may also be used more generally to solve systems of linear simultaneous equations. If **C** is a known square and nonsingular matrix, **b** is a known vector or matrix, and **x** is a vector or matrix of unknowns, then the solution of the system of linear simultaneous equations $\mathbf{Cx} = \mathbf{b}$ is $\mathbf{x} = \mathbf{C}^{-1}\mathbf{b}$, which is computed in R by

```
> solve(C, b)

[1] 2.875 2.375 4.500
```

as we may easily verify:

```
> solve(C) %*% b

      [,1]
[1,] 2.875
[2,] 2.375
[3,] 4.500
```

8.2.3   EXAMPLE: LINEAR LEAST-SQUARES REGRESSION

To illustrate the application of matrix operations in R, we compute the least-squares coefficients for a linear model with model matrix **X** and response vector **y**, using the Canadian occupational-prestige data as an example:

```
> X <- cbind(1, as.matrix(Prestige[ , 1:3]))   # model matrix
> y <- Prestige[ , "prestige"]  # the response vector
> head(X)   # first 6 rows
```

```
                    education income women
gov.administrators  1    13.11  12351 11.16
general.managers    1    12.26  25879  4.02
accountants         1    12.77   9271 15.70
purchasing.officers 1    11.42   8865  9.11
chemists            1    14.62   8403 11.68
physicists          1    15.64  11030  5.13
```

```
> head(y)
```

```
[1]  68.8 69.1 63.4 56.8 73.5 77.6
```

Selecting the single column for the response `prestige` from the data frame `Prestige` produces a vector rather than a one-column matrix because R by default drops dimensions with extent one. We can circumvent this behavior by specifying `drop=FALSE` (see Section 2.3.4 on indexing), which not only produces a matrix (actually, here, a data frame) with one column but also retains the row labels:

```
> head(Prestige[ , "prestige", drop=FALSE])
```

```
                    prestige
gov.administrators    68.8
general.managers      69.1
accountants           63.4
purchasing.officers   56.8
chemists              73.5
physicists            77.6
```

Although some R functions are fussy about the distinction between a vector and a single-column matrix, in the current example either will do.

The usual formula for the least-squares coefficients is $\mathbf{b} = (\mathbf{X'X})^{-1}\mathbf{X'y}$. It is simple to write this formula directly as an R expression:

```
> solve(t(X) %*% X) %*% t(X) %*% y
```

```
              [,1]
          -6.794334
education  4.186637
income     0.001314
women     -0.008905
```

This approach of forming and inverting $\mathbf{X'X}$ can be numerically inaccurate in some instances, and there are numerically superior methods for solving least-squares problems. We may do a bit better in large data sets by forming squares and cross-products as `crossprod(X)` and `crossprod(X, y)`, but computations via the QR decomposition (Section 8.2.5) of the model matrix $\mathbf{X}$, for example, will be more numerically stable in ill-conditioned problems—as when the columns of $\mathbf{X}$ are nearly collinear (see Weisberg, 2005, Appendix A.9; Chambers, 1992). This is the approach taken by the lm function. Unless the data are ill-conditioned or the data set is very large, however, the computation will go through just fine, as we may verify via the lm function for the current illustration:

```
> lm(prestige ~ education + income + women, data=Prestige)

Call:
lm(formula = prestige ~ education + income + women, data = Prestige)

Coefficients:
(Intercept)     education       income        women
   -6.79433       4.18664      0.00131     -0.00891
```

8.2.4 EIGENVALUES AND EIGENVECTORS

The `eigen` function calculates eigenvalues and eigenvectors of square matrices, including asymmetric matrices, which may have complex eigenvalues and eigenvectors. For example, an eigen-analysis of the correlation matrix for the predictors in the Canadian occupational-prestige regression is provided by the following commands:

```
> R <- with(Prestige, cor(cbind(education, income, women)))
> R   # correlation matrix

          education  income    women
education   1.00000  0.5776   0.06185
income      0.57758  1.0000  -0.44106
women       0.06185 -0.4411   1.00000

> eigen(R)

$values
[1] 1.6977 1.0596 0.2427

$vectors
          [,1]      [,2]     [,3]
[1,] -0.5611   0.60527   0.5647
[2,] -0.7213  -0.02271  -0.6923
[3,]  0.4062   0.79569  -0.4493
```

The eigenvectors are the columns of the list-component $vectors returned by `eigen`; each eigenvector is normalized to length 1 and, therefore, the eigenvectors give the *loadings* for a principal-components analysis based on the correlations, while the eigenvalues give the collective variation accounted for by each component. Principal-components analysis can also be performed by the `princomp` and `prcomp` functions.

8.2.5 MISCELLANEOUS MATRIX COMPUTATIONS

Other matrix factorizations available in R include the singular-value, QR, and Cholesky decompositions: See the online help for `svd`, `qr`, and `chol`.

The determinant of a square matrix may be computed in R by the `det` function: for example,

```
> det(R)

[1] 0.4365
```

Depending on its argument, the `diag` function may be used to extract or to set the main diagonal of a matrix, to create a diagonal matrix from a vector, or to create an identity matrix of specified order:

```
> diag(R)   # extract diagonal

education     income      women
        1          1          1

> diag(R) <- NA   # set diagonal
> R

          education   income     women
education        NA   0.5776   0.06185
income      0.57758       NA  -0.44106
women       0.06185  -0.4411        NA

> diag(1:3)   # make diagonal matrix

      [,1] [,2] [,3]
[1,]     1    0    0
[2,]     0    2    0
[3,]     0    0    3

> diag(3)   # order-3 identity matrix

      [,1] [,2] [,3]
[1,]     1    0    0
[2,]     0    1    0
[3,]     0    0    1
```

The **MASS** package includes a function, `ginv`, for computing generalized inverses of square and rectangular matrices. Advanced facilities for matrix computation, including for efficiently storing and manipulating large, sparse matrices, are provided by the **Matrix** package.

8.3   Program Control: Conditionals, Loops, and Recursion

8.3.1   CONDITIONALS

The basic construct for conditional evaluation in R is the `if` statement, which takes one of the following two general forms:

1. if (*logical.condition*) *command*

2. if (*logical.condition*)*command* else *alternative.-command*

   - In these expressions, if the first element of *logical.condition* evaluates to TRUE or to a nonzero number, then *command* is evaluated and its value is returned.
   - If *logical.condition* evaluates to FALSE or 0 in the first form, then NULL is returned.

- If *logical.condition* evaluates to FALSE or 0 in the second form, then *alternative.command* is evaluated and its value returned.
- In either case, *command* (or *alternative.command*) may be a compound R command, with the elementary commands that compose it enclosed in braces and separated by semicolons or new-lines; when a compound command is evaluated, the value returned is the value of its last elementary command.

The if statement is commonly used in writing functions. Here, for example, is a simple function that returns the absolute value of a number:

```
> abs1 <- function(x) if (x < 0) -x else x
> abs1(-5)

[1] 5

> abs1(5)

[1] 5
```

Of course, in a real application we would use the abs function in R for this purpose.

When abs1 is applied to a vector, it does not produce the result that we probably intended, because only the first element in the condition x < 0 is used. In the illustration below, the first element is less than 0, and so the condition evaluates to TRUE; the value returned by the function is therefore the negative of the input vector. A warning message is also printed by R:

```
> abs1(-3:3)   # wrong! the first element, -3, controls the result

[1]  3  2  1  0 -1 -2 -3

Warning message:
In if (x < 0) -x else x :
  the condition has length > 1
  and only the first element will be used
```

The ifelse function in R provides a vectorized conditional, as required here:

```
> abs2 <- function(x) ifelse(x < 0, -x, x)
> abs2(-3:3)

[1] 3 2 1 0 1 2 3
```

The general format of ifelse is

```
ifelse(vector.condition, true.vector, false.vector)
```

The three arguments of ifelse are all vectors of the same length, although a scalar value for *true.vector* or *false.vector* will be extended to the length of *vector.condition*. Wherever an element of *vector.-*

condition is TRUE, the corresponding element of *true.vector* is selected, and where *vector.condition* is FALSE, the corresponding element of *false.vector* is returned.

More complex conditionals can be handled by cascading if/else statements. For example, the following function returns −1, 0, or 1 according to the sign of a number—negative, zero, or positive, respectively:

```
> sign1 <- function(x) {
+     if (x < 0) -1
+        else if (x > 0) 1
+             else 0
+ }
> sign1(-5)

[1] -1
```

Once again, this is an artificial example, because this functionality is provided by the sign function in R.

The same technique may be applied to the ifelse function, for example to provide a vector of signs:

```
> sign2 <- function(x){
+     ifelse (x < 0, -1,
+         ifelse(x > 0, 1, 0))
+ }
> sign2(c(-5, 0, 10))

[1] -1  0  1
```

Alternatively, complex conditionals can be handled by the switch function: for example,

```
> convert2meters <- function(x,
+     units=c("inches", "feet", "yards", "miles")) {
+     units <- match.arg(units)
+     switch(units,
+         inches = x * 0.0254,
+         feet = x * 0.3048,
+         yards = x * 0.9144,
+         miles = x * 1609.344)
+ }
```

The default value of the argument units appears to be a vector of values, c("inches", "feet", "yards", "miles"). The match.arg function in the body of convert2meters, however, selects one of these elements. If the user doesn't specify units, then the first element, in this case "inches", is returned. If the user provides one of the other elements in the list, or an abbreviation that uniquely determines the element, then units is set equal to that value. If the user specifies a value of units that matches *none* of the elements of the default vector, then an error is produced, and so this is a procedure that limits the allowed choices for a function argument.

The switch function picks which branch to execute according to the value of the units argument; for example:

```
> convert2meters(10) # uses "inches" by default

[1] 0.254

> convert2meters(10, "inches") # equivalent to default

[1] 0.254

> convert2meters(3, "feet")

[1] 0.9144

> convert2meters(100, "y") # we can abbreviate values if unique

[1] 91.44

> convert2meters(5, "miles")

[1] 8047

> convert2meters(3, "fathoms")   # produces an error!

Error in match.arg(units) :
  'arg' should be one of "inches", "feet", "yards", "miles"
```

8.3.2 ITERATION (LOOPS)

The `for`, `while`, and `repeat` statements in R are used to implement loops. Consider computing the factorial of a nonnegative integer,

$$n! = n \times (n - 1) \times \cdots \times 2 \times 1 \text{ for } n \geq 1$$
$$0! = 1$$

```
> fact1 <- function(x){
+     if (x <= 1) return(1)
+     f <- 1  # initialize
+     for (i in 1:x) f <- f * i  # accumulate product
+     f  # return result
+ }
> fact1(5)

[1] 120
```

This, too, is an artificial problem: We can calculate the factorial of n very easily in R, as `factorial(n)`; or as `gamma(n + 1)`; or, for $n > 0$, less efficiently as `prod(1:n)`. In `fact1`, we initialize the local variable `f` to 1, then accumulate the factorial product in the loop, and finally implicitly return the accumulated product as the result of the function. It is also possible to return a result explicitly—for example, `return(1)` in the first line of the `fact1` function—which causes execution of the function to cease at that point.

The function `fact1` does not verify that its argument is a nonnegative integer, and so, for example,

```
> fact1(5.2)
```

```
[1] 120
```

returns $5! = 120$ rather than reporting an error. This incorrect result occurs here because `1:5.2` expands to the values `1, 2, 3, 4, 5`, effectively replacing the argument `x=5.2` by truncating to the largest integer less than or equal to `x`. To return an incorrect answer would be unacceptable in a general-purpose program. For a quick-and-dirty program written for our own use, however, this might be acceptable behavior: We would only need to ensure that the argument to the function is always a nonnegative integer.

Here is another version of the program, adding an error check:

```
> fact2 <- function(x) {
+       if ((!is.numeric(x)) || (x != floor(x))
+            || (x < 0) || (length(x) > 1))
+          stop("x must be a non-negative integer")
+       if (x <= 1) return(1)
+       f <- 1  # initialize
+       for (i in 1:x) f <- f * i  # accumulate product
+       f  # return result
+ }
```

```
fact2(5.2)
```

```
Error in fact2(5.2) : x must be a nonnegative integer
```

The function `stop` ends execution of a function immediately and prints its argument as an error message. The double-*or* operator `||` differs from `|` in two respects:

1. `|` applies element-wise to vectors, while `||` takes single-element logical arguments.

2. `||` evaluates its right argument only if its left argument is FALSE. This second characteristic can be exploited to prevent the evaluation of an expression that would otherwise cause an error—for example, in the illustration, `x != floor(x)` is not evaluated if `x` is not numeric.

Analogous comments apply to the double-*and* operator `&&`: The right argument of `&&` is evaluated only if its left argument is TRUE.

The general format of the `for` statement is

```
for (loop.variable in values) command
```

In executing the loop, `loop.variable` successively takes on the values in the vector or list `values`; `command` is usually (but not in the preceding example) a compound command enclosed in braces, `{ }`, and is evaluated each time through the loop using the current value of `loop.variable`.

In contrast, `while` loops iterate (repeat) as long as a specified condition holds true; for example:

```
> fact3 <- function(x){
+     if ((!is.numeric(x)) || (x != floor(x))
+         || (x < 0) || (length(x) > 1))
+       stop("x must be a non-negative integer")
+     i <- f <- 1  # initialize
+     while (i <= x) {
+        f <- f * i  # accumulate product
+        i <- i + 1  # increment counter
+        }
+     f  # return result
+ }
> fact3(5)

[1] 120
```

The indentation of the lines in the function reflects its logical structure, such as the scope of the `while` loop. R does not enforce rules for laying out functions in this manner, but programs are much more readable if the program code is indented to reveal their structure.

The general format of a `while` loop is

$$\text{while } (\textit{logical.condition}) \textit{ command}$$

where `command`, which is typically a compound command and therefore enclosed in braces, is executed as long as `logical.condition` holds.

Finally, `repeat` loops iterate until a `break` is executed, as illustrated in the function `fact4`:

```
> fact4 <- function(x) {
+     if ((!is.numeric(x)) || (x != floor(x))
+         || (x < 0) || (length(x) > 1))
+       stop("x must be a non-negative integer")
+     i <- f <- 1  # initialize
+     repeat {
+        f <- f * i  # accumulate product
+        i <- i + 1  # increment counter
+        if (i > x) break  # termination test
+        }
+     f  # return result
+ }
> fact4(5)

[1] 120
```

The general format of a `repeat` loop is simply

$$\text{repeat } \textit{command}$$

The `command` must be compound, and one of its components must be a termination test, or else the `repeat` could continue forever.

8.3.3 RECURSION

Recursive functions call themselves. Recursion is permissible in R and can provide an elegant alternative to looping. We ignore error checking for clarity:

```
> fact5 <- function(x){
+     if (x <= 1) 1  # termination condition
+     else x * fact5(x - 1)  # recursive call
+ }
> fact5(5)

[1] 120
```

This recursive implementation of the factorial relies on the properties $n! = n \times (n-1)!$ for $n > 1$, and $0! = 1! = 1$. We can use the `trace` function to report the recursive calls, followed by `untrace` to turn off tracing:

```
> trace(fact5)
> fact5(5)

trace: fact5(5)
trace: fact5(x - 1)
trace: fact5(x - 1)
trace: fact5(x - 1)
trace: fact5(x - 1)
[1] 120

> untrace(fact5)
```

A potential pitfall of having a function call itself recursively is that the name of the function can change by assignment (here to `fact6`):

```
> fact6 <- fact5
> remove(fact5)
> fact6(5)  # tries to call the removed fact5

Error in fact6(5) : could not find function "fact5"
```

Consequently, a safer, if less readable, approach is to use the special `Recall` function in place of the function's name to implement the recursive call:

```
> fact7 <- function(x) {
+     if (x <= 1) 1
+     else x * Recall(x - 1)  # recursive call
+ }
> fact7(5)

[1] 120

> fact8 <- fact7
> remove(fact7)
> fact8(5)  # still works with fact7 removed

[1] 120
```

In contexts in which we know that a function will not be renamed, we prefer not to use `Recall`.

8.4   apply and Its Relatives

Avoiding loops and recursion can make R programs more compact, easier to read, and sometimes more efficient in execution. R provides several facilities that we have already encountered—for example, matrix functions and operators, and vectorized functions—that encourage us to write loopless expressions for tasks that might require loops in lower-level programming languages, such as Fortran and C. The apply function, and its relatives lapply, sapply, mapply, and tapply, can also help us avoid loops or recursion. In addition, the Vectorize function uses mapply to create a vectorized version of a function that normally takes scalar arguments.

The apply function invokes or *applies* another function over specified coordinates of an array. Although this is a useful facility for manipulating higher-dimensional arrays, such as multi-way contingency tables, in most instances the array in question is a matrix or data frame, with the latter treated as a matrix.

By way of example, consider the data frame DavisThin in the **car** package. The data represent the responses of 191 subjects to a 7-item *drive for thinness* scale and are part of a larger data set for a study of eating disorders. Each item is scored from 0 to 3, and the scale is to be formed by adding the 7 individual items (DT1 through DT7) for each subject:

```
> head(DavisThin, 10)   # first 10 rows

   DT1 DT2 DT3 DT4 DT5 DT6 DT7
1    0   0   0   0   0   0   0
2    0   0   0   0   0   0   0
3    0   0   0   0   0   0   0
4    0   0   0   0   0   0   0
5    0   0   0   0   0   0   0
6    0   1   0   0   0   0   0
7    0   2   2   0   2   2   0
8    2   3   3   2   3   3   3
9    0   0   0   0   3   0   0
10   3   3   2   1   3   3   0

> dim(DavisThin)

[1] 191   7
```

We can calculate the scale score for each subject by applying the sum function over the rows (the first coordinate) of the data frame:

```
> DavisThin$thin.drive <- apply(DavisThin, 1, sum)
> head(DavisThin$thin.drive, 10)

 [1]  0  0  0  0  0  1  8 19  3 15
```

We have chosen to add a variable called thin.drive to the data frame rather than to define the scale in the working data; consequently, the new eighth column of the data frame is named thin.drive and has values that are the row sums of the preceding seven columns.

Similarly, if we are interested in the column means of the data frame, they may be simply calculated as follows, by averaging over the second (column) coordinate:

```
> apply(DavisThin, 2, mean)

        DT1           DT2          DT3         DT4         DT5         DT6
     0.4660        1.0209       0.9581      0.3403      1.1099      0.9319
        DT7   thin.drive
     0.5654        5.3927
```

In these two simple cases, we can more efficiently use the functions row-Sums and colMeans; for example:

```
> colMeans(DavisThin)

        DT1           DT2          DT3         DT4         DT5         DT6
     0.4660        1.0209       0.9581      0.3403      1.1099      0.9319
        DT7   thin.drive
     0.5654        5.3927
```

There are similar colSums and rowMeans functions.

To extend the example, imagine that some items composing the scale are missing for certain subjects; to simulate this situation, we will eliminate thin.drive from the data frame and arbitrarily replace some of the data with NAs:

```
> DavisThin$thin.drive <- NULL   # remove thin.drive
> DavisThin[1, 2] <- DavisThin[2, 4] <- DavisThin[10, 3] <- NA
> head(DavisThin, 10)

   DT1 DT2 DT3 DT4 DT5 DT6 DT7
1    0  NA   0   0   0   0   0
2    0   0   0  NA   0   0   0
3    0   0   0   0   0   0   0
4    0   0   0   0   0   0   0
5    0   0   0   0   0   0   0
6    0   1   0   0   0   0   0
7    0   2   2   0   2   2   0
8    2   3   3   2   3   3   3
9    0   0   0   0   3   0   0
10   3   3  NA   1   3   3   0
```

If we simply apply sum over the rows of the data frame, then the result will be missing for observations with any missing items, as we can readily verify:

```
> head(apply(DavisThin, 1, sum), 10)

 1  2  3  4  5  6  7  8  9 10
NA NA  0  0  0  1  8 19  3 NA
```

A simple alternative is to average over the items that are present, multiplying the resulting mean by 7 (to restore 0–21 as the range of the scale); this procedure can be implemented by defining an *anonymous function* in the call to apply:

```
> head(apply(DavisThin, 1, function(x) 7*mean(x, na.rm=TRUE)), 10)

    1     2     3     4     5     6     7     8     9    10
 0.00  0.00  0.00  0.00  0.00  1.00  8.00 19.00  3.00 15.17
```

The anonymous function has a single argument that will correspond to a row of the data frame; thus, in this case we compute the mean of the nonmissing values in a row and then multiply by 7, the number of items in the scale. The anonymous function disappears after `apply` is executed.

Suppose that we are willing to work with the average score if more than half of the 7 items are valid but want the scale to be NA if there are 4 or more missing items:

```
> DavisThin[1, 2:5] <- NA  # create more missing data
> head(DavisThin, 10)

   DT1 DT2 DT3 DT4 DT5 DT6 DT7
1    0  NA  NA  NA  NA   0   0
2    0   0   0  NA   0   0   0
3    0   0   0   0   0   0   0
4    0   0   0   0   0   0   0
5    0   0   0   0   0   0   0
6    0   1   0   0   0   0   0
7    0   2   2   0   2   2   0
8    2   3   3   2   3   3   3
9    0   0   0   0   3   0   0
10   3   3  NA   1   3   3   0

> makeScale <- function(items) {
+     if (sum(is.na(items)) >= 4) NA
+     else 7*mean(items, na.rm=TRUE)
+ }
> head(apply(DavisThin, 1, makeScale), 10)

    1     2     3     4     5     6     7     8     9    10
   NA  0.00  0.00  0.00  0.00  1.00  8.00 19.00  3.00 15.17
```

The `lapply` and `sapply` functions are similar to `apply` but reference the successive elements of a list. To illustrate, we convert the data frame `DavisThin` to a list:

```
> thin.list <- as.list(DavisThin)
> str(thin.list)  # structure of the result

List of 7
 $ DT1: int [1:191] 0 0 0 0 0 0 0 2 0 3 ...
 $ DT2: int [1:191] NA 0 0 0 0 1 2 3 0 3 ...
 $ DT3: int [1:191] NA 0 0 0 0 0 2 3 0 NA ...
 $ DT4: int [1:191] NA NA 0 0 0 0 0 2 0 1 ...
 $ DT5: int [1:191] NA 0 0 0 0 0 2 3 3 3 ...
 $ DT6: int [1:191] 0 0 0 0 0 0 2 3 0 3 ...
 $ DT7: int [1:191] 0 0 0 0 0 0 0 3 0 0 ...
```

The list elements are the variables from the data frame. We used `str` (see Section 2.6) to avoid printing the entire contents of `thin.list`. To calculate the mean of each list element eliminating missing data:

```
> lapply(thin.list, mean, na.rm=TRUE)

$DT1
[1] 0.466

$DT2
[1] 1.026

$DT3
[1] 0.9577

$DT4
[1] 0.3439

$DT5
[1] 1.116

$DT6
[1] 0.932

$DT7
[1] 0.5654
```

In this example, and for use with apply as well, the argument na.rm=TRUE
is passed to the mean function, so an equivalent statement would be

```
> lapply(thin.list, function(x) mean(x, na.rm=TRUE))
```

The lapply function returns a list as its result; sapply works similarly,
but tries to simplify the result, in this case returning a vector with named
elements:

```
> sapply(thin.list, mean, na.rm=TRUE)

   DT1    DT2    DT3    DT4    DT5    DT6    DT7
0.4660 1.0263 0.9577 0.3439 1.1158 0.9319 0.5654
```

The mapply function is similar to sapply but is multivariate in the sense
that it processes several vector arguments simultaneously. Consider the
integrate function, which approximates definite integrals numerically and
evaluates an individual integral.[5] The function dnorm computes the density function of a standard-normal random variable. To integrate this function
between -1.96 and 1.96:

```
> (result <- integrate(dnorm, lower=-1.96, upper=1.96))

0.95 with absolute error < 1.0e-11
```

The printed representation of the result of this command is shown above. The
class of the returned value result is "integrate", and it is a list with
five elements:

---

[5]This example is adapted from Ligges and Fox (2008). For readers unfamiliar with calculus, integra-
tion finds areas under curves—in our example, areas under the standard-normal density curve, which
are probabilities.

```
> names(result)

[1] "value"        "abs.error"     "subdivisions" "message"
[5] "call"
```

The element `result$value` contains the value of the integral.

To compute areas under the standard-normal density for a number of intervals—such as the adjacent, nonoverlapping intervals $(-\infty, -3)$, $(-3, -2)$, $(-2, -1)$, $(-1, 0)$, $(0, 1)$, $(1, 2)$, $(2, 3)$, and $(3, \infty)$—we can vectorize the computation with `mapply`:

```
> (low <- c(-Inf, -3:3))

[1] -Inf   -3   -2   -1    0    1    2    3

> (high <- c(-3:3, Inf))

[1]   -3   -2   -1    0    1    2    3  Inf

> (P <- mapply(function(lo, hi) integrate(dnorm, lo, hi)$value,
+      lo=low, hi=high))

[1] 0.00135 0.02140 0.13591 0.34134 0.34134 0.13591 0.02140
[8] 0.00135

> sum(P)

[1] 1
```

This is an artificial example because the vectorized `pnorm` function is perfectly capable of producing the same result:

```
> pnorm(high) - pnorm(low)

[1] 0.00135 0.02140 0.13591 0.34134 0.34134 0.13591 0.02140
[8] 0.00135
```

The `Vectorize` function employs `mapply` to return a vectorized version of a function that otherwise would be capable of handling only scalar arguments. We have to tell `Vectorize` which arguments of the function are to be vectorized. For example, to produce a vectorized version of `integrate`:

```
> Integrate <- Vectorize(
+      function(fn, lower, upper) integrate(fn, lower, upper)$value,
+      vectorize.args=c("lower", "upper")
+      )
> Integrate(dnorm, lower=low, upper=high)

[1] 0.00135 0.02140 0.13591 0.34134 0.34134 0.13591 0.02140
[8] 0.00135
```

Finally, `tapply` (table `apply`) applies a function to each cell of a *ragged array*, containing data for a variable cross-classified by one or more factors. We will use Moore and Krupat's conformity data (from Section 4.2.3) for an example:

```
> some(Moore)   # randomly sample 10 observations

    partner.status conformity fcategory fscore
7             low         12    medium     51
13            low          7       low     28
19            low         23      high     57
20            low         13      high     55
27           high         23       low     15
33           high         15       low     30
36           high         12       low     22
38           high         14    medium     42
39           high         17    medium     41
45           high         15    medium     44
```

The factor `partner.status` has levels `"low"` and `"high"`; the factor `fcategory` has levels `"low"`, `"medium"`, and `"high"`; and the response, `conformity`, is a numeric variable. We may, for example, use `tapply` to calculate the mean `conformity` within each combination of levels of `partner.status` and `fcategory`. We first redefine the factor `fcategory` so that its levels are in their natural order rather than in the default alphabetical order:

```
> Moore$fcategory <- factor(Moore$fcategory,
+     levels=c("high", "medium", "low"))
> with(Moore, tapply(conformity,
+     list(Status=partner.status, Authoritarianism=fcategory), mean))

        Authoritarianism
Status  high medium  low
  high 11.86  14.27 17.4
  low  12.62   7.25  8.9
```

The factors by which to cross-classify the data are given in a list as the second argument to `tapply`; names are supplied optionally for the list elements to label the output. The third argument, the `mean` function, is applied to the values of `conformity` within each combination of levels of `partner.status` and `fcategory`.

8.4.1   TO LOOP OR NOT TO LOOP?

Because R code is executed under the control of the R interpreter rather than compiled into an independently executable program, loops that perform many iterations can consume a great deal of computing time. It is not our object, however, to encourage a neurotic avoidance of loops. The primary goal should be to produce clear, correct, and reasonably efficient R code. It is at times difficult to write vectorized code, and vectorized code may be opaque or may yield a small speed advantage at the cost of a large increase in memory consumption.

If you do use loops in your program, it is advisable to adhere to the following rules:[6]

---

[6]The material in this section is adapted from Ligges and Fox (2008).

INITIALIZE OBJECTS TO FULL LENGTH BEFORE THE LOOP

If an element is to be assigned to an object in each iteration of a loop, and if the final length of that object is known in advance, then the object should be initialized to full length prior to the loop. Otherwise, memory has to be allocated and data copied unnecessarily at each iteration, potentially wasting a great deal of time.

To initialize objects, use functions such as logical, integer, numeric, complex, and character for vectors of different modes, as well as the more general function vector, along with the functions matrix and array.

Consider the following example, in which we introduce three functions, time1, time2, and time3, each assigning values element-wise into an object: For $i = 1, \ldots, n$, the value i^2 is inserted into the ith element of the vector a. In time1, the vector a is built up element by element in a loop:

```
> time1 <- function(n) {  # inefficient!
+      a <- NULL
+      for (i in 1:n) a <- c(a, i^2)
+      a
+ }
> system.time(time1(30000))

   user  system elapsed
  3.664   0.104   3.784
```

Here, we use the system.time function to measure execution time.[7] In time2, the vector a is initialized to full length prior to the loop:

```
> time2 <- function(n) {  # better
+      a <- numeric(n)
+      for (i in 1:n) a[i] <- i^2
+      a
+ }
> system.time(time2(30000))

   user  system elapsed
  0.096   0.000   0.095
```

Finally, in time3, a is created in a vectorized operation (i.e., without a loop):

```
> time3 <- function(n) {  # best
+      a <- (1:n)^2
+      a
+ }
> system.time(time3(30000))

   user  system elapsed
  0.000   0.000   0.001
```

---

[7]The system.time function reports three numbers, all in seconds: *user time* is the time spent executing program instructions, *system time* is the time spent using operating-system services (e.g., file input/output), and *elapsed time* is clock time. Elapsed time is usually approximately equal to, or slightly greater than, the sum of the other two, but because of small measurement errors, this may not be the case.

It is generally advisable to initialize objects to the right length if the length is known in advance. The relative advantage of doing so, however, depends on how much computational time is spent in each loop iteration. Consider the following code, which creates ten thousand 100×100 matrices, each filled with numbers sampled from the standard-normal distribution, and which pertains to an example that we will develop shortly:

```
> system.time({
+     matrices <- vector(mode="list", length=10000)
+     for (i in 1:10000) matrices[[i]] <-
+                             matrix(rnorm(10000), 100, 100)
+ })

   user  system elapsed
 21.669   0.684  22.362
```

In contrast, as we explained, deliberately building up an object piece by piece is much slower, because the entire object is copied at each step. Compare the preceding result with the following code, which, reflecting our impatience, executes only 1,000 rather than 10,000 iterations (and thus, for comparison, the system time should be multiplied by 10):

```
> system.time({  # inefficient!
+     matrices <- list()
+     for (i in 1:1000) matrices <-
+         c(matrices, list(matrix(rnorm(10000), 100, 100)))
+ })

   user  system elapsed
 42.507   0.612  43.119
```

Initializing the list reduces the run time by about 95%.

MOVE COMPUTATIONS OUTSIDE THE LOOP

It is inefficient to perform a computation repeatedly that can be performed once, possibly in a vectorized fashion. Consider the following example, in which we apply a function (here $\sin$) to $i = 1, \ldots, n$ and multiply the results by 2π. Imagine that the $\sin$ function is not vectorized (which, of course, is not the case), so that we need to perform the computation in a loop:

```
> time4 <- function(n) {  # (slightly) inefficient!
+     a <- numeric(n)
+     for (i in 1:n) a[i] <- 2 * pi * sin(i)
+     a
+ }
> system.time(time4(100000))

   user  system elapsed
  0.448   0.000   0.450

> time5 <- function(n) {  # better
+     a <- numeric(n)
+     for (i in 1:n)
```

```
+            a[i] <- sin(i)
+        2 * pi * a
+ }
> system.time(time5(100000))

   user  system elapsed
  0.368   0.000   0.368
```

Saving about 25% in computation time is probably unimportant by itself, but in functions with many steps, savings like this can add up.

DO NOT AVOID LOOPS SIMPLY FOR THE SAKE OF AVOIDING LOOPS

Some time ago, a question was posted to the R-help e-mail list asking how to sum a large number of matrices in a list. To simulate this situation, we will use the list matrices of ten thousand 100×100 matrices that we had created previously. One suggestion was to use a loop to sum the matrices as follows, producing, we claim, simple, straightforward code:

```
> system.time({
>       S <- matrix(0, 100, 100)
>       for (M in matrices) S <- S + M
> })

   user  system elapsed
  0.832   0.148   1.169
```

In response, someone else suggested the following ostensibly cleverer solution, which avoids the loop:

```
> # opaque and wastes memory!
> system.time(S <- apply(array(unlist(matrices),
+       dim = c(100, 100, 10000)), 1:2, sum))

Error: cannot allocate vector of size 762.9 Mb
In addition: Warning messages:
1: In unlist(matrices)  :
  Reached total allocation of 1535Mb: see help(memory.size)
. . .
```

Not only does the second solution fail for a problem of this magnitude on the system on which we tried it, a 32-bit Windows system, but it is also slower on smaller problems. We invite the reader to redo this problem with ten thousand 10×10 matrices, for example.

A final note on the problem:

```
> # opaque & wastes memory!
> S <- rowSums(array(unlist(matrices),
+       dim = c(10, 10, 10000)), dims = 2)
```

is approximately as fast as the loop for the smaller version of the problem but fails on the larger one.

The lesson: Avoid loops when doing so produces clearer and possibly more efficient code, not simply to avoid loops.

8.5   Illustrative R Programs*

With the exception of the introductory `inflPlot` function in Section 8.1, all the preceding programming examples have been trivial; their purpose was transparency. The purpose of the current section is to demonstrate the application of the programming techniques described in this chapter to more complex problems.

8.5.1   BINARY LOGISTIC REGRESSION

Although they are more realistic, the examples in this section are in another sense artificial, because logistic regression is handled perfectly well by the `glm` function (as described in Section 5.3). Indeed, checking results against `glm` will tell us whether our programs work properly.

ESTIMATION BY THE NEWTON-RAPHSON METHOD

Estimation of parameters for GLMs using maximum likelihood is one of many problems that require a numerical algorithm for the maximization. One general technique is called the *Newton-Raphson method*. Suppose that we have a function $g(\beta)$, where β is for now a scalar, and we want to find a value of β that will maximize $g(\beta)$ given a current guess b_t, starting with iteration $t = 0$. The Taylor series approximation to $g(\beta)$ is

$$g(\beta) = g(b_t) + (\beta - b_t)\frac{dg(\beta)}{d\beta} + \frac{1}{2}(\beta - b_t)^2 \frac{d^2g(\beta)}{d\beta^2} + \text{remainder} \quad (8.1)$$

All the derivatives in Equation 8.1 are evaluated at b_t. The Taylor series approximates $g(\beta)$ using the quadratic polynomial in β on the right side of Equation 8.1. The remainder represents the error in approximation. We do this because finding the maximum of a quadratic polynomial when we ignore the remainder is easy: Simply differentiate the right side of Equation 8.1 with respect to β, set the result to 0, and solve to get

$$(\beta - b_t) = \left[-\frac{d^2g(\beta)}{d\beta^2} \right]^{-1} \left[\frac{dg(\beta)}{d\beta} \right]$$

The next iterate, b_{t+1}, is then

$$b_{t+1} = b_t + \left[-\frac{d^2g(\beta)}{d\beta^2} \right]^{-1} \left[\frac{dg(\beta)}{d\beta} \right] \quad (8.2)$$

Provided that the second derivative is negative, b_{t+1} is the new guess at the maximizer of g; we repeat this procedure, stopping when the value of b_{t+1} doesn't change much. The Newton-Raphson algorithm works remarkably well in many statistical problems, especially problems with a well-behaved likelihood like most GLMs.

The generalization of Newton-Raphson to many parameters starts with a vector version of Equation 8.1,

$$g(\boldsymbol{\beta}) = g(\mathbf{b}_t) + (\boldsymbol{\beta} - \mathbf{b}_t)' \frac{\partial g(\boldsymbol{\beta})}{\partial \boldsymbol{\beta}} + \frac{1}{2}(\boldsymbol{\beta} - \mathbf{b}_t)' \frac{\partial^2 g(\boldsymbol{\beta})}{\partial \boldsymbol{\beta}(\partial \boldsymbol{\beta})'}(\boldsymbol{\beta} - \mathbf{b}_t)$$
$$+ \text{remainder} \tag{8.3}$$

again with the derivatives evaluated at $\mathbf{b}_t$. Here, $\boldsymbol{\beta}$ and $\mathbf{b}_t$ are $(k + 1) \times 1$ vectors.[8] The vector of first derivatives in Equation 8.3 is $(k + 1) \times 1$ and is called the *gradient* or *score vector*. The second derivatives multiplied by -1 compose the $(k + 1) \times (k + 1)$ *Hessian matrix*. The Newton-Raphson update is

$$\mathbf{b}_{t+1} = \mathbf{b}_t + \left[-\frac{\partial^2 g(\boldsymbol{\beta})}{\partial \boldsymbol{\beta}(\partial \boldsymbol{\beta})'} \right]^{-1} \left[\frac{\partial g(\boldsymbol{\beta})}{\partial \boldsymbol{\beta}} \right] \tag{8.4}$$

We set $g(\boldsymbol{\beta})$ to be the log-likelihood function evaluated at the data and $\boldsymbol{\beta}$. For the binary logistic-regression model (as presented in Section 5.3), the gradient vector and Hessian matrix are given, respectively, by

$$\text{gradient} = \mathbf{X}'(\mathbf{y} - \mathbf{p}_t)$$
$$= \sum(y_i - p_{it})\mathbf{x}_i \tag{8.5}$$
$$\text{Hessian} = (\mathbf{X}'\mathbf{V}_t\mathbf{X})^{-1} \tag{8.6}$$

where $\mathbf{X}$ is the model matrix, with $\mathbf{x}_i'$ as its ith row; $\mathbf{y}$ is the response vector, containing 0s and 1s, with ith element y_i; $\mathbf{p}_t$ is the vector of fitted response probabilities from the last iteration, the ith entry of which is

$$p_{it} = \frac{1}{1 + \exp(-\mathbf{x}_i'\mathbf{b}_t)}$$

and $\mathbf{V}_t$ is a diagonal matrix, with diagonal entries $p_{it}(1 - p_{it})$. Equation 8.4 becomes

$$\mathbf{b}_{t+1} = \mathbf{b}_t + (\mathbf{X}'\mathbf{V}_t\mathbf{X})^{-1} \mathbf{X}'(\mathbf{y} - \mathbf{p}_t) \tag{8.7}$$

Equation 8.7 is fit repeatedly until $\mathbf{b}_t$ is close enough to $\mathbf{b}_{t-1}$. At convergence, the estimated asymptotic covariance matrix of the coefficients is given by the inverse of the Hessian matrix $(\mathbf{X}'\mathbf{V}\mathbf{X})^{-1}$, which is, conveniently, a by-product of the procedure.

An implementation of Newton-Raphson for the binary logistic-regression problem is shown in Figure 8.3. Input to the function consists of a matrix X of the regressors and a vector y of the 0-1 responses, and so this function works for *binary* logistic regression, not the more general *binomial* logistic regression. The next two arguments control the computation, specifying the maximum number of iterations and a convergence tolerance. Newton-Raphson is remarkably stable for GLMs, and leaving `max.iter` at its default value of

---

[8]We anticipate applications in which $\boldsymbol{\beta}$ is the parameter vector in a regression model with a linear predictor that includes k regressors and a constant.

```
lreg1 <- function(X, y, max.iter=10, tol=1E-6, verbose=FALSE){
   # X is the model matrix
   # y is the response vector of 0s and 1s
   # max.iter is the maximum number of iterations
   # tol is a convergence criterion
   # verbose: show iteration history?
   X <- cbind(1, X)   # add constant
   b <- b.last <- rep(0, ncol(X)) # initialize coefficients
   it <- 1  # initialize iteration counter
   while (it <= max.iter){
      if (verbose) cat("\niteration = ", it, ": ", b)
      p <- as.vector(1/(1 + exp(-X %*% b))) # fitted probabilities
      V <- diag(p * (1 - p))
      var.b <- solve(t(X) %*% V %*% X)   # inverse Hessian
      b <- b + var.b %*% t(X) %*% (y - p)  # update coefficients
      if (max(abs(b-b.last)/(abs(b.last) + 0.01*tol)) < tol) break
      b.last <- b  # update previous coefficients
      it <- it + 1  # increment counter
   }
   if (verbose) cat("\n")  # newline
   if (it > max.iter) warning("maximum iterations exceeded")
   list(coefficients=as.vector(b), var=var.b, iterations=it)
}
```

Figure 8.3   The `lreg1` function implementing the Newton-Raphson algorithm for binary logistic regression.

10 is usually adequate. The final argument is a flag for printing information about the values of the estimated parameters at each iteration, with the default being not to print this information.

The function only fits models with an intercept, and to accomplish this, a vector of 1s is appended to the left of X in the first noncomment line in the function. The next line initializes the current and previous values of b to vectors of 0s. Unlike most problems to which Newton-Raphson is applied, setting the starting values $b_0 = 0$ is good enough to get convergence for most GLMs. The Newton-Raphson algorithm proper is inside the `while` loop. We continue as long as neither convergence nor `max.iter` is reached. If `verbose=TRUE`, the `cat` function is used to print information; \n is the *newline character* and is required because `cat` does not automatically start each printed output on a new line. The remainder of the loop does the computations. The `if` statement is the test for convergence by computing the maximum absolute proportional change in the coefficients and comparing it with the value of `tol`; if convergence is reached, then `break` is executed and the loop is exited.[9] Finally, the returned value is a list with the components `coefficients`, `var` for the inverse of the Hessian, and `it` for the number of iterations required by the computation.

---

[9]The convergence test could be incorporated into the termination condition for the `while` loop, but we wanted to illustrate breaking out of a loop. We invite the reader to reprogram `lreg1` in this manner. Be careful, however, that the loop does not terminate the first time through, because b and b.last both start at **0**.

This function uses both memory and time inefficiently by forming the $n \times n$ diagonal matrix $\mathbf{V}$, even though only its n diagonal elements are nonzero. More efficient versions of the function will be presented later in this chapter (particularly in Section 8.6.2).

To illustrate the application of `lreg1`, we return to Mroz's labor force participation data, employed as an example of logistic regression in Section 5.3:

```
> head(Mroz)   # first 6 observations

  lfp k5 k618 age  wc hc     lwg     inc
1 yes  1    0  32  no no 1.21016 10.910
2 yes  0    2  30  no no 0.32850 19.500
3 yes  1    3  35  no no 1.51413 12.040
4 yes  0    3  34  no no 0.09212  6.800
5 yes  1    2  31 yes no 1.52428 20.100
6 yes  0    0  54  no no 1.55649  9.859
```

The response variable, `lfp`, and two of the predictors, `wc` and `hc`, are factors. Unlike `glm`, the `lreg1` function will not process factors, and so these variables must be converted to numeric dummy regressors (but see Section 8.8, where we explain how to write functions that use R model formulas). This task is easily accomplished with `ifelse` commands:

```
> Mroz$lfp <- with(Mroz, ifelse(lfp == "yes", 1, 0))
> Mroz$wc <- with(Mroz, ifelse(wc == "yes", 1, 0))
> Mroz$hc <- with(Mroz, ifelse(hc == "yes", 1, 0))
> mod.mroz.1 <- with(Mroz, lreg1(cbind(k5, k618, age, wc, hc, lwg,
+      inc), lfp, verbose=TRUE))

iteration =  1 :  0 0 0 0 0 0 0 0
iteration =  2 :  2.57 -1.18 -0.0449 -0.051 0.655 0.0758 0.491 -0.0270
iteration =  3 :  3.13 -1.44 -0.0626 -0.0619 0.795 0.108 0.596 -0.0338
iteration =  4 :  3.18 -1.46 -0.0646 -0.0629 0.807 0.112 0.605 -0.0344
iteration =  5 :  3.18 -1.46 -0.0646 -0.0629 0.807 0.112 0.605 -0.0344
```

Convergence was achieved in five iterations, typical for a GLM. Finally, we extract the coefficients from `mod.mroz.1`, compute their standard errors, and print the coefficients and standard errors as a matrix with two columns:

```
> out <- with(mod.mroz.1,
+      cbind(Estimate=coefficients, "Std. Error"=sqrt(diag(var))))
> rownames(out)[1] <- "Intercept"
> out

          Estimate Std. Error
Intercept  3.18214   0.644375
k5        -1.46291   0.197001
k618      -0.06457   0.068001
age       -0.06287   0.012783
wc         0.80727   0.229980
hc         0.11173   0.206040
lwg        0.60469   0.150818
inc       -0.03445   0.008208
```

We invite the reader to compare these values with those computed by `glm` and reported in Section 5.3 (p. 236).

```
lreg2 <- function(X, y, method="BFGS") {
    X <- cbind(1, X)
    negLogL <- function(b, X, y) {
        p <- as.vector(1/(1 + exp(-X %*% b)))
        - sum(y*log(p) + (1 - y)*log(1 - p))
    }
    grad <- function(b, X, y) {
        p <- as.vector(1/(1 + exp(-X %*% b)))
        - colSums((y - p)*X)
    }
    result <- optim(rep(0, ncol(X)), negLogL, gr=grad,
        hessian=TRUE, method=method, X=X, y=y)
    list(coefficients=result$par, var=solve(result$hessian),
        deviance=2*result$value, converged=result$convergence == 0)
}
```

Figure 8.4 Binary logistic regression using `optim`.

ESTIMATION BY GENERAL OPTIMIZATION

Another approach to fitting the logistic-regression model is to let a general-purpose optimizer do the work of maximizing the log-likelihood,

$$\log_e L = \sum y_i \log_e p_i + (1 - y_i) \log_e (1 - p_i)$$

where, as before, at iteration t, $p_i = 1/[1 + \exp(-\mathbf{x}_i' \mathbf{b}_t)]$ is the fitted probability of response for observation i.

Optimizers work by evaluating the gradient vector of partial derivatives of the log-likelihood at the current estimates of the parameters, iteratively improving the parameter estimates using the information in the gradient. Iteration ceases when the gradient is sufficiently close to **0**. Information from the Hessian may be used as well. Depending on the optimizer, expressions for the gradient and Hessian may be supplied by the user, or these quantities may be approximated numerically by taking differences. If expressions for the derivatives are available, then it can be advantageous to use them, although in complicated problems, writing programs to compute derivatives may introduce errors.

Several general-purpose optimizers are available in the standard R distribution. We will illustrate how to proceed using the `optim` function.[10] By default, `optim` *minimizes* an objective function, and so we work with the *negative* of the log-likelihood, which is half the deviance, and with the negative gradient. The `optim` function will use an analytic gradient if a function is provided to compute it; the formula for the gradient is given in Equation 8.5 (p. 387). Our `lreg2` function, which uses `optim`, is shown in Figure 8.4:

---

[10]In addition to the `optim` function, the standard R distribution includes `nlm` and `nlminb` for general optimization. The functions `constrOptim`, for constrained optimization, and `mle` (in the **stats4** package), for maximum-likelihood estimation, provide front-ends to the `optim` function. The `optimize` function does one-dimensional optimization. Additional optimizers are available in several contributed packages. See the *CRAN Optimization Task View* at `http://cran.r-project.org/web/views/Optimization.html`.

- The negative log-likelihood and the negative gradient are defined as *local functions*, negLogL and grad, respectively. Like local variables, local functions exist only within the function in which they are defined.
- Even though X and y are local variables in lreg2, they are passed as arguments to negLogL and grad, along with the parameter vector b. This is not strictly necessary (see the discussion of lexical scoping in R in Section 8.9), but doing so allows us to show how to pass additional arguments through the optimizer.
- The optim function in R provides several general optimizers. We have had good luck with the BFGS method for this kind of problem, and consequently, we have made this the default, but by providing a method argument to lreg2 and passing this argument down to optim, we also have made it easy for the user of lreg2 to substitute another method. See ?optim for details.
  - The first argument to optim gives starting values for the parameter estimates, in this case a vector of 0s.
  - The second argument gives the *objective function* to be minimized, the local function negLogL, and the third argument gives the gradient, gr=grad. The first argument of the objective function and gradient must be the parameter vector—b in this example. If the gradient is not given as an argument, optim will compute it numerically.
  - Specifying hessian=TRUE asks optim to return the Hessian, the inverse of which provides the estimated covariance matrix of the coefficients. The Hessian is computed numerically: optim does not allow us to supply an expression for the Hessian. Because we know the Hessian from Equation 8.6 (p. 387), we could have computed it outside of lreg2, but in many optimization problems the Hessian will be much more complicated, and letting the optimizer approximate it numerically is usually a reasonable approach.
  - As explained, the method argument specifies the optimization method to be employed.
  - The two remaining arguments, the model matrix X and the response vector y, are passed by optim to negLogL and grad.
- optim returns a list with several components. We pick out and return the parameter estimates, the Hessian, the value of the objective function at the minimum (which is used to compute the deviance), and a code indicating whether convergence has been achieved.

Trying out lreg2 on Mroz's data produces the following results:

```
> mod.mroz.2 <- with(Mroz, lreg2(cbind(k5, k618, age, wc, hc, lwg,
+      inc), lfp))
> mod.mroz.2$coefficients

[1]  3.18211 -1.46290 -0.06457 -0.06287  0.80727  0.11173  0.60469
[8] -0.03445
```

```
> sqrt(diag(mod.mroz.2$var))
```

```
[1] 0.644443 0.197001 0.068000 0.012786 0.229980 0.206039 0.150817
[8] 0.008209
```

```
> mod.mroz.2$converged
```

```
[1] TRUE
```

One interesting feature of the lreg2 function in Figure 8.4 is that no explicit error checking is performed. Even so, if errors are committed, error messages will be printed. For example, suppose that we replace the response variable, lfp, by a character vector with "yes" and "no" elements:

```
> Mroz$LFP <- ifelse(Mroz$lfp==0, "no", "yes")
```

Trying to use this character variable as the response produces an error:

```
> mod.mroz.2a <- with(Mroz, lreg2(cbind(k5, k618, age, wc, hc, lwg,
+       inc), LFP))
```

```
Error in y * log(p) : non-numeric argument to binary operator
```

The functions called by lreg2 do check for input errors, and in this case, the error occurred when the negLogL function was first executed by optim. The error message was informative, but unless we build in our own error checking, we can sometimes produce very obscure error messages.

ESTIMATION BY ITERATED WEIGHTED LEAST SQUARES

A third approach to the problem, which we will leave as an exercise for the reader, is to use IWLS to compute the logistic-regression coefficients, as glm does. The relevant formulas for binomial logistic regression are given in Section 5.12. For GLMs with canonical link functions, which includes logistic regression, IWLS provides identical updates to Newton-Raphson (McCullagh and Nelder, 1989, p. 43).

8.5.2   NUMBERS INTO WORDS

The program described in this section, which is adapted from Fox (2005a), originated in a question to the R-help e-mail list asking how to translate numbers into English words. The program that we develop in response to the question exemplifies the divide-and-conquer strategy of recursion.

The numbers from *one* to *nineteen* are represented by individual words; the numbers from *twenty-one* to *ninety-nine* are formed as compound words, with components for the tens and units digits—with the exception of multiples of ten (*twenty*, *thirty*, etc.), which are single words. The *Chicago Manual of Style* tells us that these compound words should be hyphenated. Numbers from 100 to 999 are written by tacking on a phrase such as "six hundred", at the left— that is, composed of a number from *one* to *nine* plus the suffix *hundred* (and there is no hyphen). Above this point, additional terms are added at the left, representing multiples of powers of 1,000. In American English, the first few powers of 1,000 have the following names, to be used as suffixes:

$$1000^1 \quad \textit{thousand}$$
$$1000^2 \quad \textit{million}$$
$$1000^3 \quad \textit{billion}$$
$$1000^4 \quad \textit{trillion}$$

Thus, for example, the number 210,363,258 would be rendered "two hundred ten million, three hundred sixty-three thousand, two hundred fifty-eight." There really is no point in going beyond trillions, because the double-precision floating-point numbers used by R can represent integers exactly only to about 15 decimal digits, or hundreds of trillions (see Section 2.6.2). Of course, we could allow numbers to be specified optionally by arbitrarily long character strings of numerals (e.g., "210363258347237492310"). We leave that approach as an exercise for the reader: It would not be difficult to extend our program in this manner by allowing the user to specify the additional necessary suffixes (quadrillions, quintillions, etc.).

One approach to converting numbers into words would be to manipulate the numbers as integers, but it seems simpler to convert numbers into character strings of numerals, which can then be split into individual characters: (1) larger integers can be represented exactly as double-precision floating-point numbers rather than as integers in R; (2) it is easier to manipulate the individual numerals than to perform repeated integer arithmetic to extract digits; and (3) having the numerals in character form allows us to take advantage of R's ability to index vectors by element names, as we will describe shortly.

We therefore define the following function to convert a number into a vector of characters containing the numerals composing the number. The function first converts the number into a character string with `as.character` and then uses `strsplit` to divide the result into separate characters, one for each digit.

```
> makeDigits <- function(x) strsplit(as.character(x), "")[[1]]
```

Here are some examples of the use of this function:

```
> makeDigits(123456)

[1] "1" "2" "3" "4" "5" "6"

> makeDigits(-123456)

[1] "-" "1" "2" "3" "4" "5" "6"

> makeDigits(1000000000)

[1] "1" "e" "+" "0" "9"
```

The second and third examples reveal that `makeDigits` has problems with negative numbers and with large numbers that R renders in scientific notation. By setting the `scipen` (scientific-notation penalty) option to a large number, we can avoid the second problem:

```
> options(scipen=100)
> makeDigits(1000000000)

 [1] "1" "0" "0" "0" "0" "0" "0" "0" "0" "0"
```

It is also useful to have a function that converts a vector of numerals in character form back into a number:

```
> makeNumber <- function(x) as.numeric(paste(x, collapse=""))
> makeNumber(c("1", "2", "3", "4", "5"))

[1] 12345
```

We next construct several vectors of number words:

```
> ones <- c("zero", "one", "two", "three", "four", "five", "six",
+     "seven", "eight", "nine")
> teens <- c("ten", "eleven", "twelve", "thirteen", "fourteen",
+     "fifteen", "sixteen", " seventeen", "eighteen", "nineteen")
> names(ones) <- names(teens) <- 0:9
> tens <- c("twenty", "thirty", "forty", "fifty", "sixty",
+     "seventy", "eighty", "ninety")
> names(tens) <- 2:9
> suffixes <- c("thousand,", "million,", "billion,", "trillion,")
```

The vector of suffixes includes a comma after each word.

Because the names of the elements of the first three vectors are numerals, they can be conveniently indexed: for example,

```
> ones["5"]

     5
"five"

> teens["3"]

       3
"thirteen"

> tens["7"]

       7
"seventy"
```

Figure 8.5 lists a function for converting a single integer into words; we have added line numbers to make it easier to describe how the function works. First, here are some examples of its use:

```
> number2words(123456789)

[1] "one hundred twenty-three million,
      four hundred fifty-six thousand,
      seven hundred eighty-nine"

> number2words(-123456789)
```

```
[ 1]   number2words <- function(x){
[ 2]       negative <- x < 0
[ 3]       x <- abs(x)
[ 4]       digits <- makeDigits(x)
[ 5]       nDigits <- length(digits)
[ 6]       result <- if (nDigits == 1) as.vector(ones[digits])
[ 7]       else if (nDigits == 2)
[ 8]           if (x <= 19) as.vector(teens[digits[2]])
[ 9]               else trim(paste(tens[digits[1]], "-", ones[digits[2]], sep=""))
[10]       else if (nDigits == 3) {
[11]           tail <- makeNumber(digits[2:3])
[12]           if (tail == 0) paste(ones[digits[1]], "hundred")
[13]           else trim(paste(ones[digits[1]], "hundred", number2words(tail)))
[14]       }
[15]       else {
[16]           nSuffix <- ((nDigits + 2) %/% 3) - 1
[17]           if (nSuffix > length(suffixes) || nDigits > 15)
[18]               stop(paste(x, "is too large!"))
[19]           pick <- 1:(nDigits - 3*nSuffix)
[20]           trim(paste(number2words(makeNumber(digits[pick])),
[21]               suffixes[nSuffix], number2words(makeNumber (digits[-pick]))))
[22]       }
[23]       if (negative) paste("minus", result) else result
[24]   }
[25]   trim <- function(text){
[26]       gsub("(^\ *)|((\ *|-|,\ zero|-zero)$)", "", text)
[27]   }
```

Figure 8.5   The number2words function.

```
[1] "minus one hundred twenty-three million,
    four hundred fifty-six,
    thousand seven hundred eighty-nine"

> number2words(-123456000)

[1] "minus one hundred twenty-three million,
    four hundred fifty-six thousand"
```

The first five lines of the function are essentially self-explanatory. The rest of the function probably requires some explanation, however:

[6]   If the number is composed of a single digit, then we can find the answer by simply indexing into the vector ones; the function as.-vector is used to remove the name (i.e., the numeral used as a label) of the selected element.

[7-9]   If the number is composed of two digits and is less than or equal to 19, then we can get the answer by indexing into teens with the last digit (i.e., the second element of the digits vector). If the number is 20 or larger, then we need to attach the tens digit to the ones digit, with a hyphen in between. If, however, the ones digit is 0, ones["0"] is "zero", and thus we have an embarrassing result, such as "twenty-zero". More generally, the program can produce spurious hyphens,

commas, spaces, and the strings ", zero" and "-zero". Our solution is to write a function `trim` to remove the unwanted characters. The `trim` function on lines [25-27] makes use of R's ability to manipulate text by processing *regular expressions* (see Section 2.4).

[10-14] If the number consists of three digits, then the first digit is used for hundreds, and the remaining two digits can be processed as an ordinary two-digit number. This is done by a recursive call to `number2words`, unless the last two digits are both 0, in which case, we don't need to convert them into words. The hundreds digit is then pasted onto the representation of the last two digits, and the result is trimmed. The `makeNumber` function is used to put the last two digits back into a number (assigned to the variable `tail`). We do not bother to use the `Recall` mechanism for a recursive function call because eventually `number2words` will become a local function, which is therefore not in danger of being renamed.

[15-22] If the number contains more than three digits, then we are in the realm of thousands, millions, and so on. The computation on line [16] determines with which power of 1,000 we are dealing. Then, if the number is not too large, the appropriate digits are stripped off from the left of the number and attached to the proper suffix; the remaining digits to the right are recomposed into a number and processed with a recursive call, to be attached at the right.

[23] Finally, if the original number was negative, then the word "minus" is pasted onto the front before the result is returned.

Figure 8.6 displays a function, called `numbers2words`, that adds some bells and whistles. The various vectors of names are defined locally in the function; the utility functions `trim`, `makeNumber`, and `makeDigits` are similarly defined as local functions; and the function `number2words`, renamed `helper`, is also made local. Using a helper function rather than a direct recursive call permits efficient vectorization, via `sapply`, at the end of `numbers2words`. Were `numbers2words` to call itself recursively, the local definitions of objects (such as the vector `ones` and the function `trim`) would be recomputed at each call, rather than only once. Because of R's lexical scoping (see Section 8.9), objects defined in the environment of `numbers2words` are visible to `helper`.

The function `numbers2words` includes a couple of additional features. First, according to the *Oxford English Dictionary*, the definition of "billion" differs in the United States and (traditionally) in Britain: "1. orig. and still commonly in Great Britain: A million millions. (= U.S. trillion.) ... 2. In U.S., and increasingly in Britain: A thousand millions." Thus, if the argument `billion` is set to "UK", a different vector of suffixes is used. Moreover, provision is made to avoid awkward translations that repeat the word "million," such as "five thousand million, one hundred million, ...," which is instead, and more properly, rendered as "five thousand, one hundred million, ..."

```
numbers2words <- function(x, billion=c("US", "UK"),
    and=if (billion == "US") "" else "and") {
    billion <- match.arg(billion)
    trim <- function(text){
        gsub("(^\ *)|((\ *|-|,\ zero|-zero)$)", "", text)
    }
    makeNumber <- function(x) as.numeric(paste(x, collapse=""))
    makeDigits <- function(x) strsplit(as.character(x), "")[[1]]
    helper <- function(x) {
        negative <- x < 0
        x <- abs(x)
        digits <- makeDigits(x)
        nDigits <- length(digits)
        result <- if (nDigits == 1) as.vector(ones[digits])
            else if (nDigits == 2)
                if (x <= 19) as.vector(teens[digits[2]])
                    else trim(paste(tens[digits[1]], "-", ones[digits[2]],
                    sep=""))
            else if (nDigits == 3) {
                tail <- makeNumber(digits[2:3])
                if (tail == 0) paste(ones[digits[1]], "hundred")
                    else trim(paste(ones[digits[1]], trim(paste("hundred",and)),
                        helper(tail)))
            }
            else {
                nSuffix <- ((nDigits + 2) %/% 3) - 1
                if (nSuffix > length(suffixes) || nDigits > 15)
                    stop(paste(x, "is too large!"))
                pick <- 1:(nDigits - 3*nSuffix)
                trim(paste(helper(makeNumber(digits[pick])),
                    suffixes[nSuffix], helper(makeNumber(digits[-pick]))))
            }
        if (billion == "UK"){
            words <- strsplit(result, " ")[[1]]
            if (length(grep("million,", words)) > 1)
                result <- sub(" million, ", ", ", result)
        }
        if (negative) paste("minus", result) else result
    }
    opts <- options(scipen=100)
    on.exit(options(opts))
    ones <- c("zero", "one", "two", "three", "four", "five", "six", "seven",
        "eight", "nine")
    teens <- c("ten", "eleven", "twelve", "thirteen", "fourteen", "fifteen",
        "sixteen", " seventeen", "eighteen", "nineteen")
    names(ones) <- names(teens) <- 0:9
    tens <- c("twenty", "thirty", "forty", "fifty", "sixty", "seventy",
            "eighty", "ninety")
    names(tens) <- 2:9
    suffixes <- if (billion == "US")
                    c("thousand,", "million,", "billion,", "trillion,")
                else
                    c("thousand,", "million,", "thousand million,", "billion,")
    x <- round(x)
    if (length(x) > 1) sapply(x, helper) else helper(x)
}
```

Figure 8.6   The numbers2words function.

Second, we understand that outside North America, it is common to write or say a number such as 101 as "one hundred and one" rather than as "one hundred one." We have therefore included another argument, called `and`, which is pasted into the number at the appropriate point. By default, this argument is set to `" "` when `billion` is `"US"` and to `"and"` when `billion` is `"UK"`. Here are some examples:

```
> numbers2words(c(1234567890123, -0123, 1000))

[1] "one trillion, two hundred thirty-four billion,
        five hundred sixty-seven million,
        eight hundred ninety thousand,
        one hundred twenty-three"
[2] "minus one hundred twenty-three"
[3] "one thousand"


> numbers2words(c(1234567890123, -0123, 1000), billion="UK")

[1] "one billion, two hundred and thirty-four thousand,
        five hundred and sixty-seven million,
        eight hundred and ninety thousand,
        one hundred and twenty-three"
[2] "minus one hundred and twenty-three"
[3] "one thousand"


> numbers2words(c(1234567890123, -0123, 1000), and="and")

[1] "one trillion, two hundred and thirty-four billion,
        five hundred and sixty-seven million,
        eight hundred and ninety thousand,
        one hundred and twenty-three"
[2] "minus one hundred and twenty-three"
[3] "one thousand"
```

Finally, another challenge to the reader. At present, `numbers2words` rounds its input to whole numbers. Modify the program so that it takes a `digits` argument (with default 0), giving the number of places to the right of the decimal point to which numbers are to be rounded, and then make provision for translating such numbers (e.g., `1234567.890`) into words.

8.6   Improving R Programs*

Computer programs are written by people, and people often make mistakes and poor choices.[11] Programming in R is no exception to this rule. This section consequently takes up two related topics: (1) debugging, that is, locating and fixing errors; and (2) measuring the execution time and memory usage of programs to improve their efficiency.

---

[11]Lest we be accused of cynicism, let us explain that we extrapolate here from our own experience.

```
# bugged!
lreg3 <- function(X, y, max.iter=10, tol=1E-6, verbose=FALSE) {
    X <- cbind(1, X)
    b <- b.last <- rep(0, ncol(X))
    it <- 1
    while (it <= max.iter){
        if (verbose) cat("\niteration = ", it, ": ", b)
        p <- 1/(1 + exp(-X %*% b))
        V <- diag(p * (1 - p))
        var.b <- solve(t(X) %*% V %*% X)
        b <- b + var.b %*% t(X) %*% (y - p)
        if (max(abs(b - b.last)/(abs(b.last) + 0.01*tol)) < tol) break
        b.last <- b
        it <- it + 1
    }
    if (it > max.iter) warning("maximum iterations exceeded")
    if (verbose) cat("\n")
    list(coefficients=as.vector(b), var=var.b, iterations=it)
}
```

Figure 8.7   The bugged `lreg3` function.

8.6.1 DEBUGGING R CODE

R offers several effective facilities for debugging programs using the `browser` command. The `browser` function halts the execution of an R program and allows the programmer to examine the values of local variables. The `browser` function can be invoked directly by inserting calls to `browser` in the function code or indirectly via the `debug` and `debugger` commands.

To see how all this works, consider the flawed version of the logistic-regression function `lreg1` (introduced in Figure 8.3, p. 388), named `lreg3` and shown in Figure 8.7. Before proceeding, we invite readers to examine this function to see whether they can spot the error, and lest you think that this example is artificial, the bug in `lreg3` was present when we first wrote `lreg1`.

Trying `lreg3` produces the following error:

```
> mod.mroz.1b <- with(Mroz,
    lreg3(cbind(k5, k618, age, wc, hc, lwg, inc), lfp))

Error in t(X) %*% V : non-conformable arguments
```

The `traceback` function supplies a little more information about the context of the error:

```
> traceback()

6: solve(t(X) %*% V %*% X)
5: lreg3(cbind(k5, k618, age, wc, hc, lwg, inc), lfp)
4: eval(expr, envir, enclos)
3: eval(substitute(expr), data, enclos = parent.frame())
2: with.default(Mroz, lreg3(cbind(k5, k618, age, wc, hc, lwg, inc),
      lfp))
1: with(Mroz, lreg3(cbind(k5, k618, age, wc, hc, lwg, inc), lfp))
```

```
# still bugged!
lreg3 <- function(X, y, max.iter=10, tol=1E-6, verbose=FALSE) {
    X <- cbind(1, X)
    b <- b.last <- rep(0, ncol(X))
    it <- 1
    while (it <= max.iter){
        if (verbose) cat("\niteration = ", it, ": ", b)
        p <- 1/(1 + exp(-X %*% b))
        V <- diag(p * (1 - p))
      browser()
        var.b <- solve(t(X) %*% V %*% X)
        b <- b + var.b %*% t(X) %*% (y - p)
        if (max(abs(b - b.last)/(abs(b.last)+0.01*tol)) < tol) break
        b.last <- b
        it <- it + 1
      }
    if (it > max.iter) warning("maximum iterations exceeded")
    if (verbose) cat("\n")
    list(coefficients=as.vector(b), var=var.b, iterations=it)
}
```

Figure 8.8   The bugged `lreg3` function, with a call to `browser` inserted.

The problem is apparently in the command `var.b <- solve(t(X) %*% V %*% X)` in `lreg3`, but what exactly is wrong here was not immediately clear to us.

Using an editor or the `fix` function, we insert a call to `browser` immediately before the error, as shown in Figure 8.8. We have "outdented" the line containing the call to `browser` to help us remember to remove it after the function is debugged. Executing the function now causes it to pause before the offending line:

```
> mod.mroz.1b <- with(Mroz,
+       lreg3(cbind(k5, k618, age, wc, hc, lwg, inc), lfp))

Called from: lreg3(cbind(k5, k618, age, wc, hc, lwg, inc), lfp)
Browse[1]>
```

The `Browse[1]>` prompt indicates that the interpreter is waiting for input in browser mode. We can type the names of local variables to examine their contents or, indeed, evaluate any R expression in the environment of the `lreg3` function; for example, entering the `objects()` command would list the function's local objects. We can also type any of several special browser commands followed by the Enter key:

- c, cont, or just Enter: Continue execution. In our case, this would simply result in the original error.
- n: Enter a step-by-step debugger, in which the function continues execution one line at a time, as if a call to `browser` were inserted before each subsequent line. In the step-by-step debugger, the meaning of the c and cont browser commands changes: Rather than execution continuing to the end of the function, it instead continues to the end of

the current context—essentially the next right brace } —such as the end of a loop. Moreover, n and the Enter key simply execute the next command.

- where: Indicates where execution has stopped in the stack of pending function calls—similar to the output produced by traceback.
- Q: Quit execution of the function, and return to the R command prompt.

One complication: If you want to examine a variable named c, cont, n, where, or Q, you will have to enclose it in an explicit call to print, for example, print(n).

In the current case, we want to discover why t(X) and V are not conformable for matrix multiplication, and so we examine these local variables; because both should be large, we use str (see Section 2.6):

```
Browse[1]> objects() # in local environment of lreg3

[1] "b"        "b.last"    "it"    "max.iter" "p"        "tol"
[7] "V"        "verbose"   "X"     "y"

Browse[1]> str(X)

num [1:753, 1:8] 1 1 1 1 1 1 1 1 1 1 ...
- attr(*, "dimnames")=List of 2
  ..$ : NULL
  ..$ : chr [1:8] "" "k5" "k618" "age" ...
```

As expected, X is a 753 × 8 matrix. We next examine V:

```
Browse[1]> str(V)

num 0.25
```

Unexpectedly, V is a single number (0.25) rather than a 753×753 ($n \times n$) diagonal matrix. To understand why V was not computed correctly, we proceed to evaluate commands in the environment of the stopped function; V is simply diag(p*(1 - p)), and so we take a look at p and p*(1 - p):

```
Browse[1]> str(p)

num [1:753, 1] 0.5 0.5 0.5 0.5 0.5 0.5 0.5 0.5 0.5 0.5 ...

Browse[1]> str(p * (1 - p))

num [1:753, 1] 0.25 0.25 0.25 0.25 0.25 0.25 0.25 0.25 0.25 0.25 ...
```

The source of the problem is now clear: p is a 753×1 matrix, not a vector, and thus p*(1 - p) is also a 753×1 matrix. In some instances, R treats vectors and single-row or single-column matrices differently, and this is one of those cases. The diag function applied to a vector of length n returns an $n \times n$ diagonal matrix, while the diag function applied to an $n \times 1$ or $1 \times n$ matrix returns the "diagonal" of the matrix, which is just the [1, 1] element. The solution is to coerce the product to a vector, `p <- as.vector(1/(1 + exp(-X %*% b)))`, returning us to the correct definition of `lreg1` (in Figure 8.3, p. 388).

As an alternative to inserting calls to `browser` into the source code of a function, we can instead invoke the `debug` function—for example, `debug(lreg3)`. When we next execute `lreg3`, we can use the step-by-step debugger commands to move through it, examining the values of local variables, and so on, as we proceed.

Another alternative to inserting calls to `browser` is to set the `error` option to `dump.frames`. We can subsequently use the postmortem `debugger` function to examine the local state of a program at the point of an error. In the current illustration, a dialog with `debugger` might begin as follows:

```
> options(error=dump.frames)
> mod.mroz.1b <- with(Mroz,
+       lreg3(cbind(k5, k618, age, wc, hc, lwg, inc), lfp))

Error in t(X) %*% V : non-conformable arguments
> debugger()
Message:  Error in t(X) %*% V : non-conformable arguments
Available environments had calls:
1: with(Mroz, lreg3(cbind(k5, k618, age, wc, hc, lwg, inc), lfp))
2: with.default(Mroz,
       lreg3(cbind(k5, k618, age, wc, hc, lwg, inc), lfp))
3: eval(substitute(expr), data, enclos = parent.frame())
4: eval(expr, envir, enclos)
5: lreg3(cbind(k5, k618, age, wc, hc, lwg, inc), lfp)
6: solve(t(X) %*% V %*% X)

Enter an environment number, or 0 to exit   Selection: 5

Browsing in the environment with call:
   lreg3(cbind(k5, k618, age, wc, hc, lwg, inc), lfp)
Called from: debugger.look(ind)

Browse[1]> str(X)

 num [1:753, 1:8] 1 1 1 1 1 1 1 1 1 1 ...
 - attr(*, "dimnames")=List of 2
  ..$ : NULL
  ..$ : chr [1:8] "" "k5" "k618" "age" ...

Browse[1]> str(V)

 num 0.25

Browse[1]> Q
```

Very similar results are obtained by setting `options(error=recover)`; see `?recover` for details.

8.6.2 PROFILING R FUNCTIONS

Now that the `lreg1` function is working again, we can reasonably consider its efficiency in the use of computing time and memory. As before, we employ the `system.time` command to compare the time required by `lreg1` (in Figure 8.3, p. 388), `lreg2` (in Figure 8.4, p. 390), and `glm`. To provide a meaningful comparison of the three functions, we begin by constructing a suitably large logistic-regression problem, with 5,000 observations and 10 explanatory variables, which is about as big as `lreg1` can handle on the 32-bit Windows machine on which these timings were performed. This is in itself problematic, because a logistic regression with 5,000 observations and 10 explanatory variables is not a very big problem—but more about that later.

```
> set.seed(12345)  # for reproducibility
> X <- matrix(rnorm(5000*10), 5000, 10)
> y <- rbinom(5000, 1,
+         prob=1/(1 + exp(- cbind(1, X) %*% rep(1, 11))))
```

The values of the explanatory variables (in X) are generated by sampling independently from the standard-normal distribution, and the value of the response (y) is generated according to a logistic-regression equation in which all the regression coefficients, including the constant, are equal to 1.

The timings proceed as follows:

```
> system.time(mod.1 <- lreg1(X, y))

   user  system elapsed
   7.78    2.59   10.48

> mod.1$coef

[1] 1.1194903 1.0927021 1.0320458 1.0694751 0.9978092 0.9832376
[7] 0.9575331 1.1162508 1.0137408 1.1149053 1.1113571


> system.time(mod.2 <- lreg2(X, y))

   user  system elapsed
   0.35    0.08    0.42


> mod.2$coef

[1] 1.1194897 1.0927029 1.0320447 1.0694760 0.9978114 0.9832366
[7] 0.9575326 1.1162490 1.0137425 1.1149041 1.1113554


> system.time(mod.glm <- glm(y ~ X, family=binomial))

   user  system elapsed
   0.11    0.02    0.12

> coef(mod.2)

[1] 1.1194897 1.0927029 1.0320447 1.0694760 0.9978114 0.9832366
[7] 0.9575326 1.1162490 1.0137425 1.1149041 1.1113554
```

The three functions produce the same answer within rounding error, and the estimated regression coefficients are all close to 1, as anticipated, but lreg1 is extremely inefficient relative to the other two functions.

The Rprof function *profiles* R code; that is, it provides an accounting of where a function spends its time and where it allocates memory. Profiling is not infallible, but it generally helps locate bottlenecks in execution time and problematic memory use. Profiling lreg1 produces these results:

```
> (tmp <- tempfile()) # create temporary file

[1] "c:\\temp\\Rtmpf05glc\\file460110d"

> Rprof(tmp, memory.profiling=TRUE) # turn on profiling
> mod.1 <- lreg1(X, y)
> Rprof() # turn off profiling
> summaryRprof(tmp, memory="both") # summarize results

$by.self
        self.time self.pct total.time total.pct mem.total
array        8.06     73.1       8.06      73.1     334.0
diag         1.72     15.6       9.80      88.9     453.3
%*%          1.20     10.9       1.20      10.9       0.8
+            0.02      0.2       0.02       0.2       0.0
t            0.02      0.2       0.02       0.2       0.0
lreg1        0.00      0.0      11.02     100.0     454.1
solve        0.00      0.0       1.22      11.1       0.8

$by.total
        total.time total.pct mem.total self.time self.pct
lreg1        11.02     100.0     454.1      0.00      0.0
diag          9.80      88.9     453.3      1.72     15.6
array         8.06      73.1     334.0      8.06     73.1
solve         1.22      11.1       0.8      0.00      0.0
%*%           1.20      10.9       0.8      1.20     10.9
+             0.02       0.2       0.0      0.02      0.2
t             0.02       0.2       0.0      0.02      0.2

$sampling.time
[1] 11.02

> unlink(tmp) # delete temporary file
```

Profiling is started by a call to the Rprof function. Rprof interrupts the execution of lreg1 at regular intervals, with a default of 20 milliseconds; writes information about the current state of the computation to a file; and optionally tracks changes in memory allocation. A second call to Rprof turns off profiling. The summaryRprof function summarizes the time and memory audit created by Rprof.

In our example, we use the tempfile command to create a temporary file to hold the results; this file can grow very large for a lengthy computation and is later deleted by the unlink function. The argument memory="both" to summaryRprof asks for a summary of all memory allocated in each function call. The summaryRprof command reports several kinds of information:

```
lreg4 <- function(X, y, max.iter=10, tol=1E-6) {
    X <- cbind(1, X)
    b <- b.last <- rep(0, ncol(X))
    it <- 1
    while (it <= max.iter){
        p <- as.vector(1/(1 + exp(-X %*% b)))
        var.b <- solve(crossprod(X, p * (1 - p) * X))
        b <- b + var.b %*% crossprod(X, y - p)
        if (max(abs(b - b.last)/(abs(b.last) + 0.01*tol))<tol) break
        b.last <- b
        it <- it + 1
    }
    if (it > max.iter) warning("maximum iterations exceeded")
    list(coefficients=as.vector(b), var=var.b, iterations=it)
}
```

Figure 8.9 Another modification of `lreg1`, without computing the diagonal matrix `V`.

- `total.time`: The time in seconds spent in each function, including the time spent in functions called by that function.
- `total.pct`: The percentage of total time spent in each function, again including the time spent in functions called by the function.
- `self.time`: The time spent in each function exclusive of the time spent in functions called by the function.
- `self.pct`: The percentage of total time spent exclusively in each function; these percentages should sum to 100.
- `mem.total`: The total amount of memory, in megabytes, allocated in each function.

The list returned by `summaryRprof` contains three elements: sorting the results by `self.time` and by `total.time`, and indicating the total execution time (`sampling.time`). The results are incomplete in the sense that not every function called in the course of the computation is represented; for example, `cbind` is missing. If we decreased the sampling interval, then we would obtain a more complete accounting, but if the interval is made too short, the results can become inaccurate. As we would expect, 100% of the time is spent in the `lreg1` function and in the functions that it calls. Beyond that observation, it is clear that most of the time, and almost all the memory, is consumed by the computation of the diagonal matrix `V`. Because all the off-diagonal entries of this $n \times n$ matrix are 0, repeatedly forming the matrix and using it in matrix multiplication are wasteful in the extreme.

Figure 8.9 displays a version of the logistic-regression function that avoids forming `V` and that also substitutes the slightly more efficient function `crossprod` for some of the matrix multiplications:[12]

```
> system.time(mod.1c <- lreg4(X, y))

   user   system  elapsed
  0.024   0.000    0.026
```

---

[12] `crossprod` multiplies its second argument on the left by the transpose of its first argument.

```
> mod.1c$coef
```

```
[1] 1.1195 1.0927 1.0320 1.0695 0.9978 0.9832 0.9575 1.1163
[9] 1.0137 1.1149 1.1114
```

Here is how `lreg4` works: Because **V** is a diagonal matrix, the product **VX** is a matrix the same size as **X** whose *i*th row is the product of the *i*th diagonal element of **V** and the *i*th row of **X**. We can therefore compute $\mathbf{X'VX} = \mathbf{X'(VX)}$ without actually forming **V**, instead using only its diagonal elements. Our redesigned `lreg4` function is not only much faster than the original `lreg1`, it is also faster than `glm` for this problem. The amount of memory used is drastically reduced as well:

```
> tmp <- tempfile()
> Rprof(tmp, memory.profiling=TRUE, interval=0.002)
> mod.1c <- lreg4(X, y)
> Rprof()
> summaryRprof(tmp, memory="both")$by.total
```

	total.time	total.pct	mem.total	self.time	self.pct
lreg4	0.024	100.0	1.2	0.000	0.0
solve	0.014	58.3	0.7	0.000	0.0
crossprod	0.012	50.0	0.6	0.004	16.7
as.vector	0.010	41.7	0.5	0.000	0.0
*	0.008	33.3	0.4	0.008	33.3
-	0.006	25.0	0.4	0.006	25.0
exp	0.004	16.7	0.2	0.004	16.7
as.matrix	0.002	8.3	0.1	0.002	8.3
solve.default	0.002	8.3	0.1	0.000	0.0

```
> unlink(tmp)
```

Indeed, `lreg4` is so fast for our relatively small problem that we had to reduce the sampling interval (to 2 milliseconds) to get the profiling to work!

8.7   Object-Oriented Programming in R*

Quick-and-dirty programming, which is the principal focus of this chapter, generally does not require writing object-oriented functions, but understanding how the object system in R works is often useful even to quick-and-dirty R programmers. We described the basics of the S3 object system in Section 1.4, which you may wish to reread now. In the current section, we explain how to write S3 generic functions and methods and how the more sophisticated and formal S4 object system works.

8.7.1   THE S3 OBJECT SYSTEM

Figure 8.10 shows an S3 object-oriented version of our logistic-regression program, a modification of the `lreg4` function (in Figure 8.9, p. 405).

Anticipating an extension of this example, we write `lreg` as an S3 *generic function*, for which `lreg.default` is the *default method*.[13]

Almost all S3 generic functions have the same general form; here, for example, are the `summary` and `print` generics:

```
> summary

function (object, ...)
UseMethod("summary")
<environment: namespace:base>

> print

function (x, ...)
UseMethod("print")
<environment: namespace:base>
```

By convention, method functions have the same arguments as the corresponding generic function—in Figure 8.10, the arguments are X and . . .—but may have additional arguments as well—y, predictors, max.iter, tol, and constant for lreg.default. The first two arguments of lreg.default are the model matrix X and the response vector y of 0s and 1s. In rewriting the function, we provide for predictor names, which by default are the column names of the model matrix X, and allow the regression constant to be suppressed. The function begins by performing some checks on the data and returns a list of coefficients, the coefficient covariance matrix, and other interesting results. The returned list is assigned the class "lreg".

Applying `lreg` to Mroz's data:

```
> mod.mroz.3 <- with(Mroz,
+     lreg(cbind(k5, k618, age, wc, hc, lwg, inc), lfp))
> class(mod.mroz.3)

[1] "lreg"

> str(mod.mroz.3) # to avoid printing the entire object

List of 6
 $ coefficients: num [1:8] 3.1821 -1.4629 -0.0646 -0.0629 ...
 $ var         : num [1:8, 1:8] 0.41522 -0.06305 -0.02303 ...
  ..- attr(*, "dimnames")=List of 2
  .. ..$ : chr [1:8] "Constant" "k5" "k618" "age" ...
  .. ..$ : chr [1:8] "Constant" "k5" "k618" "age" ...
 $ deviance    : num 905
 $ converged   : logi TRUE
 $ predictors  : chr [1:8] "Constant" "k5" "k618" "age" ...
 $ iterations  : num 5
 - attr(*, "class")= chr "lreg"
```

We may now write "lreg" methods for standard generic functions, such as `print` and `summary`, as shown in Figure 8.11:

---

[13] See Section 1.4 for an explanation of how S3 object dispatch works.

```
lreg <- function(X, ...){
    UseMethod("lreg")
    }

lreg.default <- function(X, y, predictors=colnames(X), max.iter=10,
        tol=1E-6, constant=TRUE, ...) {
    if (!is.numeric(X) || !is.matrix(X))
        stop("X must be a numeric matrix")
    if (!is.numeric(y) || !all(y == 0 | y == 1))
        stop("y must contain only 0s and 1s")
    if (nrow(X) != length(y))
        stop("X and y contain different numbers of observations")
    if (constant) {
        X <- cbind(1, X)
        colnames(X)[1] <- "Constant"
    }
    b <- b.last <- rep(0, ncol(X))
    it <- 1
    while (it <= max.iter){
        p <- as.vector(1/(1 + exp(-X %*% b)))
        var.b <- solve(crossprod(X, p * (1 - p) * X))
        b <- b + var.b %*% crossprod(X, y - p)
        if (max(abs(b - b.last)/(abs(b.last) + 0.01*tol)) < tol) break
        b.last <- b
        it <- it + 1
    }
    if (it > max.iter) warning("maximum iterations exceeded")
    dev <- -2*sum(y*log(p) + (1 - y)*log(1 - p))
    result <- list(coefficients=as.vector(b), var=var.b,
        deviance=dev, converged= it <= max.iter,
        predictors=predictors, iterations = it)
    class(result) <- "lreg"
    result
}
```

Figure 8.10 An object-oriented version of our logistic-regression program, with `lreg` as an S3 generic function and `lreg.default` as its default method.

```
> mod.mroz.3

Constant        k5       k618        age         wc         hc        lwg
 3.18214  -1.46291  -0.06457  -0.06287    0.80727    0.11173    0.60469
     inc
-0.03445

> summary(mod.mroz.3)

          Estimate  Std.Err z value Pr(>|z|)
Constant   3.18214  0.64438    4.94  7.9e-07
k5        -1.46291  0.19700   -7.43  1.1e-13
k618      -0.06457  0.06800   -0.95  0.34234
age       -0.06287  0.01278   -4.92  8.7e-07
wc         0.80727  0.22998    3.51  0.00045
hc         0.11173  0.20604    0.54  0.58762
lwg        0.60469  0.15082    4.01  6.1e-05
inc       -0.03445  0.00821   -4.20  2.7e-05

Deviance = 905.3
```

```
print.lreg <- function(x, ...) {
    coef <- x$coefficients
    names(coef) <- x$predictors
    print(coef)
    if (!x$converged) cat("\n *** lreg did not converge ***\n")
    invisible(x)
}

summary.lreg <- function(object, ...) {
    b <- object$coefficients
    se <- sqrt(diag(object$var))
    z <- b/se
    table <- cbind(b, se, z, 2*(1-pnorm(abs(z))))
    colnames(table) <- c("Estimate", "Std.Err", "z value", "Pr(>|z|)")
    rownames(table) <- object$predictors
    result <- list(coef=table, deviance=object$deviance,
        converged=object$converged)
    class(result) <- "summary.lreg"
    result
}

print.summary.lreg <- function(x, ...) {
    printCoefmat(x$coef,signif.stars=FALSE)
    cat("\nDeviance =", x$deviance,"\n")
    if (!x$converged) cat("\n Note: *** lreg did not converge ***\n")
    invisible(x)
}
```

Figure 8.11   print and summary methods for objects of class "lreg".

Our print.lreg method prints a brief report, while the output produced by summary.lreg is more extensive. The functions cat, print, and printCoefmat are used to produce the printed output. We are already familiar with the generic print function. The cat function may also be used for output to the R console. Each *new-line character* (\n) in the argument to cat causes output to resume at the start of the next line. The printCoefmat function prints coefficient matrices in a pleasing form. As we explained, it is conventional for the arguments of a method to be the same as the arguments of the corresponding generic function, and thus we have arguments x and ... for print.lreg, and object and ... for summary.lreg.

It is also conventional for print methods to return their first argument as an invisible result and for summary methods to create and return objects to be printed by a corresponding print method. According to this scheme, summary.lreg returns an object of class "summary.lreg", to be printed by the print method print.summary.lreg. This approach produces summary objects that can be used in further computations. For example, summary(mod.mroz.3)$coef[, 3] returns the column of z values from the coefficient table.

8.7.2   THE S4 OBJECT SYSTEM

The S4 object-oriented programming system, while broadly similar to the S3 object system, is more formal and consistent. The S3 and S4 object systems coexist largely harmoniously in R.

In S4, classes are defined globally, via the `setClass` function. Adapting the preceding example, we define a class `"lreg5"` of objects to contain the results of a logistic regression:

```
> setClass("lreg5",
+     representation(coefficients="numeric", var="matrix",
+         deviance="numeric", predictors="character",
+         iterations="numeric"))

[1] "lreg5"
```

The first argument to `setClass` is the name of the class being defined, here `"lreg5"`. The second argument calls the `representation` function to define the *slots* that compose objects of class `"lreg5"`; each argument to `representation` is a slot name and identifies the kind of data that the slot is to contain—for example a numeric vector, a matrix, or a character vector.

Our S4 object-oriented logistic-regression program, named `lreg5` and displayed in Figure 8.12, is similar to the S3 function `lreg.default` (Figure 8.10, p. 408). The `lreg5` function creates the class `"lreg5"` object `result` by calling the general *object-constructor function* `new` and supplying the contents of each slot, which are automatically checked for appropriateness against the class representation. The `lreg5` function terminates by returning the object `result`.

Let us try out `lreg5` on Mroz's data:

```
> mod.mroz.4 <- with(Mroz,
+     lreg5(cbind(k5, k618, age, wc, hc, lwg, inc), lfp))
> class(mod.mroz.4)

[1] "lreg5"
attr(,"package")
[1] ".GlobalEnv"

> slotNames(mod.mroz.4)

[1] "coefficients" "var"          "deviance"     "predictors"
[5] "iterations"

> str(mod.mroz.4)

Formal class 'lreg5' [package ".GlobalEnv"] with 5 slots
  ..@ coefficients: num [1:8] 3.1821 -1.4629 -0.0646 -0.0629 ...
  ..@ var         : num [1:8, 1:8] 0.41522 -0.06305 -0.02303 ...
  .. ..- attr(*, "dimnames")=List of 2
  .. .. ..$ : chr [1:8] "Constant" "k5" "k618" "age" ...
  .. .. ..$ : chr [1:8] "Constant" "k5" "k618" "age" ...
  ..@ deviance    : num 905
  ..@ predictors  : chr [1:8] "Constant" "k5" "k618" "age" ...
  ..@ iterations  : num 5
```

```
lreg5 <- function(X, y, predictors=colnames(X), max.iter=10,
        tol=1E-6, constant=TRUE, ...) {
    if (!is.numeric(X) || !is.matrix(X))
        stop("X must be a numeric matrix")
    if (!is.numeric(y) || !all(y == 0 | y == 1))
        stop("y must contain only 0s and 1s")
    if (nrow(X) != length(y))
        stop("X and y contain different numbers of observations")
    if (constant) {
        X <- cbind(1, X)
        colnames(X)[1] <- "Constant"
    }
    b <- b.last <- rep(0, ncol(X))
    it <- 1
    while (it <= max.iter){
        p <- as.vector(1/(1 + exp(-X %*% b)))
        var.b <- solve(crossprod(X, p * (1 - p) * X))
        b <- b + var.b %*% crossprod(X, y - p)
        if (max(abs(b - b.last)/(abs(b.last) + 0.01*tol)) < tol) break
        b.last <- b
        it <- it + 1
    }
    if (it > max.iter) warning("maximum iterations exceeded")
    dev <- -2*sum(y*log(p) + (1 - y)*log(1 - p))
    result <- new("lreg5", coefficients=as.vector(b), var=var.b,
        deviance=dev, predictors=predictors, iterations=it)
    result
}
```

Figure 8.12   An S4 version of our logistic-regression program.

In S3, typing the name of an object or entering any command that is not an assignment causes the generic `print` function to be invoked. Typing the name of an object in S4 similarly invokes the `show` function. Because we have not yet defined a `"show"` method for objects of class `"lreg5"`, the default method—which in S4 is the function simply named `show`—would be invoked and would just display the values of all the slots of `mod.mroz.4`. The `show` S4 generic function has the following definition:

```
> show

standardGeneric for "show" defined from package "methods"

function (object)
standardGeneric("show")
<environment: 0x12da7c0>
Methods may be defined for arguments: object
Use  showMethods("show")  for currently available ones.
(This generic function excludes non-simple inheritance; see ?setIs)
```

We proceed to define a `"show"` method for objects of class `"lreg5"` using the `setMethod` function:

```
> setMethod("show", signature(object="lreg5"),
+     definition=function(object) {
+             coef <- object@coefficients
+             names(coef) <- object@predictors
+             print(coef)
+         }
+     )

[1] "show"
```

The first argument, `"show"`, to `setMethod` gives the name of the method that we wish to create. The second argument indicates the *signature* of the method—the kind of objects to which it applies. In our example, the function applies only to `"lreg5"` objects, but S4 permits more complex signatures for functions with more than one argument. The final argument to `setMethod` defines the method function. This may be a preexisting function or, as here, an anonymous function defined on the fly. Methods in S4 must use the same arguments as the generic function, for example, the single argument `object` for a `"show"` method. The @ (at sign) operator is used to extract the contents of a slot, much as $ (dollar sign) is used to extract a list element.

Let us verify that the new method works properly:

```
> setMethod("summary", signature(object="lreg5"),
+     definition=function(object, ...) {
+             b <- object@coefficients
+             se <- sqrt(diag(object@var))
+             z <- b/se
+             table <- cbind(b, se, z, 2*(1-pnorm(abs(z))))
+             colnames(table) <- c("Estimate", "Std.Err",
+                                  "Z value", "Pr(>z)")
+             rownames(table) <- object@predictors
+             printCoefmat(table)
+             cat("\nDeviance =", object@deviance,"\n")
+         }
+     )

[1] "summary"
```

The `"show"` method for objects of class `"lreg5"` reports only the regression coefficients. We next define a `"summary"` method that outputs more information about the logistic regression:

```
> setMethod("summary", signature(object="lreg5"),
+     definition=function(object, ...) {
+             b <- object@coefficients
+             se <- sqrt(diag(object@var))
+             z <- b/se
+             table <- cbind(b, se, z, 2*(1-pnorm(abs(z))))
+             colnames(table) <- c("Estimate", "Std.Err", "Z value", "Pr(>z)")
+             rownames(table) <- object@predictors
+             printCoefmat(table)
+             cat("\nDeviance =", object@deviance,"\n")
+         }
+     )

[1] "summary"
```

Because the generic `summary` function has two arguments, `object` and `...`, so must the method, even though `...` is never used in the body of the method. The argument `...` can be used to soak up additional arguments for different methods in both S3 and S4 generic functions. Applying `summary` to the model produces the desired result:

```
> summary(mod.mroz.4)

           Estimate  Std.Err  Z value  Pr(>z)
Constant   3.18214   0.64438     4.94  7.9e-07 ***
k5        -1.46291   0.19700    -7.43  1.1e-13 ***
k618      -0.06457   0.06800    -0.95  0.34234
age       -0.06287   0.01278    -4.92  8.7e-07 ***
wc         0.80727   0.22998     3.51  0.00045 ***
hc         0.11173   0.20604     0.54  0.58762
lwg        0.60469   0.15082     4.01  6.1e-05 ***
inc       -0.03445   0.00821    -4.20  2.7e-05 ***
---
Signif. codes:  0 '***' 0.001 '**' 0.01 '*' 0.05 '.' 0.1 ' ' 1

Deviance = 905.3
```

Finally, a word about inheritance in S4. Recall that in S3, an object can have more than one class. The first class is the object's primary class, but if a method for a particular generic function does not exist for the primary class, then methods for the second, third, and so on, classes are searched for successively. In S4, in contrast, each object has one and *only one* class. Inheritance is a relationship between classes and not a property of objects. If one class *extends* another class, then the first class inherits the methods of the second. Inheritance is established by the `setIs` function: `setIs("classA", "classB")` asserts that `"classA"` extends, and therefore can inherit methods from, `"classB"`; put another way, objects of class `"classA"` also belong to class `"classB"`.

The object-oriented programming system in S4 is more complex than in S3—indeed, we have only scratched the surface here, showing how to do in S4 what we previously learned to do in S3. For example, unlike in S3, S4 method dispatch can depend on the class of more than one argument, and instances of S4 objects are checked automatically for consistency with the class definition. The S4 object system has been used to develop some important R software, such as the **lme4** package for fitting linear and generalized linear mixed-effects models.[14] Nevertheless, most current object-oriented software in R still uses the older S3 approach.

8.8   Writing Statistical-Modeling Functions in R*

The logistic-regression programs that we have presented thus far put the burden on the user to form the response vector **y** of 0s and 1s; to construct the

---

[14]Mixed-effects models are discussed in the online appendix to the text.

```
lreg.formula <- function(formula, data, subset, na.action, model = TRUE,
    contrasts = NULL, ...) {
    call <- match.call()  # returns the function call
    mf <- match.call(expand.dots = FALSE)  # the function call w/o ...
    args <- match(c("formula", "data", "subset", "na.action"),
        names(mf), 0)  # which arguments are present?
    mf <- mf[c(1, args)]
    mf$drop.unused.levels <- TRUE
    mf[[1]] <- as.name("model.frame")
    mf <- eval.parent(mf)  # create a model frame
    terms <- attr(mf, "terms")  # terms object for the model
    y <- model.response(mf)  # response variable
    values <- sort(unique(y))
    if (length(values) != 2) stop("the response variable is not binary")
    y <- as.numeric(y == values[2])  # higher value coded 1, lower coded 0
    X <- model.matrix(terms, mf, contrasts)  # model matrix
    mod <- lreg.default(X, y, predictors=colnames(X), constant=FALSE, ...)
    mod$na.action <- attr(mf, "na.action")
    mod$contrasts <- attr(X, "contrasts")
    mod$xlevels <- .getXlevels(terms, mf)
    mod$call <- call
    mod$terms <- terms
    if (model)  mod$model <- mf
    mod
}
```

Figure 8.13   A formula method for `lreg`, which uses the standard arguments for R modeling functions.

model matrix **X**—including generating dummy variables from factors, creating interaction regressors, and handling polynomials in a numerically stable way; to select cases to use in a particular analysis; and so on. In addition, our functions make no provision for missing data, an annoying oversight that will plague the data analyst in most real problems. Most, but not all, of the modeling functions we use in R do these things for us, and in a more or less consistent way.

We illustrate these ideas here based on our S3 logistic-regression function `lreg` (in Figure 8.10, p. 408).[15] We earlier introduced a default method, `lreg.default` (also in Figure 8.10), which takes a numeric model matrix as its first argument. Figure 8.13 shows a formula method, `lreg.formula`, for the `lreg` generic, the first argument of which is an R model formula.[16]

The first few lines of `lreg.formula` handle the standard arguments for modeling functions: `formula`, `data`, `subset`, `na.action`, `model`, and `contrasts` (see Section 4.8). Comments in the code indicate the purpose of each of the special commands for manipulating statistical models.

---

[15]More details are available in the *R Project Developer Page* at http://developer. r-project.org/model-fitting-functions.txt.

[16]Even though the first argument of the S3 generic function `lreg` is X, it is permissible to use the name `formula` for the first argument of the formula method `lreg.formula`. The other argument of the generic, ..., also appears in `lreg.formula`, at it should, and is passed through in the call to `lreg.default`.

Although you can simply regard this procedure as an incantation to be invoked in writing a statistical-modeling function in R, an effective way to see more concretely what the various lines in the function do is to enter the command debug(lreg.formula) (Section 8.6.1), call the lreg function with a formula argument, and then step through lreg.formula line by line, examining (via str) the result of each operation. It is also instructive to consult the help pages for match.call, eval.parent, and so on.

The lreg.formula function works by setting up a call to lreg.-default, passing to the latter the model matrix X and response vector y. Because the model matrix will already have a column of 1s if the model formula implies an intercept, the constant argument to lreg.default is set to FALSE, to avoid attaching a second column of 1s. The names of the columns of the model matrix are passed to lreg.default in the predictors argument. Finally, any other arguments to lreg.default (e.g., max.iter or tol) are passed through via . . . .

We already have print and summary methods for "lreg" objects, but to make the lreg function more useful, we should also write methods for standard generic functions associated with statistical models, such as coef, vcov, anova, and residuals, among others, or, where appropriate, allow objects of class "lreg" to inherit default methods. We illustrate with a vcov method:

```
> vcov.lreg <- function(object, ...) {
+     object$var
+ }
```

Let us try out the new functions:

```
> remove(Mroz) # delete modified Mroz data set
> mod.lreg <- lreg(lfp ~ ., data=Mroz) # Mroz will be found in car
> mod.lreg
```

```
(Intercept)           k5          k618          age         wcyes
    3.18214     -1.46291      -0.06457     -0.06287       0.80727
      hcyes          lwg           inc
    0.11173      0.60469      -0.03445
```

```
> str(vcov(mod.lreg))  # i.e., an 8 x 8 matrix
```

```
 num [1:8, 1:8] 0.41522 -0.06305 -0.02303 -0.00767 0.01282 ...
 - attr(*, "dimnames")=List of 2
  ..$ : chr [1:8] "(Intercept)" "k5" "k618" "age" ...
  ..$ : chr [1:8] "(Intercept)" "k5" "k618" "age" ...
```

```
> coef(mod.lreg) # inherits coef.default
```

```
[1]   3.18214 -1.46291 -0.06457 -0.06287  0.80727  0.11173  0.60469
[8] -0.03445
```

In addition to writing new statistical-modeling functions with a formula interface, the ideas in this section can be applied to provide formula interfaces for existing functions. For example, the glmnet function in the **glmnet**

```
Glmnet <- function(formula, data, subset, na.action, ...) {
    call <- match.call()  # returns the function call
    mf <- match.call(expand.dots = FALSE)  # the function call w/o ...
    args <- match(c("formula", "data", "subset", "na.action"),
        names(mf), 0)  # which arguments are present?
    mf <- mf[c(1, args)]
    mf$drop.unused.levels <- TRUE
    mf[[1]] <- as.name("model.frame")
    mf <- eval.parent(mf)  # create a model frame
    terms <- attr(mf, "terms")  # terms object for the model
    y <- model.response(mf)  # response variable
    X <- model.matrix(terms, mf, contrasts)  # model matrix
    intercept <- which(colnames(X) == "(Intercept)") # location of intercept
    if (length(intercept > 0)) X <- X[ , -intercept] # remove intercept
    glmnet(X, y, ...)
}
```

Figure 8.14   A friendly front-end to the `glmnet` function.

package contains very fast computer code for using the *lasso* and the *elastic net* for selecting variables in linear models, binomial-regression models, and some multinomial-regression models (see `?glmnet`; Friedman et al., 2008). The arguments for this function are as follows:

```
> library(glmnet)
> args(glmnet)

function (x, y,
    family = c("gaussian", "binomial", "poisson", "multinomial",
            "cox"),
    weights, offset = NULL, alpha = 1, nlambda = 100,
    lambda.min = ifelse(nobs < nvars, 0.05, 1e-04),
    lambda = NULL, standardize = TRUE, thresh = 1e-04,
    dfmax = nvars + 1, pmax = min(dfmax * 1.2, nvars), exclude,
    penalty.factor = rep(1, nvars), maxit = 100,
    HessianExact = FALSE, type = c("covariance", "naive"))
NULL
```

The first argument, x, is a numeric matrix of predictors, and the second, y, is the response variable; the remaining arguments control the details of model fitting.

The function Glmnet in Figure 8.14 acts as a front-end to glmnet, facilitating the specification of the model and data. The ellipses argument . . . in Glmnet is used to pass arguments to glmnet. The response, on the left side of the model formula, should be a numeric variable for family= "gaussian"; a two-column matrix, a factor with two levels, or a vector of 0s and 1s for family="binomial"; or a factor with more than two levels for family="multinomial".

For example, applying Glmnet to the Prestige data in the **car** package:

```
> g1 <- Glmnet(prestige ~ income + education + women + type,
+      data=Prestige)
> class(g1)

[1] "glmnet" "elnet"
```

The `Glmnet` command uses the model formula to create the arguments `x` and `y` for `glmnet` from the `Prestige` data frame. For example, the factor `type` in the data frame is converted into dummy variables. In constructing the matrix of predictors, the column for the intercept is suppressed, because the `glmnet` function includes an intercept in the model: Having a vector of 1s in the predictor matrix `x` would be redundant. The last line of `Glmnet` is a call to `glmnet`, and so the `Glmnet` function returns the result produced by `glmnet`; the object `g1`, therefore, contains all the output from `glmnet`, which we do not describe here but which can be plotted or otherwise examined in the usual manner.

8.9 Environments and Scope in R*

The material in Section 2.2 that describes how objects are located along the R search path should suffice for the everyday use of R in data analysis. Sometimes, however, the behavior of R seems mysterious because of the scoping rules that it uses. In this section, we provide further discussion of scoping rules, in particular with respect to the manner in which the values of variables are determined when functions are executed. This material, while relatively difficult, can be important in writing R programs and in understanding their behavior.

8.9.1 BASIC DEFINITIONS: FRAMES, ENVIRONMENTS, AND SCOPE

Several general concepts are useful for understanding how R assigns values to variables. These definitions are adapted from Abelson et al. (1985), where they are described in much greater detail. Abelson et al.'s usage conflicts with the terminology usually employed to discuss scoping in R but, we believe, facilitates an understanding of the subject; we note the differences below so that the reader can consult the R documentation with minimal confusion.

- A variable that is assigned a value is said to be *bound* to that value. Variables are normally bound to values by assignments, for example, `x <- 5`, or by passing values to function arguments, for example, `f(x=2)`. In the latter instance, the binding is local to the function call, which means that inside the function the variable `x` has the value 2 but outside the function the variable `x` could have a different value or no value at all.
- A *frame* is a set of bindings. A variable may have at most one binding in a particular frame, but the same variable may be bound to different values in different frames. In R, the same variable may be bound in a particular frame both to a function definition and to an object of another mode, such as a numeric vector or list. The R interpreter is able to distinguish between the two values by context. In standard R usage, a frame is called an "environment," but we reserve the term *environment* for a different purpose, as will be discussed shortly.

- If a variable is *unbound* in a particular frame it is said to be a *free variable* in that frame. For example, when the function f <- function(x){ x + a } is called as f(2), x is bound to the value 2 in the local frame of the function call but a is a free variable in that frame. Likewise, the assignment x <- 5 made at the R command prompt binds the value 5 to x in the global frame. In standard R usage, the global frame is called the "global environment" or the *workspace* and is kept in memory. This usage conflicts with the definition of the term *environment* given below, and consequently in this section (though not more generally in the book), we will refer to the R workspace as the *global frame*.
- *Scoping rules* determine where the interpreter looks for values of free variables. In the example function f, assuming that f was defined in the global frame, the R interpreter would look for the free variable a in the global frame and subsequently on the rest of the search path.
- An *environment* is a sequence of frames. A value bound to a variable in a frame earlier in the sequence will take precedence over a value bound to the same variable in a frame later in the sequence. The first value is said to *shadow* or *mask* the second. This idea is familiar from the discussion of the R search path in Section 2.2. Indeed, the frames on the search path, starting with the global frame, are at the end of the frame sequence of *every* environment. Therefore, variables that are bound to values in frames on the search path are globally visible, unless shadowed by bindings earlier in the sequence. We will term the sequence of frames beginning with the global frame and proceeding along the search path the *global environment*. This usage conflicts with standard R terminology, in which the *single* frame of the workspace, in our usage the *global frame*, is called the "global environment."
- The *scope* of a variable binding is the set of environments in which the binding is visible.

8.9.2   LEXICAL SCOPING IN R

In R, the environment of a function, which is the environment created by a function call, comprises the local frame of the function call followed by the environment in which the function was defined. The latter environment is called the *enclosing environment*. This rule is called *lexical* or *static scoping*.[17] A function together with its environment is termed a *closure*. The following examples (some adapted from Tierney, 1990, sec. 3.5) elucidate lexical scoping.

We begin with a simple illustration, introduced in the preceding section:

```
> f <- function(x) x + a
```

[17] Another common rule is *dynamic scoping*, according to which the environment of a function comprises the local frame of the function followed by the environment from which the function was *called*, not, as in lexical scoping, the environment in which it was *defined*. Dynamic scoping, which is not used in R, is less powerful than lexical scoping for some purposes, but it is arguably more intuitive.

```
> a <- 10
> x <- 5
> f(2)
```

```
[1] 12
```

When f is called, the local binding of $x \equiv 2$, shadows the global binding $x \equiv 5$. The variable a is a free variable in the frame of the function call, and so the global binding $a \equiv 10$ applies. To avoid confusion, we use $\equiv$ to represent a binding in place of the ordinary $=$ sign.

Now consider an example in which one function calls another:

```
> f <- function(x) {
+       a <- 5
+       g(x)
+ }
> g <- function(y) y + a
> f(2)
```

```
[1] 12
```

We use different names for the arguments of f and g—respectively, x and y—to emphasize that argument names are arbitrary. In this example, the global binding $a \equiv 10$ is used when f calls g, because a is a free variable in g, and g is defined at the command prompt in the global frame. The binding $a \equiv 5$ in the local frame of f is ignored.[18]

The next illustration employs a locally defined function:

```
> f <- function(x) {
+       a <- 5
+       g <- function(y) y + a
+       g(x)
+ }
> f(2)
```

```
[1] 7
```

The local function g is defined within the function f, and so the environment of g comprises the local frame of g, followed by the local frame of f, followed by the global environment. Because a is a free variable in g, the interpreter next looks for a value for a in the local frame of f; it finds the value $a \equiv 5$, which shadows the global binding $a \equiv 10$.

Lexical scoping can be quite powerful and even mind-bending. Consider the following function:

```
> makePower <- function(power) {
+       function(x) x^power
+ }
```

The makePower function returns a *closure* as its result (not just a function, but a function *plus* an environment):

---

[18]If R were dynamically scoped, as described in Footnote 17, then when g is called from f, the interpreter would look first for a free variable in the frame of f.

```
> square <- makePower(2)
> square

function(x) x^power
<environment: 0x3d548b8>

> square(4)

[1] 16

> cuberoot <- makePower(1/3)
> cuberoot

function(x) x^power
<environment: 0x3c8b878>

> cuberoot(64)

[1] 4
```

When `makePower` is called with the argument 2 (or 1/3), this value is bound to the local variable `power`. The function that is returned is defined in the local frame of the call to `makePower` and therefore inherits the environment of this call, including the binding of `power`. Thus, even though the functions `square` and `cuberoot` *look* the same, they have different environments: The free variable `power` in `square` takes on the value 2, while the free variable `power` in `cuberoot` takes on the value 1/3.

We conclude this section with one additional example. *Tukey's test for non-additivity* is computed by the `residualPlots` function in the **car** package (as described in Section 6.2). The outline of the test is as follows: (1) fit a linear model; (2) compute the squares of the fitted values corresponding to the original data points, $\widehat{y}^2$; (3) update the model by adding $\widehat{y}^2$ to it as a new regressor; and (4) compute Tukey's test as the t value for the additional regressor, with a p value from the standard-normal distribution. For example, using the Canadian occupational-prestige data from the **car** package:

```
> m1 <- lm(prestige ~ income + education + women + type,
+      data=na.omit(Prestige))
> yhat2 <- predict(m1)^2
> m2 <- update(m1, . ~ . + yhat2)
> test <- summary(m2)$coef["yhat2", 3]
> pval <- 2*pnorm(abs(test), lower.tail=FALSE)
> c(TukeyTest=test, Pvalue=pval)

TukeyTest     Pvalue
-2.901494   0.003714
```

The small p value suggests that the linear predictor does not provide an adequate description of the expected value of `prestige` given the predictors. We used `na.omit(Presige)` to replace the original data frame with a new one, deleting all rows with missing values; otherwise, because of missing data in `type`, the fitted values `yhat2` would have been of the wrong length (see Sections 2.2.3 and 4.8.5).

Tukey's test is sufficiently useful that we might want to write a function for its routine application. Copying the code for the example almost exactly, we have

```
> tukeyTest <- function(model) {  # bugged!
+     yhat2 <- predict(model)^2
+     m2 <- update(model, . ~ . + yhat2)
+     test <- summary(m2)$coef["yhat2", 3]
+     pval <- 2*pnorm(abs(test), lower.tail=FALSE)
+     c(TukeyTest=test, Pvalue=pval)
+ }
```

If we are careful to delete the variable named `yhat2` from the global frame before trying to run this program, we get

```
> remove(yhat2)
> tukeyTest(m1)

Error in predict(model) : object 'yhat2' not found
```

The problem is that `yhat2` is defined in the local frame of the function, while `update` is acting on `model`, which is in the global frame, and thus it can't find variables in the local frame. The result is the error message.

A quick-and-dirty solution to this problem is to define `yhat2` in the global frame and then delete it before leaving the function:

```
> tukeyTest <- function(model) {
+     yhat2 <<- predict(model)^2  # note the use of "<<-"
+     m2 <- update(model, . ~ . + yhat2)
+     test <- summary(m2)$coef["yhat2", 3]
+     pval <- 2*pnorm(abs(test), lower.tail=FALSE)
+     rm(yhat2, envir=globalenv())
+     c(TukeyTest=test, Pvalue=pval)
+ }
> tukeyTest(m1)

TukeyTest    Pvalue
-2.901494  0.003714
```

Because no variable named `yhat2` is visible in the environment of `tukeyTest`, the special operator `<<-` makes an assignment to this variable in the global frame (see `help("<<-")`) for details). An obvious problem with this solution, however, is that if a global variable named `yhat2` exists prior to calling `tukeyTest`, then `tukeyTest` will overwrite it and subsequently delete it. More generally, for a function to make a change to the global frame as a side effect is a questionable programming practice, to which we should resort only in exceptional circumstances.

A more elegant solution is to obtain the test statistic without using `update`, so all quantities are in the same frame. One way to do this is to compute the regression of the Pearson residuals on the residuals from the regression of $\hat{y}^2$ on the regressors in the original model. Apart from a correction for df, the t statistic for the slope in this regression is Tukey's test. The `tukeyNonaddTest` function in the **car** package takes this approach:

```
getAnywhere(tukeyNonaddTest)
```

```
A single object matching 'tukeyNonaddTest' was found
It was found in the following places
  namespace:car
with value

function (model)
{
    qr <- model$qr
    fitsq <- qr.resid(qr, predict(model, type = "response")^2)
    r <- residuals(model, type = "pearson")
    m1 <- lm(r ~ fitsq, weights = weights(model))
    df.correction <- sqrt((df.residual(model) - 1)/df.residual(m1))
    tukey <- summary(m1)$coef[2, 3] * df.correction
    c(Test = tukey, Pvalue = 2 * pnorm(-abs(tukey)))
}
<environment: namespace:car>
```

The function `getAnywhere` can find objects that would otherwise be hidden in the namespace of a package. The `tukeyNonaddTest` function isn't *exported* from the **car** package because it isn't meant to be called directly by the user.[19]

8.10   R Programming Advice

Programming is a craft. Like most crafts, it is a combination of art and science; and as is true of most crafts, facility in programming is partly the product of practice and experience. The purpose of this section is to give general, miscellaneous, and mostly unoriginal advice about the craft of programming in R, organized as brief points:

- *Program experimentally:* One of the advantages of programming in an interpreted environment such as R is the ability to type expressions and have them immediately evaluated. You can therefore try out key parts of your program, and correct them, before incorporating them into a program. Often, you can simply copy a debugged command from the *R Console* into your program editor or from one editor window into another.
- *Work from the bottom up:* You will occasionally encounter a moderately large programming project. It is almost always helpful to break a large project into smaller parts, each of which can be programmed and debugged as an independent function. The function `numbers2words` (developed in Section 8.5.2) provides a case in point. In a truly complex project, functions may be organized hierarchically, with some calling others. If some of the small functions are of more general utility, then you can maintain them as independent programs and reuse them. If the small functions are unique to the current project, then they may eventually be incorporated as local functions. Traditionally, large projects were

---

[19]Package namespaces are discussed in the *Writing R Extensions* manual (R Development Core Team, 2009b).

programmed from the top down—beginning with the highest level of generality—but a functional, interpreted programming language such as R makes it easier to build the language up to the program.[20]

- *If it is possible and reasonable, avoid loops:* Programs that avoid loops may be easier to read and often are more efficient, especially if a loop would be executed a very large number of times. Some processes such as numerical optimization are intrinsically iterative, but in many other cases, loops can be avoided by making use of vectorized calculations, matrix operations, functions such as `apply` (see Section 8.4), or even recursion (Section 8.3.3). Sometimes, however, a loop will be the most natural means of expressing a computation (see Section 8.4.1).

- *Test your program:* Before worrying about speed, memory usage, elegance, and so on, make sure that your program provides the right answer. Program development is an iterative process of refinement, and getting a program to function correctly is the key first step. In checking out your program, try to anticipate all the circumstances that the program will encounter, and test each of them. Furthermore, in quick-and-dirty programming, the time that you spend writing and debugging your program will probably be vastly greater than the time the program spends executing. Remember the programmer's adage:[21] "Make it right before you make it faster." (And emphasize the "quick"—in the sense of quick program development—as opposed to the "dirty.") Tools for measuring time and memory use in R were introduced in Section 8.6.2.

- *Learn to use debugging tools:* It is rare to write a program that works correctly the first time that it is tried, and debugging is therefore an important programming skill. Working in an interpreted environment simplifies debugging (as described in Section 8.6.1).

- *Document the program:* Unless your program is to be used only once and then discarded, its use should be documented in some manner. The best documentation is to write programs in a transparent and readable style. You should use descriptive variable names, avoid clever but opaque tricks, not pack too many operations into one line of program code, and indent program lines (e.g., in loops) to reveal the structure of the program. You can also add a few comments to the beginning of a function to explain what the function does and what its arguments mean (as in Figure 8.3, p. 388). It is our assumption that, at least most of the time, you will be programming for yourself rather than for others, and this decreases the burden of preparing documentation, but you want to understand your own programs when you return to them a month or a year later.

- *Use the R package system:* The infrastructure for creating packages is one of the great strengths of R. Writing an R package is often worth-

---

[20] See Graham (1994, 1996) for an eloquent discussion of these points in relation to another functional programming language—Lisp.

[21] This dictum, and a great deal of other good advice on programming, originates in Kernighan and Plauger (1974); also see Kernighan and Pike (1999).

while even if you do not intend to distribute it to other people: The package-checking system and provisions for documentation make it easier to maintain functions in packages.[22]

8.11   Complementary Reading and References

There are now many books that deal in whole or in part with R programming.

- Possibly the most comprehensive, if somewhat dated, treatment remains Venables and Ripley (2000), a companion volume to Venables and Ripley (2002), which also has some information on programming in R.
- The manual *Writing R Extensions* (R Development Core Team, 2009b), which is distributed with R and is also available on the Internet, includes information on using programming languages such as C and Fortran with R, writing packages, preparing documentation, and more. Be warned, however, that this manual can be difficult to read if you are unfamiliar with the language of computer science.
- A volume edited by Chambers and Hastie (1992), known colloquially as "the white book," includes the original description of the S3 object system; an earlier book on S by Becker et al. (1988), "the blue book," is still of interest.
- Two books by John Chambers (1998, 2008), who is the principal architect of the S language, deal with a variety of topics but focus on the S4 object system. The treatment in these books (the first of which is called "the green book") is both deep and relatively difficult.
- Despite its title, *R Programming for Bioinformatics*, by Robert Gentleman (2009), is a thorough and at points challenging treatment of programming in R by one of the cofounders of the R Project.
- In addition, there are several books that treat traditional topics in statistical computing—such as optimization, simulation, probability calculations, and computational linear algebra—using R, though the specific coverage of the books varies: Braun and Murdoch (2007), Jones et al. (2009), and Rizzo (2008). Of these books, Braun and Murdoch's is the briefest and most accessible.

---

[22]The process of creating an R package is described in the *Writing R Extensions* manual (R Development Core Team, 2009b).

References

Abelson, H., Sussman, G. J., and Sussman, J. (1985). *Structure and Interpretation of Computer Programs*. MIT Press, Cambridge, MA.

Adler, D. and Murdoch, D. (2010). *rgl: 3D visualization device system (OpenGL)*. R package version 0.89.

Agresti, A. (2002). *Categorical Data Analysis*. Wiley, Hoboken, NJ, second edition.

Agresti, A. (2007). *An Introduction to Categorical Data Analysis*. Wiley, Hoboken, NJ, second edition.

Agresti, A. (2010). *Analysis of Ordinal Categorical Data*. Wiley, Hoboken, NJ, second edition.

Andrews, F. (2010). *playwith: A GUI for interactive plots using GTK+*. R package version 0.9-45.

Atkinson, A. C. (1985). *Plots, Transformations and Regression: An Introduction to Graphical Methods of Diagnostic Regression Analysis*. Clarendon Press, Oxford.

Becker, R. A., Chambers, J. M., and Wilks, A. R. (1988). *The New S Language: A Programming Environment for Data Analysis and Graphics*. Wadsworth, Pacific Grove, CA.

Becker, R. A. and Cleveland, W. S. (1996). *S-Plus Trellis Graphics User's Manual*. Seattle.

Becker, R. A., Wilks, A. R., Brownrigg, R., and Minka, T. P. (2010). *maps: Draw Geographical Maps*. R package version 2.1-4.

Berk, R. A. (2008). *Statistical Learning from a Regression Perspective*. Springer, New York.

Berndt, E. R. (1991). *The Practice of Econometrics: Classic and Contemporary*. Addison-Wesley, Reading, MA.

Birch, M. W. (1963). Maximum likelihood in three-way contingency tables. *Journal of the Royal Statistical Society. Series B (Methodological)*, 25(1):220–233.

Bowman, A. W. and Azzalini, A. (1997). *Applied Smoothing Techniques for Data Analysis: The Kernel Approach with S-Plus Illustrations*. Oxford University Press, Oxford.

Box, G. E. P. and Cox, D. R. (1964). An analysis of transformations. *Journal of the Royal Statistical Society. Series B (Methodological)*, 26(2):211–252.

Box, G. E. P. and Tidwell, P. W. (1962). Transformation of the independent variables. *Technometrics*, 4(4):531–550.

Braun, W. J. and Murdoch, D. J. (2007). *A First Course in Statistical Programming with R*. Cambridge University Press, Cambridge, UK.

Breusch, T. S. and Pagan, A. R. (1979). A simple test for heteroscedasticity and random coefficient variation. *Econometrica*, 47(5):1287–1294.

Campbell, A., Converse, P. E., Miller, P. E., and Stokes, D. E. (1960). *The American Voter*. Wiley, New York.

Chambers, J. M. (1992). Linear models. In Chambers, J. M. and Hastie, T. J., editors, *Statistical Models in S*, pages 95–144. Wadsworth, Pacific Grove, CA.

Chambers, J. M. (1998). *Programming with Data: A Guide to the S Language*. Springer, New York.

Chambers, J. M. (2008). *Software for Data Analysis: Programming with R*. Springer, New York.

Chambers, J. M., Cleveland, W. S., Kleiner, B., and Tukey, P. A. (1983). *Graphical Methods for Data Analysis*. Wadsworth, Belmont, CA.

Chambers, J. M. and Hastie, T. J., editors (1992). *Statistical Models in S*. Wadsworth, Pacific Grove, CA.

Cleveland, W. S. (1979). Robust locally weighted regression and smoothing scatterplots. *Journal of the American Statistical Association*, 74(368):829–836.

Cleveland, W. S. (1993). *Visualizing Data*. Hobart Press, Summit, NJ.

Cleveland, W. S. (1994). *The Elements of Graphing Data, Revised Edition*. Hobart Press, Summit, NJ.

Clogg, C. C. and Shihadeh, E. S. (1994). *Statistical Models for Ordinal Variables*. Sage, Thousand Oaks, CA.

Cook, D. and Swayne, D. F. (2009). *Interative Dynamic Graphics for Data Analysis: With R and GGobi*. Springer, New York.

Cook, R. D. (1977). Detection of influential observation in linear regression. *Technometrics*, 19(1):15–18.

Cook, R. D. (1993). Exploring partial residual plots. *Technometrics*, 35(4):351–362.

Cook, R. D. (1998). *Regression Graphics: Ideas for Studying Regressions Through Graphics*. Wiley, New York.

Cook, R. D. and Weisberg, S. (1982). *Residuals and Influence in Regression*. Chapman and Hall, New York.

Cook, R. D. and Weisberg, S. (1983). Diagnostics for heteroscedasticity in regression. *Biometrika*, 70(1):1–10.

Cook, R. D. and Weisberg, S. (1991). Added variable plots in linear regression. In Stahel, W. and Weisberg, S., editors, *Directions in Robust Statistics and Diagnostics, Part I*, pages 47–60, New York. Springer.

Cook, R. D. and Weisberg, S. (1994). Transforming a response variable for linearity. *Biometrika*, 81(4):731–737.

Cook, R. D. and Weisberg, S. (1997). Graphics for assessing the adequacy of regression models. *Journal of the American Statistical Association*, 92(438):490–499.

Cook, R. D. and Weisberg, S. (1999). *Applied Regression Including Computing and Graphics*. Wiley, New York.

Cunningham, R. and Heathcote, C. (1989). Estimating a non-gaussian regressino model with multicolinearity. *Australian Journal of Statistics*, 31:12–17.

Davis, C. (1990). Body image and weight preoccupation: A comparison between exercising and non-exercising women. *Appetite*, 15:13–21.

Davison, A. C. and Hinkley, D. V. (1997). *Bootstrap Methods and Their Application*. Cambridge University Press, Cambridge.

Efron, B. (2003). The statistical century. In Panaretos, J., editor, *Stochastic Musings: Perspectives from the Pioneers of the Late 20th Century*, pages 29–44. Lawrence Erlbaum Associates, New Jersey.

Efron, B. and Tibshirani, R. J. (1993). *An Introduction to the Bootstrap*. Chapman and Hall, New York.

Ericksen, E. P., Kadane, J. B., and Tukey, J. W. (1989). Adjusting the 1990 Census of Population and Housing. *Journal of the American Statistical Association*, 84: 927–944.

Fienberg, S. E. (1980). *The Analysis of Cross-Classified Categorical Data, Second Edition*. MIT Press, Cambridge, MA.

Fox, J. (1987). Effect displays for generalized linear models. In Clogg, C. C., editor, *Sociological Methodology 1987 (Volume 17)*, pages 347–361. American Sociological Association, Washington, D.C.

Fox, J. (1991). *Regression Diagnostics: An Introduction*. Sage, Newbury Park, CA.

Fox, J. (2000a). *A Mathematical Primer for Social Statistics*. Sage, Thousand Oaks, CA.

Fox, J. (2000b). *Nonparametric Simple Regression: Smoothing Scatterplots*. Quantitative Applications in the Social Sciences. Sage, Thousand Oaks, CA.

Fox, J. (2003). Effect displays in R for generalised linear models. *Journal of Statistical Software*, 8(15):1–27.

Fox, J. (2005a). Programmer's Niche: How do you spell that number? *R News*, 5(1):51–55.

Fox, J. (2005b). The R commander: A basic-statistics graphical user interface to R. *Journal of Statistical Software*, 14(9):1–42.

Fox, J. (2008). *Applied Regression Analysis, Linear Models, and Related Methods*. Sage, Thousand Oaks, CA, second edition.

Fox, J. (2009). Aspects of the social organization and trajectory of the R Project. *The R Journal*, 1(2).

Fox, J. and Andersen, R. (2006). Effect displays for multinomial and proportional-odds logit models. *Sociological Methodology*, 36:225–255.

Fox, J. and Guyer, M. (1978). "Public" choice and cooperation in n-person prisoner's dilemma. *The Journal of Conflict Resolution*, 22(3):469–481.

Fox, J. and Monette, G. (1992). Generalized collinearity diagnostics. *Journal of the American Statistical Association*, 87(417):178–183.

Freedman, D. and Diaconis, P. (1981). On the histogram as a density estimator. *Zeitschrift fur Wahrscheinlichkeitstheorie und verwandte Gebiete*, 57:453–476.

Freedman, J. L. (1975). *Crowding and Behavior*. Viking, New York.

Friedman, J., Hastie, T., and Tibshirani, R. (2008). Regularization paths for generalized linear models via coordinate descent. unpublished.

Gentleman, R. (2009). *R Programming for Bioinformatics*. Chapman and Hall, Boca Raton.

Gnanadesikan, R. (1977). *Methods for Statistical Data Analysis of Multivariate Observations*. Wiley, Hoboken, NJ.

Graham, P. (1994). *On Lisp: Advanced Techniques for Common Lisp*. Prentice Hall, Englewood Cliffs, NJ.

Graham, P. (1996). *ANSI Common Lisp*. Prentice Hall, Englewood Cliffs, NJ.

Harper, E. K., Paul, W. J., Mech, L. D., and Weisberg, S. (2008). Effectiveness of lethal, directed wolf-depredation control in minnesota. *Journal of Wildlife Management*, 72(3):778–784.

Hastie, T., Tibshirani, R., and Friedman, J. (2009). *The Elements of Statistical Learning: Data Mining, Inference, and Prediction*. Springer, New York, second edition.

Huber, P. and Ronchetti, E. M. (2009). *Robust Statistics*. Wiley, Hoboken, NJ, second edition.

Ihaka, R. and Gentleman, R. (1996). R: A language for data analysis and graphics. *Journal of Computational and Graphical Statistics*, 5:299–314.

Jones, O., Maillardet, R., and Robinson, A. (2009). *Introduction to Scientific Programming and Simulation Using R*. Chapman and Hall, Boca Raton.

Kernighan, B. W. and Pike, R. (1999). *The Practice of Programming*. Addison-Wesley, Reading, MA.

Kernighan, B. W. and Plauger, P. J. (1974). *The Elements of Programming Style*. McGraw-Hill, New York.

Landwehr, J. M., Pregibon, D., and Shoemaker, A. C. (1980). Some graphical procedures for studying a logistic regression fit. In *Proceedings of the Business and Economics Statistics Section, American Statistical Association*, pages 15–20.

Leisch, F. (2002). Sweave, part I: Mixing R and LaTeX. *R News*, 2(3):28–31.

Leisch, F. (2003). Sweave, part II: Package vignettes. *R News*, 3(2):21–24.

Lemon, J. (2006). Plotrix: a package in the red light district of R. *R News*, 6(4):8–12.

Ligges, U. and Fox, J. (2008). R help desk: How can I avoid this loop or make it faster? *R News*, 8(1):46–50.

Little, R. J. A. and Rubin, D. B. (2002). *Statistical Analysis with Missing Data*. Wiley, Hoboken NJ, second edition.

Loader, C. (1999). *Local Regression and Likelihood*. Springer, New York.

Long, J. S. (1997). *Regression Models for Categorical and Limited Dependent Variables*. Sage, Thousand Oaks, CA.

Long, J. S. and Ervin, L. H. (2000). Using heteroscedasticity consistent standard errors in the linear regression model. *The American Statistician*, 54(3):217–224.

Mallows, C. L. (1986). Augmented partial residuals. *Technometrics*, 28(4):313–319.

McCullagh, P. and Nelder, J. A. (1989). *Generalized Linear Models, Second Edition*. Chapman & Hall, London.

Moore, D. S. and McCabe, G. P. (1993). *Introduction to the Practice of Statistics, Second Edition*. Freeman, New York.

Moore, J. C., Jr. and Krupat, E. Relationship between source status, authoritarianism, and conformity in a social setting. Sociometry, 34: 122–134.

Mosteller, F. and Tukey, J. W. (1977). *Data Analysis and Regression: A Second Course in Statistics*. Addison-Wesley, Reading, MA.

Mroz, T. A. (1987). The sensitivity of an empirical model of married women's hours of work to economic and statistical assumptions. *Econometrica*, 55(4):765–799.

Murrell, P. (2006). *R Graphics*. Chapman and Hall, Boca Raton.

Murrell, P. and Ihaka, R. (2000). An approach to providing mathematical annotation in plots. *Journal of Computational and Graphical Statistics*, 9(3):582–599.

Nelder, J. A. (1977). A reformulation of linear models. *Journal of the Royal Statistical Society. Series A (General)*, 140(1):48–77.

Nelder, J. A. and Wedderburn, R. W. M. (1972). Generalized linear models. *Journal of the Royal Statistical Society. Series A (General)*, 135(3):370–384.

Ornstein, M. D. (1976). The boards and executives of the largest Canadian corporations: Size, composition, and interlocks. *Canadian Journal of Sociology*, 1: 411–437.

Phipps, P., Maxwell, J. W., and Rose, C. (2009). 2009 annual survey of the mathematical sciences. *Notices of the American Mathematical Society*, 57:250–259.

Powers, D. A. and Xie, Y. (2000). *Statistical Methods for Categorical Data Analysis*. Academic Press, San Diego.

Pregibon, D. (1981). Logistic regression diagnostics. *The Annals of Statistics*, 9(4):705–724.

R Development Core Team (2009a). *R: A Language and Environment for Statistical Computing*. R Foundation for Statistical Computing, Vienna, Austria. ISBN 3-900051-07-0.

R Development Core Team (2009b). *Writing R Extensions*. R Foundation for Statistical Computing, Vienna, Austria.

Ripley, B. D. (2001). Using databases with R. *R News*, 1(1):18–20.

Rizzo, M. L. (2008). *Statistical Computing with R*. Chapman and Hall, Boca Raton.

Sall, J. (1990). Leverage plots for general linear hypotheses. *The American Statistician*, 44(4):308–315.

Sarkar, D. (2008). *Lattice: Multivariate Data Visualization with R*. Springer, New York.

Sarkar, D. and Andrews, F. (2010). *latticeExtra: Extra Graphical Utilities Based on Lattice*. R package version 0.6–11.

Schafer, J. L. (1997). *Analysis of Incomplete Multivariate Data*. Chapman and Hall, New York.

Silverman, B. W. (1986). *Density Estimation for Statistics and Data Analysis*. Chapman and Hall, London.

Simonoff, J. S. (2003). *Analyzing Categorical Data*. Springer, New York.

Spector, P. (2008). *Data Manipulation with R*. Springer, New York.

Stine, R. and Fox, J., editors (1996). *Statistical Computing Environments for Social Research*. Sage, Thousand Oaks, CA.

Swayne, D. F., Cook, D., and Buja, A. (1998). XGobi: Interactive dynamic data visualization in the X Window system. *Journal of Computational and Graphical Statistics*, 7(1):113–130.

Tierney, L. (1990). *Lisp-Stat: An Object-Oriented Environment for Statistical Computing and Dynamic Graphics*. Wiley, Hoboken, NJ.

Tufte, E. R. (1983). *The Visual Display of Quantitative Information*. Graphics Press, Cheshire, CT.

Tukey, J. W. (1949). One degree of freedom for non-additivity. *Biometrics*, 5(3): 232–242.

Tukey, J. W. (1977). *Exploratory Data Analysis*. Addison-Wesley, Reading, MA.

Urbanek, S. and Wichtrey, T. (2010). *iplots: iPlots—interactive graphics for R*. R package version 1.1-3.

Velilla, S. (1993). A note on the multivariate box-cox transformation to normality. *Statistics and Probability Letters*, 17:259–263.

Venables, W. N. and Ripley, B. D. (2000). *S Programming*. Springer, New York.

Venables, W. N. and Ripley, B. D. (2002). *Modern Applied Statistics with S*. Springer, New York, fourth edition.

Wang, P. C. (1985). Adding a variable in generalized linear models. *Technometrics*, 27:273–276.

Wang, P. C. (1987). Residual plots for detecting nonlinearity in generalized linear models. *Technometrics*, 29(4):435–438.

Weisberg, S. (2004). Lost opportunities: Why we need a variety of statistical languages. *Journal of Statistical Software*, 13(1):1–12.

Weisberg, S. (2005). *Applied Linear Regression*. John Wiley & Sons, Hoboken, NJ, third edition.

White, H. (1980). A heteroskedasticity-consistent covariance matrix estimator and a direct test for heteroskedasticity. *Econometrica*, 48(4):817–838.

Wickham, H. (2009). *ggplot2: Using the Grammar of Graphics with R*. Springer, New York.

Wilkinson, G. N. and Rogers, C. E. (1973). Symbolic description of factorial models for analysis of variance. *Journal of the Royal Statistical Society. Series C (Applied Statistics)*, 22(3):392–399.

Wilkinson, L. (2005). *The Grammar of Graphics*. Springer, New York, second edition.

Williams, D. A. (1987). Generalized linear model diagnostics using the deviance and single case deletions. *Applied Statistics*, 36:181–191.

Yeo, I.-K. and Johnson, R. A. (2000). A new family of power transformations to improve normality or symmetry. *Biometrika*, 87(4):954–959.

Zeileis, A., Hornik, K., and Murrell, P. (2009). Escaping RGBland: Selecting colors for statistical graphics. *Computational Statistics & Data Analysis*, 53:3259–3270.

Author Index

Subject Index

Command Index

Data Set Index

Package Index

About the Authors

John Fox is a professor of sociology at McMaster University in Hamilton, Ontario, Canada. He was previously a professor of sociology and of mathematics and statistics at York University in Toronto, where he also directed the Statistical Consulting Service at the Institute for Social Research. He earned a PhD in sociology from the University of Michigan in 1972. He has delivered numerous lectures and workshops on statistical topics, at places such as the summer program of the Inter-University Consortium for Political and Social Research and the annual meetings of the American Sociological Association. His recent and current work includes research on statistical methods (e.g., work on three-dimensional statistical graphs) and on Canadian society (e.g., a study of political polls in the 1995 Quebec sovereignty referendum). He is author of many articles, in journals such as *Sociological Methodology*, *The Journal of Computational and Graphical Statistics*, *The Journal of the American Statistical Association*, *The Canadian Review of Sociology and Anthropology*, and *The Canadian Journal of Sociology*. He has written several other books, including *Applied Regression Analysis, Linear Models, and Related Methods* (Sage, 1997), *Nonparametric Simple Regression* (Sage, 2000), and *Multiple and Generalized Nonparametric Regression* (Sage, 2000).

Sanford Weisberg is a professor of statistics at the University of Minnesota, Twin Cities. He is also director of the University's Statistical Consulting Service for Liberal Arts and has worked with literally hundreds of social scientists and others on the statistical aspects of their research. He earned a BA in statistics from the University of California, Berkeley, and a PhD, also in statistics, from Harvard University, under the direction of Frederick Mosteller. The author of more than 60 articles, his research has primarily been in the areas of regression analysis, including graphical methods, regression diagnostics, and statistical computing. He is a fellow of the American Statistical Association and former Chair of its Statistical Computing Section. He is the author or coauthor of several books, including *Applied Linear Regression*, third edition (2005), *Residuals and Influence in Regression* (with R. D. Cook, 1982), *Applied Regression Including Computing and Graphics* (with R. D. Cook, 1999). He has several publications in areas that use statistics, including archeology, plant sciences, wildlife management, fisheries, and public affairs.